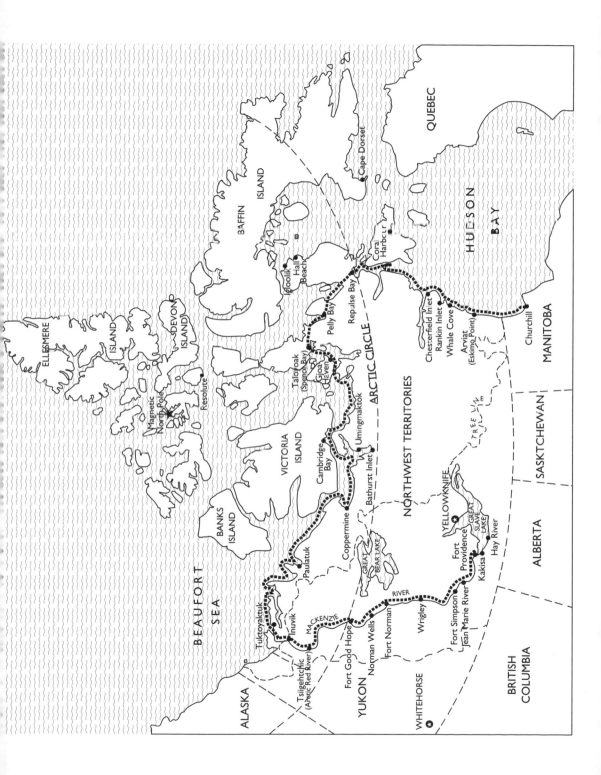

Kabloona in the Yellow Kayak

KABLOONA
in the
YELLOW KAYAK

One Woman's Journey Through
the Northwest Passage

VICTORIA JASON

Turnstone Press

Turnstone Press
607-100 Arthur Street
Winnipeg, Manitoba
Canada   R3B 1H3

Turnstone Press gratefully acknowledges the assistance of the Canada Council and the Manitoba Arts Council.

Cover photographs: Don Starkell and Victoria Jason

Author photograph: David R. White

Interior photographs: Victoria Jason, Don Starkell and Mike Macri

Design: Manuela Dias

The book was printed and bound in Canada by Friesens for Turnstone Press.

Canadian Cataloguing in Publication Data

Jason, Victoria, 1945–

Kabloona in the yellow kayak

ISBN 0-88801-201-2

1. Jason, Victoria, 1945–   - Journeys - Northwest Passage.
2. Northwest Passage - Description and travel. 3. Sea kayaking - Northwest Passage. 4. Jason, Victoria, 1945–   - Journeys - Hudson Bay.
5. Hudson Bay - Description and travel. 6. Sea kayaking - Hudson Bay.
I. Title.

FC4167.3.J385 1995   910'.9163'27 C95-920185-8
F1090.5.J385 1995

I dedicate this book to all my children.
To my daughter Angela, her husband Brian Everts, and my
youngest grandchild Aleia Victoria. To my daughter Debbie,
her husband Grant Peterson, and my granddaughter Denine
(Rosebud). To my daughter Teresa, her husband Gregg Davey,
and my grandsons Garrett and Keith. The best children a
mother could hope for! I write for them, so they may one day
forgive me for my wild wanderings and understand how much
I appreciated the land I had learned to love.

And to my late mother and father – Frances and Wasyl Polon.
They taught me love, respect and consideration. I felt their
presence many times during the trip.

Acknowledgements

My heartfelt thanks to the many individuals who encouraged me to write this book. How could I disappoint you? You were the source of my strength.

My thanks to Don Starkell for consenting to allow me to come on the first expedition.

My thanks to the North West Company for their much appreciated support in supplying our groceries and accommodations in the settlements, through their Northern Stores.

Special thanks to all their staff for their devoted consideration. They buoyed up our spirits so many times.

My thanks to Urban Trail for supplying me with hiking boots, to Mark's Work Warehouse for the solar fleece sweater, to Kodak Canada for the slide film in 1994, to the Nutri-Bar Company for their generous addition to my food supply.

Thanks to my friends and co-workers at CN. They worried about me, but encouraged me to follow my dream. I'm sure in their minds they believed my mental processes should be carefully examined by a shrink. However, their support was unwavering!

Thanks to my friends in the Big Lake Kayak Touring Club and the Manitoba Recreational Canoeing Association. Their enthusiasm was infectious.

Thanks to my sisters, Ann, Olga, Wilma, Nadia and Christine. They must have wondered why a farm girl from the Swan River Valley would be so interested in the Arctic. Their questions were always polite. I love them all dearly!

Thanks to Geoff Ball, Director of Purchases and Materials at CN, for having the nerve to sign my leave of absence forms four years in a row.

Thanks to the many people I met on my journey. Each individual was a treasure. They left me with memories money cannot buy!

Thank you to Steve Hawyluk for allowing me the use of his lovely cottage, where I found the solitude to start my writing. A daunting task indeed!

And last, but certainly not least, my deep appreciation goes to Louise Ferris for having the courage to decipher my handwriting and type it into the word processor. An excellent job, my dear friend!

Table of Contents

The strong life that never knows harness;
    The wilds where the caribou call;
The freshness, the freedom, the farness –
    Oh God! how I'm stuck on it all

—Robert Service

1991

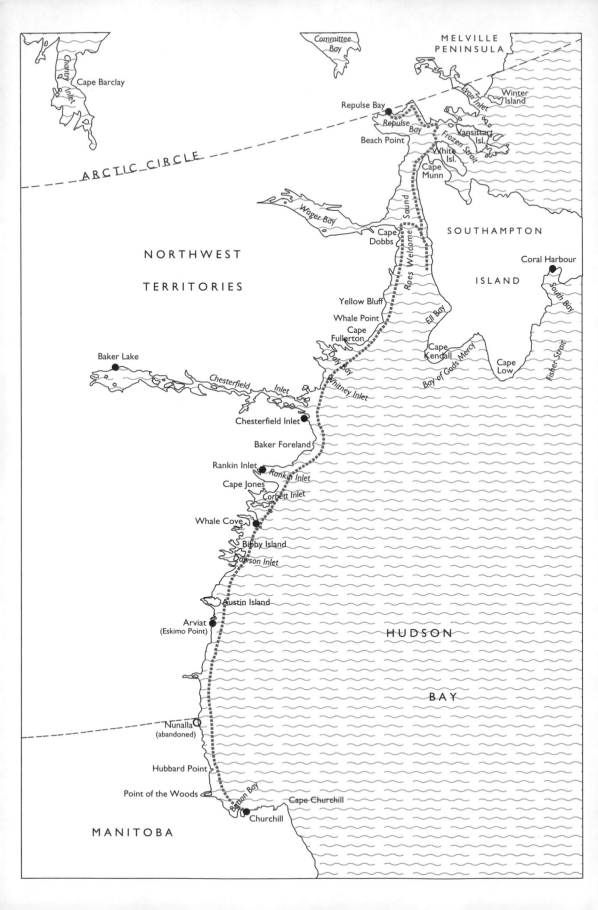

Chantry Inlet

Cape Barclay

Committee Bay

MELVILLE PENINSULA

Repulse Bay

Winter Island

Lyon Inlet

Repulse Bay

Vansittart Isl.

Beach Point

Frozen Strait

White Isl.

ARCTIC CIRCLE

Cape Munn

Wager Bay

SOUTHAMPTON

Roes Welcome Sound

Cape Dobbs

Coral Harbour

ISLAND

NORTHWEST

Yellow Bluff

Ell Bay

South Bay

Whale Point

Cape Fullerton

TERRITORIES

Cape Kendall

Cape Low

Bay of Gods Mercy

Daly Bay

Fisher Strait

Baker Lake

Whitney Inlet

Chesterfield   Inlet

Chesterfield Inlet

Baker Foreland

Rankin Inlet

Rankin Inlet

Cape Jones

Corbett Inlet

Whale Cove

HUDSON

Bibby Island

Dawson Inlet

Austin Island

Arviat
(Eskimo Point)

BAY

Nunalla
(abandoned)

Hubbard Point

Point of the Woods

Button Bay

Cape Churchill

MANITOBA

Churchill

I will not dwell greatly on the history of the North as I write. Much research has been done by professionals and many history books written. Reflections are entered here and there only because they were of interest to me.

This book is about a true adventure that haunted me for half my lifetime. To experience the North from a kayak was beyond my wildest hopes and dreams.

I suppose I should try to explain the magnetic attraction that drew me to the North, but perhaps it doesn't need an explanation. Perhaps it was just the passion for feeling free.

I came by the love of kayaking quite accidentally. My ex-husband Dennis and I had done a great deal of canoeing in our seven years together, but when we divorced in 1989 he took the canoe, boats, and the all-terrain vehicle along. It turned out to be the nicest thing he ever did for me. It forced me to search for something I could handle on my own. I would try kayaking!

I was 45 years old and had never seen a kayak, except in pictures. Being a touch claustrophobic, I was leery about sitting in something that looked so confining. Gary Brabant at Wave Track changed my mind. He was very patient. He demonstrated the proper technique for getting in and out, and we hashed over pros and cons. Instantly, the idea of owning a kayak took hold.

I had one more concern. "If I flip over, will I be able to get out easily?" I asked Gary.

"Yes," he replied, "the kayak is a very stable craft, but if you flip over, the law of gravity says you will fall out."

That was all I needed to know. I went home with a *Canoeing & Kayaking* magazine containing an article, "A Primer on Paddling Strokes." I bought a thirteen-foot yellow River Runner and on May 5, 1990, I slipped it into the water for the first time at Willard Lake in Ontario. With the open magazine in my lap, I followed the instructions step by step. By evening I was completely hooked on kayaking.

Leroy and Betty Goodell, the owners of Pleasant Point Lodge, became like family to me, and I spent every weekend in 1990 on Willard Lake or the surrounding area, portaging from one lake to another. Having so much freedom was exhilarating. I would wonder no longer what was around the next bend. I would find out on my own. Never in my life had I felt better. I was strong, lean and deeply tanned from the days on the water.

One Monday in July, the office at work was abuzz at an article in *The Winnipeg Sun* about a fellow by the name of Don Starkell. Louise Ferris handed me the paper.

"You like kayaking. Look at this!" The picture of Don in his kayak amid the ice in the Churchill River hit me like a ton of bricks.

I had read his famous book, *Paddle to the Amazon.* It had said that he wanted to do a trip by canoe from Churchill, paddle the Northwest Passage and end up in Tuktoyaktuk. Most people thought his trip was a stupid idea. I thought it was grand and remarkable. Canoeing didn't appeal to me – but this! Every day I scanned both local papers for news on how he was progressing. Nothing. Then came the sad news that he had to abort the attempt because of a capsize two days out of Churchill. An article in the paper said he did not want to go back up north. I hoped I could meet him and change his mind.

We met on the Red River in late September of that same year. I asked Don if he was considering going north again.

"I don't know if I would. I definitely wouldn't go alone," he replied.

"If you go," I persisted, "would you consider taking a woman along?"

His answer was definite. "No! It's no place for a woman."

Well, I love being a woman, I love being treated as one, but I don't like being excluded because I am one. I would bide my time.

In November, I questioned him again. "Has anyone volunteered to join you, if you go?"

The answer was "no."

"If no one volunteers, may I go?" I asked.

The answer was "no!"

Then came Christmas. Lots of roast turkey and trimmings and a few glasses of wine put Don in a mellow mood. "If you go north, may I come along?" I asked.

Then the answer I was hoping for: "Maybe. Depends on how hard you train in the spring."

He didn't know it, but I had half my equipment ordered and packed.

Merry Christmas!

My experience of the North began in 1961. My first husband worked on the railroad. He relieved foremen up and down the Lynn Lake and Hudson Bay Line, as it was called back then. We travelled with not much more than a bedroll, a sack of potatoes and two babies. Then came a permanent position at Mile 412 on the Hudson Bay Line. Herchmer was a mere flagstop situated 100 miles south of Churchill, Manitoba. Besides ourselves and the other foreman we had approximately thirty Cree neighbours. The nearest grocery store, hospital, and school were at Churchill. We got along well and helped each other as best we could.

I was sixteen years old with two babies under two years old, trapped into a marriage by my own naiveté, to a man I hated. However, the magic of the North captured my heart immediately, so what my miserable marriage lacked was compensated for by the silence, tranquillity, and openness.

Life was simple. The only running water was in the Owl River nearby. A pot-bellied coal heater kept out the cold. Kerosene lamps provided the light and, for relief, there was an outhouse at the end of a path. The four years went by quickly. The winters were long, I'll admit, but there was plenty to do. In March of '66 we were transferred to Winnipeg.

My love affair with the North did not end there. I vowed one day, when my children were grown, I would return. I never imagined it would come about in such a dramatic way.

The winter was hectic. Don was over every weekend. We studied maps. He taught me how to use a compass. I sewed nylon bags for our gear, collected supplies, made lists, packed and repacked, trying to eliminate weight and bulk. We weighed every piece of equipment and supplies. My spare moments were taken up by reading about the North. My children got caught up in the act. Between them, my sisters and my friends, I ended up with the best of equipment. All the time, in the back of my mind, I was afraid something would happen and I would have to stay behind.

Don came over one day. I could tell he had something on his mind.

"Something bothering you?" I questioned.

"Yeah, well, we're going to be involved in this project for a long time," he hedged.

"And?" I waited for him to go on, my heart full of dread.

"Well, you're not my type. Looks are very important to me. I like my women younger and slimmer," he answered. I was already twelve years his junior. I wondered when he had last looked in a mirror. Perhaps it doesn't hurt to have a big ego.

"Are you trying to tell me you want to be dating someone?" I asked.

"Yes, that's it," he agreed.

"Will it affect my chances of going north with you?"

He replied, "No."

I was so relieved! "You have my blessing. You can date whomever you want."

It was good to get the situation into the open. Now we had no commitments except the expedition. A week later he demanded I not date while we were in this together. Obviously the rule didn't include him. I didn't feel bound by it either.

Then another change in plans. Freddie Reffler, a friend of Don's, had been trying all winter to talk me out of doing the trip. When he couldn't talk me out of it, he decided to come along. Now there were three of us. Our departure was set for June 11, 1991.

Another surprise. My daughter Teresa and her husband Gregg announced they were expecting their second baby on June 3rd. Eight days of grace. I wanted desperately to see my new grandchild before I left.

Spring of 1991 came early. On the 24th of March, Don, Freddie and I were at Winnipeg's North Perimeter Bridge, putting our kayaks into the Red River. We headed north to Lockport. What a grand feeling to be paddling! The current was swift. Don is a very serious kayaker. There wasn't any time to slack off or stop to rest. The morning started to cool and the snow came down in big fluffy flakes.

A mile from St. Andrew's Church an odd sensation came over me. A warning light was flashing in the back of my mind. The twinge of pain in my left side worried me. Not another stroke! I was still recovering from speech impairment and short-term memory loss from the last one. This was a bad situation. The ice along the river bank prevented me from landing. Both Don and Fred were far ahead of me. I paddled to the edge of the ice and rested one end of the blade on it. The stab of pain hit hard on the left side of my chest. I couldn't call out. From my chest it moved up the back of my neck and I was sure the back of my head would explode. From there it went to my right temple, across half my forehead, and stopped at the bridge of my nose. I remember touching my eye to see if it was still there. Nausea welled up inside. Just as I felt I would faint, the pain released. I felt incredible heat in my hips. It travelled down the length of my legs and to my toes. I was drenched in sweat. The river water looked very appealing.

By the time Don and Freddie came back, I was breathing much better.

Freddie stabilized my kayak while I removed my jacket. We paddled back in the falling wet snow. I didn't mention my problem to either of them. They were both cold, so I told them to go ahead. I felt too weak and too hot to hurry. By the time we returned to the cars, six inches of snow covered them. I drove home, had a bath, and slept for sixteen hours.

My family doctor sent me to a neurologist who immediately ordered a CAT scan. When he heard about the trip, his comment was: "If you were my patient, I wouldn't let you go."

"This can't be happening," I told myself. "No!"

I wasn't sure if my doctor had the authority to keep me from leaving on the trip. I couldn't take a chance. I didn't return for the results. Each day I felt better. My speech seemed to improve and my memory was better.

On March 30th, I purchased my touring kayak. She was a beauty. I named her Windsong. By June 11th, five months of preparing and planning had flown by.

Don, Freddie and I, along with family and numerous friends, were at the VIA Rail station waiting for the "all aboard" signal for Churchill.

According to Don's plans, we would be kayaking from Churchill north along the west coast of Hudson Bay to Repulse Bay on the Arctic Circle. Then we were to cross the Rae Isthmus overland to Committee Bay. Next, from the north end of Committee, overland to Spence Bay (now called Taloyoak) and the Arctic Ocean. The plans also included paddling the Northwest Passage to Tuktoyaktuk in the western Arctic.

Big plans, big dreams! We didn't know how much the odds were stacked against us.

Departure was an anxious moment for me. Saying goodbye to the children was hardest. The responsibility of leaving Teresa, already eight days overdue with her baby, lay heavily on my heart. I began to question the kind of mother I was. I knew if I let my guard down, I would decide not to go. Ann and Mel Davey, her in-laws, promised to take good care of her. If only I could have seen the baby at least once!

We boarded amid many tears. All three of us were left with our own thoughts. What lay ahead? None of us knew. Don was hyper, Fred never stopped smiling, and I was wondering what had driven me to such insanity.

The calming force was Don's friend, Gloria Pearen. She and her daughter Melissa were accompanying us to Churchill to see us off.

At 7:00 a.m. on the morning of June 13th the train rumbled past Mile 412, where this had all begun. The only thing I recognized was the bridge over the Owl River. Where the section house had stood on the tundra were two prefab trailers on a massive bed of gravel. Behind them was the hydro line to Churchill, and in front, a huge satellite dish. My favourite tamarack tree was gone.

June 13th – 9:00 a.m. It had been 25 years since I had last seen Churchill. As I stepped off the train, I tipped my head back to smell the ocean and to feel the wind. It could have been just yesterday.

By the time Herb Hinks, the Northern Store manager, had us settled into the staff quarters, the call from home came through. Yes, Teresa was fine. I was the proud grandmother of a handsome boy by the name of Keith William, my third grandchild. What a day to celebrate! A healthy new baby boy, my grandson Garrett's fifth birthday, and the beginning of an exciting adventure.

Churchill is a unique town. It is a fully modern community situated 1,100 kilometres north of Winnipeg, on the rugged southwest edge of Hudson Bay at the mouth of the Churchill River. It is the only seaport in the prairie provinces and the only Arctic seaport in Canada. It also serves as the re-supply point for many communities in the eastern Northwest Territories. Tonnes of supplies move from Churchill by tug and barge to the more isolated northern towns.

The town is surrounded by tundra, with a sparse covering of coniferous trees. Most have branches only on the south side due to the strong northern winds. I remember they made good Christmas trees, because they could be placed flat against the wall. In the spring and summer the town is alive with tourists. They come to watch the polar bears, beluga whales, seals and caribou. Close to 200 species of birds arrive in the spring. The tundra and the seashore come to life with their calls.

The area holds nearly 400 years of history. Henry Hudson, in his ship *Discovery* in 1610, discovered the Hudson Bay. He had been hoping to find a way to Asia. Samuel Hearne, at the age of 22 years in 1767, stencilled in stone a record of his passing. It can be seen till this day in Sloop's Cove, on the west shore of the Churchill River.

Fort Prince of Wales is another interesting feature. It is situated across the Churchill River on the Eskimo Point peninsula. It is a partially restored 18th-century stone four-flanker fort with 40 cannon. My father helped in its restoration. We have a picture of him and the rest of the crew sitting on the wall in 1928 or 1929. He also helped to dredge the harbour after quitting the railroad since it was his turn to do the cooking. Sometimes I can relate to that.

We didn't get a chance to see much of the town. The river was free of ice. Don was anxious to be on the way. We would be leaving with the first high tide at 8:30 p.m. Mike Macri supplied us with the tide tables for June, July and August. We came to depend on them religiously. Don appointed me tide-master. It was my responsibility to know the level and time of the tide. By 3:30 we were on the banks of the river trying to figure out how to load the huge pile of supplies into three kayaks. We each had our own personal supplies. Freddie carried his own food. Don and I split ours between us. I must have ended up with an extra box of groceries. My kayak weighed a ton compared to Don's.

It takes a great deal of ingenuity to pack a kayak for a long journey. Every square inch of space is used. I was thankful for my large hatch openings. A crowd had gathered around us as we packed. Gloria and Melissa were with us, Mike Macri and son David, Paula and Mike Cook, and Bob Taylor and his group of bird-watchers from Boston.

Excitement was rising, as was the wind. Nothing to do but wait for the tide to rise. There was a threat of rain from the southwest. Paula lent me Mike's big parka. I couldn't tell if the shivers were from the cold or the excitement.

Time to go. With a raspy goodbye from the gravel, our kayaks slid further into the water and drifted free from shore.

Our destination was the fort, 45 minutes away. Don wanted to be away from town. Away from influence, negative statements, and advice.

Hurriedly, we set up our tents and went to the protection of the fort to cook supper. Don handed me a protein pill. He had a litre of them. "You might as well use these too," he said. It was horrible. I reached for the 7-Up bottle nearby and took a mouthful. Before I could rinse and spit, my head nearly exploded. One more rinse before I realized I was rinsing with methyl hydrate. The wood alcohol and the water were in identical bottles. Don had neglected to mark them. I felt too foolish to mention it, yet I worried about the possible side effects.

The next day was overcast, cold and windy. After a hurried breakfast, we dismantled the wet tents, loaded the kayaks, and pushed off into three-foot waves. We were all heavily loaded, determined to carry enough food and supplies for thirty days in case of delay. Don had estimated it would take us six days to get to Arviat, formerly Eskimo Point.

Compass bearings were set at 288°. We started across Button Bay, a large bay west of the promontory on which the fort is located. It is at least ten miles across. Don was quite concerned about Button Bay. In 1990, he had almost lost his life on it.

Off to the west, a storm was brewing, with the thunder and lightning coming closer. Before long the rain started and the wind picked up. I wasn't prepared for the waves splashing into the cuffs of my rain jacket. The water ran down to pool at the elbow, where it was soaked up by my sweatshirt. My arms became heavier by the minute. Don had some rubber bands around his wrist and I asked for two of them. He relented and passed them to me. "Be more prepared next time," he said.

We paddled in unison, 25 feet apart, always trying to be aware of what was happening to one other. Don was unable to look back because of the instability of his kayak, so we called to him to keep in touch. Our greatest fear was of capsizing. We would have to get the capsized person out of the water immediately, but in these rough seas it would be hard to get into position in time to help. Wind, waves, and tides are the obvious hazards, but they don't kill. Cold water kills. The shock of immersion is profound. Breathing is interrupted, balance is disturbed, and the initial automatic gasp fills your lungs with ice-cold water. If you don't succumb to shock within a few seconds, hypothermia claims you within a few minutes. The temperature of the water was probably -1° Celsius. If it weren't salty, it probably would have been frozen solid. We weren't wearing wet suits or life-jackets. Both would have been too hot for twelve hours of strenuous paddling. Besides, if we capsized, we'd be dead before we had time to drown.

The toughest thing about paddling on the Hudson Bay is the tide. The shoals extend far into the ocean, up to ten miles in some places. You must leave on the high tide and paddle on the outside edge of the shoal area until the next high tide twelve hours later. Only then can you return to solid ground.

Don kept asking me to look back at the elevators. Were they getting smaller? Were we still on our bearing? Slowly, they slid away below the horizon. We were really on our way. I was committed. Of my own free will, I had accepted the possibilities of disaster and my responsibility to the expedition and to my companions. Still, my responsibility was also to my beautiful daughters. Safety was my main priority. I would not let anyone jeopardize that without a battle. Although it is normal human nature to worry, I wished I had the power to dissolve the fears they had for my safety. The compelling urge to see the North had overrun my usual sound way of thinking and I begged their forgiveness for getting caught up in its spell!

I paddled a Bluewater Huron kayak purchased at Wave Track in Winnipeg. A symbol of the spirit Misshipeshu was on my bow. He would guide my way. Misshipeshu is a reminder of the great power and beauty that nature and the elements possess and a symbol that you travel prepared in mind and body.

Don was paddling a We-No-Nah Seal kayak. It was six inches longer than mine and very sleek and narrow. He was a very accomplished paddler. He was also our confirmed leader. This was his trip, one he had planned for ten years.

Freddie was paddling a We-No-Nah Sea Otter, a very stable, high volume kayak, but my Huron outshone them both when it came to large waves.

Fred is a serious sort, perhaps a little nervous. A very talented man with his hands, he could fix anything. It was good to have him along. His wry sense of humour brightened up many moments.

The tide was dropping and we were forced further east to bypass rocks that were appearing all around. Soon we were paddling among floes caught up in the shallows. Although we were miles from shore our paddles occasionally touched the ocean floor. Enormous icebergs could be seen in the distance. Before long, we were paddling among those mountains of ice. I was in awe of their size and beauty. We were dwarfed by them and I felt we should be whispering as we paddled our way through the maze. With a thunderous crack a berg split in two and capsized into the water near Fred and me. As it sank, it made a huge cavity. I had never paddled uphill before, but I leaned forward and did my best. As the iceberg bobbed to the surface, the surge of the backwash pushed me out of the crater. A ride like that cannot be duplicated. I glanced back at Freddie. He had managed to stay on the rim. His eyes were like saucers. I don't know why my first reaction was to laugh.

Land appeared to our left and it was a comfort to be in sight of it. The comfort didn't last long. Fog rolled in. We paddled on, relying on our compasses for a northerly bearing. Past the main area of the bergs and as the fog shifted, we glimpsed massive boulders. We had to go further to sea to bypass them. The water carried much silt so it was impossible to see below the surface. Fred and I both hit rocks with our bows. The force of the incoming tide was strong. It was a constant mental challenge to avoid the rocks. Pass a rock before the tide carried the kayak into it, or break the rhythm and allow the tide to carry you behind the rock?

We had our eyes peeled on the land for a knoll that was supposed to be very prominent. Don was hoping to camp at a shack he had found the year before. It was called the Seal River Goose Camp and was supposed to be five miles from the knoll. The fog separated for a second: the knoll. It lifted our spirits. At the same time Don spotted a riptide, heading toward us.

"Get out of here," he yelled. "We're in the mouth of a river."

We had accidentally paddled into the mouth of the Seal River. The incoming tide and the outgoing current were colliding, agitating the water. We raced back through the boulder-strewn tidal estuary.

We didn't find the shack that night. We blundered on in the fog, letting the tide bring us closer to shore, and before long small, willow-covered islands appeared. We headed in, cold, wet, and hungry. Suddenly the incoming tide stabilized and reversed itself. We grabbed the nearest little island. I do mean grabbed! I had to hold on to the turf to keep my kayak from being sucked away by the outgoing tide and current. Within minutes there was only six inches of water surrounding the island.

Freddie tasted the water. "It's fresh," he announced. "We're in a river again."

The island was fifty feet square, covered in thick wet willows and tern nests. Don and Fred had been at each other's throats for the last half hour, but tensions eased as we pulled out our wet tents and set them up. Our main concern was to get warm. We draped our wet clothes over the willows and crawled inside. Fred fell asleep without making supper. He had refused an invitation to join us. Don and I heated beans and corned beef, and made hot chocolate. It was the warmth from the little alcohol stove, as much as the food, that turned the evening around.

The temperature stabilized at 2° Celsius. In the meantime the fog was getting heavier. The terns we had upset were shrieking round the island. We were all chilled. I crawled into my mummy-bag, dressed in wind pants, heavy jacket, socks, and mitts. My hood covered my head. As warmth started to return, I drifted off into an exhausted sleep.

High tide was due at 10:35 a.m. We planned to sneak out 2½ hours ahead of it. Don and Fred retrieved their clothes from the willows and put them on. I packed mine away and wore a dry set. The men were angry. They warned me I would have two sets of wet clothes by nightfall. Still, I could not bring myself to change. The fog was thicker. We were certain we must be in the mouth of Little Seal River.

Don was very paranoid of launchings and landings. He became more hyper as the tide crept in. He paced, yelled, and swore. The terns were shrieking. So much for my beloved solitude! Don was much easier to take once we were paddling. If nothing else, I could stay out of range of his voice.

Again the tide clashed with the river's flow. It made it extremely difficult to maneuver among the boulders. Don was off in the distance, calling for us to catch up. His compass wasn't working properly. He was waiting for a bearing from mine. Freddie had become pinned against a rock by the current. He spent a few frantic moments getting out of the predicament. I didn't want to leave him alone. We all needed to clear the shoal area as quickly as possible.

As the wind rose and the fog began to thin a shape on shore caught our attention. "That's my shack," Don yelled. It was too early to stop. The bergs were larger and more numerous. We wound our way along the channels between them. The sun came out. The shore was visible. We paddled on. Don wasn't stopping to allow for photography, so I wanted to file the scenes in my mind. The silhouettes of the bergs had an unearthly beauty against the blue of the water. The craggy rock shores in the distance provided a perfect backdrop. The ice was keeping the ocean fairly calm. Before long the wind switched to an easterly direction, pushing the ice toward shore. It was not good for us.

Don and Freddie were freezing. Their wet clothes and the wind had drawn away too much of their body heat. Freddie's spray skirt didn't fit well enough. Besides his wet clothes, he was sitting in a few inches of water. My fingers were frozen to the first knuckle and cramped around the shaft of the blade. Rather than sacrifice a firm grip on the shaft I had been paddling without gloves. The combination of ice-cold salt water and the rising wind was torturous. The crowding ice was closing up the channels ahead. We could not chance being cut off from shore.

"Watch for an opening to shore!" Don yelled.

Finally we spotted one. In the background was a cove with a high sandy beach. We were four hours ahead of high tide. The water level would be rising for a while. We staked our kayaks on the tidal flats, dug out our tents, sleeping bags, and stoves, and walked onto the beach.

Don and I started fighting about our tent's location. I wanted to camp on the beach below an embankment to get some protection from the wind.

Don was yelling, "I had enough sand on my South American trip. I don't want the tent on the sand!" So we set it up on the wet grass on the bluff, in the direct force of the miserably cold wind coming off the ice-fields.

Don crawled into his sleeping bag and stayed there the whole evening, the night, and the next day. Freddie and I kept restaking the kayaks as the tide rose and brought them closer. There was no reason for both of us to watch them. I sent Freddie to his tent.

The fog started rolling in again. There was plenty of driftwood along shore. Before long I had a huge bonfire going. I had started out in dry clothes, so I was not in the state of hypothermia that Don and Freddie were. Except for my fingers I could function well. The bonfire was a cheery sight. I sat in front toasting first one side, then the other. I collected Don's and Freddie's clothes and, on racks made of scraps of lumber and double-blades, hung them to dry. Every fifteen minutes, I would restake the kayaks, until at 9:00 p.m. the tide stabilized and they were safely above the high-tide mark.

Freddie tried to warm up inside his tent. His moans and groans suggested no success.

"Come sit by the fire," I called. Another groan.

Finally, he came out. He seemed to be wearing every article of clothing he possessed. Even the waterproof bags from his sleeping bag and air mattress were on his feet. I handed him a spare fly sheet to wrap around himself.

"I'm so cold and miserable, Vicki," was the first thing he said.

"Freddie, holidays are like that sometimes," I replied.

No amount of encouragement would bring Don out of the tent.

The heat and sound of the fire brought contentment. I sat near, trying to thaw my fingers slowly. The tingling was just bearable. The possibility of gangrene setting in worried me. A weary but happy tiredness came over me. I stacked the dry clothes in the tent. It was good to get into the sleeping bag at last. I put on my mitts and drifted off to the sound of the flapping tent and crackling fire.

Sunday, June 16th. There would be no travelling. The tents were whipping in the wind and rain. At Don's suggestion, we crawled back into our sleeping bags.

Monday wasn't any better. More cold wind from the northeast. Fog too.

Feeling had not returned to my fingertips yet. I kept my mitts on and drifted in and out of sleep. In my dream I held my new grandson. What had possessed me to leave behind the comforts of home and family?

We reassured each other that the wind would change and push the ice to sea again. We would see it all better when the fog lifted.

The sun woke us on Tuesday. Don came out of the tent for first time since our arrival.

"I was the only smart one!" he announced proudly. "I stayed in my bag and conserved my heat and energy."

Fred and I exchanged glances. I vowed to myself that if he wanted something from his kayak from then on he would have to get it himself.

Visibility at last. We were totally iced in to the east and north. A solid ice-field stretched endlessly to the distant horizons, nothing but white. Along the shore, the ice was rafted and hummocked by the pressure of the ice-field forcing it over the shoals and reefs. It spelled disaster.

Our main concern was finding fresh water. There were many ponds nearby, but they were contaminated by the hundreds of geese in the area. Their collective chorus had been with us day after day. More were arriving. We could see them silhouetted against the spring sky.

Through binoculars we could see a cabin to the southwest. We decided that would be a good place to start looking. Being cooped up in the tent for so long had made us all a bit edgy. It was a relief to be exploring. Along our way we discovered bits and pieces of garbage. Anything we could use we stacked along the return trail. The cabin belonged to the Research Council of Canada. It had been abandoned for a while. The windows were broken, garbage was strewn around. During the winter the snowdrifts must have reached the kitchen window. An arctic hare had filled the sink with droppings. We did find water in a makeshift well nearby. As we were leaving, we spotted a second cabin farther to the west. On our way back, we collected a piece of chicken-wire fencing, a few metal rods, and a chunk of tent canvas.

Our next excursion was to the north end of the peninsula. A half-mile walk brought us to a high prominent piece of land. All across the top were ancient stone tent rings and cleverly constructed meat caches. The rings of rocks had long ago secured the skin walls of Inuit tents. The meat caches numbered at least thirty. They were built of rocks piled in a circle to a depth of three or four feet. None had collapsed. They bore mute testimony to the survival skills of a hunting people. This was all they had left to tell of their passing. I felt like tiptoeing even more after we found a human skull in one of the caches. It reinforced that in the North, the margin for error is slight.

One glance to the north proved that we would not be going anywhere in the near future. Don tried to encourage us by saying the wind would change and blow the ice away. At the moment it looked permanent.

"Look at the seals!" Looking closer we could see hundreds basking in the sun on the flat ice. I was amazed there could be so many seals in this world, much less in one spot. Back to camp we trudged, discouraged but optimistic.

At high tide, the more adventurous seals started coming into the cove in front of our camp. Fred was carrying a 410/22 shotgun, over and under. As we were about to make supper, Freddie yelled, "Get that seal, Vicki. It wouldn't hurt to have fresh meat if we are here a while." To this day I do not know why I shot it. Freddie butchered it. We barbecued it on the wire fencing, over an open fire. When it was done we cut all the meat off and put it into ziploc bags. We found it to have a very strong fishy, salty taste. I guess one has to acquire a taste for it. We used it up by adding it to our soups. We had fashioned a type of refrigerator with the materials on hand. We dug a large hole in the sand and lined the sides and bottom with ice. The meat stayed well-chilled.

Signs of the approaching summer increased rapidly. The tundra was studded with wild flowers. All the flowers were low and tiny, but vibrant and perfect. One minute there would be a green clump on the ground. A few hours later it would be a cushion of colour. The air was filled with the sound of birds. Big Canada geese, snow geese, the raspy croaking sounds of cranes, the gulls, terns, and many species of ducks.

Our camp was beginning to look more permanent by the day. Don had finally consented to bringing our tent down, out of the wind. Freddie did likewise. We had a fridge, a woodpile covered in tent canvas, and a pit for melting ice for drinking water. If we chopped the ice from the top of the floes on our beach, after the salt had seeped down, we could use it like fresh water. It would melt quickly in the large black garbage bag in the hollow. We found a small fuel drum on the tundra and hauled it home for a stove. It already had a square hole cut out near the bottom of one end. We could build a fire inside it and do all of our cooking.

The ice closed in from the south. We no longer had the choice of returning to Churchill. We started rationing food and fuel.

I had been cold during the nights. Don growled every time I moved closer to him, so instead I planned to use my spare flysheet to wrap around my sleeping bag.

"Your bag will get damp!" he warned me.

I didn't care. I was just at the point of being cozy when we heard drips. Our tent was leaking. I had the ideal solution. For a moment I smirked to myself. Fred heard us and admitted his tent was leaking too. I would have to give up my flysheet and get my ground sheet for Freddie's tent.

No one volunteered to do it. I crawled out of my warm bag, and covered and staked both tents in the rain. After Don fell asleep, I put my rain-suit over my clothes and got back into my bag. It worked! I slept till morning.

Each day we went exploring. The second cabin did not give us any clues as to our location. Freddie and I were positive we were at Hubbart Point. Don insisted we had paddled further up the coast. Twice a day at high tide Don and I walked to the north end of the peninsula to check for open water. The sun was hot. The floes along the shoreline were beginning to melt. What we needed was a strong west wind combined with an outgoing tide. I was surprised at how calm Don was. I was more anxious than he to be on the way. I didn't want my northern journey to end. Freddie was restless. He would take his gun and wander away for long stretches at a time. He and Don were at each other's throats quite often, so it was just as well. Surpisingly, if I voiced a thought of my own, he was quick to side with Don. Sometimes, I walked with Freddie, even though his careless handling of the gun frazzled me. Twice he had fired it accidentally, narrowly missing Don both times.

By June 20th the weather was hot and sunny. I dug out my cut-offs and T-shirt and strolled down the wide sand beach that edged the cove. I settled in on a pile of rocks. The view was spectacular. The wind off the ice-field was fresh. My thoughts mingled with the sounds of the waves slapping the shore at my feet. Sometimes I was overcome by homesickness. My girls would be worrying. We were already overdue at Arviat.

Don walked down to meet me. He seemed to think I was unhappy, which was not the case. I am basically a solitary soul. I don't mind being alone. At times I crave solitude.

"You've changed, Vicks. You don't do as much for me anymore," he announced.

At first I was stunned, then furious. I hadn't minded hauling his kayak in or fetching articles from it, while he was safe and warm in his sleeping bag, but I certainly wasn't about to make a permanent habit of it. I felt an obligation to the expedition and had no intention of shirking my responsibilities, but I was not going to wait on him hand and foot. I bit my tongue. We still had a long way to go.

The tides seemed to be getting higher each day. Jagged ice boulders were lined up on the reef on the outskirts of our cove. Every so often, the pressure of the ice-field would push one over the reef. It would come sailing to our shore to be left there by the falling tide. Twice each day the scenery changed. In a moment of fun, I waded to an ice-floe, climbed up and posed in my bikini.

The floes were pretty in the hot sun. As they melted, droplets of water formed around their perimeters and fell to the ocean in rapid succession, like strands of the finest pearls. The ice-field was beginning to creak and groan. Finally, a narrow lead showed a half mile from shore. We watched carefully twice each day. At high tide it would open; at low tide it closed again. On the 22nd of June, Freddie and Don trekked to the knoll to check the incoming tide.

When they returned, Don announced, "Pack up, we're leaving at high tide."

"Has it really opened that much in the last couple of hours?" I asked amazed.

"Freddie seems to think so" was all Don would say. It was not like Don to allow someone else to make the decision.

I suggested we leave ahead of high tide. If we couldn't get through, at least we would have a chance to return before the lead closed on us. Agreed! We paddled out of the little cove and over the reef. Single file we entered the ice-field. The ice was keeping the water fairly calm. We went little by little, winding our way among the floes. We stayed close together, so as not to lose sight of one another. If we did find enough open water, we would be paddling through the night to 5:30 a.m. Don set a fast pace. That suited me. It was exhilarating to be amid the ice. We only had four hours in which we could return safely. It was better to find out quickly whether we were likely to get through.

Freddie began having trouble. Worried about paddling through the night, he had dressed too heavily. I had commented on it back at camp.

"Freddie, do you really need all those clothes?" I had asked. His lethal stare told me to mind my own business.

Before long Freddie's face was beet red, the veins in his neck were distended, and large beads of perspiration were forming on his forehead and upper lip. I called to Don to hold up.

"That's his problem!" he yelled and kept paddling.

But it wasn't just Freddie's problem. If we were a team, it was our problem. If he succumbed to heat exhaustion or cardiac arrest we would be in big trouble. If we couldn't get out of there on time we would be smeared all over the grinding ice.

"Stop, Freddie. I'll stabilize your kayak. You have to get some of those clothes off," I told him.

"But what about Don?" he worried.

My answer was fertilized by a few abusive words.

Layer after layer came off. He was soaked to the skin. He removed his thick Irish wool toque. I gave him my baseball cap. I only wore it to keep the glare out of my eyes. I preferred to have the wind in my hair anyway. He returned to normal very quickly. By the look on his face, I could tell he was grateful.

We began to have difficulty picking our way through the ice. An hour and ten minutes later we came to a halt. The openings between the floes were too narrow to get our kayaks through. Don had proved a point to Freddie. If the timing had been out, it would have cost us our lives! We were approximately one mile out to sea and 4½ miles north of the knoll behind our cove. It was still prominent against the southern sky line. We wasted no time in turning back.

I was in my glory. I love the smell of the ice on the breeze, the tinkle of the shards as they slip off the floe edges and knife into the sapphire water. All around us was a good sign of melting. Seals played hide and seek among the floes. We dodged amongst the small floes. Some lunged at us with the current. Others, because of the melting, changed their centre of gravity and rolled over. Resounding cracks came from the ice-field. The tide was coming in full force now. The wind had also increased, which it always seemed to do when the tide was incoming. The waves were getting rougher too. I loved it. My kayak seemed to be responding to the challenge on its own. It sliced through the water effortlessly. I found a fairly long channel and Don called for me to lead. At the end of the channel was an opening to shore. One more mile. The cove was in sight. The tide was still right. I guess in my exuberance I set too fast a pace. I could hear Freddie's voice ricocheting off the icebergs. In a preacher's Bible-thumping voice, he was yelling to Don, "Follow that woman and she'll lead you straight to Hell!"

We were back to our original camp. The wind switched to south and southwest. The days were hot but the nights were cold. I was still having trouble staying warm. Don suggested eating a chocolate bar before bedtime and it became our routine for the rest of the trip. If we didn't choose the same type of bar, we would cut each in half and trade. They became our comfort food. If things went wrong during the day they were our peace treaty. Actually, the boost of sugar did increase body heat.

The situation around camp was more relaxed. We all knew we weren't going anywhere until conditions were better.

June 24th dawned with an overcast sky and rain. Freddie dressed in a rain-suit and left camp with his gun. Hours later he came back with a goose. I wrapped it in double tin foil, added water, and set it on the drum stove to roast. A thin layer of stones protected it from the top of the stove and a piece of half-flattened stovepipe made a perfect cover. It was done to perfection. I don't remember a meal I enjoyed more. It was such a good break from canned food.

The mosquitoes came in hordes. We had to wear bug-hats out on the tundra to keep them out of our noses and mouths. Freddie and I decided to check out a cabin. We headed out in a direct line. Before long we were detouring around muskeg and water. The mosquitoes were following in a maddening cloud and I kept tripping on the arctic willows that were hugging the ground. I'd had enough. Fred was far ahead. I knew he could hear me call him, but he wouldn't turn or answer. So I yelled.

"Go back then!" he retorted angrily. I was in a foul mood too. I was suffocating in my bug-hat. I snagged my foot on a trailing willow as I turned. Down I went. A ptarmigan erupted from the willows, in front of my face. It took to the air with a staccato beat of wings. Startled, I sent a few choice words after Freddie, who was long gone.

I headed south toward the Caribou River to find some easier walking. Once I reached high ground the hat came off. How I hate things that are confining! A mile later, I reached the river and turned east towards the coast. The river sand was a lively rusty colour. High willows and the odd coniferous tree grew along the banks. It was fairly wide. The sound of rapids was pleasing. I sat on a rock and leaned over to wash my face. The water was much warmer than the ocean. Warm enough for a serious swim, in fact. I stripped, swam, rinsed my T-shirt and underwear, and shampooed my hair. I felt normal again. The walk back was pleasant. The geese were feeding on the tidal flats as I crossed. They stepped out of the way and kept a wary eye on me. The nesting geese on the tundra would stretch their necks, take a look, then lie absolutely motionless as I passed. I pretended not to see them.

I wasn't in a hurry. I loved the openness, the wind, the coolness. The meadows were numerous shades of green. Tiny flowers grew everywhere. The ocean in the background was glinting in the sun. I was happy!

From a distance, I could see Don on the rise above camp. Something was wrong. I started to hurry, not really knowing why. As I got closer, I could see he had Freddie's gun over his shoulder, the bear bombs across the other, and his belt knife at his waist. His hand was on a can of Bear Spray.

"You hunting bear?" I inquired.

"No, one was visiting me," he replied. "Where's Fred?"

He then proceeded to tell me how he was sitting on some turf, sharpening his knife. He felt he was being watched. He turned to see a polar bear strolling toward our camp. The gun was in a case in Fred's tent, halfway between the bear and Don. In his panic, he ran towards the bear, screaming and yelling and waving his arms. Luckily, the bear thought it over and left. He had probably smelled the bones from the seal. I had wanted to burn them, but Don and Fred had been disgusted that I was always cleaning up. "Do something useful" or "save your energy for paddling" was how they put it. Five minutes later Don was helping me pick up and burn each one. I never had trouble getting them to keep a clean camp after that. Don retold the story when Fred returned.

Fred's first question was "Did you get a picture?"

He didn't believe the story. He went to look for the tracks. He found them. His comment was "There's nothing to be afraid of!" That night, though, he had a fish line strung across the sand in the direction the bear had come. On it was an aluminum pan. The loaded gun was outside the door of his tent, leaning on a piece of driftwood and pointing at our tent four feet away.

Don bawled us out properly for leaving the camp unprotected. The rule would be "One person will always stay in camp."

Later Don and I left to check the ice conditions. When I glanced back, Freddie was loading his camera.

At supper time Freddie said, "Vicki, at 7:00 I want you to bring your camera and come with me. It will only take a minute." I glanced at Don, but he didn't say a word.

"Where are we going, Freddie? How far is it? What are we going for?" No answer.

Camp was nearly a mile back already.

"How much farther?" I asked.

Freddie exploded, "If you're so afraid of bears go back to Transcona where you belong!" It wasn't the bear I was concerned about.

"I should have let you drown in your tent, you little sucker!" I turned on my heel and returned to camp. If the tent door had been solid, I would have slammed it shut behind me. I plugged in my cassette player and drifted off to sleep to "The Strawberry Roan." Thanks, Pilgrim!

Every day we heard thunderous cracks from the ice-field. As yet there was no movement. Each trip to the knoll was more interesting. I looked forward to these strolls with Don. We had some of our more interesting talks along the way. One day he was carrying Fred's gun. A goose raised her head from among the rocks. Don fired. The bullet ricocheted off the rocks. I could hear the panic in the goose's call. She didn't fly but moved quickly into the open and exposed her goslings.

"Don't shoot, Don! She has babies!" The shotgun blast was trauma enough for them, but Don herded the goslings together for a group picture. Seconds later the parents had them back.

The seals were still out on the ice. More and more they came to visit our cove at high tide.

Freddie was becoming restless again. I helped him get his kayak down to meet the tide and he paddled off into the bay. We watched him wind his way along the edge of the ice-field. He was singing little religious songs to the seals and eider ducks, making them up as he went along. From a mile away his voice echoed back to us, crystal clear, across the water. He returned very happy and put us all in good spirits.

My sunburn had turned to a deep tan. Each day I got darker. I could have worn my shorts every day, if it hadn't been for the black flies. Often we would have to make a smudge with seaweed to get some relief. Each day there was enough to do. We gathered driftwood, checked and repacked our diminishing supplies, did minor repairs to clothes, tents, and kayaks, melted ice for drinking water or hauled it in. We also kept a hopeful eye on the ice-field and a cautious one open for polar bears. Freddie was really beginning to enjoy himself. He would disappear down to the Caribou River and try fishing. Often he could see the fish, but they wouldn't bite. He always came back in a super mood. He looked comical in the bottom half of his woolly white underwear, toque, and bare feet. Sometimes he wore a red wool shirt with the ensemble. With his white beard and big smile he looked like a wild trapper. He began to think he would like to live here forever. He claimed it brought back his childhood. He swore there could only be one improvement and that was to have Gundela, his wife, with him.

Don left camp with the gun one evening. After eight shots he came back with one mud hen. He had also wounded one. We returned to end its misery. They both ended up in the soup.

Saturday, June 29th, turned out to be a bright, warm, and windy day. The wind was coming from the west across the tundra. It carried the faint aroma of the land in bloom. Subconsciously, I felt an anxiety and a restlessness. We were already eleven days overdue in Arviat. I worried about what my family and friends might be thinking. It was also Freddie's 56th birthday. He took his gun and left for the day. Don and I were hoping he would be back early, so we could have supper together. By 5:00 p.m. he hadn't returned.

The sound of a low-flying plane reached our ears.

"Yes, yes, there it is!" I was so excited I could barely contain myself. It was definitely a search plane, flying low and following the coastline closely. It flew over us and Don warned me not to wave first, so they wouldn't think we were in trouble. In the window I could see an officer's blue shirt and the R.C.M.P. shoulder patch. They buzzed us once, then flew out over the ice, back, and then once more. At that point Freddie came over the ridge. They must have been counting heads. Now there were three. I waved and Don gave them the thumbs-up sign. The ice-field filled in the rest of the story. The wings rocked from side to side. The plane banked to the left and they were gone. My legs weakened and my eyes blurred with tears. I felt relief knowing that within the hour our families would know we were safe. We were to learn later that we were only 35 air miles out of Churchill and an ambulance was waiting for the plane's return.

I made Freddie a bannock birthday cake to celebrate the occasion. It was decorated with a Happy Birthday sign and a candle. We toasted him with wine I had along for the occasion. He made his wish and blew out the candle. He was beaming.

"This is the best birthday I've ever had," he exclaimed.

There must have been magic in his wish, for the explosions in the ice-field were louder and more frequent than ever. They echoed like a barrage of cannon fire across the water, and the tremors vibrated through the ground like a giant heartbeat. It was music to my ears.

Before turning in for the night I went for a stroll down the beach. I felt I was walking a foot off the sand. Freddie caught up to me.

"What's up, Freddie?" I asked.

"It's that man with the rose who sent the search plane," he stated.

"So?" I waited for him to go on.

"Do you know how much that could cost?" he asked.

"No, but don't worry, Freddie, you won't have to pay for it," I replied before I walked away. "It will be taken care of. It's worth it to me."

The explosions lulled me to sleep that night.

June 30th. "The ice-fields are breaking up!"

With the winds and the changing tides the broken floes reared up and tilted to form islands of floating ice. They shone an iridescent cobalt in the bright sunshine. More and more bergs were shoved and pushed over the reef. They came waltzing to our shore on the waves. The best part was the amount of blue water showing amid the ice. The strangest sort of images appeared on the horizon to the south and east, and sometimes to the north. It was a mirage, but it looked as though the ice was lifting into cliffs hundreds of feet high. Thank goodness it was not constant. It was so unnerving. I was taking pictures, but unfortunately it was an optical illusion for the eye only.

July 1st. A few toots on the noise-makers. Happy birthday, Canada!

The wind had shifted to strong and warm from the west. The pressure on the massive ice-field was easing with each outgoing tide. The giant floes were beginning to pull apart and the channels of water between them widened.

On his little short-wave radio, Don heard that Michael Landon had passed away. We had all liked Little Joe Cartwright on *Bonanza*.

July 2nd, Tuesday. At 6:00 a.m. we were awake. Hurriedly, Don and I walked to the knoll. Yes! Yes! Yes! There was a trail of blue showing amid the ice all the way to the horizon in the north. In the excitement we were tripping over ourselves. High tide was at 10:45 p.m. We planned to leave at 9:00. As departure time drew nearer, Don became more hyper. He was adding confusion to a very routine job. We shared the task of getting the kayaks down to meet the tide. It felt good to be settling snugly into the cockpit. Pushing away from shore, we dropped our rudders. It was a comfort to find them operating well. At last, after sixteen days, we were free. My muscles began working rhythmically. I felt the satisfying bite of the double-blade through the crystal clear water. Don led the way over the reef and out to sea. As soon as he spotted a fairly long clear channel, we headed north. We settled into a rhythm that would continue for the next twelve hours. Seals frolicked in the water as we paddled along. They had no fear of us. The banter was light-hearted. We all felt the relief of being on the move. The width of the channels among the floes did not allow paddling side by side. I'm sure in the back of all our minds was the thought that we might not be able to get to shore at the end of the day. We watched for large chunks of transparent ice, riding so low in the water they couldn't be readily seen in the breaking sea. Hitting one was like connecting with a rock. Riding one's kayak onto a chunk was even more dangerous. The call went out: ice to the left, ice to the right. There was ice all around us, but the meaning was understood. Teamwork counted.

Don was the first to spot the whales. Belugas! They were caught up in exuberant play in the ice. Don and I were six feet apart. "Watch for the clear ice, Don," I cautioned. But the ice moved. It was a beluga. It swam between our kayaks and dove into the depths. I could have touched it. Then two gray whales came up from my left, side by side, in perfect, graceful rhythm. First came one short spout, then the curve of their backs cleared the water, and last their flukes, as they disappeared into the next gentle swell. I couldn't imagine more delightful paddling companions.

At times we could spot land to our left. Halfway through the day we were confronted once more by chaotically jumbled pack ice. Again there were many seals resting on the floes. The floes were smeared with feces and the smell was strong. I kept watching for polar bears. Seals and bears are a combo. It would have been a touchy situation if one had spotted us squeezing through the narrow openings. We paddled in very close quarters. We could not afford to lose sight of each other. Some openings were so narrow that the ice scraped the kayaks on both sides. We used our hands to pull through, often to discover there was no exit.

Don would start yelling. "Just shut up for a minute," I'd yell back. "It's not easy to turn a kayak in such a confined space." Usually Freddie would be in the best position to exit first, then I, followed by Don. Much as we hated to, we paddled farther out to sea to skirt the ice-field. Though the water was much rougher, it was a relief to have more space. Three hours later we were past the worst. The bergs were floating free and loose. The current was strong and conflicting. Huge chunks would come by, catch the current, twirl away, and head back in the direction they came from. It became quite a challenge and some fun too. I'd break the rhythm of my stroke, judge the angle of approach, look in both directions, and accelerate at the opportune moment to sneak through. Nothing can top a responsive kayak in these conditions.

The farther north we paddled, the more beautiful the scenery became. The tide was on the rise. We were able to head nearer to a friendly shoreline. The green tundra sloped to the ocean. Watching the shoreline fascinated me. I loved the ice and the experience of paddling in it, but it was the land I had come north to see.

We left the floe-ice behind. Even the icebergs were scattered. My eyes were watering and sore from the glare of the shiny bergs. Still, I watched in a trance. They came sailing majestically before the wind, so heavy they barely rocked on the climbing waves.

We had been paddling steadily for nearly twelve hours. "Watch for a good landing spot," Don called.

On a high point of land extending into the water, I spotted a tower. If there was a tower, there might be a radio phone. With much enthusiasm, we headed for it. It took us another hour of paddling and, in the process, we crossed the 60th parallel from Manitoba into the Keewatin District of the Northwest Territories.

As we neared, I couldn't contain my excitement. "Look, a cabin by the tower and people running toward the cabin!" We made our way through the rock-strewn shoals to a protected cove and pulled up to shore. Again, Don went berserk. "Pull up your rudders, undo your spray skirt. Get out, grab the kayaks." I scrambled out of the cockpit. My legs were numb. They buckled and I fell backwards into the water. Instantly my temper flared. My first impulse was to take a swing at Don with my double-blade, but I managed to suppress the urge.

Don ranted on, "Grab the kayaks, lift, carry, get the tent!"

Fred and I had a system by which we looped a wide strap under the back of the kayak and lifted together. In the confusion, I lifted before he was ready. The strap slipped through his hands and rubbed the blisters off. He screamed in agony. I reached for his hands and turned them palms up. I was sick at the sight of the broken, bloody blisters covering his palms and fingers.

I glared at Don. He backed off.

The minute the tent was up and Don was inside, I exploded. "Don't you ever do that to us again!"

"I'm paranoid of launching and landing from my South American trip," he whined.

I'll admit I lost control. "Well, this is not South America!" I shouted. "We are in a protected cove, in six inches of water, with a favouring tide. What in hell is the panic about? If you don't stop this hysteria, someone is going to be seriously hurt and it may even be you!" He promised to control himself. Secretly, I hoped he would never take to leading sky-diving expeditions.

I was trembling from the cold as much as from anger. We had been paddling at full speed for twelve hours without a single break. While paddling, we generated a great deal of heat. Once we stopped the wind and our wet clothes immediately sucked the last of the heat from our bodies. The unplanned dip in the ice-cold water didn't help.

After a quick change into dry clothes, I went to check the tower. It turned out to be a six-foot mast from a Peterhead boat. The cabin was the top two feet of the boat's cabin. The people were Canada geese. Emotions went from inflated to deflated in a matter of seconds. The north plays such wicked optical tricks. Still the day held a special reward. We were treated to the most spectacular sunset ever. It came across the ocean, highlighting the icebergs with rims of fire. With it came a certain amount of peace.

I went to Freddie's tent to help him with his hands. We got them bandaged. How he would be able to paddle the next day, I didn't know.

While we waited for the tide to rise the next morning, we had time to explore. Don found a huge polar bear skull which he tied to the front of his kayak. He did it quite sheepishly, after having griped at me for carrying extra weight in mine.

We discovered the rest of the Peterhead boat. The top deck was flat on the sand. The Cummins engine block was halfway up the shore rocks. Across the top of the point lay parts of thousands of soda-pop cans. Don's comment was, "Whoever camped here sure liked pop." I showed him the lids. The pull tabs had not been opened.

In Arviat later on, we discovered the boat had belonged to Simon Kaumak. He was freighting ten tonnes of soda-pop from Churchill to Arviat in 1970, when the boat's engine failed during a terrible storm. He and his son and companion were able to bail out in a canoe before the Peterhead smashed up on the rocks.

Manitoba was two miles to the south of us. Till the end of the trip we would be paddling in the immense Northwest Territories. Almost a third of Canada, yet home to only 54,000 people, the Northwest Territories stretch from the 61st parallel to the 84th and from the Yukon to the Davis Strait, over 3200 kilometers in each direction. It was a first visit for all three of us.

July 3rd, Wednesday. We shivered as we packed our kayaks. I was always the last to finish because I was carrying the tent and it was always the last article to be put away. Don was ready and pacing, but almost in control. I was proud of his attempt. It would make it much more pleasant for us. Freddie's hands were painful. He didn't complain, but I doubted whether he had been able to sleep. Carefully, we made our way through the rocks. Don was a good navigator. We followed single file, two feet apart. The day was hot, the sea untroubled by the wind. We were out two hours ahead of high tide. For the next two hours and for two hours after high tide we were assured of high water, so we stayed nearer to shore. Once the tide was edging toward low, we had to follow the outgoing tide to deeper water. The shoals were wide. Most of the day we were four to five miles from shore. We had left the ice far behind.

Halfway through the day, we passed the Tha-Anne and Thlewiaza Rivers. Their deltas nearly combined as they entered the Hudson Bay. The mirages played tricks again, projecting small objects into large, as we strained our eyes to make some sense of the scene. We were entertained through the day by old-squaw ducks. Flocks of them beat their wings in perfect rhythm as they cut sharply across the front of our kayaks, circled again, then flew off to settle in the water far ahead. There the mirage magnified them to the size of boats. In the silence, their loud, persistent vocalization could be heard over the water.

The glare off the water had left us all with red eyes. Don asked me to lead so he could have a darker object to rest his eyes on. This was fine for a while, but it is not in his nature not to be in the lead. He overtook me and we were back to normal. Up to this point we had kept all exposed rocks to our left. Now, two hours before high tide, we were edging our way toward shore. Again the navigation became tricky. The water to our left did not have a headland behind it. Freddie figured it out for us. He tasted the water.

"This water is fresh," he announced. "Let's fill our water bottles." We were again in the mouth of a river. Freddie spotted a cabin on the opposite shore and wanted to head for it. Don gave me the lead. I could hear the tip of my rudder hitting the rocks below. Freddie was cursing behind me. We came to a standstill in the twilight. Again Fred yelled to Don, "I told you, if you follow that woman, she'd lead you straight to Hell!" I was furious. "It was your bloody idea to go for the cabin, Fred." I turned my kayak toward a peninsula at the mouth of the river, away from the cabin. There we found a huge sandy beach.

"Do you want to stay here?" I asked.

"No, too much sand," Don answered. "Head around the point."

Clouds were moving in. The sky darkened. We had to strain to see the shoreline. Judging distance was difficult. Because of the shallows, we ended up paddling far out to sea to get around the point. Once we had rounded it, we had no choice. We must make it in with the tide or we would perish. Don was in the lead again. He gauged a way through the rock-strewn shallows toward shore in the deepening twilight. As we paddled toward it, the sea consumed the land with each incoming wave. We caught up at last and came to a halt. There was still about twelve inches of water, but the rocks were too numerous. We would have to walk in. I sucked in my breath, anticipating the cold of the water as I stepped out. Instead, it was pleasantly warm. The air was warm. The sea was gentle. The surge of the tide was strong but smooth. Each incoming swell lifted the kayaks – less our weight – and took them over the rocks beneath. A rather beautiful ending to a 13¼-hour paddle.

We headed toward a dark object on the tidal flats. It turned out to be a three-foot-high bed of seaweed. The water ended at its base. I suggested lifting the kayaks onto it to give us time to walk in to high ground and set up the tents. For once, there was no argument. We collected our tent, sleeping bags and some food and trudged a quarter of a mile to solid ground. An arctic fox appeared out of the shadows. He stopped to sniff at our gear, but apparently he found nothing of interest. He trotted off into the darkness. Quickly we erected the tents, then returned for the kayaks. There was a foot of water around the bed of seaweed by then. It was an easy chore to pull them down and walk them in as far as the water allowed. They were staked and left again. It was 11:00 p.m. Don crawled into his sleeping bag and started cooking. That awful habit made me nervous. If the camp stove had ever tipped, he would have been trapped with his feet stuck in the mummy-bag.

Freddie was exhausted. I volunteered to bring the kayaks in so he could cook supper. No, he was too tired. He would cook the next day, which Don promised would be a rest day. Between mouthfuls of supper, I made trips to pull the kayaks closer. Freddie took turns too. After he scared me in the dark, I suggested he turn in for the night. There was no need for both of us to be up. He gratefully accepted. An hour later, at midnight, the kayaks were next to the tents and the tide was receding. I fell into an exhausted sleep to the chorus of disturbed geese. The fox must have been tormenting them.

Don woke me hurriedly. "Look at the caribou!" I fell out of the tent in my haste. There he was! Just a magnificent set of racks. Absolutely huge. His big eyes were bulging with curiosity. He took a few more running steps toward the tent. He stopped with legs spread wide, stretched his neck out, and emitted a sharp snort. Then he turned quickly and ran off in a loose, even trot, his head held high and tail erect. The pounding of my heart must have frightened him.

That wasn't the end. Again, Don roused me. "Look at this. Fred, Fred, look at this!" Just a groan came from Freddie's tent. Thousands and thousands of snow geese were parading by our tents. They were all paired off, with two little fluffy yellow goslings each. They walked by keeping a wary eye on us. A cautious honk, honk came from some. They must have been feeding on the tidal flats at dawn and were on their way to the meadows. I stood riveted to the spot, dizzy. I felt I had been caught up in a ground blizzard as they swept by. The meadows and the hills to the west were a moving mass of white.

We crawled back in the tent. As the sound of the passing geese faded away, we enjoyed the symphony of mosquitoes outside our tent. It was only 6:00 a.m. I was too excited to sleep.

We checked our maps and realized we were camped on the McConnell River Bird Sanctuary, between the two branches of the river. It is the nesting ground for some 400,000 snow geese.

The surprises weren't over yet. As I went to my kayak for my toothbrush, I glanced east toward the ocean, but there wasn't any water to be seen. Not to the north, not to the east or to the south. Nothing but boulders stretching to the horizon. I took my binoculars and climbed a rise. No water! In a panic I called Don. "Look what has happened!"

He wasn't surprised. "The water will come back," he promised. I felt better when I saw it seeping among the rocks three hours later.

Drinking water was going to be a problem again, with all the geese around. It was too far to hike to the river, so we strained some of the brown water from the oil-slick-covered ponds, hoping we'd find better water before we needed to use it.

July 4th. Fred had unloaded a good portion of his kayak. He was planning to do some serious cooking. The day was starting out calm and very warm. I was not surprised when Don changed his mind. "We are going to paddle today," he stated. "I'm sorry, but I feel we should go." I was game. Those tidal flats had really unnerved me.

I felt sorry for Freddie. He had so much packing to do. I could only help by carrying a few loads to his kayak. His hands were still raw from the blisters. He was the only one carrying a spare double-blade. I noticed he was switching to his heavier, wooden, unfeathered double-blade. I doubted it was the paddle that caused his blisters. It was probably his ill-fitting gloves. He was not one to tolerate advice from a woman either, so I tried to keep my mouth shut. Obviously, his wrist was giving him trouble too. He wrapped a tensor bandage around his lower arm and wrist and asked me to pin it for him.

"Good God, Freddie. Isn't that much too tight?" I ventured. The daggers that shot from his eyes warned me that I had stepped out of line again. I pinned it where he requested it.

We couldn't cheat on the tide. The shores were so flat that we had to wait until high tide to wedge our way out.

Once we got to deeper water the water was very clear and we could stay near shore for at least two hours. The shoreline quickly became steeper. The caribou trotted down to the water's edge and dashed back and forth trying to get a better look at us. They made me laugh. I was paddling in a short-sleeved T-shirt. The sun felt good on my back. "Good decision," I complimented Don.

He was in a good mood too. Fred was a different story. He was nervous about the rocks below the surface. We were clearing them nicely. I watched the sand, rocks, and seaweed on the ocean floor. I kept calling out the countdown to low tide. Before 6:00 p.m. we must be over deeper water. We were approximately four miles from shore, paddling near the outer edge of the shoals. The dark blue of the deeper water was about a quarter mile to our right. The sea was flat. No rocks to be seen. "If you start seeing rocks popping up or hear the sound of rushing water, head for the dark blue water," explained Don.

Hardly had he spoken when the rocks started popping up, like popcorn in a popper, all around us. "Rudder right, rudder right. Go! Go! Go!" Don yelled. Our reflexes were instant. At full speed we tried to keep up with the receding tide. We weren't fast enough. We heard a sound like a monstrous bathtub draining, and within seconds we had three kayaks sitting flat on the ocean floor. It was hilarious. We had stopped 300 feet short of deep water.

"Get out and go!" Don kept yelling. We jumped out of our cockpits onto the hard-packed ocean floor. I grabbed my tow rope and started running and pulling my kayak along a skinny rivulet that was quickly draining in the direction of the disappearing tide. Freddie was right behind. We made it to the edge of the deep water. Don was a ways back. He didn't have a tow rope. He was pulling the kayak along by its bow and trying to hold up his pants at the same time.

I laughed until my sides hurt when Freddie described how he was pulling the kayak, holding his pants up, running, taking a pee, and eating in the short space of time it took to run the 300 feet. We looked so ridiculous! We were out of sight of land, standing on the ocean floor, laughing. Then Freddie gave Don and me a blast.

"Don't you guys ever need to eat, drink, or pee?" he yelled.

"Okay," Don answered. "We'll have lunch as soon as we get back in the kayaks."

"Hey, that sounds nice. This will be the first time we stopped for lunch since we left Churchill," I commented.

We edged our bows into the deeper water, got in, and pulled away, still chuckling.

I fitted the spray skirt around the cockpit and was opening my chocolate bar when Don yelled, "Let's go!"

"Hey, I thought we were going to have lunch!" I said.

"Yeah," he yelled back, "but don't stop paddling." I thought he was kidding. He wasn't. He was serious and mad. And I don't use the term loosely. Freddie and I glanced at each other. "What can I say?"

Freddie was shivering uncontrollably. "I'm so cold," was his desperate comment. I was still only wearing a T-shirt. The fact that he hadn't eaten well in the last two days was probably starting to affect him. The lack of sleep also.

The storm that was hanging over the land on the horizon hit us full force before we had gone far. We bent to the task of riding it out. There was no way to get to shore. The light breeze shifted into a stormy wind. I really could have used my jacket, but it would have been too dangerous to try to get it on. We paddled on four-foot waves for at least an hour. The wind was in our favour and I think we made good time. The outer edge of the storm was all that got us. Before long we were back to calmer seas and sunshine.

I was longing to see a shoreline again. Only one spot on the horizon was visible. From out on the ocean, it appeared as a long black mound. I half expected it to be a mirage and disappear, but it was constant all day long. It was a good focal point for our progress. The shoals were littered with massive, rounded boulders sticking out above the water. Even at high tide I would hate to have to navigate a powerboat through.

Soon even the boulders were blocked from sight. We had paddled behind what could be best described as the Great Wall of China. It was a reef that looked like it had been designed by an ingenious engineer. It was perfectly straight, wide and flat on top. It ran parallel to shore, each stone placed as though by hand to a height of six to ten feet above water. God only knows how deep it went. How incredible to be travelling five miles from shore on the outside of these barriers for hours at a time with no way to pass through or over. Luckily, we were blessed with agreeable weather. When a break in the wall finally appeared, we paddled through to the grand sight of land not too far away. The shoreline was high and sandy. It even had a tower on it. This time I wasn't fooled. In order to stay out of the shallows, we kept to the right of all exposed boulders. By 8:00 p.m. we came to a long reef projecting across our path. It stretched at least three quarters of a mile into the ocean. Because of its angle and the incoming tide, it churned the water into a seething, boiling mass all along its length. At first Don planned to pass around it, then he changed his mind. "Stay close behind me, do as I do," he commanded. I passed the message on to Freddie. Don was very good at judging the water and waves. We paddled along until he yelled, "Now! Once you commit yourself, you go."

Don got a lifting wave and went through. I picked the next one. No problem! My rudder rattled on a few rocks with no harm done. I turned my kayak to watch Freddie. My heart stopped as he came in on a bad angle. The wave held him suspended, his bow and rudder clear of the water. To make matters worse, he raised his arms high to ward off the wave. I called to Don to wait, but he was out of range. I fully expected Fred to go over. He slammed down at an awkward angle and recovered. He had just missed breaking his neck. We carried on at a relaxed pace. It was 10:30 p.m. and we were waiting for the tide to rise. Rain was falling to the east, south and west of us. Storm clouds were darkening the sky and the shore was in shadows.

Freddie exclaimed, "Look, a light!"

Don figured it out. "It must be the beacon at Arviat. Yes, it has to be."

We had paddled steadily for twelve hours already and were exhausted. Still, the beacon was a drawing card. The thought of a warm soft bed, instead of setting up in the rain, provided wonderful motivation. Don warned us, "It looks close, but I guess it's fifteen miles away."

"Okay, fifteen miles it is."

The storm caught up to us, northern style, instantly. The ripples on the water ballooned into five-foot waves. We headed into a strong north wind, side by side, with nothing in mind but the beacon. The rain came. Big, warm drops splattered on our faces. I was proud of the way my kayak handled those waves. Feeling the surge and strength of the current through the shaft of the double-blade made my adrenaline flow faster.

The sky was dark, the clouds were crowding the quarter moon. What little light broke through was reflected across the tops of the waves. The wind was calming. Instead of full force, it became moderate. The breezes turned warm carrying the smell of rain off the land. They caressed my face and lifted the wet hair off my neck.

Don was incredibly tense. His kayak did not respond well in the waves. We called back and forth to keep in touch. I'm sure in the back of all our minds was the thought, "If one falters, we're all dead. At least it will be quick."

"Don't become hypnotized by the beacon," Don yelled. "Look away from it." I tried, but my eyes were drawn back automatically to the light.

Midnight. The seas were calming and the tide was reversing. We had been able to see more lights of the town. Now, one by one, they were extinguished. I felt a loneliness, like no one expected me home this night. Fred called for an easier pace. We slowed down, but we were getting chilled. I only had my short-sleeved T-shirt under my rubberized rain jacket. The waves had come in past the collar and every inch of me was drenched. Rocks were popping up all over. We could feel the sandy ocean floor with some paddle strokes. I was bringing up the rear. Don was in high gear again. He hated being cold. I was doing my best to encourage Fred to stay with us. He tried to joke back but his retorts were lame. All I could see of Don were the tips of his double-blade flashing in the moonlight in the distance. I started to hate him. This was supposed to be a team. I called to Fred. No answer. The moon broke through momentarily and I spotted Fred. He was sagged forward, leaning on his paddle and dozing. My heart went out to him.

"Come on, Fred. We can make it. Let's go. Stay close. It can't be far now." He was too tired to care.

The shoreline was in long dark shadows. I suggested going in and setting up the tents. It was 2:00 a.m. Don was furious at the idea. Around the peninsula we went. From one point to the next. High on the headland, we could see tents silhouetted against the sky. Don called up. No answer. We rounded a point and started into a bay where Don thought Arviat was. We were only fifty feet from shore. All of a sudden came the sound of a big slurp. In seconds, the outgoing tide sucked the water out from under us and we were sitting on the ocean bottom again.

"Turn around. Head out to sea, head out to sea," Don kept shouting.

"What are we going to use for water?" I screamed back. "I'm going to shore now!" I got out and dragged my kayak to the shore, then went to help Fred. His arm was puffy and blue. We helped each other lift the kayaks to higher ground. Don was stomping around, cursing, insisting he could have made it. We were all hypothermic. I was shivering uncontrollably. Freddie could hardly keep his eyes open. Don was walking around in circles and blabbering incoherently. I was near tears, and at that point it would have been nice to have a strong wide shoulder to lean on and a dry sleeve to wipe my nose in.

"I've had enough of this bullshit. I'm pulling out in Arviat," were Freddie's only words.

"Me too!" I answered.

Don was shouting commands at me, as I tried setting the tent up. "Don't put it on the sand, put it here, put it there." Shouting back I said, "Just shut up. If you're not going to help, go get your sleeping bag."

He came back without it. Again, he was cursing and babbling incoherently.

"Where's your sleeping bag?" I asked.

"My fingers are too cold to open the hatches," was his answer. I went to open his hatches and finished the tent. He crawled in, got into his sleeping bag, and seconds later was as placid as a baby as he sucked on a spoonful of peanut butter.

I collected the food we needed, checked on Freddie, and with relief crawled into the tent. All I wanted was to sleep. Don insisted on making a full meal. We hadn't eaten for 17½ hours. We had paddled fifteen hours and 53 minutes of that. Eating, I struggled to keep my head out of my plate. "Help me with the maps," Don insisted. "Fuck off," was all I could manage. I fell asleep, physically, emotionally, and mentally exhausted.

July 5th, Friday, came in with an overcast sky, cold and windy. A fellow named Bernie spotted us and came by on his Honda. I traded a couple of packs of cigarettes for some help getting the kayaks down to meet the tide. He promised to tell the Northern Store manager, Gordon Main, that we were on our way.

The tent was wet, we were wet, the ground was wet. We packed ourselves into the kayaks and headed for Arviat. The waves were high and ice was still packed along shore in some places. Four miles later, as we paddled into town, some Inuit were waiting on the shore. They asked us where we had come from. We said, "Churchill." They were smiling and all started to clap. What a warm welcome it was!

At the Northern Store, Gordie and Martha and their children were waiting, along with others. They gave us a royal reception. It certainly did raise our spirits. Our kayaks were put away and we were hustled into warm, clean staff quarters of the Northern Store. Beautiful people, food, dinner invitations, a chance to do laundry. Piece of heaven!

First of all I wanted to phone my daughters and friends. I caught up on the news about my new grandson. And even mail. Teresa had sent pictures of the baby. I was thrilled.

What a luxury it was to soak in a tub of hot water! As I soaked, the skin on my fingers came off like little condoms. They had been frozen deeper than I thought. I still didn't have much feeling in them but at least they still functioned.

The first evening Gordie, Martha, and their children – Jim, John and twins Fiona and Heather – had us over for an arctic char supper. It was the first time I had tasted char. It was delicious! To top if off we had pineapple upside-down cake and coffee.

We missed part of their barbecue party the next evening. The R.C.M.P. caught up with us. We had to fill out Wilderness Travel Forms, which Don, in his childish revolt against rules, refused to do in Churchill. The female officer reprimanded us sternly for the thoughtlessness.

For two days the wind and waves were wicked.

Fred was definitely pulling out. His arm and wrist were very painful.

I was torn between leaving and carrying on. The insatiable desire to know what lay beyond the next point was too powerful. I decided to continue.

Arviat, formerly Eskimo Point, has a population of 1100 people, mostly Inuit. The Inuit have abandoned the lifestyle of the nomadic hunter and live now in modern, energy-efficient homes, in communities that have sprung up in this century. The people were very friendly and I was excited to see the mothers carrying their babies in traditional Amautis. They are parkas in which the baby cuddles next to the mother's back, with a hood that will cover both baby and mother. The young girls were so beautiful they attracted immediate attention.

We asked to speak to a local person who could give us advice about the coast to the north. It turned out to be Simon Kaumak, the Inuit captain of the Peterhead we had found wrecked on the shore. When we mentioned it he answered, "Yes, I know it. It was my boat," and told us the story. Simon told us the worst was over. From now on, we would have deeper water and better shoreline. He pointed out an island we could camp on for the first night out. All the news was encouraging.

July 8th, Monday. Gordie and Martha bade us goodbye at 2:00 a.m. It was cool in the twilight of the night, yet it was pleasant to be on the way again. The seas were calm and stretched forever away to the horizon. We headed between Sentry Island and the island off its west point to avoid the riptides. We had learned to respect them. We knew the Maguse River was deep in the bay where we could hear the cackling of the old-squaw ducks. The prominent headland of Maguse Point guided us in the twelve-mile crossing. The next bay was full of reefs and shoal areas. The heat shimmers danced and blurred the islands. We were looking for a specific one.

Don called a halt. "Come look at this map. Tell me if that is the island Simon meant." The island he was pointing to was a wavering black mirage on the horizon to the north. One minute it was long and low, the next it was short and high. The sun was so bright, the water so calm, that nothing looked real.

"I don't know, Don. According to the map the island is eleven miles away. Why don't we paddle closer? Then we'll know," I offered.

He exploded with curses. "You don't care about the map. You don't want to help."

"Listen, Don, the island is to the north. We have to go north anyway. We aren't getting anywhere paddling in circles and yelling," I said.

He was still terribly angry. "I don't want to be paddling across the ocean without knowing where I'm going!" he shouted. Ironically, he saved that for later in the trip.

The discord between us was draining my strength. I paddled north. He paddled past. I could tell he was still angry by his quick, jerky paddle strokes. I was glad he couldn't look back, because the situation had struck me as comical. I couldn't help laughing.

Two and a half hours later we landed on the island. It was the right one. The beaches were good. A few stranded floes rested on shore. We'd have drinking water. The island was high, flat, and covered in long green grass. The minute we stirred the grass we were attacked by clouds of mosquitoes. We dashed back to our kayaks and made a hasty exit and headed to the distant shore instead.

We had put in a 12¼-hour, 46-mile day. It seemed much easier to paddle with just the two of us. Our camp was ten miles northeast of the Wallace River on a sand esker that ended in the ocean and looked like a roadbed under construction. Our clothes were soaked from perspiration and paddle drip. We spread them on the sand and weighted them down with rocks. We were not able to find fresh water nearby; however, we were carrying enough for supper and the next day. After corned beef, creamed corn, and instant mashed potatoes, we had our tea, then got on with the map work. We always worked on it together. The time travelled, location, and distance were all recorded. I'd mark the two high and low tides for the next day, write it in big numbers, put it in a ziploc bag and snap it under the deck elastic next to my compass.

July 9th – High Tide – 3:15 a.m. One nice thing about starting a paddling day in the wee hours of the morning was the early afternoon quits. We always woke 1½ hours before departure. This allowed a 45-minute breakfast and 45 minutes for dismantling and packing. Don would not tolerate a minute past a specific departure time. Although he was a little more kind at departures, I could tell by his pacing and watch checking that he was near a volatile explosion at the drop of a hat.

As promised, the shoals were narrower, only hundreds of yards instead of miles. The water was deeper, crystal clear, and a turquoise blue. Getting to shore would not be a problem. There would be no need to stay out twelve hours at a time. Lots of islands too. The land was mostly solid rock or sand. We spotted a yellow cabin along the coast. At Sandy Point we spotted Simon's white cabin. The Inuit have not forgotten their traditional love for the land. They spend many days camping, hunting, and fishing.

Past Angusko Point, we headed twelve miles across Dawson Inlet. Our eyes were strained from the glare and the distance of those open stretches. It was a relief to reach Bibby Island, a quite unique mass of rusty-coloured boulders. We were thinking about fresh water for our supper. There was the odd little floe around. Don asked for my hatchet and decided he would chop off a chunk of an overhang into a black plastic bag. I came alongside and stabilized his kayak. He chopped too hard. The whole projection broke off and narrowly missed his kayak. It was a close call for both of us, also an important lesson.

On the east shore of Bibby we spotted a white cabin with a red roof at the end of a path. I was wondering if it had belonged to the Hudson's Bay Company. As we paddled around the northeast corner of Bibby we were confronted by ice. It blocked our way to the Morso Islands. We would have to find a good position to get a new compass bearing. The only channel open to us was due north through Nevill Bay. Reefs to the seaward were holding back the ice-pack. They were shaped like massive horseshoes. All were joined together to form totally impassable barriers and lined up in a north-south direction. We paddled north aided by a strong tailwind. What would have caused such formations? They protected us from the ice for a ten-mile stretch.

"Watch for an island with a flat top,'" Don instructed. We were hoping it was called Flattop for the right reason. The sun and sea were playing tricks on us again. Every island looked like it had a flat top, and there were many. The islands would lift from flat to mushroom shaped, distort, and shrink to actual size. It was eerie and frustrating, until we spotted one that remained constant. We had found Flattop. We had to wind our way through trapped ice along the shore, but had no trouble landing. We carried our kayaks up to the last high-tide mark and set up camp on the sandspit.

We decided to climb Flattop and get our bearing for the Morso Islands, which were our halfway point to the hamlet of Whale Cove. A large snowdrift extended most of the way up on the south side. We trudged up alongside it. Don was in the lead. He disappeared over the embankment. I looked up for a better handhold in time to duck a brown missile coming for my face. Don had frightened an eider duck off her nest. One foot higher and she would have hit my face. She probably would have broken her neck and mine. Don reached down and helped me over the edge. My heart was pounding from the climb and the sight. All around us was a turquoise sea dotted with brilliant white ice-floes. We had an idea of the direction of the Morso Islands from the mirages that rose and faded to the east. There seemed to be fairly solid ice in that direction, but the wind could change things overnight.

Don loved exploring. We walked the mile-long island. Even here there were ancient stone tent rings. We discovered more eider ducks' nests. Three large eggs nestled in the piles of down. We took some photographs, got our bearings, and left the ducks in peace.

July 10th. The smell of ice was heavy on the wind. We tackled the rough sea with enthusiasm. My kayak seemed to love the wind, as I do. It responded to slight touches on the rudder. As we passed the northern tips of the Morso Islands the wind was starting to whip the tops of the waves into foam. I kept flexing my fingers to keep the circulation going. The wind was trying to wrench the double-blade from my grasp.

Don called, "What's your compass bearing?"

I answered back, "I can't get one. The compass is going nuts." And it was. It was spinning wildly. Again he started cursing and yelling. I hated the way he exploded when things weren't just right. "Shut up and keep your shirt on! We're over a reef. That may be the cause," I retorted. Sure enough, as we paddled away from the reef, the compass settled into the 47° bearing that would take us to Whale Cove.

Don's compass wasn't working. He had left it outside all winter on his overturned kayak. He and Freddie had taken it apart at Hubbart Point, but couldn't fix it properly. I didn't mind calling the bearing to him periodically through the day. By 9:00 a.m. we were in Whale Cove. A group of men walked out on the tidal flat to meet us. After we exchanged greetings, they picked up our kayaks and carried them to shore. Don and I were very grateful. Both of us were drenched and chilled. The last few miles had been rough.

The hamlet of Whale Cove is the smallest community in the Keewatin District of the Northwest Territories. It is home to 255 Inuit, many of whom moved to the hamlet when the inland caribou numbers dropped. When I mentioned that we had a tough time finding it, one of the Inuit asked me, "Didn't you see the inukshuks on the land?"

"What are inukshuks?" I asked.

"They're markers made of piled stones that guide you to shelter," they explained.

We had seen them as we paddled in, but were ignorant of their purpose. On the rest of the trip they always lifted my spirits wherever I spotted them.

The evening high tide, with the help of the south wind, brought pack ice into the cove and blocked it tightly. We spoke to Lewis Voisey, who had grown up in the area. He told us we might be able to escape through to the north. We would have to get through a channel called Hell's Gate. The timing would have to be perfect. We studied the maps. Don figured out a plan. Hell's Gate has four channels. The rising tide would come from four directions into a central bay area. We would have to enter as near to peak high tide as possible, then be ready the minute the tide reversed itself. Lewis told us, "Don't panic if you feel like you're paddling uphill, because you will be. The force of the incoming tide will lift the water in the central area." That sounded tricky but there was more. "If you have to exit through the longest channel be prepared. The current runs at fourteen knots. If the entrance is blocked by ice, you will not be able to return against the current."

Don timed the tide perfectly. We made our way through the floes to the beginning of the south channel. Now we were committed. I could feel the lift and surge on my kayak. We headed for the north exits, two miles away. Both were blocked by jumbled pack ice. I didn't feel safe there. I didn't want us to be in the way if it all let loose. Our only hope now was the long channel. We found it in time. We were ready at the entrance just as the tide reversed. We came down that chute dodging the islands and paddling like mad to keep the rudder from overtaking the bow. Within minutes we had cleared the two miles and were spat out into the ocean, but there was nowhere to go. Pack ice crowded the bay. I led the way along the shore, around a big island, and back into Whale Cove. The experience was fun. We were feeling our oats, so to speak. We raced, joked and laughed all the way back to town. Besides, it was good to know what an overloaded touring kayak could do in fast water.

The ice conditions became worse. We were stranded in Whale Cove for four days. One could feel the excitement in town. With the ice would come the seals and whales.

This turned out to be a good time to repair my rudder. A weld on the rudder assembly had cracked on the way in. I felt better after one of the fellows at the hamlet garage fixed it. The rest was good for us. Don and I hiked many miles over the rocks to check ice conditions. Our legs needed it, after so many hours in the kayaks.

On the 12th of July, it was so warm, Don and I were in T-shirts and bare feet. One group of kids felt sorry for Don when they saw his big, bare feet. "Don't you have any shoes?" they asked shyly.

We were lucky to get a room in an unoccupied construction trailer. The door wouldn't close properly and the mosquitoes became a nuisance. In the next two days of rain, I caught up on my sleep while Don went exploring.

Andy Kowtak came by one day to tell us he had just flown in from Rankin. From the plane he had seen open water along the shore to the north. If we stayed in close we could get around it.

Andy was overcome by Don's constant chatter, questions, and hyper-ness. "Why do you ask so many questions?" he asked.

"I want to learn," was Don's answer.

"In our way, we learn by listening and watching," was Andy's reply.

Don mentioned he had written a book and Andy clammed up for good. The next day, when Don walked toward him, he put up his hands and said, "I don't feel like talking today."

I was on the beach working on my kayak.

Andy stopped by and we had a pleasant conversation.

"Is Don another Farley Mowat?" he asked.

I laughed, "Not likely!"

"I hope you aren't married to that man," was the last thing he said before he walked away. I strolled back to the trailer and turned to look back at the ocean. The sun beat down on the pack ice. Yes, we would be on the way soon.

Don stepped out of the trailer and grabbed my arms from behind. He pulled them back so hard my elbows almost touched.

"Ouch!" I screamed, "What are you doing?"

He led me to the stairs and leaned me over the edge.

"Tell me how much you love me or I'll push you over," he warned.

The remark caught me off guard. I also knew that he had had a pressing call from nature at that very spot. I didn't want to end up down there!

"Ouch, lots, lots, let me go!" was all I could manage, before I broke up with laughter.

He let go and turned to go inside, leaving me to figure out the meaning of the moment.

The first time we tried pilot biscuits was in Whale Cove. They are like a hard tack bread, dry but very filling. I bought some to add to our food supply.

Then, to my horror, I discovered I was bleeding from the bowel. It could only be from my ulcers acting up, from the tension of the last few weeks. I was afraid Don would insist I stay behind, so I didn't tell him. I didn't want to go home yet.

Mary Jane Ford worked at the hamlet office. I'll never forget how kind she was. She and her daughter Amanda came for a visit one day. Amanda was only 22 years old but had worked on a farm in Ontario and worked in Venezuela for a while. She played hockey and had won a canoe race at the last tournament of Inuit games in Baker Lake. She had a laugh that was infectious. They invited us to their home for a delicious caribou supper. We met Mary Jane's husband, Joe. He was tall, slim, and very dark. He was also very soft-spoken and shy. Mary Jane lovingly interpreted back and forth, but there was amusement in her eyes the whole time. I had a sneaking suspicion Joe could speak English if he had a mind to. Suddenly, Joe glanced at the clock and started searching for something. I asked, "Are you looking for your toque, Joe?"

"Yes," he replied.

"Where are you off to, Joe?" I handed him the toque.

"To a meeting," he quickly answered. There was a twinkle in his eye as he went out the door.

I had time to write and phone home during this break. Continuing past Repulse Bay in 1991 was starting to seem less possible. Already we were twenty days behind schedule. Still, I was enjoying every day that was granted to me. The trip had already brought out reserves I didn't realize I had. If nothing else, I had learned to bite my tongue. That had never been one of my strong points. I was enjoying my sabbatical from civilization but I remained conscious of my responsibility to all those who, for one reason or another, valued my life. I assured everyone we would be very careful. I planned to come home alive.

July 16th. Time to leave. Mary Jane came running with a much appreciated present of caribou meat.

The plan was to try Hell's Gate again. This time we were able to use one of the north-end chutes. We had to get out of our kayaks, pull them through the ice jam, and then paddle to the sea. The pack ice was still out there, grinding and groaning. Its days were numbered, though. It was rotten. Big chunks were falling off, to end up as slush on the water.

I was shocked when Don headed into the thick of it.

"Where are you going, Don? Andy said to stick close to shore," I yelled. I was yelling a lot lately. Anyway, I followed him. We ended up blundering around for an hour. After becoming totally blocked, we turned back to our starting point. We followed the shore, and before an hour was out we had skirted the pack with free passage to Dunne Foxe Island.

We turned into the strong head wind. The ice-pack had been steadying the water. In the open, the wind was whipping the waves to foam. We worked hard. The power of waves should never be underrated. Don's kayak was so different from mine. The speed that was good for him was not necessarily good for me. It was hard to get a good rhythm going in the short chop. Each time I punched through a wave by mistake, my kayak lost its momentum and needed to be accelerated again. If I wasn't careful the odd crest would leap up, plunge onto the kayak, rush to hit me in the chest, then pool on the spray skirt. Sometimes rogue waves broke over my head. I would feel the cold as the water slid past my collar to drain down between my breasts in front and my shoulder blades at my back. I ended up sitting in a pool for the rest of the day. I would feel the tang of salt on my lips and the sting of it in my eyes. Then to top it off, if I took a split second to raise my hood, the last of the wave, accumulated in the hood, would spill down my back. Deep in our hearts all of us realize paradise is where we are happy.

For most people, paradise is easier to find while smearing on suntan lotion at a beach than battling ice-cold waves in a kayak. I honestly would not switch. It is no wonder my dear children find it hard to understand me. Someday, I want to be a proper mother and grandmother. Someday, I might get the North out of my system. Then, maybe not!

After hours of intense effort we had gained Dunne Foxe Island. Don veered off for the mainland six miles away. I was impressed by the tenacity and courage he showed in crossing long distances of open water. He was driven, I know, by his compulsion to save miles.

The wind was stronger. A storm was brewing in the east. At least our direction was better since we were angling into the waves. Windsong responded immediately. We had good speed and rhythm. The hardest part was holding onto the double-blades. We fooled the wind somewhat by keeping them low. I flexed my fingers, one hand at a time, to keep them functioning. The wind was forcing us off the water again. Just in time Don turned into a long channel between two islands. Once out of the wind, the kayaks glided in the calm water. We rested the blades on the cockpit to let the tension out of our arms. "Well done, Pal," we complimented each other.

We were in five hours ahead of high tide. We followed a little channel and hauled out on the flat rocks of Igloo Island. My sweat-soaked clothing was cooling down quickly. I was chilled and shivering. Don too, but he insisted on getting the tent up before changing clothes. He held it down while

I collected rocks to set inside, around the perimeter. Once that was done we hauled rocks and made a wind barrier around the outside. Dry clothes and supper made us feel a lot better. We decided to explore. When we glanced back, we saw our island being turned into two islands by the rising tide. We hurried back. This was not a night to be separated from the tent. As I jumped the narrow channel, I slipped on seaweed and exposed some mussels fastened to the gravel.

"Let's try them," Don said. He was all excited about the prospect. While we had been in Whale Cove, we had mentioned to our Inuit friends that we had eaten sik-siks, which are like our gophers on the prairies. They are actually an Arctic ground squirrel.

Wide-eyed, they would ask, "Were you starving? Before you eat sik-siks you should eat mussels." They considered the sik-sik in the category of a rat. The only mussels I had ever seen were through the glass of a jar at Safeway. We gathered our pockets full. Don boiled them. I tried one. With butter, salt, and pepper, they were good. Don ate the rest. The shells were in a pile near our tent.

"Don, Don, a boat!" Sure enough. It was turning into the flooding channel. I dashed down to steady the bow as two Inuit fellows stepped out. We introduced ourselves.

"Are you planning to camp here?" I asked.

"No," James said, "we spotted your tent and came to see how you were."

"Can you stay for tea?" I offered.

"No, we have to make it to Whale Cove for high tide," was his answer. "We're just coming back from Rankin."

They took time to look the kayaks over, then came to the tent to meet Don. While they were talking, they kept looking at the pile of mussel shells. I was hoping it wasn't illegal to pick them. "Are you starving?" Ross asked. We assured them we weren't. It was comforting to know people would stop. The rising wind prompted them to leave. The resounding thud of their boat, as it hit the mounting waves, dwindled into the wind. I wished them "God bless" and a safe journey home.

Again, "Don, Don, I hear a boat!" This one was heading north. It was a big freighter canoe with a cabin on it. We recognized it as the *Evening Star.* It had been anchored at Whale Cove. The women were waving. Don warned me not to wave back. "They might think we need help," was his logic. I am sorry I listened. They cruised to a stop and cut their engines. After refuelling they continued on their way.

The tide kept rising. We moved the kayaks higher. Once again, the water caught up. Once again, Don and I were fighting. I wanted them much higher. Don would only help move them a few feet. He got mad and crawled into his sleeping bag. Before long the waves were splashing the kayaks again. It was with much trepidation that I woke him. We moved them to higher ground. By that time I was angry at myself for putting up with this. I could have been warm and resting in my sleeping bag too, instead of guarding them. No wonder my ulcers were bleeding.

After 10:00 p.m., when the tide had shown real signs of receding, I crawled into my sleeping bag, clipped on my headset, and allowed my favourite songs to drain the anger away.

For three days we were trapped on the island. Ahead of us lay the thirteen-mile crossing of Corbett Bay. We had to wait for good weather.

The storm held. All night we could hear the surf exploding, as it hit the rocks around us and churned the ocean to froth. The storm clouds rolled, and with the wind came the sound of distant thunder. The scene was moody but spectacular. The guillemots enjoyed the storm. They are birds the size of large ducks with feathers of the darkest black. They have brilliant white oval patches on their wings. The most amazing part is their bright red feet. The insides of their beaks and their throats are scarlet also. They dived repeatedly into the foaming curl of the surf, then circled and did it again. It seemed they were doing it for fun. They probably were feeding. I watched their crazy antics and laughed until I was soaked from the fine mist dusting my face and the tears in my eyes. The storm worsened and even the guillemots became subdued. The waves became huge, rolling breakers. We could hear them spilling over their crests as they came rolling in. I had my doubts whether the island would be high enough. The one alternative would be to escape to the mainland, across the protected channel.

When the tide was in, we only had a small area to walk in. On one excursion we found a dandelion clump. Swiftly came thoughts of home and the stable life I had left behind.

By the 19th of July the sky was clearing. Shafts of sunlight pierced the gloom. I was thankful. Though I love the wind and water, the constant sound of it was beginning to grate on my nerves. "Come and see the sunset, Don. We'll be travelling tomorrow." The sky was red, and as the little poem says, "Red sky at night is a sailor's delight."

Don relaxed with his little short-wave radio, I with the cassettes Pilgrim had taped for me. I was sound asleep when I heard Don call, "Vic."

"Yes?" I hadn't heard the alarm. "What's wrong?"

"Do you mind if we talk for a while?" he asked.

Four o'clock in the morning. It had to be important; probably be about tomorrow's crossing.

"What do you think about Joe Clark's ideas on the Referendum?" he asked.

Groan! "Joe Clark! It's four o'clock in the morning and you want to talk about Joe Clark? I don't even like Joe Clark!" Once Don has an audience, he doesn't quit. He had definitely being listening to CBC too long. Maybe I should smash his radio? In my frustration I turned up the cassette player.

July 20th. What a classic paddling day! The sea was smooth except for the last four miles of the crossing. My heart went out to Don. He should have been enjoying the trip. Instead, he was incredibly tense on the water. His capsize on the 1990 trip had made him paranoid. To watch him paddle, one would never guess the tension he was under. His clean, strong strokes hid the fact. It was his sharp, sarcastic retorts to any statement or question that gave him away. We crossed the bay in a record 2½ hours. As we headed more northerly, the wind calmed. The sky was clear, totally untouched by clouds. We paddled suspended on long transparent turquoise swells that flowed as smoothly as molten metal. The silence was breathtaking. I didn't want anything to spoil these moments for me. Don must have felt the same. He looked happy. We didn't speak, just smiled a whole lot.

It didn't last forever. Two hours later, the first simmers were showing on the surface. Then waves. Then came the breakers that were forming on the reefs out at sea. They started to roll. They came cascading in, in sets of two, gathering speed and size until they could contain no more and broke, sending volumes of foam ahead of themselves. We had to time our paddling in order to get through between the sets. With Don's skilful guidance we cleared the reef area.

"I hear a boat," I called. Don heard it too and flagged it down. The Inuit fellow was surprised to see us. He confirmed that Papik Point was now to our left. He was on his way to bring in his fishing nets.

Half an hour later, another boat. It was coming out of Rankin Inlet. Again, Don flagged it down with his double-blade.

On board were an Inuit man, an elderly lady, and three young boys. We grabbed onto their big freighter canoe. They looked down at us in utter amazement. We introduced ourselves. We were pleased to meet Peter, his mother, and his children.

"Where are you coming from?" Peter asked.

"From Churchill," Don answered.

"Oh shit! In that boat?" He couldn't believe it.

I had become mesmerized by the elderly lady. I would guess her age at 80 years. She was wearing a burgundy babushka with large colourful flowers on it. She was smiling tenderly and serenely. The colour was fading at the edges of her kind, sad eyes. I detected a tiredness and wisdom there. Eyes that had seen a whole lot of life. A life that could not have been easy. The shock of it was, she could have passed for my mother!

I was brought back by Peter's question. "Where are you going?"

"Repulse Bay," answered Don.

"In that boat?" Still he was amazed. "Where are you camping?"

"We are going to Crane Island tonight," said Don. "Tomorrow we'll be on Rabbit Island."

"Oh, good," said Peter. "I'll get on the CB radio and tell my friends where you are."

I couldn't keep the tears from my eyes. I waved. The lady nodded gently. It was as though she understood.

From Papik Point we headed east. We had planned to pass among the Mirage Islands to Crane Island, but the tide was three hours into low. Each channel we chose became blocked by reefs. We were forced southward until we could pass around the bottom end of the whole pretty mess. The islands were composed of jagged, rusty rock ridges that probably disappeared at high tide. Hence their name.

We headed up the channel toward the north end of Crane Island. We could detect the faint motion of the wind. I could feel the salt crust on my face. My sweat-laden clothes were sticking to my skin. I tossed my head to help the wind lift the hair off my neck. Don cursed the wind. One hour later, three-foot waves escorted us to the shore.

We spread our salt-crusted clothes over the rocks to dry. Our neoprene reef boots were probably our most prized pieces of clothing. I couldn't imagine paddling in anything else. To enter our kayaks each day we had to step into the ice-cold water. The shock of it takes one's breath away, but within minutes our body heat warmed the neoprene and our feet stayed toasty warm all day. Wet, but warm.

Our camp life was becoming very routine. Haul the kayaks in above the high-tide line. Haul the gear to the tent site. (If I got my way, that was next to the kayaks. Our lives depended on the gear in those two seventeen-footers. I didn't like to be out of sight of them.) Set up the tent. Change into dry clothes and put the wet ones to dry on the rocks. Don would search for fresh water and I'd arrange the tent, putting the silver thermal blankets down first to cover the floor. Next came the two therma-rest mattresses. Then the mummy-bags. All the gear from my kayak stayed on my side and all the gear from Don's on his. We left room between the two mattresses for the camp stove. We had been cooking inside the tent, because of the constant wind. We shared the chore of making meals. Don was much better at planning meals. Protein, carbohydrates, fats, sweets. I left the chore to him. The kitchen had never been the favourite room in my house. I think back to my dear ex-husband Dennis. He was a terrific handyman. As we sat at the kitchen table having coffee, he wondered out loud, "How can we make this kitchen larger?"

My reply was, "Why don't we eliminate it?"

It was a few minutes before he could find any humour in that.

Don was not successful in finding fresh water. We would have to do with what we had left. My ears picked up a familiar sound. It was the raspy, croaking sound of a crane.

"Don, I hear a crane," I told him.

"Of course, this is Crane Island," he laughed.

We were anxious to finish our chores. Marble Island was visible thirteen miles to the east of us. We had heard so much about it and we wanted time to scan it with binoculars. A young Inuit fellow in Whale Cove had explained to us that, on one's first visit to Marble Island, it is customary to crawl up the light-greyish rock on one's knees and elbows to appease the supernatural spirits that guard it. Marble Island is the final resting-place of a number of nineteenth-century whaling ships. Near to Marble, on ghostly Deadman Island, lay the bones of many seamen. They had come to open the North or to trade with the Inuit, and perished in their attempt to winter in the harsh conditions. Marble Island is now being developed as a historical site. We would have liked to visit the island, but Don was forfeiting this side trip for a direct eighteen-mile crossing to Rabbit Island. We were looking forward to having Peter's friends visit us there.

It was already the 21st of July. We pushed away from Crane Island and started across Rankin Inlet. Our compasses were useless, due to the terrific magnetic disturbance surrounding Marble Island. It didn't really matter since we had the noonday sun directly behind us. Before long, a dark spot on the horizon began to rise from the sea. It was Rabbit Island and we headed for it eagerly. We completed the four-hour crossing and were left with the afternoon and evening to explore.

Don called out, "Look, Vicks, a rabbit."

I jumped at the chance to get him back. "Of course, it's Rabbit Island!"

We set up quickly on a sandy beach, out of reach of high tide, and hiked to the summit. Hauntingly mysterious Marble Island was now five miles south of us. It looked like pink and grey marble in the afternoon sun. Green meadows graced the top of our island. Rough rock ridges poked through, adding contrast. Bunches of very bright yellow flowers grew on the ledges. The good Lord really has talent when it comes to designing rock gardens. Three deep turquoise bays cut into the island, each bordered by sandy beaches. It was such a beautiful, peaceful scene. An arctic fox appeared silently above us, then melted back into the landscape. He must have been watching the arctic hare in the meadow. We were able to fill our water containers from a pool high in the rocks.

There were many traditional graves about. I tiptoed respectfully past. A skull or a heavy femur bone were the only clues these carefully piled mounds of rocks held. I could see why the burials were described as "stone set."

I chose to sit on a stone on the perimeter of a tent ring while Don went exploring. I imagined I could smell the hides and the fumes of the oil lamp. I listened to hear the whispers of the ancient spirits on the breath of the wind, the voices of mothers, of children, of hunters. If I could just for one minute be granted the chance to go back in time and reverse the changes civilization has brought.

I was awakened from this reverie by the sound of a boat. I caught up to Don and we ran towards the sound. I could feel how strong my legs were, how effortlessly my lungs worked. With the wind in my face, I felt light-hearted and free.

The boat pulled to shore in the bay. Leo Minialik and his wife were from Chesterfield Inlet. They were on their way to Rankin to return their grand-children after a holiday. Leo wanted to see the kayaks. The kayaks always drew much attention. We all started along the rocks to our camp, but a curt word from Leo sent his wife back to make tea. The children were asking questions about the kayaks, tent, and various equipment. I handed out the last of our granola bars. Don was not pleased. I promised to buy him more in Chesterfield Inlet.

Before long some hunters pulled in. They had been after whale near Marble Island but were not successful. Instead, they saw a polar bear on the shoreline. Another family arrived. We recognized the boat as the *Evening Star* from the channel at Igloo Island. Paul, Martha, and their daughter, Louise Pudnak, were returning to Chesterfield. All the families knew each other. There was much excitement in the greetings.

They all had such warm hands. Especially Martha's. I told her so. She took my hands in hers and held them tightly while we talked. That was the first time since Churchill that my hands had been warm.

"We saw you at Igloo Point," Martha said, "but you didn't wave back at us. We thought you were stuck-up." I assured her that wasn't the case.

Louise was wearing an amautik. I asked her if she had a baby. Yes, she would love to show her to me. We walked down to the boat where Renee Kayya Kabloo Pudnak was asleep in the cabin. Louise proudly explained her baby was named after her great-grandmother, Kabloo Kabloona, who was a New Year's baby 81 years ago. It was important in their culture to have a child carry on the name of an elder. Louise was proud of her ancestry. Her people still travel out on the land to honour their hunting traditions. She said one of her favourite treats is muktuk. It is whale's skin with a thin layer of fat. To her it is delicious. Louise said that long ago the Inuit would come to Rabbit Island to collect soapstone for their carvings from the ocean floor when the tide was out. The men joined us at the boat and before they left they handed us an arctic char. Louise promised to write to me and it was a great pleasure to get her letters and pictures.

Leo was still with us. He insisted he could run into the town of Rankin and get us some groceries. "No, we have plenty," we answered. He looked at the kayaks and still was skeptical. I guess compared to their big freighters and their eighty-horsepower motors the kayaks did look puny.

He made us another offer. "I'll take my family to Rankin. I'll come and load your kayaks in the canoe and take you to Chesterfield."

"No," said Don, "we've paddled this far. We want to say we paddled the whole way by ourselves."

Innocently he replied, "I will not tell anybody." I am sure he would not have. We thanked him kindly and walked him to the boat.

I felt sad at leaving Rabbit Island. In such a short time, I had collected many memories.

July 22nd. Both Don in his kayak and the sky were so perfectly mirrored in the still water that either could be reversed. I looked at Don and he was smiling down at me. I looked in the water and the reflection was smiling up at me. I had to look away and concentrate on the shoreline to keep from getting seasick. The shoreline was friendly. Long, rolling, grassy hills with wide meadows ended at the sea. I felt at ease. Lyrics from half-forgotten songs popped into my head. I hummed. I dreamt. All too soon the eighteen-mile crossing was behind us. We would pass Baker Foreland and turn to a northerly direction.

Baker Foreland itself is a narrow ridge of grey rock. We sneaked though the narrow, shallow channel, between the point and an island. The tide was rising. The wind was soft, somewhat tropical. The water was a fabulous, clear turquoise colour and rising into gentle, foot-high waves. Through the clear water I was able to see the ocean floor. This area could easily pass for a coast on some tropical island. The sand extended far out to sea. Here and there a rock could be seen resting on the bottom.

I touched my right rudder. I felt the tautness for a moment, then instant release. Oh no, my rudder cable! "Don, wait up. Please see what's wrong with my rudder," I called.

With a few swift strokes he was there. He broke into a volley of violent curses.

"What happened?" I asked.

"Shut your mouth," he yelled.

I thought the worst had happened. I must have pulled the cable out of sight into the channel. He wouldn't give me an answer. He wouldn't let me tell him I had wire, wire-cutters, and needle-nose pliers in my cockpit. He went absolutely, totally *berserk*. He cursed and raved. I couldn't see what had happened or what he was doing. Finally, I just couldn't stand the stupidity. "Leave it alone," I yelled. "I'm going to shore to fix it myself."

This was definitely not an emergency. The water was only three feet deep, the tide was in our favour, the shore 200 feet away, and I could still paddle. There was nothing in the situation that would justify the madness. I began to realize just how dangerous he could be. If he totally came apart for something that turned out to be trivial, what did I have to look forward to if we had a real emergency? During all the cursing, he had tied the broken end of the cable to the rudder with wax string. In half an hour we were on our way. I had seen him fly off the handle because of pain in his heel, sand in the tent, or water in his hatches, but this was downright scary. The rest of the day was spoiled by the tension.

Storm clouds started rolling in from the land. Streaks of rain showed in the west. We began looking for a campsite. As we rounded a narrow peninsula I pointed to a protected sandy beach. Still angry, Don wasn't going to let me make the decision, so he paddled on deeper into the bay. There wasn't anything but jumbled rocks as far as I could see. Again, he was screaming and cursing that we had to set up before the rain came.

"If you don't want to get wet," I said, "we better get back to the beach in a hurry." I turned my kayak and headed back. He overtook me. A mile later he turned toward the little beach. While he was wildly shouting landing instructions I stepped out of the cockpit into eight inches of water and slipped my kayak over wet seaweed to the high-tide line. A shudder rumbled through my body from head to toe. If it hadn't started to rain I would have gone for a long, long walk, alone. The caribou tracks in the sand reminded me what this trip was really all about. I sent a thankful sigh to the heavens. Thank you for the subtle reminders.

Once the tent was up and Don was in his sleeping bag he was a changed person. As usual, he comforted himself with spoonfuls of peanut butter, sugar, or a handful of peanuts. I hauled in the gear, then went to check the damage on the rudder. Don swore it would hold, but I reinforced it with more waxed string just in case.

Rain fell intermittently through the night. The alarm rang at 2:00 a.m. High tide was at 3:00. Don decided, because of the rain, not to leave on this tide. Then while we were having breakfast he changed his mind.

The sea was rough, but I agreed. "Let's paddle inside the bay. We might add a few extra miles, but at least we will be protected by the peninsula," I bargained.

The tide had been dropping for four hours by then. Another two hours and it would be at its lowest level. Don was back to his hyper self once more. We dismantled in record time, packed, and tried launching. One minute we would have twelve inches of water under us, but by the time we got into the cockpits the receding tide would leave us grounded. Again, we would jump out and chase the tide into knee-deep water, hold onto rocks for stability, slide into the cockpits, and again find the water too shallow. The tide was dropping fast. Don managed to get in and began poling with his double-blade. I didn't want to risk breaking mine, so once more I dragged Windsong, chased the tide, and hopped in. At last we gained the freedom of deeper water.

As promised, Don set a course into the bay to get relief from the wind, but nature was not finished with us yet. All around us the dropping tide was revealing barrier reefs. Their jagged tops were ripping the waves apart as if with anger from within. I felt the same anger boiling inside. I couldn't understand why Don was purposely making a journey that could be so incredible so unpleasant and difficult. Our biggest concern at the moment was to stay clear of the reefs. The water action against the sharp rocks would have shred us to pieces. There were too many reefs barring our way back to shore and not enough water. That option was eliminated. We kept ruddering to the right to escape. Half a mile later, we were cast into the unprotected sea, where the waves were cresting to ten feet.

"There's supposed to be an island eight miles to the northeast," Don shouted over the sound of the waves. "We have to head into the wind toward it. Do you see an island?"

"Not yet," I called back.

This was like a roller coaster. Up one wave, then down into a trough. With attention focused on each mountain of water, there wasn't much time for sightseeing. Before long I called back, "I can't see the island, Don, but I see a tower to the northeast." The height of the waves hid the land.

"Good," yelled Don. "The map says Fairway Island has a beacon on it. That must be it. We have to head for it to get a good angle on the waves. We can't let the current carry us past the island." I didn't have to ask why.

"Follow me," Don yelled.

That was easier said than done. He disappeared over the next wave and, although I knew he was shouting, I couldn't hear what he was saying. The rush of the wind in my ears erased all sound. I was on my own. The waves seemed to come in sets of two. I would rudder right up the front side in a diagonal line, let the crest pass under the kayak, and rudder left down the back side across the trough and up the next. It was a game of anticipating and reacting naturally to the condition presented.

Don was shouting instructions again. "I'm behind you. Don't worry, I'm doing okay," I yelled every so often, or just plain "Yes" to unheard commands.

I was paddling one wave back and to the left side of him. He wanted me to keep calling to him, because he couldn't look back. It was a futile effort. The wind was increasing. The waves were higher and more of them were breaking. Every time I called I had to spit out salt water. My lips and mouth were raw.

I was duly impressed and quickly humbled by the monstrous waves when

I misjudged a breaker and the foaming curl slammed down on the bow, lifting the back of the kayak, making the rudder useless. The wave carried on, slammed into my upper body, and broke in my face. I stabilized, ruddered left, and slid down the back side. Quickly I realized the narrowness of the permissible margin of error. I knew chances of survival plummet after a single moment of exposure. If disaster came, each of us would be alone. Still, the chance to ride those waves was exhilarating. I was mesmerized by their lethal beauty. I was so proud of the way my kayak handled. It excels in rough seas. It responded quickly and slid over the crests like a sedate eider duck. I was grinning. My heart was thumping from the excitement. The only thing that bothered me was that my rudder was held together by string. Losing the rudder would have meant instant death.

I didn't call to Don often enough. He yelled for me to paddle closer to him. "Okay, I'm right behind you. Don't worry. I'm right behind you, I'm here."

"Keep talking," he insisted.

For a change of pace, I said, "When we get to the leeward side of the island we'll get some protection." He thought I was losing my nerve.

"Shut your fucking mouth and keep paddling," he screamed.

For the first instant I was hurt. It was for his sake I was babbling into the wind. I started to laugh. He was so scared he was ready to snap.

Paddling alongside Don was too dangerous. I preferred to stay behind and off to the left of him. This way I could keep an eye on what was happening and be ready to react if necessary. He would go shooting up the wave, his kayak would wallow like a log, and it was anybody's guess which side of the wave he would come down on. No wonder he was so terrified. I couldn't understand why he chose to take a flat-bottomed kayak on the Hudson Bay in the first place. Our danger was not only from colliding or tipping, but also from missing the outside edge of Fairway Island. There was nothing but open ocean beyond. We angled sharply into the waves, but it would still be touch and go, whether we would catch the tip of the island on the present bearing.

I started making alternative plans by hanging back and experimenting. Would Windsong run with the waves as well as she did against them? To my relief she handled well again. The only problem was I couldn't tell as easily if the wave I was on would be a breaker. Going against it, that wasn't a problem. If the wave was going to break, it would start pushing foam over the edge before it crested. This would be warning enough to adjust the paddle stroke to let it pass. I was confident I would manage to get to the leeward of the island one way or the other. Still, I was most relieved when Don finally started doing longer parallel runs in the troughs.

We kept skirting the rollers at a respectful distance or sneaking through between the sets, until after five hours of effort we glided into the protection of Fairway Island. We paddled at a slower pace to catch our breath. Both of us were soaked to the skin. I had taken a few waves over my head. Parts of each were pooled on my seat.

"Let's have a chocolate bar," I suggested.

As I looked up, I saw the prettiest, most welcome sight. It was the red and white buildings of the Northern Store on the mainland.

"Don, look, it's Chesterfield," I squealed.

"Don't be so sure," he answered.

"What else could it be? Look at the big fuel tanks," I replied.

It was Chesterfield Inlet. I wondered how many times through the years the sight of those red and white buildings had brought relief to weary travellers.

"We can camp here," Don suggested.

I didn't want to camp. If we carried on, we would have the protection of Fairway for at least two miles. We could catch our second wind and paddle the last eight miles to the harbour.

As we passed the reefs off the northwest tip of Fairway, we were again at the mercy of ten-footers. The angle of the waves was bad. If we could have stayed in the troughs we could have headed straight in. Instead, we had to play hopscotch from side to side across the troughs. We had passed the worst of the rollers and into the protection of the peninsula when the fog landed on us. I checked the bearing on the compass just as the Northern Store disappeared from sight. The waves came like ghosts out of the fog. We couldn't tell we were on them until we felt the lift. I lost sight of Don, but when we emerged from the fog we were both only yards from the beach. The tide was still rising so I stayed with the kayaks while Don walked across the beach to the manager's house.

He must have told Chris the whole story of his Amazon trip. By the time he got back, I was hypothermic. We carried the kayaks to an empty warehouse and went to join Lynn Rudd, Chris's wife, at the staff house.

She asked us what we wanted for lunch. I had to confess to a terrible craving for a hot dog. Chris and Lynn were relieving a manager's position that was vacant because of vacation. I was so impressed by these two young people. They were so mature and dedicated to their position. I wished them well in their permanent posting at Kuujjuaq in northern Quebec.

Chesterfield Inlet, with a population of 250 people, is the oldest community in the Keewatin District of the Northwest Territories. It lies in a protected bay, at the mouth of a long inlet of the same name. We resupplied our groceries at the Northern Store. I repaired my rudder with wire. I bought four litres of methyl hydrate for our stove, then, on second thought, returned for three more.

The fact that I hadn't told Don that I was bleeding from the bowel was bothering me. If he thought it would jeopardize his trip he had a right to go on alone, so I told him. He wasn't concerned or else was ignorant of how serious it could be. At least I felt better with it off my chest. I made three attempts to go to the nurse's station. I chickened out each time. I wasn't sure how much authority they had to prevent me from continuing.

Leo and his family arrived back from Rankin after the storm settled. He tried to talk us into aborting the trip and heading home. He was concerned about the report of heavy ice blocking Daly Bay and that we might not be able to cross Wager Bay due to the crosscurrents and riptides. He claimed he had trouble powering through with his eighty-horsepower outboard. When he realized we weren't carrying a gun, he was even more insistent that we cash in at Chesterfield. "There will be many polar bears on shore," he warned. "You must have a gun. I'll give you mine." Don kept changing the subject until Leo was totally frustrated.

I assured him we would be all right; we understood what he was saying and we appreciated his concern. I could understand Don's reluctance to have a gun along after his close calls with Freddie.

On the way back to the staff house we stopped at the store to buy granola bars. There weren't any in stock. I knew I would never hear the end of it.

July 25th. We were already well into 24 hours of daylight. Chris was planning on helping us carry the kayaks to the beach at 7:00 a.m., but when I glanced out at 3:30 a.m., the water was so peaceful. I took a picture of the full moon over the harbour, then woke Don. We dressed quietly, left a note, and went to see if the two of us could lift the kayaks and carry them to the beach.

Don's wasn't a problem. Mine was a back-breaker. I was half expecting it to sink out of sight in the water. I always ended up paddling the heaviest load. I was totally self-contained. If the two of us separated I would have everything I needed, except the maps. I could travel without them. After all, if I kept the shore to my left and headed north I would surely get to Repulse. My extras included the stove fuel, the tent, extra fly and ground sheet, first-aid supplies, binoculars, repair kit and tools, warm mitts and socks, lots of film, duct tape, nightgown, butane curling iron, makeup, pictures of my family, and one silk rose.

We paddled away on a satin sea. Except for a very strong current coming out of Chesterfield Inlet, our crossing to Promise Island, then north to Pintail Island and around Cape Silumiut, was uneventful. The last sixteen miles we were again battling waves and finally forced off the water on the shore of Whitney Inlet. We pulled out on smooth, solid rock. It felt good on my bare feet. The rusty striped pattern was unique. The tent was set against a tiny ridge to get some protection from the wind. The ancient Inuit tent rings we saw there were on high ground, exposed to the wind. They were certainly tougher than we. The graves in the area attested to the fact it was too tough for some.

July 26th. We spent the day wind-bound on Whitney. On one of our walks we discovered a massive whale bone. It probably had been weathering for decades, but was still so heavy Don and I could barely lift it. The one strange thing Don found was a pair of wool melton pants folded carefully and laid under a rock. They were the ¾-length type with poofy thighs, narrow below the knee and laced. I remember my father wearing them long ago, inside high-top felt socks. We refolded and replaced them.

Don was studying Depot Island eight miles away. He was anxious to explore there. Depot Island, whose Inuk name is Pitsiulak, meaning guillemot, has a long history. It was used by whalers as a blubber-rendering station. It is a small island approximately two miles square and 75 feet above sea level at the north end. Through the binoculars Don could see two buildings. He was sure the largest must be the whaling factory. As usual, he was wanting to find artifacts.

July 27th. We were literally blown to the island. With a favouring, strong southwest wind we made the crossing in one hour. Don hurried to the upper levels of the island to discover the whaling factory was an 8′ x 8′ shack, and the other building a doghouse. The only evidence of the whaling factory being there were the approximately eight-foot-in-diameter iron barrel rings, lying rusting on the tundra.

The cabin was not locked. Inside was a sleeping platform and part of a broom. Don swept the cabin and wanted to spend the night there. I didn't want to be so far away from the kayaks. The cabin only had one tiny window and we would have to close the door, because of the mosquitoes. I can control my claustrophobia well, but I knew I would not get any sleep. Don wrote our names and date on the wall, just to record our passing. Finally, after the minimum of cursing, Don gave in to setting the tent on the grassy meadow near the beach. I had become so accustomed to falling asleep to the sound of the surf that I couldn't imagine being away from it.

We discovered a grave on the top of Depot. We assumed it was a whaler's grave. It also had stone around it, but was boxed in with wide planks. A bleached, human lower jawbone lay at the head of the grave. Pretty arctic wildflowers bloomed around it, probably just as they had when the seaman lost his life so far from his homeland, so long ago.

Again, we were entertained by the antics of the guillemots. They were revelling in the warm summer day just as we were. They preened and acted silly by crowding each other off the flat rocks. The arctic terns were another story. They kept dive-bombing and pecking our heads. Their eggs were all over the tundra, so it was no wonder. They were so well camouflaged one could not see them until the last moment. Don took his camera and lay on his back among the eggs. What a ruckus that created. I went to sit by the tent to get relief. When he tired of that he went to get close-ups of an eider duck on her nest. It was an hour before he gave up and allowed her to return. By then, two of her babies had hatched.

Don was determined to find an artifact and he did. It was a brass sword handle, discoloured to green. The blade had rusted away, but he was happy with it.

July 28th. I wish the tide wasn't so early. Again, a 2:00 a.m. wake-up. We had Daly Bay ahead of us this day. It was only twenty miles wide, but Leo had warned us it was jammed with pack ice. We started out into two-foot waves. There was definitely a coolness in the air. Don kept telling me to look back at Depot and see if we were drifting off our bearing. That was a nuisance for me, because, in the rough water, I would first have to stop paddling and brace my blade across the cockpit before I could look back. In the meantime, he would be paddling away at full speed. Then he would be yelling for me to catch up. Finally, I would not bother looking back. "Yes, the island is getting smaller. Yes, we are still on our bearing. Yes! Yes! Yes!" If he had replaced his compass for the few dollars it would have cost, he wouldn't have been so frustrated. Maybe.

Before long I drifted far enough away from him that he left me alone. I was left to my own thoughts and dreams. It was so good to have time to think, hum a few lines of a favourite song, and watch the waves exploding on the reefs inside the bay.

Then Don's yell broke the calm. "Get over here. Let's pretend we're on the same kayak trip."

"I'm still on the same bearing," I yelled back.

From the first long peninsula extending out of the bay we could see ice crowding the shore. Its icy breaths were already reaching us. Soon my bow was entering through little brittle pieces of loose, clear ice. To my ears came the sounds of tumbling crystals. Once we passed the heaviest ice area the water changed from the colour of skim milk to a transparent turquoise. The waves were climbing to four-footers. The wind was increasing quickly.

Don was becoming extremely nervous. "We have to get off the water," he yelled. "How far do you think it is to the next point?"

"I guess four miles," I said. He agreed.

We were paddling with the wind, but against the falling tide. I could feel the tidal surge on the kayak. If Don did, he didn't mention it. The worst part was that we had to land at low tide. As we got closer, we had few choices. The only spot that might do was a rock sloping to shore. It was protected somewhat by a small island that was diverting the worst of the waves. It would be tricky.

"Let's go in there," I suggested. I didn't wait for an answer. We got properly soaked, but at least we were safe for the moment. Don wasn't pleased that I had taken matters into my own hands. I was too cold to care, but I paid for it before the day was through.

We carried the kayaks up, then set about looking for a tent spot.

Don chose a spot on a flat stretch of rock.

"There is salt water between the cracks, Don," I said. "This won't be high enough." The tide had just stabilized at low and was about to rise. He started off, cursing. I thought I was becoming immune to it, but I could feel the tension building.

We weren't going to have much choice in a tent site either. The only other possibility was the small chute of gravel near the top of the cliff. I headed up with the tent amid a volley of curses. Don followed and glared as I made a three-quarter-circle of rocks around the bottom of the slide. When it was the circumference of the tent, I started pulling down the gravel to fill the circle. Don caught on. I handed him a slab of slate and he reluctantly helped level the foundation for the tent. It fit perfectly. The front step was eighteen inches high.

The tide was returning in full flood. We moved the kayaks twice to higher ground. The water kept rising. It covered the tent spot Don had chosen and was still rising. Don was relaxing in the tent. "Come help me move the kayaks," I asked again.

He sure was in a vile mood but he helped again. I wanted the kayaks near the top of the rock where there was a projection I could stabilize them against. He refused to move them any further. Don Starkell does not like taking orders from a woman. I was angry enough to throttle him with my bare hands by that time, but I bit my tongue. It was enough to see him looking at his choice of tent spot covered by four feet of rising, ice-cold water. He promptly returned to the tent and fell asleep. I went to the tent only long enough to get my rain-suit. I put it over my clothes to break the wind and went back to the kayaks. Already, the channel between the tent and the kayaks was filling with water. Soon this would be two islands instead of one. I was absolutely exhausted. The paddling had been the easy part. It was the mental and emotional struggle that got me down.

I tied the tow rope of my kayak around my wrist and crouched beside it to get some protection from the wind. I was not going to let the sea take my kayak. As cold as I was, I drifted off to sleep.

There is nothing that will wake you faster than frigid sea water splashing in your face. I awoke with a start. I didn't have much time. I started unloading my kayak. If I could make it light enough, I could carry it up to the top by myself. There was no way I was going to wake Don. There was only one other person in my life that I'd hated as much as I hated him at that moment. I'd get my kayak to safety and perhaps give his a nudge toward the water. It is unbelievable what anger can do to one's common sense.

Don startled me. "What are you doing?" he shouted.

"Moving my kayak," I answered.

He did not need to ask why. Both were being splashed by waves. We carried them up and I reloaded mine and tied it to my ski pole, jammed in the rocks. By then we had to rush back. The channel was getting too deep. We couldn't be separated from the tent. I was too cold! The surge of the tide wasn't lessening. "What's happening here?" I wondered. We had two islands now. The kayaks were on the tip of one. We were on the other. I glanced over the cliff behind our tent. The ice-floes were rising towards the top. From the look of the gravel chute, it wasn't the first time the floes had been pushed over the cliff by a rising tide.

Cross my fingers and wait. From the tent door I watched as the water came towards me. I started gathering up the gear. "It is going to stop," Don kept insisting. He made no move to help. I wanted to be prepared just in case, but he was right. The water did stop six inches from the door. It stabilized for half an hour and started to recede. It could have been worse. Don's chosen spot was under nine feet of water.

Our kayaks were wet from the spray, but they were safe too.

Don went for a walk and I passed out in my sleeping bag. Deep shudders kept wracking my body. I couldn't tell if they were from the hatred or the cold. I pushed the episode to the back of my mind. We still had a long way to go.

A polar bear's head rested on a rock behind our camp. The fur was still intact. Also the eyes. They were small, cold, and mean, just as Don's had been moments earlier. The paws were intact too. I would have liked to have the claws, but they were not loose. This bear definitely had not died of natural causes. The paws had been chopped off.

We prepared supper methodically as usual. Don gathered another pot of mussels and boiled them. I was tempted to try the curly seaweed Lynn had said was edible.

The sound of the pounding surf woke me in the morning. Then another sound. "Don, I hear a boat," I said.

"You don't hear a boat," he answered angrily.

"Yes, I do." I scrambled out of my sleeping bag and out the door. I had forgotten about the step and landed on my knees. A big silver cabin cruiser was coming out of Daly Bay and past our island. Two men were standing near the cabin. I waved. I was sure they saw me, but they didn't acknowledge me. Perhaps they didn't believe what they saw or didn't want to be bothered if we were in trouble. Not that they could have helped. The water was too rough. I'd much prefer to have a kayak in those waves than a powerboat. They turned northeast. The loud thud of the boat hitting the waves could be heard for a long while. They disappeared in a flash of silver against the rising sun.

Although the water was rough, we decided to leave. We carried the kayaks down to the channel. It wasn't the best site for a put-in, but we got away unharmed. There still was plenty of ice around. The gently sculptured forms came floating by like a Disneyland parade. Two hours later the ice and waves were behind us. The sea calmed. Marshmallow clouds floated by. Thoughts of my grandson, Garrett, came to mind. He had called them marshies when he was a baby. The clouds were reflected perfectly in the water and our kayaks seemed to part them as we paddled. Seals bobbed into sight, sometimes startling me. I guess my nerves were getting a little raw. My paddle connected with a solid object. I was saddened to see the body of a dead baby seal.

Paddling along we watched the ocean floor rising to meet us. I had to be careful, since it made me nauseous. Below the surface, seaweed of incredible length lazily swayed with the currents. I was surprised to see it growing in such cold water.

After we passed Cape Fullerton, I kept hearing a deep throbbing sound from behind. My concern was that I was finally losing a grip on my senses. I kept looking back. Don spotted me doing so. "What are you looking for?" he asked.

"Nothing," I answered.

Still the sound was there. Deeper, heavier, and closer. I was hoping Don would hear something. I continued to look back and out to sea. The sea was like glass. Surely, there had to be something out there.

"Don, I've been hearing a boat and there it is."

A big trawler was chugging along down the centre of Roes Welcome Sound. It was miles out to sea but it showed up picture perfect. The sound of the heavy engine stayed with us all day. I was still sane.

The old-squaw ducks kept us company too. From the distance would come their chatter. Caribou browsed on shore. Their magnificent racks were silhouetted against the sky. Before long the wind came fast and furious. It had good direction to it. The shores were whipping by. The waves were high but long, and my kayak came to life after the long stretch of flat water. The wind evaporated the sweat off my body and blew in my hair. It is pure exhilaration when kayak and paddler are evenly matched.

Then came Don's tense words. "We have to get off the water. Don't let your kayak surf!" Under my breath I cursed him and his kayak. Just as paddling was becoming effortless, he wanted to pull out. I kept my mouth shut because he was in a real panic. We landed in a pile of rocks three hours before the high tide. It was difficult to find an area flat enough for the tent. I propped runners under my Therma-Rest to level out the mattress. I wanted the kayaks moved, but Don refused. He wanted to go exploring. I kept a wary eye in their direction. If we had moved them, I wouldn't have had to put up with this anxiety. He knew I would guard them with my life. He had no worries whatsoever. What made me so upset was that he was doing it on purpose and enjoying it too. I was becoming extremely angry at myself for putting up with this crap.

Above the jumble of rocks the plateau became a huge green boulder-studded meadow. It sloped down to a cozy little cove with a sandy beach just around the corner from where we had hauled up on the rocks.

"Look at this, Don, a handsaw," I said. We hadn't seen a stick of wood in the last 600 miles. "It must have been used to cut snow blocks," I mused to myself. I set it back.

We got back just in time to lift the kayaks to higher rocks.

July 30th. The wind and waves were still in our favour the next morning. The paddling was harder though, because the waves were closer together and sharper. We approached high rocky shores. The boulders were squarish, massive, and a rich rust colour. The water was deep, so we had no trouble staying close to shore.

Don spotted our first polar bear. It was high up in the rocks, resting. "Give me your camera. I'm going to get it to come down," Don shouted. The bear never moved a muscle. He either couldn't hear or didn't care.

We paddled on. Past Whale Point we spotted another bear. "Get your camera. Be ready to take a picture," Don shouted. We headed for the white spot on the island far ahead. Three hours of paddling in high gear got us to our bear. It was a chunk of ice-floe stranded on a tiny island by the falling tide.

Again, the wind forced us off the water. We managed to get protection from a rocky reef and headed into a tiny cove behind it. We landed on a sandy beach marked by the tracks of caribou. A feeling of tranquillity I couldn't explain came over me. The silhouettes of many peacefully foraging caribou could be seen against the evening sky. Mothers with tiny babies at their sides were more cautious, but they didn't leave. We set the tent on the coarse grass growing in the sand. The heat of the sand came through the tent floor. The wind was strong but warm. The heat from the sun was penetrating my clothes. This was paradise with a whole lot of atmosphere!

Don was cursing again. He had opened his hatches to find water inside. It was nothing unusual. He had water in them every day. I felt smug about my hatches being totally waterproof.

At last, time for a walk. Actually, it was an urge to tiptoe. I did not want to mar the beauty of this incredible part of our country. It was so clean – no natural debris like we have down south. There weren't any twigs or rotting leaves. The only thing that spoiled the scene were two 45-gallon fuel drums.

The caribou seemed to be all around us. We gave up counting them. At first they were uneasy at our strange scent and preferred to shun us. Their splayed hooves were silent on the rock, but there was an audible clicking noise when they walked. Later, I learned the noise is made by the ligaments in their tarsal joints. By evening they accepted us as strangers in their midst and came fairly close to the tent. In the morning there were fresh tracks on the beach near the kayaks. They must have been feeding on the curly seaweed left by the ebbing tide.

July 31st. I was so thankful for the wind that morning. It had the sea stirred to whitecaps and we were stranded in paradise for another day. We took long hikes on the caribou trails. They were deep, well-worn paths. The site showed signs of extensive use for hunting in times long ago. Along the paths were rock-built ambuscades to conceal an Inuit hunter. They looked like one-man igloos, only the openings were waist-high. In the days before the rifle they gave the hunter the advantage with his primitive weapons. The cleverness of the Inuit is remarkable. It had to be, in a harsh land with few convenient resources. The undisturbed lichens testified to the fact these rocks had not been moved out of place for hundreds of years. Even with the winter snow and the strong north wind none had collapsed.

There were many ponds on the higher meadows. "I'm going to wash my hair and the clothes. Do you want to come along?" I asked Don.

"No," he said, "I'm too tired. I am going to sleep for a while."

I left humming a favourite song.

"Did you take your bear bombs?" he called after me.

Everything was so peaceful, I didn't think I'd need them. In the meadow, I found a pond with a black rock bottom. The water was warm compared to the ocean. I washed the clothes and took them back to the rocks within sight of camp. I returned to wash my hair. While I was washing clothes it had been easy to look up and scan the area. Doing my hair was harder. I dipped the water, stepped back from the pond, poured it over my head, dipped again, stepped back, poured. Looked up and around. My hair was long and thick and the checking was a nuisance. I would count on the caribou to warn me. Surely they would see or sense a bear long before I. I would hear them as

59

they retreated. I went back to rinsing my hair. I stepped back from the water's edge, leaned over, and started pouring the water over my head once more.

There was a hint of a sound behind me and I was suddenly aware that I was not alone. A tremble of fear ran through me; yet, if it was a bear, to run would be useless. I looked down under my extended arm, through the dripping water. I saw Don's white runner. I knew it was his, yet I couldn't quell the fear rising from within. I turned on him in fury. He yelled "Grizzly bear!" at the same time as I yelled, "You asshole! Don't you *ever* do that to me again." My knees were weak and I felt awfully faint. I didn't need this. My nerves were already at the limit of their endurance because of him. He thought he was teaching me a lesson. The tables would have been turned if he'd gotten himself killed by a bear bomb. I refused to talk to him on the way back to camp.

I sat behind the tent in the sunshine to dry my hair. It was bleached by the sun to a flaming chestnut colour. My bangs needed cutting too. It was awkward to hold the mirror and cut, so, mad as I was, I had to ask Don to hold the mirror for me. The anger melted away, but it was a long time before I forgave him.

A pair of arctic loons shared the cove. Their hoarse calls were not like the yodelling of the loons I remembered from Willard Lake. Still, they kept me thinking of home.

To the north of our tent, flights of terraced stone steps, covered in layers of orange, red, and black lichen, led to the top of a ridge. It was like standing at the top of the world. The vastness hit home. Here I was, standing on this rise, looking from horizon to horizon knowing that for hundreds of miles there was not another human being out there. Down below was a long valley, hemmed between rock ridges. The lush meadow slid from the rise to end up at the beach at the ocean's edge. We saw many caribou there and Don slid down the rocks to get pictures. The caribou spotted him and followed a path up the ridge toward me. I held my breath. The caribou stopped. I followed their gaze to where my red mitten lay on top of the rock. They veered away and before long were back to grazing.

I was sorry to leave this peaceful place, with its landscape so rich in wildlife, plants, and human history. Perhaps some day I shall return.

August 1st. We pushed off in the morning. I looked back to watch the tide erase the evidence of our passing. The space and silence were left to the caribou once more.

The seas were smooth and the wind calm. The hundreds of seals seemed to like the calm days. They were always such a delight to watch. Time after time we made long crossings from one peninsula to the next. The coastline was studded with side bays and inlets. We passed Yellow Bluff that day. It is a massive mound of rock, a definite yellow gold. We paddled past Kamarvik Harbour, where the headland disappeared, far inland among the haze.

The wind hit us instantly, and within minutes the sea was rocking with three-foot waves. Don was anxious to pull out. It wasn't that easy. It was still four hours to high tide and the shores were rocky. The next peninsula had a high headland extending to the water. Behind lay a big bay, with long rolling meadows coming right down to the shore.

"Let's go in closer, Don. We should be able to camp here. No! Look, polar bears," I called. A mother with two cubs.

"Give me your camera," Don yelled. "I'm going in for a picture."

"Slow down, Don. There's another one." This one was huge, a big male. It would have been nice to sit back and watch them for a while. Don headed in. I don't know if the female sensed us or if she was protecting the cubs from the male. She summoned them and galloped up the meadow and over the ridge. It is hard to believe something that big could move so fast.

The male was spooked for a bit. Then he lumbered up the ridge and poked around near the rocks. "Well, we won't be camping here," I said to Don.

The waves were demanding a lot of concentration, but I kept glancing at the big male. He was headed in our direction. Then he disappeared. We paddled on to the next peninsula. He was there, curled up and resting in the rocks, facing away from the water. "There's the big male," I said to Don.

"I'm going in," he said. "I want to wake him up."

"Not me," I answered.

Don yelled and growled and finally the big bear swung his head around. He was not really interested. Don kept antagonizing him. The bear rose up and swung his head to catch our scent. Don kept growling. It didn't take long for the bear to get really interested. He came down the rocks in a big lumbering gait. Don kept growling, but there was panic in his voice. He was trying to scare the bear, but by that time the bear was willing to take up the challenge and include Don in his diet.

"Get out of there, Don," I yelled. He didn't listen. Then I thought to myself if he is so stupid and has so little respect for that animal, why should I worry. The only trouble was I would have to go back to Chesterfield, to report his demise. I didn't want to go back, I wanted to go north. The bear was only fifty feet away and was coming down the gravel chute that extended into the water. The reef had only two feet of water over it. The tide was pushing Don in.

I screamed, "You stupid ass, stop growling and get the hell out of there! There's only two feet of water ahead of you!"

The bear had been so intent on Don that he didn't know I was out there. He stopped, went up part way on his hind legs, and swung his head trying to figure out where I was. He came down in a half turn and barrelled away over the rocks.

"You didn't have to yell," Don said. "I had everything under control."

"Oh, yeah, then why didn't he stop before he heard me?" I asked.

"A woman's voice will scare anything away," he answered sarcastically.

I let that comment slide. At least I didn't have to explain to his children which turds on the tundra were their father. I paddled away. I didn't wait for thanks and none came.

I shook my head at the wonder of that beautiful animal. If the polar bear is really the symbol of northern strength and beauty, then he was one prime symbol.

We knew we'd have to go far before we'd feel comfortable camping. An hour later Don was getting desperate to pull out. He wanted to camp on an island. The bear shook him up more than he wanted to admit. I hoped he had learned a lesson. Probably too much to ask for.

Don spotted a low, solid rock island.

"We'll camp there," he said. "We have to get off the water."

"It's not high enough," I answered. "The tide has to rise for three hours."

He didn't listen. He went to shore.

"Wait a minute," I said, "I'm going to check first." I got out of the cockpit and walked to the top of the island. The whole top was covered in pools of salt water. There was a bigger island further out. I could see the green grassy slopes. I had taken a few waves over my head in the last open stretch and getting out had started me shivering uncontrollably.

"Hurry up," Don was yelling. "I'm getting cold."

"Jerk," I said under my breath. "It's your lousy judgment that's got me traipsing over this rock."

"Are we staying?" he asked.

"No," I answered.

"We have to get off the water!" he screamed.

"Keep your shirt on. There is a bigger island behind. Probably only three quarters of a mile away," I yelled back. There was a boulder field connecting the island to the mainland, but as we paddled toward it, the tide was absorbing it quickly. We landed without mishap. It was a long walk across the tidal flats to a tent site. We dumped the gear on a grassy spot. I had to change clothes. I was freezing. I stripped and dressed in dry clothes.

I had a feeling we were being watched. No more than 200 feet away was one lone caribou, sporting an impressive set of antlers. He browsed and watched, shifting weight from one foot to the next. He lay down and watched some more. We went about our work and didn't notice when he silently disappeared. It was a comfort to know there probably weren't any bears on the island, with him being so calm.

Don set about preparing supper, while I brought the kayaks closer, bit by bit, as the tide allowed. The clothes were out even though the air was humid. It was late. We climbed to the top of the island and searched, but the caribou was nowhere to be found. He probably decided not to spend the night with us and swam to the mainland. The only fresh water we could find was a small pool of thick dark water. There were arctic tern tracks leading in and out along the edges, which were bordered in poop. We filled the containers, straining the water through two thicknesses of Kleenex paper towels. We hoped we would find better water soon.

From the top of the island, we could see high headlands stretching far into the ocean.

They didn't connect to our shore.

"We don't have to go there, do we?" I asked.

"I guess so," said Don. "That has to be Kamarvik Harbour."

"But we passed Kamarvik around noon today," I answered. It had been the only wide inlet on the map that day. I knew we had passed it.

"We're not as far up the map as you think," he growled. "We would have to be paddling six miles an hour for distance like that." He had been judging us at 4½ miles per hour during the whole trip.

"Whatever," I said, "but tomorrow let's stay closer to shore. We'll make a couple of extra miles, but at least it will be more relaxing." The day's long crossings had been a drain on my nerves. We were used to the wind catching us in mid-stroke, but the unpredictability played on the mind.

August 2nd, Friday. The alarm went at 5:00 a.m. The tent was in the shade of the island. Everything had dew on it. I shivered as I came out of the sleeping bag. I had to pause to boost my willpower enough to dress in my cold wet clothes. The dry ones went back into a bag behind my kayak seat.

We had our usual breakfast of granola with powdered milk and sugar covered with hot water. Our beverage in the morning was hot chocolate. We had no coffee along and only drank tea in the evening because it had a diuretic effect. Don had no problem with that. He had a bailing can that doubled as a pee can. For me it was a whole lot different. My kidneys behaved. I managed twelve-hour stretches with no problem, except twice. Once I had to step out onto a reef covered by six inches of water and the other time I just wet my pants.

We waited for high tide to flood the tidal flats. The day was already getting warm. Again, the sea was smooth as glass. We paddled north to a black wavering line on the horizon that turned out to be an island. From there the shore sloped away to the west. We didn't know it, but it was the entrance to Wager Bay. Instead of following the shore, Don headed across the water to the northeast.

"Where are you going, Don?" I asked.

"I'm heading across to that peninsula," he yelled back. "We have to save miles."

He paddled away as fast as he could. He had broken his promise to stay closer to shore and didn't want to give me the chance to remind him. Due east, long black mirages were expanding and contracting. They'd lure us, then disappear, to appear elsewhere. We were blundering first north, then east, then south. Women's intuition was telling me we shouldn't be leaving our shore. A good clue was the path of frigid water stretching to the north without a headland across the back of it. I mentioned it to Don.

"Kamarvik Harbour is deep. That's why you can't see land on the horizon," he claimed.

"We passed Kamarvik yesterday," I reminded him.

He paddled on with dogged determination. Every time I tried to say something he cut me off short with an angry, sarcastic remark. An anxious premonition compelled me to look back, over and over. I was sure we would be returning. I wanted to remember some landmarks.

Three hours later and approximately fifteen miles from the mainland we spotted something white. It couldn't be a polar bear standing on the water, so it had to be ice. The one small floe had turned dark in spots. The pungent, windblown smell warned of living creatures long before we could make out their shapes.

"Are they seals?" Don asked.

"No," I replied. "They're walrus."

The small ice-floe was nearly submerged by the weight of nine blimp-like bodies. They were lying motionless, soaking up the warmth of the sun.

"I'm going in for a picture," Don stated.

"I'm warning you," I said. "If you get in trouble in there, you are on your own."

He paddled away. I watched him go. To my left I heard a huge belch. I looked to see walrus all around in the water. Seaweed kept popping up to the surface and mixed with the excrement floating there already. The barnyard odour was very strong. Don was paddling behind the ice. I decided to move to a less populated area, just as I heard Don's panic-stricken voice.

"Victoria!" I started towards him. He appeared from behind the ice, with a walrus four feet behind. It was a blessing he couldn't look back.

"What?" I yelled. He did a 90° turn. He had become disoriented and couldn't find me on the water.

"Bring me your camera," he yelled. "Mine has seized up."

"Come and get it," I yelled back. I paddled towards him because I didn't want to upset the walrus near me. They are fast, powerful, and aggressive in the water. He went back and got some good pictures. I got a unique souvenir too: walrus dung all over the bow of my kayak.

We paddled away. I looked back and the land to the west slipped below the horizon. If Don wasn't going to turn back, then we had to get to the land ahead. Don was so excited about the walrus I couldn't get a word in. We followed the mirages to the east, then to the south. Don was so anxious to save miles that he wanted to head for the very tip of the peninsula, but it didn't stay in one spot.

My attention was diverted by the current. I was paddling forward and my kayak was drifting sideways. I looked at Don's kayak. It was at an angle too.

"Don, we're in some sort of a channel," I said. "My kayak is drifting sideways."

"I'm not having any trouble," he answered.

"Look at the seaweed," I said. Fifty-foot lengths were whipping in the current.

"It's probably the tide coming out of the bay," he answered.

We paddled hard.

"It's getting worse," I called.

"Then let's turn and paddle with it," he answered.

Although it was a relief, something was definitely wrong since we were travelling due south.

"The compass says south, Don."

"You know the compasses don't work in the North," he yelled back angrily.

"Then what's the sun doing in the south at noon?" I asked. We were heading directly into it. It was 12:20 p.m. I planted a seed and let it rest.

To the east, the only thing that remained constant on the far horizon was a huge hill. To the right of it was a mushroom-shaped knoll. I strained my eyes to focus on it through the haze.

"We aren't getting any closer to land," Don finally admitted.

"That's because we're running parallel to it," I answered. "I'm heading toward the big hill."

Don didn't want me to be making decisions. "Head for the knoll on the right. We'll save miles that way."

I just wanted to get to shore. After miles of heavy paddling, it was a relief to be released from the current. At least we were heading east instead of south. We came near land. The cliffs I had been watching flattened out into a taupe-coloured gravel desert. My immediate concern was fresh water. All we had left was that brown water from the pool on what I had dubbed "Lone Caribou Island." It had been under my deck elastics in the hot sun all day. Don veered south along the shore.

"What are you doing?" I asked him.

"We have to keep the land to our left," he answered.

"Let me see that map," I said. I pulled up to him to take a look.

"We're on South Hampton Island," I said.

He exploded. "Don't be so fucking stupid," he yelled. "Nobody in their right mind would cross Roes Welcome Sound in a kayak. It's sixty miles wide."

We had. The biggest challenge lay ahead. How would I get him to admit it?

He paddled away. I followed. Don calmed down. "If we follow the shore we will come to the end of the peninsula. We'll go around it and we'll be heading north again." The worst part was that he believed it.

The area was beautiful. If I hadn't been worrying about the drinking water, I would have been deliriously happy. The gravel shores extended down under the water, turning it a vivid turquoise colour. It could have been a shore in Hawaii, minus the tourists. Set back from the shore were gravel cliffs, with snowdrifts against them. That could be our source of water.

I was startled to see a cliff that could easily be mistaken for an ancient Greek ruin, perhaps the Acropolis. Eroded pillars held up the top layer of gravel, and behind was a huge foyer. The terraced steps were uniform. Levelled rocks extended to the ocean, where they spilled over the bank. Down the middle cascaded a stream of water, ending in a waterfall at the ocean's edge like run-off from a fountain. I asked Don to stop, pretending that I wanted to see if the water was fresh. I climbed the rocks along the waterfall and stood on the platform, fascinated. The run-off water was salty, drainage from the last high tide. I kept this picture in my mind. I knew we would be returning. It was a landmark that I would never forget. Two miles north we had crossed from the mainland.

We kept paddling south with the land to our left. Don was sure the next point and the next would be the end of the peninsula. We would go around it and head north to Repulse. I felt rather sorry for him, and, at the same time, I hated him for denying the truth and not even allowing me to reason with him.

We pulled onto a gravel beach and set up camp. I was anxious about the water situation. We took the bottles and hiked to the upper reaches of gravel.

"There's water," Don said. It was a pretty little pond with green moss and flowers bordering it. A little oasis without the palm trees. We poured out the filthy water, rinsed the bottles, and refilled them. How that coarse gravel contained the water I'll never know, but nature has a way of making miracles.

We were too tired for exploring or talking. We had crossed Roes Welcome Sound and paddled at least twenty miles going south along the Southampton coast.

Don came into the tent with a puzzled look on his face. "The sun is setting on the wrong side of the ocean," he said.

"That is a magnum clue," I thought, but all I said was, "No kidding!"

I sent my silent, nightly prayer to the good Lord to keep my children safe and sank into my sleeping bag. Don was listening to his radio and constantly switching channels. I put on my headphones, turned up the volume of my cassette player, and was sound asleep before the first song ended.

August 3rd, Saturday. We ate hurriedly, packed up, and pushed away from shore. I was shocked when Don turned south.

"Where are you going?" I asked.

"I'm not convinced we are on Southampton," he said.

It was high time he was convinced. For one thing, the terrain was so different from the mainland. We were heading south; the sun had set over the ocean instead of land. What else did he need? The seeds of revolt were beginning to sprout. I would need medication for my ulcer very soon if it didn't perforate before that. We would also run out of food and fuel if we went much further out of our way.

We headed south all day for another 46 miles. The light wind from the northeast made for a very pleasant day. Below the surface of the clear water the long seaweed swayed with the currents. Every so often my shoulders would feel a jar, if my double-blade connected with a stem. We sighted three more polar bears on separate occasions. They were roaming at a leisurely pace.

At 6:00 p.m. we stopped on a high sandy beach. Set back far from the shore were hundred-foot gravel cliffs. A narrow canyon led into them. There didn't seem to be any water nearby, so we took the containers and headed into the canyon. Within, the scenery was different, another little oasis. Not far from the entrance was a clear pond, where we filled the bottles. Little rivulets of water were trickling into the pond, and as we walked farther in we found what must have been the branches of a river that joined the pond to spill out of the mouth of the canyon during spring run-off. The moss and little flowers grew in profusion in the wet. Even the air was humid. We started back. Before the mouth of the canyon, we both stopped. In the gravel against the north ridge there was a big, shallow, round pit scooped out. It was fresh too. The undersides of the overturned stones were still damp. I wished it had been caused by a caribou browsing.

"It must be a bear's resting pit," I said.

Don immediately started up the wall.

"Where are you going?" I asked.

"If there's a bear here, I want to see it first," he said.

I followed. I was nervous with a bear in the vicinity, but that was soon set aside. The top of the cliffs gave us a magnificent vantage point over the high gravel plateaus. A plateau stretched away to the eastern horizon, dotted with hundreds of little lakes all rimmed in green. The big white birds on the water were either snow geese or swans. There were also plenty of eider ducks. As we looked closer, we saw inukshuks winding their way across the magnificent plateau. On and on they went towards the north. Even here, inukshuks stand sentinel to thousands of years of Inuit history. The markers were certainly necessary, because the plateau was cut into sections by deep canyons. Shadows hid the bottoms. I would not like to be lost in that maze. I was thankful for all I had seen so far. I would not die with regrets.

We walked back to the tent without seeing the bear. I was tired. The emotional and mental highs and lows were taking their toll. I could barely stay awake while waiting for the tide to crest. I didn't trust the ocean. I always felt better when the waters were receding. If the tide was cresting during the "night" – still daylight – I would set the alarm an hour before high tide. Then I would wait for it to crest and start receding before I went back to sleep. I had a sort of inner switch that worked in my favour. The minute my sleeping bag zipper was pulled up I could block the day from my mind. I fell asleep to the sound of the surf pounding the shore.

August 4th. Don was admiring his baseball cap. He had been collecting pins all along the trip and the hat was quite heavy. It would have been a shame to lose it, so I gave him my Northern Stores cap.

This day we would be doing a direct beach launch because of the onshore wind. We would point the kayak straight at the water. If the waves weren't too big, we would put the bow part way in the water, get in, and attach the spray skirts. As the waves came in, we would lunge forward in the cockpit. The kayak would slip down and forward until it slid free of the gravel. Then all we had to do was paddle away.

Don was in one of his states again, yelling and cursing at me to do this and that. I'd have everything under control and then I'd turn into a fumbling idiot. I could barely control my temper. I got away first and paddled away out of earshot.

As I waited, I watched him lunge his way into the water. His double-blade was high on the shore and I wondered how long it would take before he noticed he had nothing to paddle with. Before long he was paddling back with his hands to step out in the surf and retrieve his paddle. He left my hat on the shore. I didn't dare remind him.

Again he turned south. He was going to turn Southampton into a peninsula by sheer willpower. If he had to prove his point, we might as well get going.

"Slow down," he yelled. "My shoulder is giving me trouble today."

We paddled slowly. One seal popped up in the water. That was strange. We hadn't seen any since the mainland.

Suddenly, Don pointed. "Is that a polar bear coming towards us?"

"I can't see anything," I said. "Maybe it's foam."

"No, it's a polar bear. Get your camera out and get a picture," Don said.

I yanked the spray skirt off and reached for the camera.

"What am I doing? I'm getting out of here," I yelled back.

The polar bear was coming at us at an angle to cut us off from shore. All I could see was the tip of his nose, his beady eyes, and the tip of his head with the little ears lying flat. He made no wake as he slid toward us. Spontaneously we veered away toward the open sea. We had no intention of being absorbed into the food chain. Don was far ahead and there was nothing wrong with his shoulder any more. The bear raised himself to a normal swimming position and now there was a wake as the chase began.

Don yelled, "Look back and see if he is still coming."

I'd glance back. "Yes, he's still coming." I kept checking. That bear wasn't giving up. We paddled as hard as we could for an hour. Luckily, the waves were moderate and the wind was in our favour. I couldn't see the polar bear any more, so I slowed to put my spray skirt back over the cockpit. From all the furious paddling, I had water in my lap. We paddled on, but I was getting more angry by the minute.

"Let's go to shore and check the maps," I said to Don.

"No, I don't want to go to shore," Don replied. "There are probably polar bears there."

"There hasn't been one on shore, " I answered. "We would have seen it for miles."

"No," Don refused. So we rafted the kayaks together. I put my double-blade across his kayak and he put his across mine. Don took the map out and we were just about to start looking at it when Don pointed, "Is that another polar bear?"

Twenty feet from my bow in an angle from shore was a polar bear.

Don grabbed my blade. I held on. "Give me my blade," he yelled.

"That's my blade," I yelled back.

"Give me my blade," he yelled again, trying to jerk it out of my hand. I wouldn't let go.

"You can't have my blade; the other one is yours," I insisted.

Each of our blades is feathered differently. He could not paddle with mine. I was about to slap some sense into him when he finally grabbed his own. He gave my kayak a shove in the direction of the bear and paddled away like a demented windmill. I managed to stabilize my kayak from the sideward drift and started paddling. I passed within six feet of the bear's nose. I will never forget the yellow reflection of my kayak in the coldest, beadiest eyes I have ever seen. The bear took up the chase. A short time later, I heard a disgusted grunt. I turned in time to see him give up the chase and turn away.

Don was disappearing in the distance. He had never even looked back.

I felt more alone than I had ever felt in my whole life. There was hurt and disappointment too. Was I foolish to expect that we would respond together in a situation of common danger? Was I wrong to think that was part of being a team?

I was troubled, but secure at the same time. Since launching that morning, I had felt a very strong presence over my left shoulder. Could it have been a guardian angel? Each time Don had spoken, I had hesitated and glanced to my left, waiting for someone else to answer. Subconsciously, I expected the answer to be in my father's voice. The whole experience was unusual, but it was not frightening in any way. In fact, it made me smile. If I needed guidance, this certainly was the perfect time.

The shores were still friendly. Another polar bear was roaming in the background. The ocean was still crystal clear. The wind still felt good on my face, but I was fuming and extremely impatient with Don's bullheadedness. It was high time to be realistic.

I caught up to him. "This is stupid, Don," I said. "We're paddling full speed in the wrong direction. We'll end up in Coral Harbour."

Coral Harbour is the only settlement on Southampton Island. I knew it was around the southernmost tip of the island, but we had no maps of the area we were in. Don had trimmed the maps extensively to cut down on weight, eliminating Southampton except for a tiny section of shore on the northern half of the island. We didn't have enough food left to paddle the couple of hundred miles to Coral Harbour. We didn't have enough to get back to Chesterfield. Our only chance was to get to Repulse Bay. I had to get Don to turn around and head north or we would perish.

"I'm still not convinced we are on Southampton," Don stated. "We'll keep paddling until we pass the next point or two."

At the next peninsula I declared mutiny. I turned my kayak around and laid my blade across the cockpit.

"I won't paddle another stroke," I threatened, "unless I can paddle northward. We've been going south for over eighty miles already. There isn't an eighty-mile-wide bay on our route."

Don relented. "I never was good with maps," he admitted. "Dana did the navigating on our South American trip."

"Now you tell me!" I groaned.

He was in a much better mood once the decision was made.

Once we started heading north, I was aware that the presence over my left shoulder was not there any more, nor did it reoccur on this trip. I glanced sheepishly at the heavens. "Thanks, Dad, for staying by my side."

Travelling in the right direction at least we had a chance. I remembered the location on the coast where we had crossed Roes Welcome Sound. All we had to do was return to the area, wait for a calm day, and cross back. That is what I thought.

We had to sneak past the bear or bears that had chased us. They would have no fear of us. We had caused them no harm. Every piece of foam churned up by a reef, every eider duck that bobbed, every piece of seaweed that floated on the surface was suspect. We skirted all at a respectful distance until we were sure. Our eyes were straining, our neck muscles in a knot from the tension. The one good thing was our direction. The sun was in the south behind us. Don was in the lead as usual. "If you spot something, tell me," he said. "Even if you think I can see it." Back and forth we kept calling. "Something to your left." "Watch the white spot." "Straight ahead, twenty feet." So, on and on.

Don still had little respect for the polar bears. He scoffed at their being able to catch us when we were paddling. Ian Sperling, an expert on polar bears, states that they are capable of swimming up to six miles per hour for fifteen hours or more without rest. I wouldn't want to test that. A fellow in Churchill told us that polar bears paddle only with their front feet when swimming. The hind feet trail out behind and are used for steering.

"If you are attacked," he had said, "try to push the head down with your paddle. If you're lucky, they'll get frustrated and back off." It would be a tough task from a kayak, I would think, especially with only four inches of freeboard.

We passed the area where we had attracted the second bear, then the area of the first, and then our last campsite. On north we went. I had practically memorized the coastline on the way south, so now it looked familiar as we approached. I was looking forward to seeing the Acropolis again, but we were forced off the water early by a strong onshore wind. We set up the tent against an embankment, not only to get a little protection from the wind, but to keep the bright yellow from attracting unwelcome company. The kayaks we carried up to the high-tide line. There was nothing more to do until the ocean calmed. A pond supplied us with drinking water. Although we were nearly surrounded by clear blue ice-cold water, it was always a worry whether we would find drinking water or not.

I kept a wary eye on our camp as we strolled around. We were on a peninsula. The shores curved away and we couldn't see far in either direction. The gravel was contoured, piled in alternate ridges and grooves, each one a little lower than the one before. It reminded me of corrugated paper or a farmer's furrowed field. This perfectly uniform pattern curved around the high gravel cliffs to the north and south, reaching high above sea level. If they were patterned by the tide, then the water level of the ocean had been fifty feet higher at some point. Although the ridges consisted of millions of small flat stones, they were packed so tightly it was like walking on concrete.

We walked to the gravel cliffs in the background. I would have liked to see what was on top of them, but it would have been too dangerous to scale them. At the base was an igloo built of thousands of round flat stones. They were entwined with such ingenuity that none had moved. I was stunned by the resourcefulness of the ancient people. To me it was an honour to walk where they had walked, to see what their eyes had rested on. If the land could speak, what incredible stories it could tell me. How willing I would be to listen.

After supper was battle time again. I wanted to remove all the food from the tent. Don insisted it wasn't necessary. He gets great comfort from being surrounded by food. Still, this was not the place. I carried everything back to the kayaks against his protests.

Don came up with a plan after we studied a tiny part of a map. "Okay, we are on Southampton Island. Look at this shoreline. It's smoother, with fewer shoal areas. It goes almost directly north. If we follow this shore we won't have to cross Wager Bay. At the north end of the island, Roes Welcome Sound is only sixteen miles wide. There we'll be able to cross to the mainland," he said.

"That's fine with me," I said. I was enjoying Southampton, except for the scare from the bears. Before turning in, I sat for a while on the shore. The strong onshore wind was whipping the tops of the waves into foam. I considered myself very lucky to be able to sit here and dream. I savoured the sunset across Roes Welcome Sound. Then the accumulated fatigue got the best of me. I zipped up my bag and fell asleep to the rhythmic pounding of the heavy surf.

August 5th. Morning came and the high tide left without us. The ocean was a mass of huge waves capped in white. We couldn't launch, much less paddle. Being windbound wasn't that bad, except that we didn't know how many more paddling days we would lose.

My biggest concern now was the bleeding. Blood had shown up in my stool every day since Whale Cove. I was wondering how much longer I would be able to carry on. I had iron pills along and was trying to keep a grip on the anemia setting in. I had no pain. Whether I blocked it out or not, I couldn't tell. The stress would be less now that I had convinced Don to turn around. We wandered around, explored and rested the whole day.

August 6th. The water was still rough, but we would try to get away in the morning. With bears around, it was not good to stay too long. It would be a beach launch again. We carried the kayaks down to meet the tide. Don was keeping his double-blade handy. It was hard to keep Windsong pointed down into the waves. Each wave attempted to throw her back on shore. Don was screaming instructions I couldn't hear and cursing. He made it out ahead of me. Finally, I caught a lifting wave and slid free. As soon as I passed the shore waves, I let the pressure of the incoming tide hold the kayak against a rock until I checked the rudder and adjusted the spray skirt.

"Get away from the rocks! Put your rudder down." On and on he screamed.

I was getting extremely angry. I had launched and landed enough times that it was a simple routine until he started shouting. On a trip like this, a response to a command can save your life. I was geared to that. However, you respond automatically to all commands, frivolous or not. To stop him from shouting, I pushed away from the rock that was stabilizing me. A wave hit me at the same time, lifting me backwards into shallow water where the rudder jammed into the sand and rocks. With the rudder useless, I had a difficult time getting the bow pointed into the waves.

Don kept yelling. I let out a mighty curse. It brought him to his senses and he paddled away.

Once he left me on my own, I got things under control and was on the way, soaked to the skin. Fingers crossed, I checked back to see if my rudder was still attached. I caught up to Don and I warned him to leave me alone on launches and landings. He grunted.

The rough water took absolute concentration. We watched for bears in the water. Whenever my eyes felt strained, I would focus for a while on the irregular pattern of the seaweed left by the high tide along the beach. There again was my Acropolis, still as impressive as the first time I saw it. Two miles later I pointed to the spot where we had crossed from the mainland. There was no sight of the mainland to the west. White-capped breakers were rolling in. We carried on, everything new and strange again.

The shoals became wider. The gravel extending far into the ocean under the turquoise water was as dangerous as it was pretty. In shallow water the waves are closer together and sharper. In the deeper water, conditions were going from bad to worse. Ahead we could see a long, narrow sand spit extending from the point of the peninsula.

"We'll probably find a sheltered spot on the other side," Don said. We headed out and around the spit and accompanying shoals. Sticking to the darker areas of water, we headed in. The tide was dropping quickly. We couldn't stay out any longer.

We came into a little bay with a high sandy shore. I pointed to a good camp spot but Don was not having anything to do with my choice. He headed across the bay to a little opening in the end. I followed him into a tiny cove, barely big enough to turn the kayaks around in. It was like a punch bowl. The sides were high, steep, and consisted of layer upon layer of flat sand-like rocks. I jumped out of the kayak and Don held it for me while I checked the top. It was full of boulders.

"We'll kill ourselves getting the kayaks up here," I said. "I'm going back to my spot." I needed to get rid of the feeling of claustrophobia the place gave me. I headed back across the bay at full speed. The tide was dropping so quickly that with every second stroke my blade hit the ocean floor.

"If we get stranded on the flats Don will kill me," I was thinking. He wasn't far behind. I had to tow my kayak the last twenty feet. It was a relief to walk up to the beautiful sandy beach. We wrestled with the wind to set up the tent. It really took a battering. Rocks inside and a circle of rocks around the outside just kept it down. In order to keep it off the horizon, we set it up two feet from the last high-tide line.

It was a pretty spot. To the south we could see for miles – in fact, right to the gravel esker that ended on the sandspit. To the north were high gravel hills. Here and there on the flat plain were tiny clumps of flowers and moss. The taupe-coloured beaches and aquamarine water had a tropical look. The water from our bay had disappeared with the ebbing tide, leaving tiny pools in the sand. As the evening sun dipped lower, the pools sparkled like diamonds. Outside the bay, the ocean was a mass of huge, white-capped breakers. We had landed just in time.

Don was prowling back and forth as I set the last of the stones around the tent.

He caught me off guard when he said, "I should slap you one."

I answered calmly, without looking up, "Go ahead, if that's the last thing you want to do in your life."

"That's a stupid statement," he said. "You know you could never stand up to me."

"Perhaps not, while you're awake," I answered, and kept on with my work.

The incident passed and was never mentioned again. If he had ever hit me, his close calls on his South American trip would have seemed like a picnic.

Map time and the battle again.

"Where do you think we are?" Don asked. The only long sandspit on the map was near the top of Southampton. I pointed to it.

"We didn't paddle that fast. There's no way we are up that far," he yelled.

"You never believe me so why do you even ask?" I retorted.

In the end he marked us on the map below Battery Bay. Battery Bay is directly opposite Wager Bay on the mainland. Of course, the two are separated by the expanse of Roes Welcome Sound and were at least eighty miles south of our camp. If he wanted that to be the spot, I wouldn't argue.

"I'm going to walk to that hill," Don said, "and see if I can get some bearings and figure out where we are."

"I'm going to sleep," I said. I was exhausted, but not from the paddling. Don was hard to cope with and I was thankful to be away from him. The hill looked about three miles away. The distances are deceptive and he might be walking for a long time, or so I hoped. He came back minutes later, full of excitement.

"Look what I found!" he said. It was a little cast-iron stove. The name Camp Junior was stamped on it, and the patent date was in the 1800s. The bottom part must have held whale oil, and the dried remains of a four-inch-wide wick were still in the holder.

"Too bad I couldn't take it home," he said pitifully.

He had been hassling me about the extras in my kayak, so he was unsure how I would react. Suddenly there was nothing but praise for me for picking the best campsite. Because of me, he found this perfect little artifact, thank you, and all that. I just wished he would get on with his walk and leave me alone.

"Don't forget to look for water," I called as he walked away. As usual the arctic terns got stirred up as soon as they saw Don. I crawled into my sleeping bag. The sun had warmed the interior. I quickly fell asleep to the diminishing shrieks of the terns, as they followed Don away from the camp.

Three hours later I awakened to a grave-like silence. I strained to hear the sound of Don tinkering with his new toy. No terns. No sound of water. Just the wind.

I dashed outside. "Where did he get to? He always loses his sense of direction away from camp." I was mad, but intuition was telling me something was wrong. I sat on the embankment and watched. Where would I even start looking? If I couldn't find him, how long would I wait for his return? For an hour I sat, paced, and strained my eyes. Finally, far to the northwest, I saw a speck of red. He could just walk back along the shore but he was confused, forgetting the tide had gone out. He searched for the tent at the edge of the water, which was now at least a mile out to sea from where I was sitting. The tide can change the character of the shoreline dramatically, but he should have remembered we were camped on high ground. I brought out a blue tent fly. I stood flapping it in the wind until I thought my arms would fall off. Finally, he turned, spotted it, and headed towards me. I relaxed. It took him over an hour to walk back.

He told his story. He had come over a ridge, and below him was a mother polar bear with two large cubs. The wind was in her favour.

"That was the worst scare I had in my life," said Don. "I hunched down and ran along a ravine all the way to the coast. My feet never touched the ground. When I got to the coast, I didn't know if I should go left or right."

I started piling rocks near the tent.

"What are you doing?" Don yelled.

I said, "If those bears come by, I don't want to be scrambling for something to throw. Lowering your voice would help a whole lot too." He did, which was surprising. Those bears had really shaken him up. A chap in Churchill had said, "Bears are very protective of their faces. If you have no choice but to throw rocks, make sure to hit the face. They may back off. If you hit them on the body, they become insulted and infuriated. Make your aim count."

I made sure my noise bombs were loaded and the hatchet was handy. The flysheet could distract a bear's attention. I would much rather have had a gun or the option of calling 911.

As if that wasn't enough, I realized my period was starting. I hadn't bought any sanitary pads in Chesterfield, because, according to plan, we would be in Repulse before I needed them. We were already rationing the paper towels we had along. Each sheet we tore into four pieces. When I told Don my problem he willingly gave up his share and volunteered to use wet kelp leaves. If he could use kelp, so could I. There was fresh clean kelp along the tide line at almost every stop. There is no experience quite like using cold, wet sea kelp as toilet paper. It brought back vivid memories of the outhouse back on the farm and the glossy pages of the Eaton's catalogue at -35° Celsius.

Don had discovered a little pond on his way back along the coast. We gathered all the containers and headed for water. As quietly as possible we slunk along the shore. The onshore wind would easily carry any scent or sound to the bears on the tundra. At each ridge, we would peer over first to check the horizon. When we reached the water hole, movement at the water's edge made me jump back. I was relieved to see swans instead of bears. Two beautiful adult swans and four grey-coloured cygnets were swimming gracefully on the water. Their nervousness was evident. They were helpless and at our mercy because the water was only about ten inches deep. The young were much too small to fly. Both parents remained. They herded the little ones to the opposite end of the pool. We quickly filled our water bottles and left. It took our mind off bears for a while. We were in the same boat as the swans. If the bears came, there wasn't a whole lot we could do.

The wind was as strong as ever. It didn't look good for the next day either.

I set the alarm for midnight and fell asleep. The sound of the surf sucking at the beach pebbles woke me before the alarm. The tide was coming in with full force. I watched it until it touched the last high-tide mark, stabilized, and started to recede.

August 7th. From the sound of the wind and ocean, we knew we were windbound for another day. It wasn't hard to keep Don in camp. He tinkered with his stove. I sorted a few things in my kayak. I checked my first aid kit for something for my stomach pain. I found a plastic bag with Tums in it. They would have to do.

"How come you aren't sharing your candy with me?" Don asked.

"They aren't candies," I replied. "If you need them, you can have some." He decided against them.

I also found a Kotex pad. I usually carry one in the first-aid kit because they come individually wrapped and are compact, soft, and sterile. I would save this one for the next paddling day. I set aside the iron pills too. I knew I was quickly becoming more anemic. Three iron pills a day didn't seem to make much difference. I hoped I would have enough to get me to Repulse.

The day was tense. We couldn't go anywhere because our wandering on the tundra stirred up the terns too much. What bothered me more than being pecked on the head was that they were announcing trespassers on their territory. Any bears in the vicinity would surely pick up the signal. The north end of Southampton Island has one of the highest densities of denning polar bears in the whole world. In the short time we had been in the area we had seen thirteen. Except for the two that had chased us in the water, none challenged our intrustion.

I sat on the beach to watch the sun. The rhythmic sound of the surf deepened the spell of solitude and I felt at peace with the world. I rested my head on my knees to ask God to take care of my children, just as I do every night of my life. Although I am not a religious person and only go to church for weddings and funerals, I feel someone has guided my destiny and I am truly thankful.

"What are you doing?" Don yelled. He guessed I was saying a prayer, so I don't know why he couldn't spare me the privacy. He thought I was losing my nerve and asking for help.

"You're not going to die here," he added.

I answered, "I'm not afraid of dying or being killed. I only fear the suffering my children would endure until my remains were found. If we were on the mainland there would be a chance. Nobody would think of looking for us here. That's why I'm looking forward to crossing back." I almost said "back to Canada." Southampton is so beautifully unearthly that I felt like an alien on its shores.

We went to sleep very early. The next high tide would be at 2:00 a.m. The red sky in the west promised good paddling weather, even though the waves were still white-capped in the distance. Already we had pushed our luck by staying too long.

August 8th. I awoke to watch the tide come in. The onshore wind was still very strong. We decided to reset the clock for 3:30 a.m. By then the conditions changed in our favour. The tide had been receding for 2½ hours, so we had to move quickly to get out of our already shallow bay.

Don was acting up again. "Just shut up and go. I'll be right behind you," I said.

I pulled up my pant legs and stepped into the ice-cold water alongside my kayak. Not my favourite thing to do, but the heat from my feet would warm the water inside my booties and by the end of the day I knew it would be a relief to step into the water to cool them off. Quickly, I slipped into the cockpit, pulled down my pant legs, fastened the spray skirt, checked the rudder, and shoved off. The waves were pretty rough at the mouth of the bay, where the deep water met the shallows. There was no turning back. With great concentration, we paddled through without a mishap. We had the favouring wind once we turned north. The sky was clear; the sun was already sending some heat. It promised to be a nice day.

I had used the sanitary pad from the first aid kit. I felt pretty smug about this one luxury. Just as I was revelling in the thought of how smart I was, I misjudged a rogue wave. It went up and over my head, dumping loads of water down my neck, front and back. I ended up sitting on that soggy Kotex pad for ten hours that day. I chalked up one more for Mother Nature. She has a way of keeping one humble.

The ocean calmed as we paddled. "Don, look to the west. I can see the mainland!" This had been our first sighting since we had crossed over seven days ago. I knew it had to be at least sixteen miles away, but it looked so close. I could even see snowbanks against some of the ridges. "Maybe tomorrow we'll be crossing back if the weather is good!" I volunteered.

I was absolutely elated. I dredged up lyrics of half-forgotten songs as I watched the shores of Southampton and the mainland slipping past. The waves turned to nice easy swells and we were making good time. Even Don was relaxed and in a good mood. A tiny movement behind him caught my eye. A bumblebee had a bead on Don's blue toque. His stinger was visible, just like the ones in children's cartoons. The currents in the wind would slow him down, then he would gain on Don, only to be forced back again. What the poor little thing was doing a mile from shore I'll never know. He had determination and hung in for a long while. Don was under no threat, so I didn't bother telling him, just enjoyed watching. Except for the hornet in my hair at Hubbart Point, this was only the second bee I had seen on the whole trip. I have a severe allergy to bee stings, so the fewer bees the better.

After ten hours of paddling we entered a calm lagoon and set up camp on the sandy shore. We shook out our sleeping bags, turned them inside out, and spread them to dry. It was a relief to find water 200 feet from camp. The tundra had more green to it. The scattering of little lakes to the north made for a pretty sight. From the lakes came the sound of ducks and geese. The only thing that disturbed the pristine look was a half-dozen 45-gallon fuel drums.

On our walk to the higher plateaus, we spotted inukshuks. I wondered if they connected with the long chain we had seen near the canyon pond miles ago. To the northeast we could see dark mountains. They seemed to billow out, change shape, and move. As the sun moved into the evening sky they disappeared.

"There must be fairly high ground ahead of us," I said to Don, "in order to make such a large mirage."

"We'll check the map, when we get back," he answered.

The only thing that remained constant was the land to the west. I had high hopes of crossing to it in the morning. I had been having terrible pain in my stomach since we landed. The thought of my ulcers perforating was foremost in my mind. I was relieved to find that it was only a severe case of diarrhea. Not pleasant when one is rationing tissue, but preferable. Soon Don admitted to the same problem. The probable cause was our water containers. When we had dumped the brackish water from Lone Caribou Island, we had only rinsed the containers with cold water. We could only hope it would not become too serious.

August 9th. The alarm sounded at 2:00 a.m. High tide was one hour away. We had to decide whether we would be paddling. Our lagoon was filling quickly. The water remained calm because of the narrow entrance. I stumbled up the embankment to see the open ocean and my heart sank. We would not see the mainland today. The water was much too rough. I reported back to Don. We decided to go back to sleep.

Four a.m came. "Yes, let's go! We'll paddle along the shore," Don said. "We can't cross today, so we might as well head north." The strange thing was we were heading into the rising sun. The compass was reading northeast.

I called the bearing to Don. "We are probably going into Battery Bay," he answered.

We started across the bay. The high hills on the other side beckoned to us. They were hazy and black and I strained my eyes to see them clearly.

To the west the mainland was diminishing and slipping away below the horizon. I mentioned it to Don. "We're probably opposite Wager Bay now," Don replied. "That's why we can't see land there any more."

An hour into "Battery Bay," the current started sucking greedily at my kayak. I looked to the southeast. There wasn't any land across the bottom of the bay.

"Don, we're in some sort of a channel again," I said.

"It's probably just the tide," he answered. "Keep paddling."

Well, I certainly had no intention of stopping! It didn't make sense at all. The tide was heading to low. It would not be dropping into the bay; it should be pulling out instead. The direction was definitely wrong. I kept watching the bottom of the bay, hoping the headland would close it off and Don would be right. That was too much to ask. The water stayed dark in the distance and dropped off the horizon. The only consolation was the land ahead. After four hours of strenuous paddling the land began to change from black to green and to have some definite features.

"Head for the most northern point of land," Don called. The wind started rising again and the conflicting waves were wicked. And no wonder. What Don thought was a river coming into "Battery Bay" turned out to be another channel. The water came whipping around an island from two directions. I was close to the island so I was able to cut through one set of standing waves into the interior of the "V." Don was further out. He was caught at the point where the current collided. I slowed to wait for him, in case he had trouble. Finally, he headed toward me. "Go," he yelled.

There were three standing waves ahead. It was slow going, but my kayak was handling them well. Don's kayak was wallowing badly. I powered on through and waited for him. He was not in a good mood!

"Let's go to shore for a break," I suggested. I pointed to a little green meadow sloping to shore.

"No, let's go around the point," Don answered.

The east wind hit us full force as we rounded the corner. The undisguised smell of ice was in the air, and the wind switched from balmy to cold in seconds. The ice was floating everywhere. I hadn't really expected to see more ice on this trip.

"My God, do we have to go in there?" I asked Don.

"Of course, this is Battery Bay," Don yelled. I could tell he was a little strung out so I kept quiet. How many Battery Bays did he have up his sleeve? When was he going to come to his senses? I paddled alongside him. We were going directly east. There was no point talking to him. I had to get him to go to shore. We paddled past the entrance to a large sheltered cove. "Let's go in, Don," I ventured.

"We are not stopping here," he said. I think he had the feeling he would lose his nerve if he stopped.

"But I have to go to the bathroom," I answered. "I'm going in."

Suddenly, we heard an angry bellow and a large dark object came shooting out of the water slightly behind Don. It landed back in the water and churned it into a froth.

"Was that a whale?" Don stuttered.

"No, get going! It's a walrus!"

Don quickly turned into the cove. Somewhere in the North Straits there is a walrus I would like to thank properly. I answered the call of nature and it was none too soon. Across the way there was a sheltered spot for a campsite, but Don would have no part of coming to shore. "I'm not camping here," he yelled back from his kayak.

"Well, I'm not paddling into that ice without checking a map," I stated. "Where do you want to camp?"

He pointed to a gravel beach across the cove. I compromised. Landing wasn't a problem. I pulled my kayak part way out and started unloading the tent.

Don wasn't in as big a hurry as usual. His kayak still floated lengthwise, against the beach. "This is the first time that I've come in almost completely dry," Don boasted.

I grabbed my gear and started up the beach. From behind me came a violent outburst. I turned and there was Don trying to brush the water from his clothes. A wave had come in and hit his kayak broadside, and the water that didn't end up in the cockpit splashed him from knees to neck. And a second time. And a third time. It was funny, but a cloud of depression landed over me. I felt weak and tired. I've never been prone to depression and I hated the feeling. The laugh I suppressed turned to a half-sob that caught in my throat. It just stayed there and ached. I didn't bother helping him. I set the tent up while he cursed and bailed the water out of the kayak.

My first concern was to check the map. We had crossed a channel of some sort. If I was right, it would put us on White Island. The only map we had with White Island on it was a rough tourist map of the Northwest Territories. I would not say a word until I was sure. I would try to find a good time. Now was not a good time.

Don noticed I wasn't my usual self. I couldn't even bring myself to look at him. I tried hard to quell the feeling of revulsion rising within. Shudders wracked me from head to toe. I never had any false illusions about the trip and never once doubted my ability to cope, but I had come as close to the end of my rope as I ever cared to get. I remembered a saying that had stabilized me many times. It was simple. "When you reach the end of your rope, tie a knot and hang on!" That is exactly what I did.

"What's the matter with you?" Don asked.

"Don, I can't stand your violent outbursts and all that cursing any more," I answered.

"Why should it bother you?" he asked. "I'm not yelling at you."

"I know that," I said, "but when my dad was alive, he kept the whole family terrified with his violent outbursts. Now he's dead and I thought I would be free from that. You're dredging up those nightmares for me. I have tried to cope, but I can't stand it any more."

"I'll try not to do it any more," he promised. "What would you have done if you had gotten splashed?"

"I would have done what any woman would have done. I would have grabbed the bow and taken the kayak out of the water," I answered.

We had landed at noon with only seven hours of paddling behind us, but I was tired. The wind had plotted new challenges for us daily since we had come to Southampton. Today had been no exception. The current in the channel hadn't helped either. Both my shoulders had started aching.

The wind increased rapidly in the short time we were on shore. Our tent sat exposed in the middle of the hundred-foot beach. We had cliffs on both ends of the beach, but the wind was from the east and came funnelling down the chute between the rock outcroppings. We loaded down the tent with extra rocks.

When Don went for water, I quickly dug out my tourist map. We had crossed Comers Strait from the tip of Cape Munn on Southampton Island to the northernmost tip of the White Island, a sixteen-mile crossing. My hands were shaking. I knew our options were equally oppressive. Ahead was the Frozen Strait filled with ice. The map showed forty miles across. If Don could ever be talked into backtracking, we would have to cross sixteen miles of Comers Strait again back to Southampton, and then cross Roes Welcome Sound to the mainland. I didn't look forward to map-work time.

We dressed warmly, took the binoculars and map, and climbed the cliffs to assess our situation. To the north we could see land across the strait. It looked fairly close. Don guessed five or six miles.

"It's probably farther than that," I said, not wanting to tell the whole truth at the moment, "because it looks too hazy. We'll get a better look tomorrow in the morning sun."

To the east the strait was choked with broken ice-floes. That was where the wind was from. We were definitely on an island. To the south and east were more little islands and, beyond, a dark mass of high headlands. The wind was getting stronger by the minute. We would not likely be travelling next day. We might be visited by polar bears since floe-ice was in the area.

The tide was on the way out as we walked back to the tent, and a reef was starting to show near the entrance of the cove. No wonder the walrus was upset. We had probably paddled over its feeding area.

Map time.

"Where would you say we are?" Don asked. I thought maybe he knew we had crossed to White Island and didn't want to frighten me. He held a teeny corner of Southampton and wanted me to pick a spot.

"We're not on Southampton, Don. We're on White Island," I ventured.

"Don't be so stupid," he said. "We're still in Battery Bay."

Again he marked us a hundred miles south at Battery Bay on Southampton, and opposite Wager Bay. Tomorrow was another day. Although it was only 7:00 p.m. I zipped up my sleeping bag and fell asleep. The feel of wet tent nylon in my face woke me. Don was stretched out and trying to hold the tent poles with one arm and leg.

"How long have you been holding the tent up?" I asked. "What time is it?"

"It's eleven o'clock and it's been like this for a while," Don answered.

"Why didn't you wake me?" I asked.

"You were sleeping too soundly," Don said.

We sat and held the poles until 2:00 a.m. My arms were aching, as I'm sure Don's were.

"This is nuts," I said. "We have to move the tent nearer the cliff. That's where it should have been anyway!"

"I'm not moving the tent in the middle of the night," Don yelled.

"Then I will," I answered. "I'm not going to hold it up all night."

I gathered an armful of gear and stepped out into gale-force winds. The thunderous surf exploded against the shore cliffs. I hugged the ground and made my way to the cliff wall. After depositing my load in a sheltered spot, I cleared a large circle of ground to set the tent on. I piled all the rocks nearby. We would be needing them. Without the load in my arms, I was at the mercy of the wind. I leaned sideways into the wind and braced my feet against the sand to keep from sliding into the ocean. I memorized every rock in case I had to dive for one for weight.

I made two more trips from the tent to the cliffs. All that remained was Don, his sleeping bag, and all the water containers.

Don still sat in the tent, in full defiance. I wanted him to pass me his sleeping bag, but he refused. "I'm going to let the tent down," I warned him.

"No," he answered angrily, "we can carry it like it is."

"Then get out and hold it down, while I throw the rocks out," I told him.

He wouldn't let me make one last trip with the water and his bag. "Leave them in. It wouldn't make any difference," he yelled. But it did. We lifted the tent. The weight slid to the middle of the floor and sagged. At the same time came the sickening sound of fiberglass poles snapping.

"Bend down and grab the stake tabs," I yelled. The wind was taking my breath away. We half carried, half dragged the tent to shelter. I went back once more to check the kayaks. I braced them with rocks and gravel. They were pointing into the wind. They would be all right until morning. It only took minutes to rearrange the inside of the tent. We were to sleep in seconds.

August 10th. My first reaction in the mornings was always to check the kayaks. This morning I panicked when I looked out and couldn't see them. Then I remembered moving the tent during the night. I walked across the beach. They were safe. We spent most of the morning repairing the tent poles.

I was anxious to see the rest of the island. We climbed the cliffs again. Down below was disaster. The broken floe-ice was grinding and heaving. Where the water was free of ice the waves were capped in foam. Along the north shore of the Frozen Strait the ice was jammed up solidly for miles. Even if the wind calmed, we couldn't take the chance of crossing and not being able to get to shore. For the moment we were imprisoned on the island by the stormy seas. It was as though someone watched and cared, someone who knew we needed to rest. The trip ahead would not be easy.

As I sat on the rocks and looked out I wondered if the wind ever got lonely. It seemed to be searching behind every rock and boulder and through the narrowest of crevasses. What would it take to pacify the wind?

We wandered around the island. A few small, dark grey birds twittered in the leeward side of the cliffs. I thought they must be the only inhabitants. Then we spotted a caribou. One large male. As he ran toward us I could almost sense joy in his large, wide-set eyes. Just like a person who has spotted someone he hasn't seen for a while. As he came closer, he became uneasy about our scent, but perhaps the length of his solitary exile made him less cautious about approaching another living creature. He stopped short. An absolute monarch. Enormous antlers crowned his head.

"You're a beauty," I told him. As we started walking toward him, he turned majestically and trotted off, stopping every fifty feet to look back. He seemed reluctant to leave. He had to stay on the island until winter or he would have a very difficult swim, whichever way he chose to go.

The island itself was stunning. The dark lichens growing on the rocks sharply contrasted with the many turquoise ponds and coves. The mosses bordering the ponds were a brilliant emerald green. From the higher reaches, little rivulets came tumbling down. We would not lack for fresh water.

From the highest point of our island we could not see Southampton or the west shore of the Hudson Bay. Across the Frozen Strait to the north and visible this day lay the bottom of the Melville Peninsula. That, of course, is mainland Canada. If we could cross the strait safely we would nearly be home free. At the moment it didn't look possible. All day the ice had been streaming in from the east. The current had to be very strong. The gale-force winds continued. Even our protected cove was an angry mess. The plunging waves came clawing at our beach. I watched their advance up the shore and set a rock marker for the high-tide line.

During the night I woke to check on the kayaks. As I strolled the beach in the twilight of the midnight sun, I noticed the sky was less troubled. The wind had eased considerably. Whitecaps no longer crowned the waves. Butterflies stirred in my stomach. Tomorrow we might be camping on the mainland. On the way back to the tent I stopped to examine a twelve-inch piece of 2"x 4" board and a piece of a child's toy skidoo made by Coleco. These items were the only evidence of modern man we had seen since we left Chesterfield Inlet seventeen days ago. If only I could let my children and friends know we were alive. I knew they would be dreadfully worried. We were already seven days overdue at Repulse Bay. Having a radio would have been so comforting. Don's refusal to allow one along was idiotic. If we had a radio, he thought we would leave a margin for error. Even without a radio, errors were not uncommon on this trip.

August 11th. By 3:45 a.m. when we prepared to shove off from shore, the ocean had calmed. In the chill of dawn we headed out of the cove.

"Let's stay away from the reef area," I said to Don. "I don't want to upset the walrus again."

"We aren't going that way," answered Don.

"Where are we going then?" I asked.

"We have to go this way," he said, pointing east into the Frozen Strait. I couldn't figure out what was wrong with him. For the last two days we had watched the ice streaming from there. How in the world could he still believe it was Battery Bay, which was only two miles deep and four miles wide on the map? Such a small area could never have held so much ice or worked up a current so strong. I knew his ego had been thrashed by the Southampton crossing and I tried to be kind. However, I was not going to let him put my life in danger any more. I certainly had no intention of paddling eastward toward the Atlantic Ocean.

I pointed my kayak northwest at a bearing of 320°.

"I'm going northwest," I said. I was prepared to part company right there in the mouth of the cove on Cape Frigid.

I paddled away. When I looked back, he was following. Within minutes he passed me, took the lead, and we were back in our old pattern. Perhaps Don was better off not knowing we were crossing the Frozen Strait. Whether the crossing was forty miles or not, it was our only chance to get to Repulse Bay before our food ran out. It was definitely not the time to dwell on uncertainties. Upon seeing a proper map when we returned home, I found the strait to be only sixteen miles across at the narrowest point.

We rode the back of an incoming tide for the first part. I settled into a rhythm that made the miles fly. The strong winds had dispersed the jammed ice on the north shore of the strait. Although much ice was still there, we could see dark shoreline in the breaks behind the bergs.

"Look back and see if we're leaving the island behind," Don said.

"Yes," I answered. Before long all that remained was a long black mirage.

I didn't tell him that the back bearing showed a marked side-drift. Also, looking south, I could see the unmistakable taupe-coloured shore of Southampton Island. I hoped he wouldn't notice. He was much easier to deal with if he wasn't upset. The next time I looked for Southampton it had disappeared behind the mirage of White Island.

What I had worried about the most happened. We were caught up in the reversing tide coming out of Repulse Bay. I picked a large rock on the far shoreline for a marker. At first we were even with it. After an hour of hard paddling I looked back to gauge our progress. Instead of gaining on it, we were not even holding our own against the current.

"Don, we're being carried backwards," I said.

"Yes, I know that," he said calmly. "Head straight in for shore. We have to get out of this current." As usual he had been heading for the most northwest point of the peninsula and we had been bucking the full strength of the outgoing tide. By the time we got some relief from the current, we had drifted eight miles back of our original bearing.

Nearer shore, the floes churned in turmoil from the conflicting current and the outgoing tide. We had to maneuver carefully through the narrow passages in among the moving ice. We needed total concentration and could have used an extra set of eyes. Don gave me the lead. The opening I was headed for closed and we had to backtrack. We skirted the ice, going farther into the channel, and again got back on track.

There were so many whirlpools that we could not avoid them. Some of the larger floes would get caught up in them and revolved slowly, as though to some sensuous music. The smaller ones would be caught up quickly. They would do a pirouette and spin out to the outside edge of the whirlpool to be caught up by the main current.

I asked Don what he thought of the whirlpools.

"They're likely the result of the turbulence coming out of Wager Bay," he explained. "Tomorrow we can probably cross to the mainland, because we'll be past Wager."

"Oh boy," I thought, "this is scary." He really doesn't believe we are crossing the Frozen Strait.

"Don, I hear a boat," I called to him.

"You only hear a boat because you want to hear a boat," he yelled back.

"No, really I do," I said. "I'm going to fire a flare."

"Don't be stupid," he said. "There's no boat out there."

I started to get the flare, but he disappeared into the ice. I didn't want to lose sight of him and he wasn't waiting. As I started paddling, I could hear the motor accelerating and the sound disappeared to the north. I was ecstatic. There were people in the area.

I started to enjoy the whirlpools. At first I was very cautious. Because there were so many, I was getting used to the tug on the kayak as I crossed the outside edges. Then, as I got braver, I would cut closer to the middle to see how much force there was. And there was plenty. I could feel the tug on the rudder. The middle of the whirlpool was depressed and very turbulent. The outside was slightly elevated with less pull. I would paddle across the vortex, and when the cockpit was over the centre I would release the rudder and the kayak would spin with the force. The whole seventeen feet of it. It was amazing! I always ruddered out before I turned completely around. I would have hated to see Don's face if he caught me pointing backwards.

A large seal on a floating slab of ice was enjoying the sun. Don motioned for my camera. I passed it to him. He took some swift paddle strokes and then glided toward the seal. It was a bearded seal, sometimes called the square flipper. It was hard to judge the approximate weight, but it was certainly much larger than any seals we had seen so far. They can grow to over 500 pounds and are prized for their extremely tough, flexible skin. Dog-team traces, harpoon lines, and soles of boots were usually made of their skin. Also, the skin was used for covering the large Eskimo boat called the umiak. It was a thrill to see this creature, so important to the Inuit for food, clothing, and gear. Don moved his paddle to get closer. The seal spotted him and slid silently into the water, long white whiskers and all.

We carried on due west. Once we left most of the ice behind, we could feel the current more. My bladder was bursting. I had my sights set on an island in the middle of a deep inlet that extended far inland. We paddled hard but gained little. We were caught in the turbulence of the current coming out of the inlet and the one whizzing through the straits. When we did make the island shore, I stepped out briefly on wobbly legs.

As we paddled away from the island, the current became milder, deflected by the prominent cape ahead of us. Four more miles took us to the mainland.

Up to this point the water had been an icy, skim-milk colour. Now it was back to shades of turquoise or royal blue depending on the direction one looked. We rounded a cape and headed due north. The scenery was incredibly beautiful. A few icebergs left by the dropping tide lined the rusty, boulder-strewn shore. We posed for pictures in front of icebergs. The water was so clear we could gaze down at the foot of the bergs. Down, down, way down! The water reflected turquoise against the white of the ice. We were only hundreds of feet from the mainland. I was gloriously happy.

Don was the opposite. Every time I tried to say something he would sarcastically finish my sentence. Sure I would weep out of pure frustration,

I just stopped talking to him. Eventually, he asked why I wasn't saying anything.

"Don, every time I want to say something you interrupt rudely, put words in I wasn't planning to say, then answer as if I'm some sort of bimbo. I'm fed up with being treated like this." For a second, I thought I saw a bit of compassion on his face.

Don still believed we were on Southampton Island, so he expected to see Roes Welcome Sound disappear to the north. Instead, the headlands to the north closed in to make a snug bay. I looked at Don. He looked old, tired, and completely drained of his energy. He could have avoided this trauma, but his stubbornness had not allowed his mind to accept his blunder.

I spotted inukshuks guarding the high ridge on the mainland shore. I couldn't suppress my happiness.

"Look, Don, inukshuks on shore!" I called.

Later on I spotted the figure of a man.

"I think that's a person," I said. "I'm going to wave."

"It's an inukshuk," Don answered.

"I'm going to wave anyway," I answered. "If it isn't a person, the inukshuk won't tell."

The little sentinel didn't wave back.

We had been making good time in the last three hours. The tide had reversed and was heading to high, carrying us along with it. The swells were smooth as silk. Although I resented Don for treating me in such a demeaning way for so long, I couldn't keep from smiling at him whenever he looked my way. The weather was clear and calm as we passed the Hall Islands. If we followed the shore we would sooner or later get to the hamlet of Repulse.

"Don, I hear a boat!" I said with great excitement. "Do you hear one?"

He answered, "No."

We paddled on. The sound was getting clearer. Still Don didn't comment.

I strained my eyes in the direction of the sound. Far to the north along the shore I could see water churned up by a boat.

"There's the boat, Don! I see it along the shore. I'm heading in, to cut it off," I yelled.

"I can signal from here," Don called back. He started waving his double-blade.

I wasn't going to take a chance on missing whoever was out there. "I'm going to fire a flare," I told Don.

"Don't fire it!" he yelled back. "They'll think we're lost."

"Well, we are!" I answered. I held the flare over my head and fired.

Immediately the boat swerved in our direction. Don caught up to me.

"Don't ask any stupid questions. Let me do the talking," he said.

The big freighter canoe pulled up. Four handsome Inuit fellows beamed at us over the side. Introductions were made. We were happy to meet Dennis and Gabriel Kaunak, Luke Putulik, and Regan Makpak.

"We heard you were coming," they said. "We never expected to find you here." We were supposed to be coming into Repulse Bay from the west. Instead, we were on the east shore.

Don cleared his throat. "Could you tell us whereabouts on Southampton Island we are?"

"Southampton Island? You're not on Southampton! You're in Repulse Bay!" they answered and started to laugh.

My fist shot skyward. My shout of elation filled the whole bay. Don looked stunned. The fellows laughed even harder.

"Do you want some coffee?" asked Dennis.

Coffee! Out here! Dennis handed me his, already sweetened, thick with milk and steaming hot. They had a pot of it on the Coleman stove in the cabin.

"Where were you during the big storm?" they asked.

"On White Island," I answered. They looked at each other.

"Did you see any walrus?" they asked.

"Just one," I answered, "and one bearded seal on this side of the straits."

Then I asked, "Was there someone in the strait this morning? I heard a boat in the ice-field."

"Yes, a fellow from town went to check for walrus," they answered. "With the straits breaking up, there will be whales too."

"What kind?" I asked.

"Narwhal, mostly," they answered.

"Where are you going now?" I asked.

"We put our nets in for char. We were just starting out to hunt seal for a couple of hours. We saw you before your flare went off. We thought you were seals on the ice-floes," they told us.

"How far is it to Repulse Bay?" I asked. The town has the same name.

"It's about thirty miles across the bay," Dennis said. "If you follow the shore, maybe 55 miles."

"Would you tell us exactly how to get there?" I asked.

"Sure," Dennis said. He pointed due west. "There are the Harbour Islands. When you get there stay along the shore."

"Can we pass between the mainland and the islands?" I asked.

"Yes," he answered. "Then there will be two long peninsulas. At the tip of the second one there is a long thin island. When you see it, you'll also see Repulse Bay to the north."

"Will I have to look hard to see it?" I asked.

"No, it will be there," he answered patiently. I memorized every word he said.

"Please tell the Northern Store manager where we are," we said. "If the weather is good, we'll be there in two days." They promised they would.

"We're going to camp on the shore up ahead," we told them. "Do we have to worry about polar bears?"

"No, you'll find no bears here," they answered.

A warm feeling stayed with me as we parted company.

"How about that, Don? Isn't it wonderful, how things worked out?" I said.

"Let's find a camp spot," he growled.

I felt like paddling. The conditions were excellent. I suggested it to Don.

"No, we've done enough today," he said. "I'm tired." And he looked it too. It was only 2:00 p.m. We had paddled for ten hours and fifteen minutes.

We found a great beach in a sheltered bay on the east shore of Repulse Bay. As we set up the tent, another boat went past. They spotted us and circled to come in. We met Jack, Gabrielle, and a fellow whose name has slipped my mind. They had also set nets and were going to do some hunting.

"You can stay at a camp up the shore a ways," they offered. "A fellow from town owns it, but he wouldn't mind."

"Thank you," we said, "but we're used to staying in the tent. We'll be fine."

"We'll check on you on our way back," they promised.

And they did. We had finished our supper when they came. I offered to make tea. They were planning to stay, but had trouble anchoring the boat. So we talked for a while on the shore. They were lucky enough to have shot a seal. Before they departed, I asked once more for directions to Repulse and they repeated Dennis' instructions. As they left, they handed us a large arctic char. It would easily make three large meals.

My spirits were high. We were so close. Our families would know tonight that we were safe. The dreaded Frozen Strait was behind us. We had done a great job of kayaking. I was thankful to have experienced such a wide range of trials. I had learned to compensate and compromise when things went wrong. I was proud of myself too. Not once had I said, "I told you so."

I set the alarm for 4:00 a.m. I fell asleep to the sound of Pilgrim's voice coming over the cassette. "On the homeward stretch, paddle hard, paddle for home."

When the alarm rang, I left the tent to check the kayaks. They were safe, but the weather was awful. Heavy fog had set in. I couldn't see past our little bay. The wind was gusting from the west. It was an incredible change from our beautiful afternoon. I hoped the tent would last another day.

Don heard me come back in.

"Don't worry about getting up early," I said. "We won't be travelling today."

August 12th. In the chill of dawn, I looked out to find the bay still fogged in. The wind was even stronger. From the rear window of the tent we could see caribou grazing in the meadow. We lay on our stomachs and watched before starting breakfast. We tried sightseeing, but the wind-driven fog stung our faces. I went back to the tent but Don took my camera and tried sneaking up on the caribou.

I had not slept well. My shoulders were aching so badly I couldn't find a comfortable position to sleep in. I must have moved up against Don's sleeping bag, because in the morning he reminded me that I had crowded his air mattress. I hadn't done it on purpose. Certainly, I did have respect for his possessiveness. Each of us has a comfort level regarding the space around us. Sometimes, we react defensively, negatively, and even violently when someone intrudes. Under the circumstances, perhaps it was normal. We had spent sixty days, 24 hours a day, together. That was a long, long time.

During the day, another fiberglass pole snapped from the pressure of the wind. We were beginning to look as though we had been travelling too long. The tent had faded from the sunlight and salt air. My neon jacket and visor had faded to an indescribable colour. My hair was bleached from a reddish chestnut to a blazing copper. Don's beard was shaggy and white. Both of us had sore, bloodshot eyes. My ulcer needed attention. The skin across my lower back had rubbed off from the friction of the seat, which was a touch too high. Don was yelping every time his sore heels came in contact with anything. It was high time we were heading home. We settled in to an excellent supper of arctic char, instant mashed potatoes, and creamed corn.

August 13th. Windbound for another day. The fog cleared away. Instead it started to rain. I preferred the rain. Fog makes me claustrophobic.

Slowly, summer was starting to lose its grip. The sun was setting a little lower, the nights were cooler, and for the first time on the trip I had to use my penlight flashlight to check the tide table in the middle of the night.

When the rain stopped, we climbed to the top of the high ridges. On the highest ridge was an inukshuk. Down below, in the next meadow, stood the little cabin the Inuit fellows had offered to us. From this viewpoint we saw a wonderland below and to the north of us. Repulse Bay is full of spectacular coves. Meadows slope down from rock ridges to end in sandy beaches at the turquoise water. We had seen incredible scenery, but this was by far the most wonderful.

Emotion overtook me as I stood overlooking this large body of water. Here whalers and explorers had sailed their crude vessels, some for gain, others for glory. It must have been because of deep disappointment that explorer Christopher Middleton named such a beautiful place "Bay of

Repulse" in 1742, when he sailed deep into the inlet in search of the fabled Northwest Passage and failed to find it. Thirty miles across the bay lay the Harbour Islands, which we would pass on our next paddling day. The remains of 1850s whaling camps on their shores attest to the courage of men who came to make their fortune in a time when maps were few. Dr. John Rae explored and mapped in the area in the mid-1800s. His stone house stands in ruins on the North Pole River on the west side of Repulse Bay. He explored overland in search of the Northwest Passage. The Rae Isthmus and Rae Strait bear his name.

The North has a unique combination of history, culture, and beauty. I developed a great respect and sincere love for this part of our country. Spectators to glorious days and nights, we had also witnessed moments of great fury. Too soon, it would end. I had finished each day physically and emotionally drained, but my contentment was absolute. At least some of my romantic attachment to the North had been satisfied. Paddling was as natural as breathing. My body was very lean and strong. I was happy.

Caribou were grazing peacefully in the evening sun. The wind was easing. Perhaps tomorrow would be our last paddling day. The idea of going beyond Repulse Bay was no longer reasonable. Because of all the delays, the season was too far advanced. We had lost too many paddling days.

The chill of the evening sent us to the tent.

We awoke to a moderate wind. The decision was to go. We had talked about paddling along the shore instead of making the thirty-mile crossing of the bay. It started out that way. The waves were fairly high, but it was a peaceful paddle. The sandy beaches in the coves were readily accessible in case of emergencies. There wasn't a worry on my mind that day. I spent my time revelling in the beauty of the shoreline. I knew it would lure me into returning.

It wasn't long before Don changed his mind and headed directly across the bay. That was fine with me. His sarcasm was getting to me and I knew I couldn't tolerate much more. Keeping a leash on my tongue had been a strain. Thirty miles is an easy paddle. There was a good chance we would be in Repulse this day. I mentioned it to Don.

He snapped back, "We're not going to be in Repulse today, so stop thinking about it. You have to learn not to believe everything people tell you."

I tipped my head back, closed my eyes for a second, took a deep breath, and welcomed the breeze. I didn't really want this to end. I had enjoyed the wind, the water and the land, but I knew, if we didn't get to Repulse this day, one of us was going to end up stone set.

Windsong took up the challenge.

"Slow down," Don kept yelling.

The words "Paddle hard, paddle for home" kept coming to me.

I looked to the northwest. A flashback came to my mind. I thought back to the night I had gone to visit Madam Red Davis, a Winnipeg psychic, when she was recuperating in the St. Boniface Hospital. We sat and chatted and she offered to read the cards for me. She described people in my life, situations that had occurred, situations that would come to pass. Most interestingly, though, she said I would be taking a trip on the ocean. "At the beginning of the trip," she said, "there will be people in uniform." That of course had been the R.C.M.P. searching for us and then catching up to us in Arviat. I was most interested in the trip.

"Ask me a question," she said.

"This trip," I asked, "will I finish it?"

"Yes, you will end it," she replied, "but you will end it from the opposite direction from what you have planned. You will write a book and there will be financial gain from it. As always in your life, you will work hard for every dollar you get, but, as before, you will never lack for love."

She was right. In all my life, I cannot recall ever lacking love. It often came from surprising sources and caught me off guard. I appreciated all of it and I cherished the memories dearly.

The only way we could end up in Repulse Bay from the opposite direction would be to cross Roes Welcome Sound, Comers Strait, and the Frozen Strait, and paddle in from the east. Against all odds, that is exactly what we had done!

I was brought back from my memories by Don's call. "Look, a whale."

Don was pointing at a bowhead whale. I just spied the last of its spout as its long sleek shape slid gracefully out of sight beneath the water, followed by the massive flukes. It had to be at least four times the length of our kayaks. These animals have been known to weigh eighty tons. I stared, spellbound. As brief as the encounter had been, I will never forget the joy of knowing I paddled the same waters as this beautiful creature that had been on the verge of extinction before it was protected. For me it was a thrill of a lifetime to be only a couple of hundred feet from it. We were battling against a rising wind and couldn't take a chance on turning the kayaks to wait for another sighting so we carried on.

We came toward the Harbour Islands. "I think we have to go around them," Don said.

"Not me," I answered. I had every direction Dennis gave me etched in my mind. We paddled easily between the islands and mainland. I watched in anticipation for the peninsula with the long thin island at its point. All along the ridges to the north, the inukshuks stood boldly against the skyline. Something else was deep in the back of an inlet.

"Look, Don, fuel tanks," I called.

"Those aren't fuel tanks. We won't be in Repulse today, so instead of looking for it, why don't you watch for a good campsite!" he shouted. "And slow down!"

I knew I had seen fuel tanks, but if he wanted to camp then he would camp. I could paddle in alone. I pointed my kayak toward shore and he crashed into me with his.

"Where are you going?" he asked.

"Towards shore, of course. I can't see camp spots from here," I answered.

"Maybe around the next point," he said, "we can camp." I knew there would be no camping tonight. The next peninsula was the one with the long island in front of it.

"Slow down," he yelled again.

We rounded the point. "Isn't that a beautiful sight! There is Repulse!" I yelled. Just as the fellows had said. It was in plain sight.

"I'm not going to get excited until I'm sure," he answered. Hatred welled up inside me.

"What else can it possibly be?" I shrieked. "For God's sake! We're at least four hundred miles from any other town."

I couldn't figure out why he was holding back. Why did he have to take the fun out of everything? This should be a glorious triumph. Instead, I could hardly wait to get as far away from him as I could.

"Get over here," he yelled.

"I'm doing okay," I answered.

"I want you closer to shore," he yelled back. I could see he was heading for trouble. The water was streaming out of a deep inlet and colliding with the current coming around the point. To calm him down, I headed in. I took three successive waves over my head and backed off. I paddled back to a safer distance and watched him struggle through.

"I made a bad move there," he admitted, as we joined up later.

The wind and waves were getting worse by the time we found the natural harbour and paddled in. A welcoming committee was lined up on shore. Don paddled in only close enough to get directions to the Northern Store and paddled away. I found his lack of manners embarrassing. The group turned to walk along the shore in the direction of the stores. I paddled alongside. All we could do was smile back and forth. The wind took our words away. I kept looking up at them. Their dark faces were lined by the cold of many northern winters but they all looked beautiful to me.

I was a horrible sight. The last three waves over my head did nothing for my hair. I had lost so much weight that I could feel my soaked pants sliding off my hips when I stepped out of the kayak. The crotch was down by my knees.

I greeted those wonderful people with joy. Even the mayor was there to welcome us to Repulse Bay and hand us the town pin. I recognized the hunters who had found us. The story had reached town two days prior. They thought it was marvellously funny, how these Kabloonas thought they were on Southampton Island. Even the teenagers extended handshakes. I was overwhelmed!

I still could not put into words what had lured me here, but I was thankful to have come. My spirits were high. My heart felt like it would burst!

Don and I stood on the Arctic Circle and shook hands. "Good paddle!" Eleven days late, but we made it. It was 2:00 p.m., August 14th, 1991, two months and one day since we had paddled out of Churchill. This emotional roller-coaster of a journey was over.

Kayaking on the Hudson Bay is definitely best suited to lunatics. I would strongly discourage anyone from attempting it. It was only by sheer luck and the grace of God that we squeaked through.

The Northern Store manager, Rodney Rumbolt, escorted us to the staff quarters. We met Ellen and their sons Richard and George. Both boys were suffering from chickenpox. After greetings, I was so relieved to have a shower and to get into dry clothes. I had forgotten what it was like to be warm and dry and to walk on a solid floor. The most fun were the phone calls home to my family. I hope someday they will forgive me for the hell I put them through.

We enjoyed a lovely steak supper with Rodney and Ellen. They introduced us to their friends. Many were young couples from Newfoundland, working in Repulse as teachers and nurses. They had plenty of courage to come to such a remote area to make a living.

We had to wait two days for the next flight to Churchill. Repulse Bay is the most northerly community on Hudson Bay. The Inuit call it "Naujaat," which means "place of the sea gulls." A cairn at latitude 66°32' N marks the spot where the Arctic Circle runs through the community.

We prepared to fly home. Our kayaks were wrapped and our gear packed. I had promised Bill Brigden, the maker of my double-blade, that I would make Don shave. I was cutting the heavy beard with scissors when we started talking about the trip.

"I never believed you would make it all the way," Don announced.

"I wouldn't have asked to go if I didn't think I could do it," I answered.

"At least you didn't realize the danger we were in," he continued.

I was stunned.

"Don, I wasn't ignorant of the danger we were in," I told him. "I had more problems to worry about than you." That had been the truth. It had been enough to have a medical condition that needed attention. His bull-headedness had kept us on the verge of danger. His utter chauvinism had blocked all I had tried to point out to him. I knew I would have money problems once I got home. I had a keyboarding job to return to, but I still didn't have any sensation in my fingertips. If I didn't show worries, it wasn't because I had none. This type of trip seeks out one's weaknesses. I was determined fear would not be one of mine.

"How come you never looked scared or worried?" he continued.

"What did you want me to do? Scream and cry?" I asked.

"If you had cried, I might have treated you better," he replied.

I handed him the scissors to safeguard him from my potential response. I threw up my hands and walked away. "Do your own damn beard!" I growled.

"Oh Lord, show me a rubber wall," I moaned. "I need to bang my head."

Grabbing my jacket, I went out the door. I needed to get far away from him. Quickly!

Like most women, I went shopping to soothe my nerves. The local Inuit carvers produce excellent soapstone and miniature ivory sculptures. I relished holding them. The stone was cold and hard and lent me strength. I purchased some for my girls.

Calm Air came to take us away. Our kayaks would have to wait for a larger plane. Don had to be assured by the pilot that he knew how to do his job. I hadn't realized he was so nervous about flying.

Ron Gulliver worked as a weatherman at the airport. I have always been a sucker for brown eyes.

"Hi," I said.

"Welcome to Repulse," he answered. "Let me give you a certificate that confirms you crossed the Arctic Circle." From his accent, I knew he was also from Newfoundland.

"Do all the good-looking men come from Newfoundland?" I teased.

Don and I posed for a picture taken at the cairn marking the Arctic Circle. We said goodbye to the crowd in the miniature terminal. They were smiling. I had tears in my eyes.

The plane lifted off into the wind, banked, and headed for Coral Harbour on Southampton Island. I was anxious to see my children and grandchildren, especially my new grandson for the first time. He was already two months old.

I relaxed and watched the ocean below. The ice was still streaming out of the Frozen Strait. Then Southampton was below. The familiar colour of the gravel eskers showed from between hundreds of lakes. After a short stopover in Coral Harbour, we headed to Rankin Inlet. The pilot had invited us to the cockpit. As I stood looking down onto Roes Welcome Sound, what we had done overwhelmed me. All of a sudden my knees were terribly weak. I had to excuse myself and go back to my seat. Still, I could not take my eyes away from the water below. Even from the air, Southampton looked like a misplaced tropical isle. I couldn't believe we had camped on its shore.

At Rankin Inlet we had a few moments to chat with Jack Lamb, the airport manager. His family is famous in the north country. I would have liked to hear more of his stories, but we had to rush for the plane. I could tell we were heading south. Already, we were caught up by schedules.

We descended through cloud cover to Churchill airport. It had taken us 62 days to paddle to Repulse and only six hours to return. We were pleased to find Paula and Mike waiting for us. We enjoyed a lovely supper with them. Thanks to Northern Stores, we were able to stay the night at their staff quarters again. We had a full day to spend in Churchill before boarding the train for the last part of our journey home.

I had butterflies in my stomach when boarding time drew near. Pilgrim had reserved a roomette for me. I felt totally pampered. I will never forget the wonderful loving gesture. I fell asleep feeling like a princess.

Nightmares of long open-water crossings and mirages woke me. I couldn't remember where I was. The sight of trees silhouetted against the skyline broke the spell of the nightmare. The train was nearing Gillam. Each time I drifted off to sleep the dreams would come back, so I forced myself to stay awake until the sun came up. The same nightmare would haunt me for weeks after I arrived home. It was strange, because I did not experience fear during the trip. Mind control is important under stressful situations, but the tension surfaced the minute my mind relaxed. Or maybe it was from the shock of seeing the width of Roes Welcome Sound from the air? To dwell on the reasons was a waste of time. I was thankful when the nightmares stopped.

The emotional roller-coaster didn't. To my surprise Don claimed he had fallen in love with me out of respect for what I had accomplished.

"You're the first woman in my life that I have looked at past the face," he told me. At 58 years of age, he had finally found out that women are not empty-headed bimbos. I should have been flattered. From Don, that was a compliment. Instead, I wanted nothing more than to get far away from him.

I looked forward to seeing my children's faces at the train station. There they were! And my sister too! What love and happiness! My grandson Garrett was shy for a moment. Maybe he didn't recognize me. I was so dark from the wind and sun. Once he was sure, he came running and I caught him in a flying leap.

"Don't go up north again, Grandma. You stayed away too long," he told me. "Come and look at my baby." He introduced me to his little brother. Sure enough, there was my newest grandson. "What a perfect little darling you are, Keith William."

Don was busy relating stories to his friends. His sons, Dana and Jeff, had come to see him arrive.

The girls whisked me off to breakfast. We had so much to catch up with. At home, I hugged the big elm tree in my front yard. My little home was still as familiar as ever, but I had changed. I felt terribly out of place.

I tried to block the North from my mind. Still, it haunted and beckoned day and night. Would I never have peace again?

1992

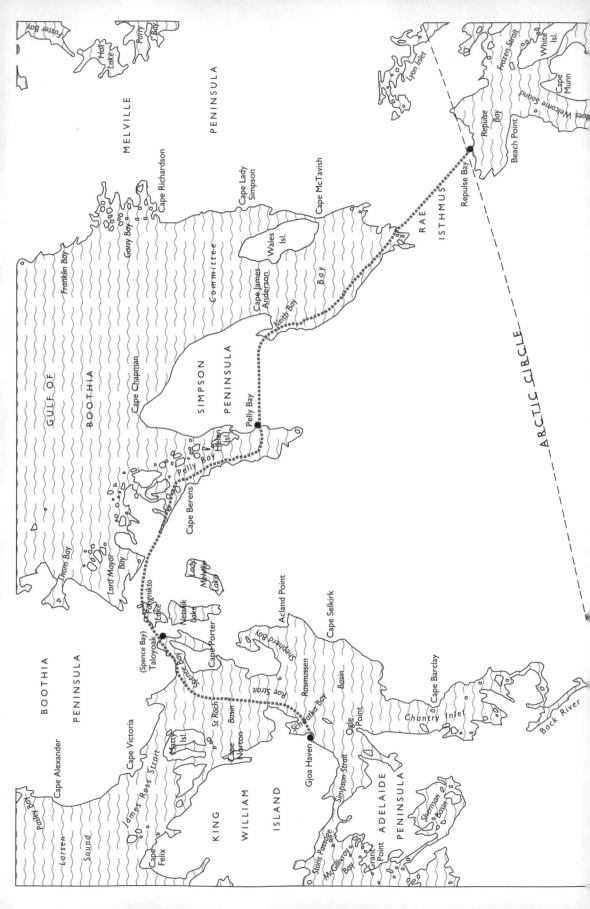

I never expected to do a long trip in the North again. I was, however, planning to go to Repulse during my holidays to kayak the shores of the bay. Don heard about it and suggested that we try to continue the trip from Repulse. He promised he would be different. I would be able to discuss situations with him. He would listen rationally. I believed him. The bitterness I felt over the way I was treated had waned during the winter. I thought I could compromise feelings and emotions for another crack at the brass ring.

Again, I applied for four months' leave of absence from my job. I skimped and saved to finance another trip.

The 1992 trip would be more difficult. Don's intent was to start at Repulse Bay on the Arctic Circle and cross the Rae Isthmus overland to Committee Bay, hauling our kayaks and gear on sleighs. We would walk north on Committee Bay to the tip of the Simpson Peninsula, then walk on the Gulf of Boothia until we were far enough north to cross to Spence Bay (now called Taloyoak). The total would be 360 miles. He insisted it could be done.

Bristol Aerospace had built a sled for Don's kayak in 1990. I had to have one built for Windsong. Again we packed, planned, and studied maps. Spring was very late, so we did very little training on the river.

In the middle of May, we shipped our kayaks off to Repulse Bay to wait for us. Ron Gulliver phoned to say they had arrived safely. He had been helpful during the winter by gleaning information from the local people. We had talked many times on the phone and he had sent me a gorgeous bouquet of roses for my birthday. I was looking forward to seeing him again.

Preparations were hectic. The completion of my sled was delayed until the last minute by problems beyond my control. I was dashing around getting my teeth fixed, buying extra life insurance, getting extra health insurance in case of a medi-vac, getting topsoil for my yard, putting in bedding plants, arranging money matters in case of problems, getting a complete check-up, and stocking up on medication for my stomach. Dr. Erenberg covered all problems that could have popped up. I had a test for TB, a booster shot for polio, one for tetanus, an E.K.G., and a chest X-ray.

I had given up my office job to work in a warehouse. I traded my high-heeled shoes for a pair of five-pound, steel-toed safety boots at the beginning of the year. For more exercise I walked to work and delivered flyers door to door. Along with that, I pumped weights at a local health spa. I was as fit as I could get and I felt good.

A friend of mine supplied a twelve-gauge shotgun. He spent hours at the rifle range coaching me to use it efficiently. My arm turned black and blue from shoulder to elbow before I qualified. I would take slugs and S.S.G.'s for close range, since I would only use it as a last resort.

Departure time was drawing nearer. I hated the thought of saying goodbye to my children and friends. From previous experience, I knew I would miss them so much. Yet the lure of the North had captured my soul once more and I waited for the moment I would set eyes on the Arctic coast.

May 28th arrived too quickly. I took a long look at my grandsons and hoped they would not change too much before I returned. I wished my granddaughter could have been there too. I had named her Rosebud when she was born, and the silk rose I carried on the trip always reminded me of how beautiful she was.

"All boar-r-rd" and flying kisses. The train pulled out on time. Excitement and trepidation all mixed together. Don had purchased the last coach seat available. I had to buy a sleeper in order to be on the same train. I sat with him for a while and we discussed our gear and plans. When I got back to my sleeping coach I was exhausted, but too restless to sleep.

I opened my notebook, and pressed between the pages was the yellow rose friends Jim and Marianne had given me at our going away party. The note with it read, "Good Luck to the Yellow Rose of the Arctic." I was carrying it to the Arctic to free the petals in the wind. By sheer coincidence a fellow in the next berth picked up his harmonica and started playing "Yellow Rose of Texas." It had to be a sign of good luck! I fell asleep as the last strains of music faded away.

Northern Stores once more supported our trip. An announcement of our coming arrival was sent to the store managers in the settlements we were to visit. Again, we were allowed to restock our food supplies. Canada Safeway had given us a $200.00 voucher for groceries. Don purchased the total amount in canned food. Vita Health Stores donated 2000 fruit roll-ups and 600 Cold-Buster Bars. We appreciated all this help immensely, but the weight of it all was astounding. At Churchill airport Calm Air seriously considered splitting the load into two separate flights.

I enjoyed seeing Paula and Mike Cook again. This couple loves Churchill and its environment. It is refreshing to see people so content.

Spring was very late. We walked to the river where a year earlier we had launched our voyage to the Arctic Circle. There was no sign of open water. The snow lay thick and heavy on the land and the river. Hudson Bay had not awakened either. Except for an open lead here and there, the surface was covered by ice and snow. Heavy pressure ridges stood where the tide and current had forced the ice to buckle and rear.

The late spring, of course, was in our favour. If we walked out of Repulse on June 3rd, we would need at the least one more month of cold weather.

June 1st. We boarded our flight to Repulse Bay. Our thoughts were our own as we watched the expanse of white slipping away below us.

During our stop in Whale Cove I phoned my friend Amanda Ford. I had not forgotten how kind her parents, Mary Jane and Joe, had been to us when we had paddled in the year before. After a short stop in Rankin Inlet we kept heading north.

Over Roes Welcome Sound we could see open water. Due to the extremely strong current the floes were broken and floating freely. There is open water there all winter, and so it is a favourite spot of polar bears, walrus, and seals.

Repulse Bay at last! We stepped down onto the Arctic Circle into -4°C temperatures, a brisk north wind, and mountains of snow. Ron Gulliver and his friend, Joe LaRose, took us in hand and hosted us royally. Ron worked for Arctic Airports and Joe was the renewable resources officer for the area.

The local Inuit had described to Ron the route they used to get to Spence Bay. It seemed the most sensible way to me. If we had problems, someone might come by. Don had his mind set on a route he had chosen. He wanted to see the stone ruins of Dr. John Rae's house on the North Pole River, so he wanted to head west, then turn north at the river and follow a series of small lakes. He thought we would travel on ice most of the way. But the ice would be covered by at least five feet of snow. It really didn't matter if we were on land or lake, since the snow disguised the boundaries. Don refused to change his mind.

Ron and Joe offered to help us by transporting what we didn't need in the first seven days to a cache point we picked on the map at Committee Bay. That was a relief!

We toasted our plans at least one time too many. For me the evening was beautiful and mellow. Every time Ron's eyes and mine met, I could see the affectionate softness there. He treated me warmly. It wasn't hard to take, after all the turmoil in my life. I excused myself from the party after midnight. Ron came to wish me good night and the chemistry was so right. I wished with all my heart that we could be alone. The music continued on into the night. I had barely closed my eyes when a noise in my room woke me.

"Good morning," Don said.

"What time is it?" I asked.

"Four o'clock," Don answered.

"Four o'clock in morning?" I asked. "Why did you wake me at 4:00? Nobody's up yet," I croaked with a groan.

"I didn't mean to wake you. I couldn't sleep, so I thought I'd come and say good morning," Don answered.

I couldn't make any sense of it, so I pulled the covers over my head. By then I was angry and couldn't sleep either. My second last day in a proper bed. How could he do this?

He was on the prowl again at six. I heard the TV go on. I went downstairs to ask him to turn it down. Ron had slept on the couch in the living-room. He was huddled at one end with his head wrapped in a pillow. His elbows were holding the pillow tightly to his ears. It really was hilarious!

We waited for Rodney, the Northern Store manager, to open the warehouse where the kayaks were stored. It would take very careful planning to pack the essentials. The gear Ron and Joe would drop off had to be packed separately.

"Leave your shotgun behind," Don told me. "We don't need two guns."

"No, I'm not parting with it," I said. It gave me a sense of security. I wanted to make sure I had something to shoot myself with if a bear came by. Don was carrying a borrowed rifle he had not even fired once. No, I did not plan to depend on him.

When all was packed we tried moving the sleds. We could barely budge them. Each had to weigh 400 pounds, and mine was much heavier than Don's.

Don was looking quite ill.

"Don't worry, Don," I said. "If things don't go well, we can always come back and see if we can hire someone to take us to Spence Bay."

He was livid! He went stomping off to vent his anger at the end of the warehouse. Mad, mad, mad!

"I planned this trip for ten years and there is no way I will accept a haul," he yelled.

"You may not have a choice," I replied. "I'm not leaving the North until

I see the Arctic coastline. If I can't walk there, I'll go by any means I can, with or without you!"

Already I knew that things would not be any different from the year before. In Don's mind, there are no alternative plans. He would not even allow discussion.

The evening was emotionally tense. Don, Ron, Joe, and I were all worried, for different reasons. Don worried whether we would make the trip in his allotted time. I wondered whether I could endure the strain of the load and Don. Ron worried we would get lost in an area no one travelled in, and Joe worried about how they would search so large an area if we did get lost.

June 3rd. Trial time. 6:00 a.m. and we had hauled the laden sleds out of the warehouse. Don got into his harness immediately and headed toward the shore. The tide had gone out so the ice had dropped, leaving a steep, ice-buckled shoreline. Joe decided to deliver my kayak to the sea-ice by snow machine and komatik. I watched Don in despair as he lunged in his harness and spun on the spot. My load was heavier and I had fifty pounds less body weight. Buckling into my harness, I thanked Ron and Joe. They looked worried, but offered no comment except "Don't eat any yellow snow!"

Being on a well-packed skidoo trail gave me more traction, and I was able to move the load. Don joined me on the trail. We struggled until 2:00 p.m. We had gained only 5½ miles. It became increasingly clear that once we left the trail, it would be twice as hard. Don kept insisting we could do ten miles per day.

Joe checked on us that afternoon. It had taken him 7½ minutes to catch up by snow machine. We talked for a few minutes. I told him I would give it another try the next day. If it wasn't easier, I'd return to Repulse and Don could carry on alone. Joe understood and was relieved.

We set up camp against an ice ridge to get shelter from the wind. The tent was barely up when the ice began to groan and creak like a rusty old hinge. It was the tide coming in. At first I was startled by the loud snaps, then quickly became accustomed to them. The ice was very thick and we weren't far from shore. Before long the water was seeping through the cracks to the surface snow. As long as we didn't tramp around and make slush, the area was stable. As the tide started to recede, the water drained back through the cracks.

Don checked our position with the Global Positioning System (G.P.S.). He refused to believe the position it called up. He was sure we had walked further, but we hadn't.

We checked the map again, weighed all possible angles, and came to the conclusion there was no way we could carry on with such heavy loads and pick up another 400 pounds at the cache in ten days' time, especially with the weather getting warmer. I was stunned when Don said he would return to Repulse without even trying another day. Ron and Joe took us in again.

At the Hamlet Office, I enquired about the chance of hiring someone to take us to Spence Bay. I got the name of a local Inuit fellow, Indigo Kukkuvak. Indigo was about to leave the same evening for Pelly Bay to purchase parts for one of his snow machines. I told him our problem and the weight of our loads, and we struck a deal. He would definitely take us to Pelly Bay and perhaps on to Spence Bay. If he decided not to continue after Pelly Bay, he could find someone to help us. He was very considerate. He would wait until the next day so we could load our kayaks and gear on his komatiks.

"Night is best for travelling," he said. "Tomorrow at 7:00 p.m."

I was so relieved. I would see the Arctic coastline after all. It wasn't any too soon, either. During the day the sun shone hot, and before long the children had gathered to play in the puddles. If we had returned a couple of days later we would not have had the option of going overland.

I told Don about the deal. Joe and Ron thought it fair to all concerned.

Don started putting on his jacket.

"Where are you going?" I asked.

"I have to talk to Indigo," he said, and stormed out the door. I followed.

"What are you going to talk about?" I asked.

"Never mind," he answered, and strode in the direction of Indigo's house. Indigo was sitting in the living-room, talking to a friend. Three little girls were playing with Barbie dolls on the floor. Don went into his speech. "We really don't have to go with you to Spence. We could still walk or we could put our kayaks on a plane and go to Spence by way of Rankin."

I couldn't believe what I was hearing. The deal had been made. I knew Indigo would not go back on his word and neither would I, even if I had to pay the whole bill and carry on alone. Indigo kept lifting his hat and scratching his head. The effort to control his anger was etched in his face. I knew I had to get Don out of there before he ruined it for me. I repeated the deal to Indigo just as we had discussed. I shook his hand and he promised he would deliver the komatiks to the warehouse.

June 5th. True to his word, the komatiks arrived. They are Inuit-built sleds. They are approximately 21 feet long and four feet wide. They consist simply of 2"x 16" runners, and crosspieces of 2"x 4", all roped together with one continuous piece of rope. This gives the sled a great deal of flexibility. The only metal used is the screws to attach the polyteflon to the bottoms of the runners. A twenty-foot tow rope completed the sled.

Indigo showed us how to spread a couple of large tarps over the sleds with the edges hanging over the sides. All the gear was stacked on, and the tarp was folded up and over it all. A long rope was used to criss-cross back and forth over the top and around the crosspieces. Nothing would be jarred loose and lost. Simple and effective.

The kayaks were on a separate komatik. They were still mounted on their own sleds to give them extra support. The excess gear was tied on wherever it fit. By 8:30 p.m. all was ready. Indigo was in charge of the heavier komatik that held our kayaks. His machine was a brand-new shiny black Yamaha Venture.

His seventeen-year-old son, Gordon, on a Yamaha Ovation, took the other komatik. On it we had the rest of our supplies, all of their camping and hunting supplies, gasoline for the trip, and the two of us riding on top of the load.

Ahead of us lay 360 miles across the ice and snow.

Indigo's wife, Maria, came to see us off. She was such a doll, so serene and soft-spoken. She was worried I'd be cold. She had me try on her daughter's sealskin coat and offered me mittens for my hands and kamiks for my feet. They are such tiny people that nothing fit. I assured her I'd be warm. The hug she sent me off with was a good start.

Don didn't have any mitts, so I gave him a spare pair of mine. The only jacket he had along was his paddling jacket. I worried that he would be freezing before long. I told him to get out his emergency blanket, but he refused, saying he didn't want to ruin it.

The minute I met Indigo, I felt great confidence. His amiable face masked the dignified, clever personality below the surface. I knew all would turn out perfectly. He proved to be as colourful as his name. Everyone had said we couldn't have picked a better person to travel with.

Excitement built as the machines were fired up. Last hugs, kisses and handshakes, and we were off. We ran alongside the sled to reduce the weight until we had crossed the last gravel street in town, then jumped on. We passed the Northern Store warehouse, cut through a ravine, and exploded out onto the tundra with all the traces of civilization behind us.

What a panorama ahead! We travelled over frozen lakes, through sloping valleys rimmed by rock ridges, across meadows, scattering herds of caribou as we went, and along rivers sheltered by high rock cliffs. I felt like Lara in *Dr. Zhivago*. The caribou hide across my knees felt as fine as sable.

Indigo was in the lead and stopped frequently for a smoke or to let the machines cool after a tough climb. I noticed he carried neither map nor compass. He pointed out places of interest and was always considerate, asking us if we were warm and comfortable. Every bone in our bodies was jarred loose, but we never admitted it.

At midnight we came to the bottom of Committee Bay. As far as we could see was jumbled, tortured, heaving pack-ice. One could imagine a giant walking through and dropping an ice jigsaw puzzle. The slush and open pools of water added to the disaster. We were to have walked this, according to the original plan. How smooth it had looked on the map. Don realized it would have been suicidal to walk, and drew his horns in. He never again mentioned he could have made it, especially when he found out what still lay ahead.

We stopped to make tea, cached gasoline for their return trip, and thoroughly enjoyed this weirdly beautiful Arctic setting. The sun at midnight is as bright as at noon. Most of the time we wore sunglasses. The only difference between night and day was the temperature. The night was a few degrees cooler.

After tea we skirted the bottom of the bay, followed Salt Lake north, then followed the west shore of Committee for about twenty miles. The plan was to cross the chaotically jumbled ice-ridges at the shore edge to the smoother sea-ice beyond. Every so often Indigo would kneel on the seat and gauge the possibility of getting through. Eventually he picked a spot and we headed in.

The sleds on their twenty-foot lead ropes required a lot of skilful maneuvering to keep them tracking. Any let-up would send them off on their own. With bone-jarring thumps we bounced off chunks of ice and held on for dear life. It was easy to see why the komatiks had to be so flexible. Up ahead Indigo had gained the smoother sea-ice. He was gesturing to Gordon for a sharp right turn. Too late! Our machine hit a large snowdrift and bogged down. The komatik swung to the left onto rotten ice. The back end started to sink. Don and I quickly got off. I yelled to Don to hold onto the ropes and head for the front. The ice was breaking away and sinking with each step. Once we got to the tow rope, we pulled hard and surprisingly were able to pull the sled forward enough for Gordon to get enough slack to gain some traction. A major victory! We had reached the flatter sea-ice.

Gordon and I set about making tea – no comments, no discussion. This is a part of their daily lives. My hiking boots were soaked. I changed into fresh socks and my hip-waders. A hot cup of tea topped it off. Indigo and Gordon raised the cowlings to let the machines cool while we stretched our legs. There was already plenty of surface water on the ice from the melt. We were lucky we weren't walking in it.

Indigo led us over the ridges guarding the shore. After approximately one mile the sea-ice became smoother. He headed north into a rising wind. The temperature was still below freezing, perfect for traction and cooling the machines. They opened them up to maximum. I could tell Don was chilled. I was comfortable. Watching Gordon made me shiver. All this time he had not been wearing a hat. His thick, jet-black hair was blowing in the wind. His parka billowed out behind him. He held on tenaciously to the machine that was tossing him around. Believe me, sea-ice is not smooth. At every hard bump he looked back to check on us. These Arctic cowboys are really a sight to see.

Indigo was kneeling on the seat and signalling for caution. We were cruising up to a four-foot-wide, open lead in the ice. The komatiks were unhooked and pushed part way across so as to straddle the lead. Don and I made our way over the load to the other side, glancing down nervously at the menacing water below. Indigo and Gordon took their machines far to the east before they found a spot narrow enough to cross. They roared back, hooked up, and off we went.

Indigo was pleased about the open water. They had come prepared for seal hunting on the way back. If it was sunny, the seals would be out on the ice along the lead. We saw many seals sunning themselves near their breathing holes, but they disappeared when they spotted us.

Before long Gordon's machine started making strange noises. "Sounds like a bearing," I said to Don. The machine started losing power and heating. Gordon signalled to Indigo. Indigo waited until we caught up. Very few words were spoken between father and son. They removed the cowling. Indigo smoked, a thoughtful look in his eyes. Gordon sat and enjoyed a chocolate bar. Don and I stretched our muscles.

Nearby was a skeleton of a very large bird. Indigo came over. "It wasn't killed by an animal," he said. "It was killed by another bird." That had to be the case. Not a single bone was broken or out of place. Every shred of flesh was picked off. It would have made a stark photograph depicting the harsh reality of life in the Arctic.

We were ready to move again. There was not much they could do to fix the problem. The cowling was left on the ice, to be picked up on the way home. We resumed our journey. Now Gordon did not even have the protection of his windshield. Before long the machine was overheating again. We waited. Everyone was calm. I loved it! Not a single curse or negative word. My admiration for them deepened.

By 4:00 a.m. on June 6th we had been awake for 22 hours. Indigo asked permission to go to shore and get some sleep. "You're the boss, Indigo," I said. "We're not in a hurry."

Skilfully he chose a path to shore. We camped on a sandy beach near the mouth of a large river that had not started to flow. Caribou were grazing in the background. At this time of the year, their hides were white with a caramel tinge. None had racks. I asked Indigo if we could use a caribou hide to sleep on. He gladly let us have one. Don and I woke at ten. There was no sound or motion from Indigo and Gordon's tent so we went for a walk. To the west was gently sloping tundra, some of it free of snow. To the east lay Committee Bay, which is seldom totally free of ice. The average is one year out of ten.

The multi-year ice makes it rougher than most ocean surfaces. It has a tide level of about eleven feet. The rising and falling tide moves the floes. They shift and freeze together at different levels. This caused most of the terrible jars on the trip. Far to the east, we could see massive icebergs frozen in the pack ice. I wondered how many years they had floated out there.

Indigo and Gordon woke at noon. Don could hardly wait to show off the Sony Global Positioning System he was carrying. "This machine," he told Indigo, "tells me exactly where I am on the map."

"I don't have a machine or a map," Indigo said, "and I know exactly where I am too!" He wasn't overly impressed.

We were precisely at the mouth of the Kuungurjuaq River, latitude 67° 36′ N and longitude 87°55′ W.

After checking the machine and doing a test run, Indigo decided not to try repairing it. He assured us that with extra stops we should make it to Pelly Bay.

Departure was set for 5:00 p.m. Don and I took armfuls of gear and headed for the komatiks. A strange noise from behind made me glance back. Our fully set-up tent came cartwheeling across the beach and passed us. If it hadn't been for the loaded komatiks in its path, it would have ended up in the water along the ice ridge. It was embarrassing, but funny. We dismantled it by the sled. The Arctic wind was teaching us a few tricks of its own.

Back to the sea-ice we went. There were slush and pooled water on the surface, but we barrelled through among the ridges with total confidence.

It was very moving to see father and son working as one. For two hours, with brief stops in between, we travelled directly north. At Colville Bay we left the sea-ice behind for the cross-country trek to Pelly Bay.

A small shack marked the junction. The door had been left open and the shack was full of snow. We stopped again to cool the machines and leave gasoline behind. From the shack we could see many caribou. Don started rubbing his stomach and mentioning how much he liked caribou meat. Indigo took his rifle out and made a spectacular shot at 350 yards, with open sights. The caribou were startled and mingled in confusion. Nothing happened!

Don wanted Indigo to shoot again.

"I don't have to," said Indigo. " I got him in the heart." At that moment the smallest lost its legs and dropped.

Gordon and I set about making tea. Indigo retrieved the carcass, and in twenty minutes he had it skinned and butchered. He held the heart out to me. Sure enough, there was a big hole right through it. He also showed me how they would strip the sinew from the back and legs. It would be used as thread for sewing. Unfortunately, at this time of the year the hide was useless. The caribou were shedding. The hair came loose by the handful. Every part except the hide and intestines was put into the body cavity and cached in the snow for the return journey. Don was handed a nice piece of meat. I wondered at Indigo's choice of shooting the smallest in the herd. Then I understood. The meat would be more tender and the bigger ones had a better chance of surviving the harsh conditions.

Indigo had decided against a more common route by way of the Kellett River. With the last few days being so warm, he was afraid of open or moving water. The land was very flat and offered no conspicuous landmarks, yet there was no doubt or wavering. Such a pleasure it was to savour the silence and enjoy the solitude of this great expanse of land. I turned a full 360° to admire the tundra sweeping in unbroken splendour as far as I could see. Indigo's eyes mirrored the pride he had for his land.

When I stomped my feet to get the chill out of my toes, he commented, "You'll never be as strong as us. Your blood is too thin."

"You have that right, Indigo," I answered with a wink.

We headed into the evening sun. Some jolts nearly shook our teeth loose. I had my arm through Don's and we kept each other from falling off. Gordon still kept checking on us. He might have enjoyed seeing us fly off, but we hung on through no great skill of our own.

We spotted a caribou running in a wild erratic manner. Behind it was something much smaller. "Don, is that a wolf?" I asked. A shadow seemed to settle over me. The trauma of death dims by comparison with the terror of the chase. I was glad when we could no longer see them.

As soon as we stopped, I asked Indigo, "Was that a wolf chasing the caribou?"

He answered, "No, it was a baby following its mother. She couldn't tell where the sound was coming from." There was nothing in the openness to baffle the sound.

Gordon and I made tea again. We had a system going. I would dig out the stove, Gordon would light it. I would fill the kettle. Gordon would get the tea bags and sugar. Within minutes the tea would be brewing. It was comfort to hold a warm cup of tea.

Everyone was hungry. We had been travelling for five hours since our last camp. Don's kayak was open, so I reached in and brought out a package of fruit roll-ups. Don came up quickly and grabbed them out of my hand.

"I don't want you to give those out," he said angrily, and started putting them back. I reached for them again. I thought he was fooling, but he wasn't. The day before he had bragged to Indigo that we had 2000 of the fruit roll-ups and 600 Cold-Buster Bars along, as well as 100 days' worth of canned food.

The worst part was Indigo facing us from four feet away and seeing it all. I felt sick to my stomach and could barely lift my head to face Indigo. When I did he caught my eye and shook his head slightly, meaning I should let it be. I couldn't. We had a seventeen-year-old boy with us, it was cold, and we all needed to eat. I went to my kayak. Don was right behind me. When I got the hatches open I took out a loaf of bread, margarine, and a can of meat. Quickly I sliced the meat, leaving an extra-thick end piece. I handed the sandwiches first to Gordon and Indigo. When I turned to make Don's, the fat slice was gone. I had never seen such possessiveness about food. I was appalled at Don's frightful breach of manners. Sharing is the foundation of traditional Inuit ethics, ethics that had kept generations of Inuit alive. In their culture it is unspeakable to hoard food. Don would likely have gotten himself killed if he had pulled such a stunt in days gone by. Didn't he remember that Indigo had handed him a large piece of caribou just hours earlier? Any respect I had for Don was left behind in that huge open space. I looked ahead and I knew, with sinking heart, that the rest of the summer would be a very long, long time.

We packed up to leave. Indigo noticed that Don never took part in setting up for tea or packing. As we stood ready to go, he faced Don across the kayaks and said, "You are a lazy man." It was a flat-out statement. I was standing behind Don, facing Indigo. I nodded my head "yes."

Indigo's eyes widened in total surprise, but he instantly gained control. Only his eyes danced with laughter. I didn't help him much because I was grinning from ear to ear. If nothing else, the incident defused a volatile situation. Don was unaware of the exchange.

"I'm not the lazy one," he said. "I was up at 10:00 this morning."

If Indigo took offence at having the tables turned on him he didn't show it as he finished preparations. I just hoped Don would leave things be, get his foot out of his mouth, and shut up for once.

After midnight, Don heard a snow machine behind us. It was Indigo's cousin, Bruno, from Pelly Bay. He had been out circling the countryside, trying to pick up our tracks because we were late. Indigo proudly introduced him. The bond of genuine affection was very visible between the two men. I guessed Bruno to be very powerful. He was short of stature, stocky, and solid. He was very well-spoken, and had an expressive face with very dark dancing eyes and a grin that lurked near the surface. His handshake was very sincere, all-encompassing, and toasty-warm. He was relieved to find Indigo and Gordon safe.

After a brief exchange of news, we were on our way. The rest of the trip was like a celebration. We dropped down into a river bed. The high shores and beautiful aqua colour of the ice made it a spectacular sight.

We wound our way into the hamlet of Pelly Bay perched high in a protective cove on the shores of St. Peter's Bay at the mouth of the Kugajuk River.

We had asked Indigo to leave us where we could set up a tent. He dropped us off at the Roman Catholic mission church. He and Gordon unhooked the komatiks and left to get some sleep at Bruno's house, promising to let us know if they would take us the rest of way to Spence Bay. We set up our tent behind the church, hoping to get some protection from the wind.

Father Henry built the small stone mission in 1941. At the time we were there it was used as a museum for storing traditional Inuit artifacts.

We fell asleep at 3:00 a.m. We were weary and thankful to have come this far.

June 7th. I stayed in the tent to keep it from blowing away, while Don went exploring. He ended up at the house of the Co-op store manager. After hearing about his lengthy Amazon trip, the family suggested that he invite me up for coffee. Mike Hart came with him. We collapsed the tent and laid rocks on top to keep it from blowing away. The invitation for coffee was very welcome.

Mike introduced me to his wife, Annette, and their two-year-old daughter, Sienna. They are friendly, warm people. Little red-headed Sienna was priceless. She was so clever, fluent in both English and German. Her Inuit name, Aupalaqtuq, described the colour of her red hair.

It was a treat to have coffee and free run of the bathroom. After showering, washing, and blow-drying my hair, I felt super. While I dried my hair and fixed my makeup, Sienna stood on the toilet seat and chattered away. She asked a million questions. It was good to have a little person near. I missed my grandchildren so. She was the tiny ray of sunshine I needed. The visit was like a little piece of heaven.

Indigo came by at 7:00 p.m. Now there were three machines. They had repaired the clutch on Gordon's machine. Indigo had some doubt the clutch was the only problem. He asked his son-in-law, Savrino Inutuinaq, to come along because of his mechanical skills. Jacobson, Indigo's stepson, came along for the ride. They were pulling a lightly loaded komatik.

We set off across Pelly Bay. The first five miles were traversed with extreme caution. Open leads were common but none was wide enough to cause a problem. We headed across the bay to Halkett Inlet at the northwest corner. As we neared the entrance to the inlet we started meeting people coming from Spence Bay. Indigo had lived in Pelly Bay before moving to Repulse, so he knew every person. The cold, relentless wind certainly didn't dampen any spirits.

Around 11:00 p.m., Gordon started having trouble with his machine. They replaced the belt on the flywheel three times, but it was getting too expensive to continue. The decision was to take it apart and fix the seized bushing on the flywheel. Jacobson and I made tea. The boys had a large bannock along. Jacobson sliced raw, frozen arctic char with a large snow knife. I sneaked chocolate bars and fruit roll-ups to the boys.

Indigo and Savrino worked for two hours to get the flywheel off. The whole process was accomplished with utmost calm. Never a harsh word was spoken. Very few words were. When one tired, the other took over. Time for tea, food, or smokes. In the tranquillity no one paid attention to the -10°C weather or the biting wind.

The bushing was mangled. They searched their parts for something that resembled a bushing. No luck! Savrino decided to make one. He cut an oil container open and fashioned a bushing out of the plastic. With a lot of trimming he had it just right. Everything went back together. I don't think there is anything that would stump these ingenious people.

My toes were getting cold. Indigo offered his extra boots.

Don pointed east toward the Gulf of Boothia. "That's where we were supposed to walk," he told Indigo.

"I know that place," said Indigo. "I go there to hunt polar bear. There's open water there."

I shuddered. It was good to be safe with him. We shared the last kettle of tea. I was really beginning to enjoy the raw char. The claim that the best char in the North comes from Pelly Bay is probably true.

A huge arctic hare and a few seagulls watched as we prepared to leave. Savrino hitched onto our komatik. Gordon took the lighter load. We gave the runners of the sled a shove to dislodge them from their icy grip and we were off.

At first everyone took it slow and easy. When it was clear the repair would work, the machines were opened up, and what a ride we had. The terrain became very hilly. Long, hard climbs and roller-coaster descents. The drivers would maneuver the komatiks off to the side on the long lead ropes. As the sleds picked up speed, they gunned their machines and drove alongside, racing for the bottom of the hill. There they took up the slack and carried on, smooth as silk.

It was often impossible to miss the rocks sticking up through the snow. Either the runners would strike and glance off them or they would pass under the komatik, gouging each crosspiece as it went over.

This part of the trip was much more scenic. The sound of the machines echoed back from the high rock cliffs that guarded the valleys or river beds.

At a high, craggy mountain of rock, Indigo stopped.

With his voice full of mystery, he said, "This mountain has spirits living in it. No Inuit will pass by if he's alone."

I looked at the mountain rising 500 feet away. I could feel the goose bumps along my arms and across my back. It did look foreboding. It was a distinct contrast to the surrounding area.

"What started the fear, Indigo?" I asked.

Before he could answer, Don interrupted by asking why the cowling was

114

Waiting for high tide at Churchill. L. to r. Don Starkell,
Fred Reffler and Victoria Jason. Photo by Mike Macri.

A moment of fun at Hubbart Point.

Vicious storm on Hudson Bay, Igloo Island.

Attempting to dry our clothes on Crane Island.

Hamlet of Chesterfield Inlet, Northern Store
and staff house in foreground (red roofs).

Walrus in the middle of Roes Welcome Sound.

Paddling in the wrong direction along the Southampton Island coast.

Komatiks straddling an open lead on Committee Bay.

Tea break at midnight. Gordon Kukkuvak and
step-brother Jacobson slicing frozen char.

Martha Quirnik making bannock, Gjoa Haven.

Inuit games,
Canada Day 1992,
Gjoa Haven.

Nicolé Mibingalok, "My Little Inuit Princess," on one of
the Couper Islands north of Coppermine.

Tee-pee frame on the MacKenzie River.

Legends in the north: Fred and Irene Sorenson at the Grandview section of the MacKenzie River.

Sacred burial grounds on the bank of MacKenzie Delta.

Stranded on Cape Bathurst by heavy surf.

up on the machine. The magic was gone. I jabbed Don in the ribs with my elbow. "Why do you think the cowling is up?" I groaned.

Tears came to my eyes unexpectedly. Indigo gave me a sidelong glance of comprehension and turned to his machine. Don ruined beautiful moments with his constant babbling. My nerves were raw.

When we came to the flat ice of Netsilik Lake, I thought we were on the Arctic Ocean at last. "Is this the ocean?" I asked Jacobson.

"No," he answered. "It's a lake, but sometimes in the spring it has seals in it. They come up the river from the ocean."

Netsilik Lake is huge. The north shore is approximately twelve miles long and absolutely straight from east to west. We made good time on that stretch. Everyone was tired. Don kept falling asleep. I had to keep waking him so he wouldn't fall off.

June 9th. The sun was renewing the lustre of its spell as we pulled into Spence Bay at 6:00 a.m. We were delivered right to the door of the Northern Store.

After unloading, the hard part began. For a short time I had shared a kinship with the ones who know the Arctic the best and love it the most. There was a lump in my throat and a tightness in my chest as we said our thanks and goodbyes to this loving father and a seventeen-year-old boy who had done a man-sized job. With one last wave the three left to get some sleep at a relative's house.

After a lifetime of dreaming, here I stood on the shores of the Arctic Ocean. Frozen solid, it was still the Arctic Ocean.

Don went to the Northern Store staff house. A pretty young girl by the name of Lisa answered and let us in to the staff quarters. She made us a breakfast of bacon and eggs, an utter luxury! We were hungry after 52 hours in the fresh air.

We met Bernie and Roslynn. They all shared the staff house. We were interested in talking with Bernie, since Gjoa Haven was our next destination. Bernie had walked from Gjoa to Spence Bay with three Inuit friends in March of 1992. They had travelled in very cold conditions, at a time of year when there was more darkness than light. They had built igloos every night. It had taken them 7½ days to walk 109 miles over the ocean surface.

Don and I went to deliver a letter to Ron Morrison, who was the renewable resources officer. We had a long chat and he promised to look at our sleds. He figured the design was all wrong.

Spence Bay is the most northerly community on mainland Canada. It is a neat hamlet set high at one end of a very long bay of the same name. The settlement began a few decades ago, when the Hudson's Bay Company chose this sheltered location for a trading post. It is surrounded by a rocky, rugged landscape and is home to approximately 500 people, mostly Inuit. Many are well-known carvers of soapstone. Others obtain income through fishing, hunting, and trapping, or hold responsible positions with federal, territorial, and municipal governments. Their warm hearts and smiles made us forget the chill of the temperature.

Ron came by after work. He had one look at our sleds and told us we needed longer runners to disperse the load over a larger area. He set up a meeting at his house with four local dog-team owners. They were sure we could walk to Gjoa Haven if we had smaller versions of the komatik. We sat in a circle around a map on the floor of Ron's living-room. They showed us the route to Gjoa by snow machine. They asked about our sleds. When Don explained the design of his sled they roared with laughter, especially a fellow called Pitseolak. He was kneeling and sitting back on his feet. Don mentioned stainless steel and Pitseolak rolled on the floor holding his stomach. He calmed down for a while, then asked Don to please explain the sled again. It set him off again. By that time we all had tears in our eyes from laughing. It was unusual for an Inuit to express so much emotion. He really enjoyed himself.

We traded our sleds for two smaller komatiks. I couldn't lift mine so it had to weigh over 100 pounds. Ron promised to deliver them to the warehouse the next day.

I met a carver by the name of Samuel Nashooratook. With the help of his son Noah, he asked if I would like to buy a pair of soapstone polar bears. He had done a beautiful job of carving and I was happy to oblige. I asked him if he could make me another animal. Samuel has a reputation for carving in sets of two. When he came back the next morning, he apologized for bringing only one musk-ox.

"I only had time to make one overnight," he said. I gladly purchased it.

The carving of the musk-ox had an ivory spear in its mouth. Don told Noah to ask his father what the spear was for. Samuel told Noah in Inuktitut and Noah translated. "A hunter went after the musk-ox and when the musk-ox was through with him, all that was left of the hunter was the spear," Noah said. I liked the story.

Don interrupted, "No, that couldn't be what he said. Ask him again."

Instead, both Samuel and Noah backed away and out the door. They were offended. I doubt Don realized what he had done.

A young Inuit lad named Moses came by. He wasn't in the house long before he headed for the skin drum hanging on the wall. The drum belonged to Bernie, but he didn't seem to mind. It was about thirty inches in diameter and looked like a large tambourine. Moses used the rolling-pin-like club to tighten the skin around the edges. He did some fine-tuning by hitting the edges of the drum against the club. In seconds he was doing a drum dance. His knees were bent and he swayed to the beat. Recounting special memories, he seemed to float into a trance. I watched his face and waited breathlessly for him to start singing. Don brought him back to reality by taking the drum from his hands. Moses appeared startled. Thinking about his grandmother, he sat near me and started talking of her.

"I was a very bad boy when I was small," he said, "but my grandmother still loved me. She always took me away and told me stories about the old days. Some stories I remember and some I forget."

June 10th. I woke early to write a letter home to my children. The polar bears and musk-ox were packed along with fuzzy white polar bears for my grandchildren. We were leaving for Gjoa Haven. The kayaks had to be loaded onto the komatiks and strapped down. Ron Morrison and his exceptionally beautiful wife, Judy, had invited us for supper to give us more time for preparations.

At the Northern Store I paused to watch a lovely Inuit girl in an amautik with a bouncing baby in the back. She was wearing Nikes, was holding a package of Pampers, and was reaching into the upright freezer for milk. How the North has changed!

On the way back to the staff house I spotted Pitseolak driving by. I had to tell him we were leaving that night and I would not be able to go on the dogsled ride he had promised me. He looked different from the day before. He was coming home from his construction job in a pickup truck. His face, hands, and hair were covered in drywall dust. His smile was still the same, as was the devilish glint in his eyes.

The last two days had been very warm. Puddles were forming along the streets. I wondered how we would be able to travel with the sleds in such slush.

Dinner at Ron and Judy's house was a lovely affair. Their one-year-old daughter, Brielle, was as beautiful as her mother. Looking at her, I was reminded of Winnipeg and my grandson Keith. He would be one year old the next day, June 12th, and Garrett would be six on the 13th. I was thankful I could phone home and wish both a happy birthday.

Ron offered to transport our extra food and supplies to Gjoa by plane, but Don refused to be parted from his food, so we loaded it all on the komatiks. Ron assured us the snow would have a crust on it by 11:00 p.m. We set that as our departure time.

Three little girls caught up to us as we were leaving Ron and Judy's house.

"Hi! What's your name?" was their first question.

Then came, "Do you colour your hair?" My hair is quite red in the sunlight. They could not understand anyone being born with any colour but black. If your hair wasn't black then it must be coloured. They all chattered away. They were pretty, their eyes dark as coal and their hair shiny black. As we neared one of the houses on the street, the smallest girl tensed up and started drawing me to the opposite side of the road.

"What's the matter, Kathy?" I asked.

"My mother died in that house," she answered.

"Did she die because she was sick?" I asked.

"Yes, she was sick. She was lying on the couch. I lay in the hallway and watched her, but she died anyway," she said sadly. I held her tightly against me. She looked up at me and smiled.

"It's not so bad," she said. "My friend's mom adopted me, so now, instead of being her friend, I am her sister." The other two comforted her immediately.

"Yes, yes," the other little girl chimed in. "She's my sister now and we are both seven years old."

They turned to Don, who was behind us.

"What's your name?" they asked.

"Donald, just like Donald Duck," he answered. They took up the chorus, "Donald Duck, Donald Duck, let's run away from Donald Duck."

They had me by the hands and we ran down the hill. They were giggling and laughing. I was happy to see them back to the carefree ways of childhood.

Don was yelling after me. "Don't run. Save your strength for pulling the sled."

"Lighten up," I thought.

We loaded our kayaks and gear onto the komatiks. A hefty 400 pounds plus, mine the heavier one again. We waited patiently for the temperature to drop.

June 11th. 10:30 p.m. -4°C. Departure for Gjoa Haven. Crust was starting to form on the snow as we said goodbye and buckled into our harnesses. The sleds pulled freely. Ron escorted us a bit to see if all was well. The three little girls ran along by my sled and pushed until they were called back. They had promised me they would look after each other until they grew up. In a way it is good to move on quickly, before the attachment becomes too deep.

Two miles later I called for a breather.

"If you'd listened to me, you wouldn't be sucking air now," Don yelled.

I exploded in a torrent of pent-up emotions.

"You inconsiderate jerk," I yelled. "It's on account of you I'm tired. You were the one that was groping at my nightclothes for the last two nights in a room with paper-thin walls. It was on account of you I had to sleep on the floor. You were the one turning the television on in the morning. You didn't have the courtesy to keep your voice down when people were sleeping. You are the most inconsiderate person I have ever known!"

Don yelled right back.

I was so furious, I was near tears. I vowed then I would make it to Gjoa in spite of him. At that point I had a sneaky suspicion he wouldn't make it easy. Oh, hell! We only had 109 miles to go.

An hour later we stopped to apologize. Cooperation and comradeship are the key to a safe expedition. We would have to count on each other's unique strengths to get through. It would be a lot easier if we were speaking to each other.

The first night we came to two open leads in the ice. We were using ski poles as walking sticks. We could probe the ice edge to find where it was solid. Because of what we'd learned from the experience with Indigo, we were able to cross without any problems. I was thankful we had long runners on the komatiks. Our original sleds were too short to span the open water and allow us to crawl over the load to the opposite side.

Navigating was not a problem. A contractor from Gjoa Haven had purchased some heavy equipment in Spence Bay. To get it back to Gjoa, he had the bulldozer cut a path over the sea-ice. The road had drifted in, but the ridges were plainly visible. We followed along the road for sixty miles.

Sometime during the night my period started. I began wondering if that, as well as the lack of sleep, had contributed to the foul mood I had been in.

After 5¼ hours and ten miles we called it quits for the night. We made breakfast, did our map work, and fell into an exhausted sleep. Camping in the snow is quite comfortable. It insulates the floor. I had no problem with the cold. I had made a fuzzy liner for my sleeping bag. The bivouac sack I purchased from Mountain Equipment Co-op really kept the heat in. We had our Therma-Rest mattresses to lie on.

Latitude 69°21′ N and longtitude 94°05′ W.

June 12th. My grandson Keith's first birthday. I hoped Teresa would allow him to sample the icing on the birthday cake with his fingers. All little children should be allowed that on their birthdays. The 13th would be my grandson Garrett's sixth birthday. I could picture the brothers sharing the same party and blowing out the candles. Before putting their pictures away, I sent them a silent wish, full of love and affection. Wish I could be there too! I recalled cold winter nights when Garrett stayed for sleep-overs with me. Before bedtime his request would be, "Grandma, take out your slides and tell me about the North." I was always thrilled to oblige.

Don was anxious to make more miles. By 4:00 p.m. we were on our way. The sleds pulled heavily. It was much too warm yet, but Don hadn't wanted to wait until evening as Ron suggested. By 10:25 p.m., when the pulling started to get easier, we were too tired to go on. We had completed another ten miles.

June 13th. We woke at 10:00 a.m. I was surprised to see seagulls sitting in the snow outside our tent. I wondered what they fed on, when everything was covered in snow. We stepped out of the tent into the brillance of a noonday sun. The heat could be felt on our backs. By 12:50 we were on our way.

"Don, we're doing this all wrong," I mentioned. "We should be resting during the day and travelling in the evening."

"As long as we can move, we will," he answered. Although I looked forward to whatever the day would bring, we expended more energy than necessary.

Most of the day I could see dark spots appear and disappear on the ice. Either my eyes were playing tricks on me or I was imagining them. Finally, I associated one dark spot with an irregular chunk of snow. When we came alongside, I stopped to investigate. There in the ice was a seal's breathing hole. I had been seeing seals coming in and out of their holes to bask in the sun. They kept the breathing hole open with the long nails of their powerful front flippers. Air-breathing mammals, they maintain an opening to the vital air above, quite a chore in itself. We looked down into the hole. The ice seemed ten feet thick.

Caribou browsed along the shore, barely interested in our passing. Don was always far ahead of me. He would stop for five-minute breathers. He would sit on the sled and wait for me. I would barely walk up, and he would yell, "Okay, let's go."

"Just a minute, I haven't had a chance to have a drink," I'd answer.

He got riled easily, so we would be on the way again. By the end of the day, I would pull up and fall flat on my back in the snow for a rest. The cold would feel so good against my back and head. Don wore the flimsy nylon shell of a jacket he had worn on his Amazon trip. It was too small for him so he always became chilled as soon as he stopped. No wonder he couldn't wait.

During the day he misjudged a narrow lead and went in up to his boot-top. He seemed to have twisted his foot a bit. He was favouring it slightly, but seemed to be okay.

The wind came from the north. At rest breaks I loved to face it, take deep breaths, and feel its caress on my face. It has such freedom to it! My thoughts also roamed freely as I walked. I thought of my children, of beautiful times spent at Willard Lake and Keyes Lake, and found the strength for the extra mile.

We had walked out of Spence Bay and turned south at the beacon on Cape Farrar, and were heading for the beacon on Cape Porter. The wind was at our backs. We followed along the snow road to Gjoa. Even though the going was harder we tallied twelve miles.

The sun was still quite warm when we set camp at 8:15 p.m. We would pull the sleds into a V and pitch the tent within. We were too far from shore to get rocks to hold the tent down, so we anchored it to the sled runners with bungee cords.

June 14th. Latitude 69°06′ N. Longtitude 94°09′ W. Each day we were leaving earlier. This morning it was only 10:45 a.m. The snow was already mushy. Before long I had to shed my jacket. I spent the day in a light cotton T-shirt, but I was perspiring profusely. Thankful for the cool wind, I couldn't understand how Don could wear a T-shirt, sweat shirt, pile sweater and a nylon shell and not die of heat exhaustion. When we came to a large slab of clear ice that was pushed onto the surface by the pressure below, I asked for a breather. I went to sit on it, took off my boots, and cooled my bare feet.

We had passed the beacon at Cape Porter. To the southwest lay De La Guiche Point. Pitseolak and his friends had told us to watch for a snow-machine trail leading across Rae Strait from that point. That was the route they used to Gjoa.

The sleds were pulling hard in the soft snow. I suggested we stop and wait for evening, but again Don refused. Somehow we had to break this cycle. The north wind came to my rescue. That night and the whole next day the north wind howled around the tent. We had no choice but to stay in. I slept for twelve hours.

June 15th. At 7:35 p.m. we set off after brushing the snowdrifts off the kayaks. The wind had left a hard crust on the snow. It was -4°C. Perfection.

We gained De La Guiche Point. From there the Inuit cross to King William Island, because this is the shortest distance across Rae Strait. Four of the Inuks we had met insisted we would see the beacon on the Beads Islands marking the halfway point across the strait. "On a clear day, you'll see all the way to King William Island, thirty miles away. Cross north of the beacon," they had warned. "There may be open water to the south."

Don was half a mile ahead of me when I came to the snow-machine trail at the point. I wondered why he had not stopped. We already had 13½ miles behind us. I checked for the beacon. The horizon to the west was shrouded in fog. Surely in the morning we would be able to spot it. I wished I had the courage to set up the tent and force him to return. I wondered what caused him to disregard advice with such bullheaded stubbornness. Toward the end of each day, he would push hard and get far ahead of me so I couldn't ask him to stop. He did it again. He had to make one more mile. It didn't seem to matter that he was heading the wrong way. Ron had suggested we allow twelve days for the trip. I suspected Don was planning to break Bernie's record of seven days.

June 16th. 6:00 p.m. A conflict was brewing. I wanted to return to the hard-packed snow-machine trail. Don refused to backtrack one mile. He headed south instead of west. He insisted we would see the beacon better.

"Don't believe everything people tell you," he warned.

"These people live and travel here. If something should go wrong, they'll be searching for us along the trail, not here," I tried to reason.

Two and a half hours later, I was really angry. He thought we were getting closer to the beacon. Instead, we were leaving it behind. Massive ice ridges obscured the horizon to the west. The map suggested we were too far south. We scanned the horizon with binoculars. With a stroke of luck, Don spotted the beacon far behind us to the northwest. We were already tired from struggling in the soft snow. The sensible thing to do would be to backtrack to the hard-packed trail. The mere suggestion sent Don into a rage.

He yelled, "I've never backtracked in my life and I'm not starting now!"

"Oh, yeah! Remember Southampton Island?" I reminded him.

He took off to the northwest in a diagonal line for the beacon on Beads Island. I looked at the massive ice ridges and snowdrifts ahead.

"My God, he'll kill us both," I thought. Psychological control has to be supreme to cope with situations like this. I got my share of practice that horrible day.

We struggled for every foot. The going was treacherous. Vast pressures build up in the ocean ice until, at points of stress, the surface buckles and jagged ridges rear up. We went over, around, up, and down. We stumbled, sank to our knees in cracks, and became bogged down in the snowdrifts extending from behind chunks of ice.

I most feared being run over by my heavy load on the declines. Don was often out of sight far ahead. He never glanced back or to the side. I could be pinned for a long time before he would even notice. Luckily, I had designed my pulling harness with buckles from car seat-belts. I could easily pop the buttons in front and leap out of my harness when the load was uncontrollable. Sometimes I would haul the komatik up a ridge until it balanced on the tip, then let it slide down the slope on its own. Every muscle screamed for relief. My whole body was soaked in sweat. I cursed Don's stubbornness. North of this ice-field was a perfectly flat, well-used trail.

In spite of all the frustrations the challenge was seductive. For years I had been drawn to the mystery and excitement of the Arctic. So far, I had not been disappointed.

Two miles from the beacon the jumble of ice became fairly smooth, except for giant slabs of clear ice leaning every which way. I imagined them to be toppled tombstones dedicated to all the courageous men who had tried to unlock the secrets of the Northwest Passage so long ago.

As we neared Beads Island and the beacon, nausea washed over me. I had a strong craving for something sour. Don had lemonade on his sled. I wished he would slow down for a second. My drinking water was reduced to a mere trickle past the frozen lump of ice inside. The hard work had made me unaware of the cold wind and the dropping temperature. Otherwise, I would have stored the water inside the covered cockpit, where the heat of the sun would have kept it from freezing.

By 2:00 a.m. we had gained the beacon on Beads Island. Two pair of huge seagulls had claimed the 100-foot-square island and were bustling around their nests. Except for a few seals earlier in the day, the gulls were the only living creatures we had seen. I had watched not only for open water during the day but for polar bears. I remembered what one Inuk had said. "When you walk on the ice, look around you very carefully. If a bear is hunting you, you may not see him until it is too late."

Don would have been an easy mark for a polar bear. He never seemed to glance around or look back. I was tempted to sneak up on him and give him a scare. At 3:05 a.m., two miles past the island, we set camp. The wind kept ripping the tent out of my hands. Don was pacing back and forth, mumbling incoherently. I could tell he was becoming hypothermic. I wasn't much better off myself. We had perspired so heavily fighting through the terrain all day that our bodies could no longer produce enough heat to counter the cooling effect of the wet gear we were wearing.

Still, the tent had to go up.

"Don, how about giving me a hand with this tent?" I yelled.

"Tell me what to do," he answered with his hands in his pockets.

"What to do?" I yelled. "What do you mean, what to do? We set this tent up 62 times last year. Why do I have to tell you what to do?"

"Well, somebody has to be the leader," he yelled back.

I was stunned. That fact had been firmly established before we departed Winnipeg.

"Obviously," I muttered.

I know I shouldn't have lost my temper, but I was running on a short fuse. If he would ease up during the day, he would have some strength left for camp chores. In the end I secured the tent to Don's sled. When I went to open it, I found the zipper frozen shut. Between blowing on the zipper and running my fingers over it, I managed to thaw it enough to get it working.

Don dived into his sleeping bag in his soaking wet socks. I passed him the gear and he started breakfast while I secured things around the kayaks. The wind wasn't easing. By the looks of the sky, we were in for a storm. Still, all was well. We had enough food for at least 150 days! The headland of King William Island was clearly visible twelve miles to the west. The ice-field was totally flat toward our destination. There was nearly enough ice out there to calm the Arctic fever in my blood. Come to think of it, another day of pulling the sled might do it too! What more could one ask for?

Although I felt hungry, sleep was more welcome. I caught myself dozing off between mouthfuls. My head would get heavy and drop towards my plate, snapping back sharply before it ruined my supper. Pure physical fatigue intruded into every bone in my body. I crawled into my sleeping bag. I sent a quick request to the good Lord to keep my children safe and was quickly lulled to sleep by the increasing wind.

June 17th. The alarm went off much too soon. My body screamed for more rest. Luckily, the wind was relentlessly battering the tent with driven snow. We wouldn't be leaving for a while. It took willpower to open the tent and step over the snowdrift to perform a duty on behalf of nature.

My eyes really felt tender and sore. I looked in the mirror. To my horror, my face and eyes were extremely puffy. Maybe I was allergic to my down sleeping bag. I filled a ziploc bag with snow, put it over my face, and went back to sleep. Occasionally the sound of ice cracking below would awaken me. It was muffled by the four feet of snow covering it.

By 8:40 p.m. we were on the road again. The wind had calmed, the snow stopped. We recovered the sleds from the snowdrifts. The tent was getting heavier every time. We couldn't get it dry between camps. This time I left the zipper open.

Except for King William Island so far away, Don and I were the only blemishes on the seascape. There was not a track on this vast white canvas. It dropped off the horizon in every direction. The sleds glided easily and silently over the hard crust, except for the occasional rasp which was carried away into oblivion.

At midnight, the glorious sun did a glancing bounce on the horizon and started rocketing upward. The snow crystals turned into a trillion dancing, twinkling prisms. The wind gently caressed my face. The air was crisp and clean. I could contain myself no longer. I snapped my harness and danced in idiotic abandon on the ice. I love it! I love it! A claustrophobic's paradise!

I turned to confront the scowl on Don's face.

"I can see you are not taking this expedition seriously," he growled. I was dumbfounded. Couldn't he see any of the beauty? I was gesturing, but the words wouldn't come. Then I took a closer look at his hands and cracked up with laughter. The serious expedition leader was wearing McGavin's bread bags to keep his hands warm.

We walked side by side for a while. He didn't affect my mood at all. Still, I was puzzled.

"Don't you enjoy any of this trip?" I asked.

"No," he said, "the only part I enjoy is when I am safe in my sleeping bag."

I couldn't understand. To go through all this agony and not to enjoy any of it was plainly tragic. I felt nothing but compassion for him.

"What do you think about while you walk?" I asked.

"Nothing," he answered. "I just keep saying I'm the mean machine and nothing can stop me, I'm the mean machine and nothing can stop me."

What a waste!

Near the King William Island shore we came upon the skidoo trail we were supposed to be on. Along it we found two igloos. It would have been special to spend a night in one, but they had drifted full of snow. Rae Strait was behind us now. It had been a much-sought-after channel in the quest for the Northwest Passage. Roald Amundsen was the first European to navigate the strait by ship in 1903, yet it bears the name of Dr. John Rae.

Ahead of us lay King William Island. The sense of excitement at being in an area that holds so much history was overwhelming. My vivid imagination recalled and replayed all the glories and tragedies of the area. It was an honour to set foot on King William Island. For so long it had been only a distant dream, inspired by a passage in a book and a picture in a magazine.

The excitement was dampened by the feeling of nausea again. The craving for lemonade came with it. Something strange was going on. Up to that point, I had been having a grand time on this perfect night. A sudden weakness overtook me and lingered for the last hour before Don called for a halt. There seemed to be a barrier. Once I pushed past the limit, my body wouldn't cooperate.

At 4:40 a.m. we set camp at latitude 68°44′ N. and longitude 95°24′ W. We had walked 16.8 miles. The temperature was still -10°C. A fantastic morning it was. We went about making supper. I thought back over the incredible day we had experienced. It was so hard to find room to absorb it all.

A strange sound caught our attention. "What was that?" I asked.

The seam in my air mattress had let go and the air had come rushing out. My sleep would not be good this night. Don had no sympathy for me. He had been sleeping on a punctured air mattress from the Hudson Bay trip.

Our supper smelled good, but my stomach was rejecting the food I attempted to swallow. I blamed it on fatigue. When the map work was completed, we realized we were only seventeen miles from Gjoa Haven. We were three days ahead of our allotted time. I was hoping Don would split it into a nine- and an eight-mile day. I knew he wouldn't. He would probably want to best the 16.8-mile record we set today.

I found it very hard to get comfortable on the deflated air mattress. As I drifted off to sleep I mused to myself. I was still the same person who, a short while ago, would never step onto the ice of a frozen lake, yet for the last two weeks I had spent nearly 24 hours a day over the cold, watery element below.

Comfortable or not, it wasn't long before my body gave in to the accumulated fatigue. It seemed I had barely closed my eyes when I woke to the sound of metal scraping on aluminum.

Don was sitting in his sleeping bag. He was crushing snow in the pot with a spoon. I looked at the alarm clock. I had slept for two hours.

"What are you doing, Don?" I asked. "Why aren't you sleeping?"

"I couldn't sleep," he replied, "so I decided to melt snow for drinking water. Somebody has to do it."

"Why didn't you melt it over the stove instead of crushing it with a spoon?" I asked.

"To save on the fuel," he replied.

"Don, we have 100 days of fuel with us. We have already saved thirty days' worth by travelling with Indigo. We can get more in Gjoa. Why make all that racket when I was sleeping?" I asked.

I tried to fall asleep again, but it was a lost cause. I lay awake, listening to Don's scraping and the sound of the wind whirling the snow crystals around the tent.

"If you're not going to sleep, we might as well travel," Don said. I muttered a few nasty words. We emerged, blinking into the bright snow-scape. The usual preparations were made for moving on. I didn't feel well. I blamed it on the lack of sleep. My face and eyes were puffy again. Handfuls of snow brought some relief. I found it difficult to squeeze my feet into my boots, yet two days ago I'd had lots of room. I mentioned it to Don. He tried to cheer me up by punching me in the shoulder. The sudden jolt caused a wave of nausea.

"Ouch, that hurt," I said as I grabbed my shoulder.

He punched me again. I knew he meant it as a playful gesture, but it really hurt.

"Please don't do that," I asked of him. "I'm serious."

However, I looked forward to the day. We would be walking along King William Island all the way to Gjoa. The snow was giving way to open areas of meadow and rock. The land was beginning to resemble a charcoal sketch. It stood solid and silent. Mystery seemed to hang like an aura over the land.

We were seeing it as Franklin, Rae, Perry, and Amundsen, to name a few, had seen it over 100 years ago. It was heartening to see land that was still in its original state after generations of use.

I thought back to the Forks in Winnipeg where the Red and Assiniboine Rivers meet. Man, in his enthusiasm to preserve a historical place, had mutilated it beyond recognition. If the Indians, Métis, or settlers of long ago were able to return to that important junction, they would be horrified to see their familiar landmark covered in concrete and lit by bulbous lamps, instead of moonlight and stars.

I returned to the task at hand. The temperature was 0°C. The sleds pulled heavily. I had opened my jacket and unzipped the vents under my arms. Still, I felt closed in. I expected my second wind to kick in as it usually did after the initial warm-up, but nothing happened. Only by sheer willpower was I able to put one foot in front of the other. I looked at the sky. I missed seeing the stars. They were invisible, even at midnight obscured by a sun that never sets. I tried to take my mind off my discomfort by thinking about the beautiful things that made my life go round.

The temperature started dropping quickly. The snow acquired a good hard crust. We could walk without breaking through. Still, I couldn't seem to get my second wind. My chest was tight and aching. I couldn't seem to draw a full breath without pain. I tried small sips of lemonade, but it was hard to swallow. "What is the matter with me?" I wondered. I was no longer perspiring. After all the water I had drunk, I found it strange that I did not have to stop to urinate.

I called for frequent breaks. Don timed them on his stopwatch. He was getting impatient. "Okay," he would say grudgingly. "You have fifteen seconds to rest." Then he would punch the stopwatch. I thought he was kidding, but he wasn't. Fifteen seconds later we were moving again.

I was surprised to see a rusty-red tricycle among the rocks on shore. We had to be nearing a camp. At Luigi d'Abruzzi Cape we stopped at an Inuit camp. No one was home except for the sled dogs. They looked happy and well fed. I knew my friends Loretta and Lorraine would be happy to know that. I wanted to camp nearby, but Don refused.

Schwatka Bay was next, ten miles across. The airport beacon at Gjoa beckoned from the top of the hill on the other side of the bay. Usually the flash of a light is a spark of life for me, but today the fire could not be rekindled. All the strength had oozed from my body, a body that felt as though it no longer belonged to me. My legs were like lead. I fixed my gaze on the beacon. One step for each rotation. Why can't I breathe properly? I must have pneumonia. If that were the case, then Don probably would not wait for me to get treatment. The fear that he would carry on without me was adding to my misery.

We started across Schwatka Bay. I knew for certain there would be no stopping until Gjoa.

The wind was at our backs; the conditions were excellent. I kept falling back. Don got so impatient he hooked my sled to his. For one or two miles he pulled both. I was thankful. He definitely had incomparable willpower. I expected to find it easier to walk, but I didn't. It was better to have the harness to lean into, so I took the sled back. The way was perfectly smooth. I guessed it was five more miles to Gjoa.

We met up with the bulldozer trail again. Don was at least a mile ahead of me. Try as I did, I could not muster the strength to go faster. Don stopped. We met up and he took hold of the ropes to help me pull. The sled was not the problem. I had simply run out of steam.

"I'll give you one day of rest in Gjoa," he threatened. "Then you better be good to me."

There was a price for the help. I felt ill.

A couple of young boys on a Honda ATV spotted us. They could barely hide their surprise. We asked them how far it was to Gjoa. "It is right around that point," they told us. We carried on and they continued their goose hunting.

Slowly, we rounded the peninsula and expected to see Gjoa Haven. There was no town to be seen. We followed along the many skidoo tracks. Another 1½ miles and there it was, nicely tucked into a little harbour. No wonder Roald Amundsen called it a haven for his ship. A line of tethered sled dogs let out a chorus of howls as we approached.

I felt so weak that exuberance was minimal. Again, the failure in our personal relations had tainted the triumph we should have felt.

June 19th. Friday. 4:45 a.m. The last of the seventeen miles was behind us.

The Northern Store buildings stood farthest into the harbour. I was relieved to spot the red and white buildings, but our trials were not over. It was going to be very difficult to get from the harbour to the buildings. Everywhere we looked there was nothing but sand, except for some sludge in a large drainage ditch. I could see Don ahead of me. He was struggling with the slush and the incline.

Out of nowhere, three young Inuit boys showed up. They helped Don up the slope. Then they hurried back to help me. I would not have made it without them. Although they were only ten and eleven years old, they were very strong and cheerful. We laughed at each other as we sank past our knees in grey slush. We pulled up alongside the warehouse. I asked them to wait until I found the chocolate bars. They gladly accepted three each.

"This is our breakfast," they said. "We're just going home to sleep." They had certainly earned them. Don didn't stop me. I would have bitten off his arm and he knew it.

A knock on the door of the manager's house brought Terry McCallum awake and ready to help. I started to untie my kayak from the sled.

"Don't do that," said Don. "We can get six strong men and carry the kayak, sled, and all."

"Dream on, Don!" I answered. "Where are you going to find six strong men at 5:00 in the morning?"

Even without the sleds, the kayaks were back-breakers. Don, Terry, and I had all we could do to carry them across the road to the empty container Terry said we could use.

Doug Hodgert at the staff house had already put coffee on. I want to extend much credit to all the wonderful Northern Stores staff. Their loyal support when our spirits were down was tremendously comforting.

Doug made excellent coffee, but I had an almost desperate craving for a carbonated drink. I am not fond of soda pop, but my hands were shaking when Doug offered me his last Pepsi. Two sips quenched the initial craving. I shared the rest with Don.

I was puzzled at the strange things my body was doing. Stranger things were ahead. I had first bid on the bathroom. A scale sat on the floor near the bathtub. Out of curiosity I stood on it to see how much weight I had lost. Instead of losing weight I had gained fifteen pounds in the last nine days.

What a shock when I undressed! (It is at most times, but this was much worse.) I looked like a blimp. The scale was not wrong. No wonder my boots were so tight. I was horribly swollen from my face to my feet. Worse still, my kidneys had stopped working. I sat on the toilet, but for the first time in my life I could not pee.

Having a shower at last was heavenly. On the way out of the bathroom I pulled my nightgown up to my knees.

"Look how swollen my legs are," I said to Don. "How come you never said anything about the way I looked?"

He just shrugged his shoulders.

I tried to get some sleep, but my whole body hurt. My skin felt like it was on fire. Every joint was extremely painful. I knew I needed help. Doug gave me directions to the nurse's station. I made it there in short, deliberate steps. Dizzy spells kept flooding over me. I focused on the door of the station and kept going. We had made it from Spence Bay in nine days instead of twelve. For me, the price was too high.

Margaret was the nurse on duty when I walked in. At first she mistook me for a fat person complaining about my weight. I assured her there was really a smaller person inside. She began tests immediately. EKG, X-ray, blood tests, etc. Her first thought was to arrange for a medi-vac to Yellowknife. She asked me to wait while she consulted with Dr. Dufresne in Cambridge.

They decided it would be too dangerous for me to fly at high altitudes in the condition I was in. Cardiac arrest was a possibility. Margaret gave me a prescription for diuretic pills and told me to drink gallons of water, go to bed, and not move a muscle for four days.

A diuretic, gallons of water, and rest are not a good combination. The bathroom door never stopped swinging. I lost four pounds per day for four days. At least my kidneys were working again.

The diagnosis was edema, due to muscle breakdown from overexertion. The swelling was from an excessive accumulation of fluid in the tissues. Edema? I thought only climbers on Everest suffered edema.

From the tests, Margaret suspected irregularities in the left ventricle. She comforted me by saying she doubted my heart had become enlarged at this stage.

"You were very lucky you stopped when you did," she told me. "You may not have any permanent damage to your heart. However, you will not be going anywhere for a long time."

"How long do you mean?" I asked, a sense of panic gripping me. "Arctic summers are not very long. I don't have time to be sick."

"When you get home," she said kindly, "get your doctor to refer you to a cardiologist."

"Home? How about if I rest faithfully? If I exercise carefully after that, how long would it take to get the muscle tone back?" I asked.

Margaret was very professional. She was kind and gentle, but she offered no false hope. I respected her for that.

How would I tell my family? I had worried them enough just by heading for the Arctic. Was I really a selfish person to want to see it all so desperately? I alone knew to what extent I had mortgaged my life to have come this far. Surely I wouldn't have to end it here, especially in this way.

Don would be carrying on alone. Possibly he was relieved to leave me behind. He couldn't understand there is such a thing as human limitations!

He needed some of the supplies I had in my kayak. I didn't want to part with my own personal gear, so Don ended up having to buy a tent and some utensils. Within 48 hours of our arrival, he was ready to be on the way again. As we stood discussing arrangements, Ron Morrison from Spence Bay walked up to us. He was in Gjoa to do some musk-ox sighting and counting for the Renewable Resources Department. We told him how well the sleds had worked and how right he had been. He would also see that the sleds were returned to their owners. Don would still be using one of them until Cambridge Bay, his next destination.

I slept in on Sunday morning after a very rough night.

Don had been sleeping on a large foam mat in the same room as I. When I awoke he was gone.

On the dresser was a note.

1. Vicki – please advise R.C.M.P.
   Depart June 21st. Arrive July 12th
   15 miles x 22 days – 330 miles?
   Route –
2. Ask N.W.Co. to wrap and mail my parcel.
3. Ask Terry to advise Northern at Cambridge – possible coming and arrival date.
4. Have food for 50 days?
5. If stuck in ice may abandon sled on land for later pickup. Will locate sled by G.P.S. and record. Will then paddle into Cambridge Bay.
6. Thanks for helping me get here – you gave it your all!! Hope you're feeling better and you have a great summer.
            Respect and regards – Don.

I dressed quickly.

At the harbour, Don was trying to get a mound of gear onto the sled and kayak. He looked scared, and well he should be. Cambridge was a long way away. The weather had turned warm. Water was pooling on the surface of the ice. His compulsion to make extra miles was getting dangerous. With no one there to slow him down, I wondered what would happen to him. We parted with mixed emotions. I'm sure a million thoughts skimmed through both our heads.

"Good luck, Don. Be good to yourself!" was all I could say.

"Bye, Vicks," he answered. "I'm going to miss you."

He hooked up his harness and started away.

"How's the weight?" we called after him. He didn't turn his head or answer. He had Cambridge Bay on his mind. "I am the mean machine. No one can stop me!"

I stood and watched with a heavy heart. To resent his ability to carry on would be unworthy, but the pang of envy burned deeply anyway.

We had shared turbulent times, Don and I. We had also shared in an incredible adventure. We would not travel together again.

I went to the R.C.M.P. office to report his departure and route to Cambridge. They promised to keep him in mind.

Later in the evening a DEW Line crew came in by snowmobile.

"Did you see anyone out on the ice?" I asked.

"Yes, we saw an old man with white hair and beard pulling a sled," they answered.

"How was he doing?" I asked.

"Good," they reported. "He wouldn't stop, so we had to run alongside of him to hear what he was saying."

"Yes, that was Don all right."

The first week disappeared in a haze. I slept almost twenty hours of each day.

I visited Margaret every day. "You really do have ankles," she commented, "and kneecaps too." Finally, my bones were showing again.

My stomach would not tolerate solid food, so I lived on a high-protein, liquid supplement. I was beginning to feel human again. Walking and climbing steps was still a problem. My muscles felt like sponge. I mentally directed my feet for each step. If I stayed on my feet too long, I would break out in a sweat. All my clothes would be soaked and absolute fatigue would wash over me.

I slept all day on June the 23rd so I could venture out in the evening to see the tee-off of the first golf tournament of the year. Gjoa Haven does have a golf course. It is called the Gjoa Haven A.G.A. Tundra Turf Golf Course and boasts that it is the only eighteen-hole golf course above the Arctic Circle. At this time of the year it had snow traps. It was not unusual to see the golfers playing in hip-waders. Tee-off was scheduled for 10:00 p.m. Delays moved the tee-off time to 11:30 p.m. It was unique to see the golfers playing with the DEW Line station and the midnight sun as a backdrop.

Little clumps of Arctic heather and purple saxifrage seemed to burst open as we stood watching. The colours were vibrant. One should appreciate the loveliness of these flowers. They struggle to survive in the harsh conditions. A pair of plovers was annoyed by all the commotion. They made low-level flights from rise to rise, faking injury, to lure the golfers away from their nests.

While I was in Gjoa, Irene, of the Northern Stores staff, was house-sitting for teachers. When her parents came from Saskatoon to visit, they brought her a small hibachi and charcoal briquettes. She decided to have a staff barbecue. I never dreamed I would be baking apple pies in the Arctic, but I did. It was a fun evening.

Doug reminded me very much of my grandson Garrett. He was very sharp, full of energy, and fun to talk to. At the age of 25, he had already led an interesting life. He was from London, Ontario. I admired his adventurous spirit.

One evening Doug, Irene, and I went to listen to the local band practise at the Recreation Centre. I recognized the popular country and western tunes, but the words were in Inuktitut. The translation was so professional one could sing along.

Each day I ventured a little further from the house. I made sure there would be people near in case I had trouble getting back. I noticed I could stay on my feet for longer periods, even though they would swell horribly. I was sure I would be well soon.

The hamlet spring clean-up day arrived. All the children were handed big garbage bags. I was to delegate the clean-up of the Northern Stores area.

The kids were good and worked hard. All the loose change we found in the sand was pooled together. There was plenty, probably because of the lousy pockets sweat pants are famous for.

Once the clean-up was done, I promised I would add money so everyone would get a chocolate bar. We enjoyed our picnic lunch. The chatter was contagious.

A fellow by the name of Eddie confronted me on the steps of the Northern Store.

"I want to shake your hand," he said.

"It would be my pleasure," I answered, "but why?"

He said, "I am 58 years old. I have lived in Gjoa most of my life. I have never walked to Spence Bay. In fact, I have trouble walking down to the harbour here in town. That's why I want to shake your hand."

We shook hands and both laughed. I liked him instantly. Eddie talked of memories of his childhood, of things his mother had taught him, about tradition and home remedies for illness and injuries. I was mesmerized. He was a well-spoken man on the precipice of two worlds, one ancient and one modern. I searched his eyes for turmoil. There seemed to be none. Either he had adapted well or had hidden it even better. His only sorrow was that very few of the young people remember the traditions and skills that kept their ancestors motivated and fed.

Everyone knows where Eddie goes. He has the only car in town. It is a yellow 1974 Plymouth. I didn't get a chance to ask him how it got to Gjoa. There were various 4 x 4's and a couple of vans, but the car stood out like a sore thumb.

On Friday, June 26th, the whole town of Gjoa Haven felt the aftershock of an earthquake from the Back River area on the mainland. This was the second one. I was at the kitchen table when it hit. The chairs started bouncing around. The house quivered and shook. Doug and I ran outside. Mothers were dashing around bringing the children in. The word spread that it had been an earthquake.

One evening a young Inuit chap by the name of Adam came to visit Doug. I made tea and asked if he would like a piece of fresh lemon pie. Well, he wasn't too sure about it. He moved it around with his fork. Yes, he decided he would like it. It was yellow like seal blubber and jiggled the same. He also advised me that the meringue would be better made of wild goose eggs.

I talked to my daughters. I assured them I would be better very soon. Word spread quickly. I began getting calls from friends and co-workers. Pilgrim, Loretta, Lorraine and Tony, Louise, Gloria, and Grace. It humbled me to realize that I had caused so many to be concerned.

A narrow lane of water was already beginning to separate the sea-ice from the shore. I wondered how Don was doing. Fog had closed in for two days.

I hoped he would not lose his way. From the look of all the sea-ice, I knew there would be no kayaking for a while. Spring was late indeed, but that did not stop people from moving to camps on the land. Who could resist the smell of the spring breeze off the tundra? On the weekend, the town was silent and still.

Gjoa Haven is a small community of approximately 700 people. The only settlement on King William Island, it lies deep in a sandy inlet. Roald Amundsen called it "the finest little harbour in the world." He named it after his ship *Gjoa*. He spent two winters making magnetic observations and exploring. From Gjoa Haven, he continued his journey to the Beaufort Sea. Between 1903 and 1906 he and his crew successfully navigated the Northwest Passage for the first time.

Sir John Franklin visited the area in the mid-1800s. The disastrous results of his expedition were discovered on King William Island's southern shores. He and 128 of his men perished.

Secrets abound on King William Island and in the surrounding waters. I was proud and honoured to be there, but I knew I had to get well and make some decisions quickly.

I couldn't have handled everything without the incredible support from my children and friends. They waited with bated breath. They would rather have had me come safely home, but they didn't pressure me. I loved them all so much.

I was not ready to leave the Arctic. I had finally come this far. Everything was at my fingertips. I felt it was only a matter of recovering enough strength to see the rest.

I planned to fly to Coppermine on Saturday, June 27th. People said there was open water there. I wasn't sure I'd be strong enough to paddle, but it would be a good place to find out. I hoped to regain enough strength to carry on to Tuk on my own. At the least, I could camp on the Arctic shoreline and recuperate just as well. I've never been at my best when I have a roof over my head. Restlessness was creeping into my bones. I was sure recovery was not far behind. I wrote a long letter home, hoping everyone would understand and forgive me for not giving up. When Doug saw the letter, he teased me that it would be a toss-up whether First Air would take it or my kayak.

Saturday came. All arrangements had been made when, at the last minute, my kayak got bumped off the cargo list in lieu of extra seats. First-Air runs a passenger-cargo combination. If there are many passengers the cargo area is reduced. The problem was my kayak's seventeen-foot length. The agent suggested I wait for Tuesday's flight. I had no choice. I could still make it to Coppermine for the Canada Day celebrations. Margaret suggested that I see the doctor at Coppermine as soon as I arrived. I promised I would.

The snow cover was disappearing very quickly. Everywhere there was soft sand. It made walking very tiring for me but the children loved it. They were playing their games in the sand in the parking lot of the Northern Store. A Honda ATV would come by, make some fresh tracks, and add a new twist to their game. Hondas are very popular here. When the Northern Store opens for business, the parking area is crowded with them, just as our cars crowd mall parking lots.

The ocean ice was turning a beautiful turquoise blue, because most of the snow cover had melted. Some snow mounds remained, looking like floating marshmallows. From the sky came the melancholy honking of the Canada geese. The signs of the approaching summer were all around.

Doug, Irene, and I were invited to join a card game at the local hotel. Eric was from Inuvik. Ted was from Connecticut. They were both doing renovations at the DEW Line station. Bob Eldridge was from Sachs Harbor on Banks Island, in the extreme western Arctic. He was managing the Amundsen Hotel. He made good coffee and excellent butter tarts. We shared many laughs and stories over pots of coffee. (Alcohol is prohibited in Gjoa Haven under the local option provisions of the Territorial Liquor Ordinance.)

June 30th. Tuesday arrived. So did the fog.

"What will happen if the fog doesn't clear up before flight time?" I asked Doug.

"The plane will bypass Gjoa," he answered.

Again, I made all the arrangements. The First-Air agents would pick up the kayak. With anxious eyes, I watched the sky. The fog cleared. The phone rang. There was no room for my kayak on this trip. There was a good chance for Thursday, the agent assured me. I shouldn't have let it get me down. I succumbed to homesickness, depression, and the question, "What am I doing?"

Doug came home for lunch. I was still sitting near the phone with my head in my hands. He didn't have to ask what had happened. He slid his glasses down to the tip of his nose, looked over the rims, and shook his finger at me. In a very British voice he said, "Now, now, young lady, you shan't look so sad!" He looked so funny with his hand on his hip, his finger wagging. His impression of a strict English professor was good. I was on the verge of tears, but laughter won out. That little episode was worth a missed flight. Doug was precious. I could have easily adopted him on the spot.

July 1st. My homesickness slipped away as I joined my new friends in celebrating Canada's 125th birthday. Doug and I joined some of the Inuit games. One of the relay races consisted of running or walking across a field with a six-inch piece of 2"x 4" between the knees. Once you got to the far side, the board would be passed to a team member, who returned to the starting position. It was no easy task in the spongy tundra. Everyone joined in. If the game was too difficult for them, the elders would still be involved as team leaders.

Most people brought lunches. One grandmother peeled goose eggs for her grandson. Dried caribou meat was laid out on clean cardboard. It was wonderful to see the sharing.

Then came the bannock- and tea-making contests. My attention was drawn to an elderly couple. I introduced myself. They told me their names were Martha and Simon Qirnik. Through a young child, they told me they were the oldest people in Gjoa Haven.

"How old are you?" I asked.

"We don't know," they answered, "but all the people that were here when we came are dead now. That's how we know we are the oldest!" No one could argue with that.

For the bannock contest, each contestant was given two cups of flour, baking powder, and lard. At a given time each contestant set about making a fire from wood scraps and a certain moss collected from off the tundra for kindling. Martha was adorable. Very tiny and flexible, she accomplished much with few movements. Simon handed her the size of sticks she called for. He was splitting them into different sizes with an ulu. An ulu has a curved blade with a T-handle in the middle. It is a design unique to the Inuit and has been used for thousands of years. Martha ended up baking the fluffiest, most golden and delicious bannock. When it was judged, she quickly acquired a nice hot piece for Simon and me.

The Northern Stores graciously donated prizes for everyone. It was a pleasant day for all. I returned to the staff house tired but very happy. I couldn't imagine a finer way to celebrate Canada's birthday.

July 2nd. Will I or won't I leave today? I walked over to the Northern Store to say my thanks and goodbyes.

A fellow stopped me as I descended the stairs. "I hear your kayak is for sale for $300.00," he said.

"NO! I mean, no, it isn't." I had to calm myself. My first thought was of a conspiracy to make me leave the kayak behind. I rushed back to the staff house to call the agent.

"Yes, there will be room for your kayak today," he assured me. I didn't breathe easily until it was on the way to the air terminal.

Eddie Kikoak was at the airport. He introduced me to his lovely wife Mary and Mark Tochiak, the R.C.M.P. officer. Both Eddie and Mark were interested in reintroducing kayaks to the North. They would have liked to buy mine, but I could not part with it. Instead, I told them to contact Wave Track in Winnipeg.

"When we get our kayak club going," Eddie said, "we'll call you back to kayak with us as our guest." I will look forward to that with all my heart.

First-Air came in on time. I watched as a huge Honda quad was unloaded from the cargo area without benefit of a ramp. Everyone pitched in to help. My kayak was loaded next. I was on my way. I snuggled into a window seat with my camera and map handy. The plane lifted away from King William Island. I thought about how I got to be there. All in all, it would have been hard to wish for a happier tragedy.

Below, the tundra spread itself out like an elaborate Oriental fabric, dotted by the thousands of still-iced lakes in many shades of blue. All this sat, like a jewel, in the turquoise ocean. How beautiful and diverse our country Canada is!

A delicate meal was provided for all passengers, along with a glass of wine. I found it refreshing to hear the on-board announcements made in Inuktitut. Travel in the North has really come a long way. Still, somewhere, 30,000 feet below, Don was trudging along pulling his sleigh. I hoped he would be careful crossing the wide leads I could spot even from this altitude.

We would be stopping over in Cambridge Bay on the way to Coppermine. As we descended, Mount Pelly stood out plainly in the limitless, flat spaces surrounding it. I can't explain how excited I was to see Coppermine. There was open water, but there was also plenty of ice in the Coronation Gulf. From the air it seemed like the Couper Islands were holding back the ice-pack. What amazed me most as we came in to the airport was how green and lush the area was. The mauve of the flowers could be seen before we landed. There were willows at least four feet tall, and cliffs, and the Coppermine River Delta. It was gorgeous and I was lucky to be there.

I didn't expect anyone to meet me so I was pleasantly surprised when a young, handsome fellow approached me and asked, "Are you Victoria?"

"Yes," I answered, rather puzzled.

"Hi! I'm Ken Mulgrew," he answered. "I'm here to give you a ride back to town." He said he was from Fort Richmond, Winnipeg. Mr. Rai, the Northern Store manager, had asked him to pick me up. That was so thoughtful and typical of northern hospitality.

At the manager's house I met Mr. Sarahjit Rai and his wife, Satinder Rai. Over coffee we discussed my plans. I assured him it would all depend on what the doctor said. I made an appointment to see Dr. Caplin on the seventh.

Every time I spoke to Satinder, she lowered her head. I didn't know whether she didn't like me, whether I had offended her by speaking directly to her, or whether she was shy.

When I was shown the room I could use, I deposited my gear, took my camera, and excused myself. I could hardly wait to get to the meadows I had seen from the plane. I hurried away from the house towards the ocean 100 feet away. Here at last was a liquid Arctic Ocean! I strolled along the beach to the west. Gentle waves were rolling in. With a rhythmic slap, they would break at my feet. The wind was in my face, blowing the hair off my neck. It was sweetened by the fragrance of the millions of flowers in the tundra meadow. I was light-hearted, free, and totally happy! When I had left the town behind, I cut away from the beach directly into the meadows. Everywhere I looked there were millions and millions of beautiful, brilliant Arctic flowers. A floral carpet spread at my feet, flowers as far as I could see. I stood mesmerized and overwhelmed.

As in a trance my mind recalled a scene in the Peterborough, Ontario, Hospital, on a stormy night in November of 1978.

My mother, Frances Vincentia Polon, was dying of cardiac failure.

She was heavily sedated with morphine. I had fallen asleep in a chair with my head on the edge of her bed. I could hear her laboured breathing. She had spoken very little in the last few days, so I awakened very quickly to the sound of her voice. She spoke only in Ukrainian. In a wondrous voice she spoke, as she weakly raised her hand and motioned in a slow arc toward the window. A storm was pelting the window with sheets of rain.

"Victosue," she said, "do you see all the beautiful flowers in the meadow?"

"Yes, Momma, I see the flowers," I answered.

"Are the flowers for me?" she asked again.

"Yes, Momma, the flowers are for you," I replied.

She smiled, her face relaxed and peaceful.

Those were the last words she spoke. She slid deeper into a coma and died later that afternoon. Six children and her husband surrounded her bed as she drew her last breath. We wished her a safe journey. She lingered with us for just a moment and headed for the meadow of flowers. Instinctively, I turned to the window, as though to see her go. At the same time the storm ceased. The sun shone through the droplets of rain on the glass. We were left with the silence and the sobs we couldn't hold back.

I know our mother would have loved this meadow too. Every meadow reminds me of her. I pray she has a meadow of her own. She certainly earned it.

The spell was broken by the sound of children's voices. A group of six had come up behind me as I day-dreamed. I was glad to see them. Introductions were made. Before long they had me by the hands and were leading me back to the beach.

"We're going to make tea," they told me. "You can have some with us."

It wasn't long before they had a driftwood fire going and the water boiling. Once it had cooled it was poured into a glass coffee jar and shared by all.

Such a treat that tearoom with atmosphere – the Arctic Ocean, a backdrop of flowers, soft sand to sit on, and six adorable smiling faces to share it with.

One little fellow found a feather and tucked it in my visor. "Wear it for good luck," he said. How much more could I hope for?

The comical little fellow, whom I dubbed Dom Deluise, decided he would teach me Inuktitut. "If you want to hang around with us, you might as well learn," is how he put it.

I caught on to "matna" quickly. Mostly because "thank you" is used many times. When I passed the tea, I'd listen carefully for "matna." I'd answer, "You are welcome."

Dom gave me an approving nod.

Then came longer words. Inuktitut is a language made up of long, single-word sentences that are built by adding suffixes to a base word. I would get the first part, but I'm afraid I don't have a good ear for languages, and the last part always trailed off. Dom would pretend to be very perturbed. He would shake his head and mutter something under his breath. I don't know what he said, but it certainly made the other children laugh. Then, like a professor, he would try again with much exaggerated patience. I noticed he always watched my face very carefully. Under all the goofiness, I knew he was one smart cookie.

Then came picture time. Everyone wanted a turn. I got my camera back after it ran out of film.

We walked back along the meadow. Melanie was picking one of each different flower we found. She showed me a fuchsia-coloured rhododendron. "I like to eat these flowers," she said. "They are my favourite dessert."

Apparently there are no poisonous plants above the Arctic Circle. Not a poisonous mushroom, root, nor berry. Most of the flowers had large blooms in relation to the length of their stems. None of the flowers seemed to grow any taller than six inches.

"What is the name of this flower?" I asked. The cluster consisted of stalks with delicate little white bells. I cocked my ear to hear clearly and impress Dom.

"Oh, those are tinker-bells," Shannon chirped. Then came banana flowers. They really did look like tiny yellow bananas.

I was exhausted but elated by the time we parted in town. What a wonderful day it had been!

Back at the house, I announced myself and went straight to my room to rest. Before long there was a cautious knock on the half-opened door. "Please come in," I said. I didn't know what to expect. Satinder came in.

"Please sit down," I said, and patted the bed near me.

She sat down.

"I have a hard time talking to people," she said. "I feel I can't speak English well enough."

I was so relieved, I could have hugged her.

"I won't have trouble understanding you," I answered. "Please don't be shy."

It was good to see her relax. She asked me where I had come from and where I was going. I pulled the maps over and showed and explained what part of the North I hoped to see.

"You must be very brave," she said sincerely.

"Tell me about your life, Satinder. How did you come to live in Coppermine?" I asked.

She told me she was a teacher back home in the Punjab province of India. Sarahjit came to India to marry her. A week after they were married he had to return to his job in Coppermine. Satinder stayed behind for six months to finish the school year. Then she came north to be with her husband.

"When I left Punjab province it was too hot. It was 40°C. When I came to Coppermine it was too cold: -40°C," she told me. It wasn't hard to imagine the shock that an 80° difference in temperature could cause.

"Satinder," I said, "you're the bravest person I know."

I laughed when she explained how hard it was to learn to walk on ice.

"Come," she said, "I will cook us some vegetables. I don't eat meat."

"Really," I told her, "I don't want to trouble you. I have food along."

"No, no," she insisted, "you will be our guest."

The aroma of the vegetables cooking made me glad I wouldn't be eating canned beans alone. I admire anyone who is skilful in the kitchen. I hope someday I will enjoy cooking, but I doubt it will happen.

Satinder warned me, "If you find the food too hot, have some sour cream."

One bite and even the tips of my ears were burning. It was hot! hot! hot!

"Have some sour cream," Satinder urged.

I had forgotten about the cream. Besides, I could barely see it through the tears in my eyes. The sour cream did the trick. The rest of the meal was smooth and mellow. After the initial shock, I discovered how delicious it was.

Sarahjit told me he had received a transfer with Northern Stores. They would be leaving the next day for Oxford House, Manitoba. All their baggage was packed and ready. The house would be empty. I could house-sit until I found out what the doctor had to say.

I was very thankful. I retired to my room. My body was screaming for mercy. I drifted into a peaceful sleep.

Fog rolled in overnight. When Sarahjit phoned the airport to confirm their flight, he was told the plane would not land in Coppermine. Their departure was delayed until Saturday. I could understand their disappointment, but it was nice to have another day with them. Ann Whittaker came to say goodbye to them. She is a nurse and had been Satinder's very good friend.

I excused myself and left them to their visiting. Ron Morrison from Spence Bay had asked me to extend a hello message to Colin and Sandy at the Department of Renewable Resources office, so I went off to find them.

"How long will it take for the ice to move?" I inquired.

"Probably not until the middle of July," they answered. We had a long discussion as we studied the wall map.

Satinder and I spent the rest of the day colouring our hair, painting each other's nails, talking about clothes. It had been a long time since I had the spare time to do girlie things with a friend. I didn't know how I would ever get the nail polish off once it started to peel. At the moment it didn't matter.

By the time they left for the airport on Saturday, we felt like sisters. All three of us had tears in our eyes. It was very difficult to say goodbye. As they drove away, I hiked to the cliffs above the town to watch their plane leave.

The scene from the cliffs presented a dramatic view of the islands rising sheer from the sea in the Coronation Gulf. Behind them the ice-pack shone brilliantly white. To the right lay the Coppermine River Delta, at the mouth of which were more islands. To the south, a range of distant hills rimmed the lush green meadows. To the west were the breathtaking meadows where I had met the children. Behind them, far to the northwest, more cliffs, the most prominent of which was Cape Kendall. Flat-topped, it made a majestic, dark silhouette against the skyline. It captured my curiosity. What is behind Cape Kendall? Everything was beautiful, even at my feet. Every crevice held bunches of tiny flowers. They huddled there, defying the wind. I barely noticed the chill of the wind coming off the ice-pack. With hands crammed in my pockets, I made my way down. Once I had gained the shelter of the buildings the mosquitoes attacked full force.

I hurried to my kayak. Now that I had my bearings I wanted to see what Windsong thought of the Arctic Ocean. I slipped her silently from the sand and turned her into the wind. It was like a challenge. We had come so far together. I had waited so long for this moment. A nagging tightness in my chest warned me that all was not well. I turned back, but nothing could quell the ecstasy I felt.

Bruce McWilliam, the relieving manager at the Northern Store, and Ken Mulgrew came by for tea in the evening. Ken was very interested in the kayak. I offered to let him try it the first chance he had. I looked forward to his visits. He shared pictures of his home and family with me. I could tell he missed the Ontario summers at his parents' cottage. I knew the area he talked about and I could understand his feelings. I showed him the pictures of my family. I missed them terribly also.

I got into a routine. I'd hike the cliffs in the morning, kayak in the afternoon, then hike the cliffs in the evening. Sometimes Ken hiked with me. I always felt better when he did. Fatigue struck at the oddest times. I was sure, if I didn't push too hard, my muscles would start responding. At the moment I was thankful to accept whatever my body was capable of.

July 7th. I kept my appointment with Dr. Caplin. Numerous tests were done – EKG, X-rays, blood tests, etc. The results would be back from Yellowknife in two days. All I could do was wait and hope.

July 8th. I packed a picnic lunch and headed for the Coppermine River. A long sand island in the mouth diverts the main channel to the west along the Arctic Ocean coastline, in front of the town. The river has deposited silt and sand as it enters the ocean so that many parts of the delta are very shallow. I followed the main channel upstream.

Samuel Hearne had first seen the Arctic Ocean from this very river. How jubilant he must have been. It was unfortunate his successful journey was marred by tragedy. History says his Indian guides massacred a complete Inuit hunting camp at the Bloody Falls, nine miles from the mouth of the river. I hoped to be strong enough to paddle to the falls within the next few days.

The river was wide and meandering. The banks were high in some places. Where the banks had slumped, the wild flowers trailed down the slope in the rich soil. They looked like our sweet-pea flowers back home, only the blooms were larger.

Whenever the pain in my chest became overwhelming, I would pause along the shore and climb the bank to the meadow. There I relaxed and watched the wind buffet millions of wild flowers as they soaked up the sun of a long summer day. I could easily become intoxicated by the perfume they produced. The absence of bees was strange, though I didn't mind at all. It would have been a monumental task for bees to pollinate so many flowers. Nature had left the job to the wind.

Back to the river I'd go. I paid careful attention to signs of fatigue. When I sensed I'd had enough paddling for the time being, it was easy to pull the kayak onto a sand bar for a rest. The current in the river would always help me back.

Joe Allan stopped me as I paddled into town. "I have a kayak too," he told me. "One day we'll paddle together." I looked forward to it, but the day he was free, I was out in my kayak. He paddled to his camp alone. I wished I had not missed the trip.

I was notified my test results were back.

"If I were in your shoes, young lady," the doctor said, "I would pack my bags and go home. That is the best advice I can give you." My heart sank. "Is there permanent damage?" I asked. "Not yet," he answered. He stood up and

I knew the conversation was over. I wanted to cry, but I couldn't. I looked to Ann Whittaker.

"I know how much you want to carry on, how much it means to you. If I thought it would make you feel better I would offer you an invitation to come with us to Tree River for three weeks," she told me.

I knew how much she needed to get away with her three little boys and her husband for a private vacation. It was sweet of her to offer, but I could never have accepted. The kindness of it all made me smile. One does not easily forget such thoughtfulness.

"Come for coffee tomorrow," Ann called after me. "Our friend Colin will be visiting. He is a prospector. You'll enjoy him."

"Thank you, I will," I answered.

I went back to the staff house and waited for the turmoil inside me to subside, but it would not. I could not accept what the doctor had said. I would hike and paddle with caution. Surely I would get stronger soon, before the ice-pack left the gulf.

Each morning I hiked carefully to the top of the cliff. I'd scan the north with binoculars. The ice-pack was still white on the horizon.

Paddling back from the west one afternoon, I passed a white barrel anchored near the beach. "Swimming Area" was written boldly on the side. Was it possible? The next day the beach was crowded with little people waiting for swimming lessons. There was also a tall, muscular, tanned, blond-headed lifeguard named Ian McCrea. Someone pinch me quick, I must be dreaming. I parked my kayak to watch. Sure enough, the children were enjoying the water. Talk about tough!

The kayak attracted much attention from the children. "Let me try!" If I stuffed a life-jacket behind them they could reach the rudder. I tied a fifty-foot rope to the back. I held the rope and walked back and forth along the beach, while they paddled parallel to shore. My legs always got numb before they were ready to give up. Sometimes Ian took over if he was off duty. He tried the kayak too, without the rope of course. It seemed the little girls could develop a natural rhythm more easily than the little boys. They weren't as aggressive and forceful. From then on, it was impossible to sneak past the swimming area.

The evening at Ann and Larry Whittaker's was most enjoyable. They have a lovely home perched on a rise at the mouth of the Coppermine River. There was a magnificent view from the huge windows. Colin was as interesting as Ann had claimed. Ann's children had collected rocks for Colin to examine. With the patience of a saint, he explained all the different characteristics to them. Colin had travelled extensively in the Arctic. I could have listened to the stories all night, but all good evenings have to come to an end. I walked back, squinting into the midnight sun.

Each day I seemed to feel stronger. My trips on the Coppermine became longer. I felt proud of myself. Maybe Dr. Caplin was wrong. Maybe I had a chance to continue on to Tuk.

The ocean beckoned. For days it had been mirror-like from evening to just before noon. Miles could easily be made in such excellent conditions. When would the ice leave? I was told to speak to Aime Ahegona. He had spent all his life travelling in the Arctic. He knew the coast to the east and west like the back of his hand.

"Would you come for tea and have a look at my maps?" I asked.

"Yes," he told me.

I was barely back when he and his wife Betty arrived. They were a pleasant couple. Aime was a sportsman's guide who had worked on the DEW Line sites and for a tourist lodge on Great Bear Lake, and had lived on the land in the traditional way. Betty nodded and confirmed or added to the conversation. They worked well together in their life.

I told him what I planned to do. He gave me a wealth of information about the coast. What to watch for, what to enjoy, where to get fresh water.

"There will be much driftwood along the coast. Save your fuel and use the wood as you go," he said. "Travel at night if the days are windy." I remembered all he said. I'm sure if I'd had an extra kayak, I would have gained a partner.

"When will the ice leave, Aime?" I asked.

"Victoria, the ice will leave on the 15th. You'll be paddling on the 16th," he told me. That left me five more days to shape up.

July 12th. Randy Turner, a reporter from the *Winnipeg Free Press,* called me in Coppermine to catch up on the news. I mentioned my plan to make an attempt for Tuk on the 16th. That is how much faith I had in Aime. Randy asked about Don.

"Don is supposed to be in Cambridge today," I told Randy. " I haven't heard from him."

Randy called Cambridge, then called back. Yes, Don had arrived safely.

I stepped up my training. Out across Four Mile Bay I'd go. After a breather I'd head back against the wind. I'd try to better my time with each run. If my chest got tight, I'd go to shore or find a handy sand bar. I was surprised to hear the call of a loon as I sat on the shore one afternoon. It brought me back to Nopiming Park, the Big Whiteshell Park, and the many lakes I visited in Ontario. The haunting beauty of a loon's call reaches to the soul like no other sound. It was like a call from home, but I couldn't leave just yet.

I was about to get back into my kayak, when I spotted an outstretched hand in the water. It was carried closer by each surging wave. I stood paralyzed; then I dashed out to grab for it. I took hold and, to my surprise, I was left holding a flesh-coloured rubber glove. I was so relieved I laughed. How the air ever got inside to hold it upright I'll never know. Now I figured my heart was strong enough for anything. That episode ended a recurring nightmare that had haunted me for many years. In the dream, I was in the North. A hand would appear in a pool of water. I would lean over to reach for it, but there would be no body attached.

Soaked to the waist, I headed home. As I passed the swimming area, the children started calling and waving. I was tempted to wave back and continue on. "I shouldn't be so selfish," I thought. "I am half-wet anyway." So I headed in. The little people quickly distracted my mind from the hand.

Joseph Kokak and Karrie Nepok stopped by for a visit. I guessed they were about seven and eight years old.

"I'll make tea," I offered.

"No, we would rather eat our candy," they answered.

They had a bag from the Northern Store, half full of treats.

"Who bought you all those goodies?" I asked.

"Our grandparents did," they answered.

I had tea. They sat on the floor and had their treats. It was good to hear them chatter away. Betty came by too. Without her husband she was quite shy. As we drank tea, she seemed comfortable and content to share the silence while I studied the maps. Whenever I thought out loud, she would nod her head and answer, "Eiyah!"

July 14th. The weather had been exceptional since I had arrived in Coppermine. Each day the temperature would reach to the mid-twenties. This day it was a hot 27°C. The Inuit did not like the heat. Many were going boating to escape the heat and the mosquitoes. A water-skier flashed by. The young chap was not wearing a wet suit. When he went down his yell resounded off the islands and ice in the gulf, and he didn't waste any time getting back up.

The river was not a good place to paddle in the evening heat. The high banks would break the wind and the mosquitoes would swarm around. Instead, I would head towards the islands. The wind coming off the ice was refreshing and cool.

At midnight, as I pulled the kayak to the beach, an elderly gentleman was watching me. He was shy, so I waved him over.

"Hello, my name is Victoria," I told him.

"Jack," he said, and we shook hands. His attention was on my kayak. He spoke only Inuktitut. We had no common language, so we used our eyes, signs, and expression. Pleasure showed in his face as he reminisced about seal hunting in his kayak. With vivid motions he showed how he'd glide near a seal with harpoon poised and then he would strike. Sometimes he missed and would be hungry. Sometimes his aim would be true and everyone would eat.

I would translate his actions into English. He realized I understood. I was proud to shake the hand of this hunter in this Arctic setting. His face beamed. He was proud of being who he was, proud of his land, and proud of the role he had played in it.

Our misty eyes met; our gaze held. We were linked for a moment by this incredible little craft with approximately 5000 years of history behind it. For him it was a bond with the past, for me a dream for the future. We parted as the midnight sun dipped its bottom edge into the ocean and started edging upwards. Sunset and sunrise, all at the same time.

July 15th. I awoke early. If Aime was right, I would be paddling the next day. I sorted my gear, got supplies from the Northern Store, mailed some soapstone carvings to my children, and prepared for leaving.

With binoculars in hand, I hiked to the top of the cliffs. The ice still blocked the gulf to the north. In the northwest the sky was in turmoil. Clouds rolled, stretched, and rolled some more. The wind carried the fresh breath of a storm. Whispers of wind simmered across the water. I dug my hands deep into my pockets and walked back.

The gale struck, rolling up a following sea. A surge of water began crashing into the shore where all the boats were beached. The owners dashed to the shore to retrieve the boats that were not already swamped. The R.C.M.P. officer used his 4 x 4 to haul the boats further up the beach. A few large drops of rain fell, but it was not even enough to settle the dust.

A soft knock on the door caught my attention. It was Betty. In her hand she held a small soapstone carving of a goose near her nest.

"Tomorrow," she said, "the ice will be gone and you will be gone. I want you to have it."

I found it hard to speak, so I hugged her instead. We shared some tea and she left as quietly as she had come. Then the phone calls started.

Angie and Brian called. Teresa and Gregg. I got to talk to my grandson. "Bring more slides home, Grandma," Garrett told me. Gloria Pearen called, along with Jean and Walter Sodomlak. Pilgrim called. He always made me laugh, and his encouragement meant so much. I called my daughter Debbie. She was quite angry with me for taking this trip. By bedtime my mind was all wound up. I couldn't sleep.

July 16th. I hurried to the cliffs in the morning. The ice had gone. Aime had been right. On my way back I stopped at the R.C.M.P. office to file a Wilderness Pursuit Plan.

I started packing my kayak. Ann and Larry Whittaker were packing their huge boat. They headed for deep water and turned east towards Tree River. I headed west towards Cape Kendall. As the sounds of civilization diminished behind me, the euphoria of paddling on alone spread through my body like a warm glow. From now on, I alone would be responsible for the consequences of my decisions, whether they be good or bad. That is part of freedom.

The wind forced me off the water early. I camped on the beach of a small island. A boat came through the channel to get protection from the wind. It swerved toward my camp as soon as its occupants spotted me.

"Are you all right?" was their first question.

"Yes," I answered.

"Do you need anything?" they asked.

"No, but would you like to have tea?" I asked. Perhaps on the way back they might, if the weather didn't get worse. They were on their way to pull in their char nets. I worried about them. The waves were high and they had too many people in the boat, including children.

I took my HF radio, which I had leased from the Hunters and Trappers Association, and climbed the bank to set up the antenna. Donald Havioyak had asked me to test it once I left town. I had never used one on my own before, so I was very proud when my call went through. It sounded like Donald was sitting next to me. On the radio I earned the handle "Kabloona in the Yellow Kayak."

The island was brilliant with fuchsia flowers. It was impossible to walk without stepping on them. I hiked to a rise to look for the people in the boat. I could see them deep in a bay. Just before midnight I heard the boat returning. The surf made it too rough to land, so they waved and headed for Coppermine. I drifted off to sleep to the sound of the surf plucking at the pebbles on the beach.

In the morning I worked the kayak back to the water before I loaded the tent and gear. I had anticipated the weight. To make things easier, I had obtained two pieces of PVC pipe from Hans Pederson at the Department of Public Works in Coppermine. I used them as rollers to bring the kayak up.

The wind had eased somewhat overnight. The ocean was beginning to calm. I was on my way. Nothing in the world compares to the magic of being on the water in a silent craft. I set the bearing for mysterious Cape Kendall. It had blocked my view from the cliffs above Coppermine. Now it could keep the secret no longer. Within two hours I would see what lay beyond.

Halfway through the crossing, an Inuit fellow and his son caught up to me in their boat.

We stopped to chat for a moment. "Where are you coming from?" I asked.

"We're returning from pulling in the nets," Jerry answered. "We were lucky today. I have nearly 400 pounds of char in my boat. Would you like to have one?"

"I'd love to have one," I answered, "but I don't have any place to carry it. My kayak is really loaded."

"Maybe just a small one then," he said, as he lifted a monstrous char.

"That will sink my kayak," I laughed. I really had to refuse.

"Do you want a tow to Cape Kendall?" he asked.

"Oh, no," I said, "I am enjoying this too much, but thank you anyway."

He asked if I had a radio. "Yes, I do," I answered.

"If you have trouble just call me and I will come to get you. My call number is Coppermine 924," he told me.

As I reached the crumbling cliffs of Cape Kendall, a falcon shrieked defiance from her nest on the cliffs. She was so well camouflaged that I had to use binoculars to spot her.

I lingered for a few moments to catch my breath. The wind was whipping around the cape. I knew it would be a tough go. Windsong took up the challenge. The waves were high but well spaced. Beyond the cape lay a huge bay. According to the map it was twelve miles to the next peninsula. I dipped into the bay instead, to get some protection from the wind. The shores were low and accessible. The flower-filled meadows extended to velvet-green ridges. Here and there, catches of snow near the bluffs highlighted the lush green.

"I can melt snow if I can't find fresh water," I thought.

The wind was rising again as I crossed an inlet at the top of the bay. I could feel a fairly strong current. On the bluffs on the opposite shore I spotted a herd of caribou coming over the rise. They were running in an erratic manner. The herd split, and then behind them came a large dark object. At first I thought it was a helicopter. Through the telephoto lens of my camera I could see it was a barrenlands grizzly. He had taken one of the caribou down. It took me another half-hour to get near shore. By then the rise in the ground obstructed my view.

A groove cut into the shore by run-off made for a simple landing. The kayak slid easily along the seaweed until only the rudder was sticking out. The tent was harder. I had to chock it half full of rocks to keep it down while I raised it. I assembled the shotgun and kept it handy. I didn't feel like cooking. I had paddled hard but had no appetite. I blamed it on the excitement of being on the way again. The wind kept up, but a peculiar silence persisted. Even the ocean was hushed by the layers of decaying seaweed on the shore.

I needed fresh water. Aime had pointed out a river on the map. The land was low and flat, and without any shrubs along the river, it was hard to tell where it entered the ocean. Finally, I discovered it. I staked Windsong near a sand bar in its mouth and walked in to fill my containers.

I needed to stop more often to relieve the tightness in my chest. Before long the nausea returned. I decided to camp early, get a good rest, and see what would happen. It took me longer than usual to pull the kayak up. If I strained just a little, a stabbing pain would shoot down my lower back and into my buttocks. It seemed I could not force the muscles past a certain point. Supper smelled good, but I had to force myself to eat.

I had no desire to look in the mirror in the morning. Already I knew my hands and feet were swollen. The symptoms were all too clear. I was devastated. Here was the end of the line for me. Elated and deflated within a span of days. Windsong sat on the beach pointing north. I felt I had let her down, that I had let down everyone who had supported me. I knew I had no choice but to turn back to Coppermine. With a heavy heart, I headed back.

I turned in again at the river to get water for the return trip. I must have startled a grizzly. His prints were in the sand. The claws were as long as my fingers. The water was just seeping back into the prints. Quickly I filled my water containers and departed.

I decided to enjoy the remainder of the trip.

Ahead of me stretched the back side of Cape Kendall to the south. The sky was mirrored in the surface of the water. The sun shone hot on my shoulders. Even the wind was resting. I was hesitant to disturb the stillness; I set the double-blade across the cockpit and rested my elbows on it. The solitude of the open water soothed some of the turmoil within. Slowly I found peace. Margaret and Dr. Caplin had been right. I was ready to accept that.

The sound of an approaching boat disturbed the silence. It was Colin and Sandy. "How are you feeling?" they asked. I guess I looked like hell. They claimed they were looking for seals, but I had a suspicion they were checking up on me. Later, I learned Donald had gone all the way to Locker Point at the entrance to Dolphin and Union Strait to make sure I made it there all right. I was a stranger in their midst but they treated me like family.

I stopped often to rest. I wanted to walk on the shores, to feel, to embrace, to know I was really there. In a special cove I found a cavern on the shore. Inside I placed a red silk rose in a ziploc bag. I vowed I would return for it someday.

I turned my back on the cove and the crumbling cliffs. Through the maze of the Couper Islands, I could see Coppermine twelve miles to the south. "Come along, Windsong. Just a few more miles today." I headed for the islands.

Children called to me as I neared the first island. I recognized Ryan from my first day in the meadow.

"Come and visit," they called. "Our grandparents are here. We'll tell them." By the time I beached the kayak they were back with a dried arctic char. I returned with them to thank the grandparents for the fish. I introduced myself and asked for permission to camp on their beach. I cherished their invitation for tea.

Millie and Andrew Nivingalok had just spent the day cleaning and slicing a few hundred pounds of char and tomcod. The fish were draped over a drying rack in front of their cabin. On one corner of the drying rack sat an effigy, what we would call a scarecrow on the prairies. This stuffed human likeness was there to frighten the gulls from stealing the fish. One or two gulls seemed braver than the rest. The children stood poised to stone them whenever they came too close.

Ryan and David and five-year-old Nicole insisted I try fishing with them. With camera along, I followed them onto the cliffs. They would catch a fish with every cast. Mostly they were tomcods, but some were an ugly little big-headed bony fish with needle-sharp spines on their fins. I thought they must be sculpins, but the kids called them devil or garbage fish. They tossed them on the rocks for the seagulls. The two boys posed with their fish as they caught them, but little Nicole, because she couldn't cast, decided she would pose with the devil fish, which she gingerly held between two tiny fingers. The look on her face showed how much she detested them.

Now it was my turn to catch a fish. I pulled in a tomcod barely two inches long. I had to stand with my trophy and have my picture taken, amid laughs and giggles. "We won't have any trouble telling which is yours," David commented.

I tried to discourage them from fishing. My heart would skip a beat every time they leaned over the cliff in the excitement of catching a fish, or as they leaped from rock to rock on the ledges. I'd haul them back and do up their shoelaces. Even tiny Nicole seemed unafraid of the cold water below. No one had a life-jacket and no one seemed concerned. Finally, I couldn't watch any longer. I told them I was going back to set up my tent. With much relief, I heard them clambering down the rocks towards me.

They sat in a semicircle around me, watched, and asked a million questions. It was nearly midnight when I set about making supper. I asked them if they would like some stew.

"We're not hungry," David said. "We had a big supper already."

"I am hungry," Nicole piped up.

"No, you're not, Nicole," David answered. "You ate so much for supper."

However, she joined me for stew, ate half of it, and made a liar out of David. She had a pudding for dessert and was halfway through an apple before she gave up and handed the rest to her brother.

Their next question was, "Can we sleep here with you?"

My body was screaming for rest. "No," I said, "but you can wake me in the morning."

They did. Very, very early.

Trying to keep their minds off fishing, I suggested a tour of the island. The island held no fresh water, but it was covered in pink flowers. We sat cross-legged, talked, and nibbled on the petals. Nicole lay among the flowers.

"May I take your picture?" I asked.

"Yes, yes," she replied. By now I knew it was her favourite thing to do. She lay in the flowers, her little face cupped in her hands. Her dark eyes sparkled and her dimples were indented deeply as she smiled.

Millie and Andrew were getting ready to go to a nearby island to collect snow for drinking water. They claimed snow water made the best tea. The children tumbled into the boat. I promised not to leave until they returned, and set about breaking camp. The family had made my last day on the ocean a very special one.

Coppermine was only five miles away.

As we parted, I promised to stay in the protection of the islands as long as possible before making the crossing. The waves were three to four feet and climbing when I reached Four Mile Bay. Fortunately, they were still far enough apart and with good direction. The heavy thud of a powerboat could be heard above the wind. Its occupants spotted me and pulled within earshot. "Are you okay?" they asked.

"Yes," I replied.

"We can load your kayak and give you a lift," they insisted.

"No, really, I'm all right. It will take me a while, but I'll paddle."

They had no idea of the weight I was carrying. It would have been a monumental task to pull the kayak aboard even if it had been empty. I would never have put them in such danger.

They left hesitantly, but a good feeling remained with me. The wind became more brutal and I worried more for the family in the powerboat than for myself. The bow of their boat was being tossed into mid-air with each wave. I felt confident in the safety of my kayak. If I did flip, I would drift to the shallows at the west end of the bay. I made the most of the troughs or zigzagged back and forth from wave to wave until I was able to gain the south shore of the bay. Coppermine was only three miles to the east, but I needed to rest. I tried inhaling deeply but failed to clear the fog in my head.

With Windsong safely on shore, I sat on the flower-studded bank to eat my lunch. It was hot, so it wasn't long before my clothes were dry and I drifted off into a relaxed sleep. The wind kept the mosquitoes away. The snooze did me good. The ache in my chest had eased. Still waiting for the wind to calm, I took a stroll along the beach. To my surprise I came to a shore rock with a sticker on it. It was the emblem of Canada's 125th birthday. I choked up when I saw it. Paddling the Northwest Passage had been Don's and my project for

Canada's 125th. I hadn't made it, and there was no way of telling yet if Don would either. Whoever had pasted the decal there had celebrated more simply. Two smaller rocks were spaced frying pan-width apart. The large rock was stained from the smoke of a fire. Someone had made bannock and had a picnic. A fair-sized piece was left on top of the rock.

I was very fortunate. I was alive and there would be time to paddle again. I had seen so much and met so many good people. I would be able to savour forever with affection the memories of both Arctic summers.

I took my time paddling past the town to the Coppermine River to set up the tent. "Tomorrow," I thought, "I will come back into town to make arrangements to return to Winnipeg."

I left a gallon of stove fuel behind for Don to use on the last part of his journey. The food supplies I left at the Northern Store staff house. I lightened my baggage as much as possible. I felt too weak to lift even the smallest parcels. The edema was returning with a vengeance.

July 21st. Windsong went out on the morning plane and I on the afternoon one.

Amid a puff of brown dust the plane lifted from the runway and banked to the south. Below lay Coppermine, the river delta, the Arctic Ocean shoreline stretching east, and my dreams.

Don would be coming in along that shore. I hated him! Hated him for being able to go on! Hated him because I might never be able to paddle again!

I watched the tundra lakes pass below and set to the task of sorting out my emotions.

Mike, Annette, and Sienna Hart from Pelly Bay were on the same flight. They were surprised to see me. I explained what had happened and that Don was on his way to Coppermine from Cambridge. We parted company in Edmonton.

I stood at the Air Canada ticket counter, making arrangements to Winnipeg. The agent, Cliff Oatway, was very helpful and kind in arranging for an early morning flight. I knew it was most urgent that I get home. I was swelling quickly and dreadfully.

"By the way, here's a voucher for the hotel," he said. "I think you need to rest. The shuttle bus will be here in ten minutes." How kind to do that for a stranger! I expressed my appreciation and turned toward the door.

"There's something wrong," I said before thinking.

"Like what?" he asked.

"It's dark outside."

"It usually is at 10:30," he said.

"Of course, I forgot. I haven't seen darkness for two months," I apologized, and he laughed.

July 22nd. As sick as I was, I could feel rebellion rising as the plane circled the Winnipeg airport. I would get better and I would return to the Arctic. I knew I had to go back for the rose and the bits of my soul I had left behind.

Everyone was well and the grandchildren had grown so much. Seeing my family was special! Except for that, the first three days at home were a nightmare. I was sicker than I ever remember being in my lifetime. Dr. Erenberg prescribed a diuretic to reduce the swelling and made an appointment for me to see a cardiologist immediately. I was ordered complete rest until the amount of damage to the heart muscle could be determined.

Meanwhile, Don was heading for Coppermine. Things were not going too well for him, according to the newspaper article. He had climbed a ridge and carelessly loosened a rock, which landed on his foot, crushing two toes.

Our last conversation had been in Gjoa Haven. As the autumn wore on, I expected to hear the news that he had arrived in Tuk. The middle of September passed and still no news. Then a call came from Dana Starkell, Don's son. He was worried. During his last call, Don had bragged about the big chances he was taking and getting away with. Now he was overdue and the weather in the western Arctic had turned very cold. "Would you speak to the R.C.M.P.?" he asked.

An appointment was made. With maps in hand and a complete list of equipment I last saw in Don's possession, I went to speak to the officer in charge.

Very quickly they understood he was not prepared for harsh weather. He hadn't bothered to take the extra fuel I left behind for him in Coppermine. He didn't have warm clothes or mitts. At that point, I didn't know he had left his winter boots behind and had sent the rifle back to Winnipeg. The homemade knife he had along had a blade one could bend into a horseshoe shape.

"No," I insisted, "he's not equipped for winter survival." Still, I did not want to be responsible for initiating a search. One of the things I remember Don saying was, "I don't ever want to have to be rescued."

The R.C.M.P. started the search. Dana's intuition that something was wrong was correct. After a fruitless try or two, Don was located near Hutchinson Bay on the Tuktoyaktuk Peninsula. After a successful rescue, word came back that he was alive, but had ten badly frozen fingers. Some toes too. Shortly before Christmas of 1992, all of Don's fingers and the affected toes were amputated.

I was allowed to return to work on October 20th. The long road to a full recovery took seven months.

In different ways, this adventure had brought us as close to death as we would ever want to come.

So ended 1992.

1993

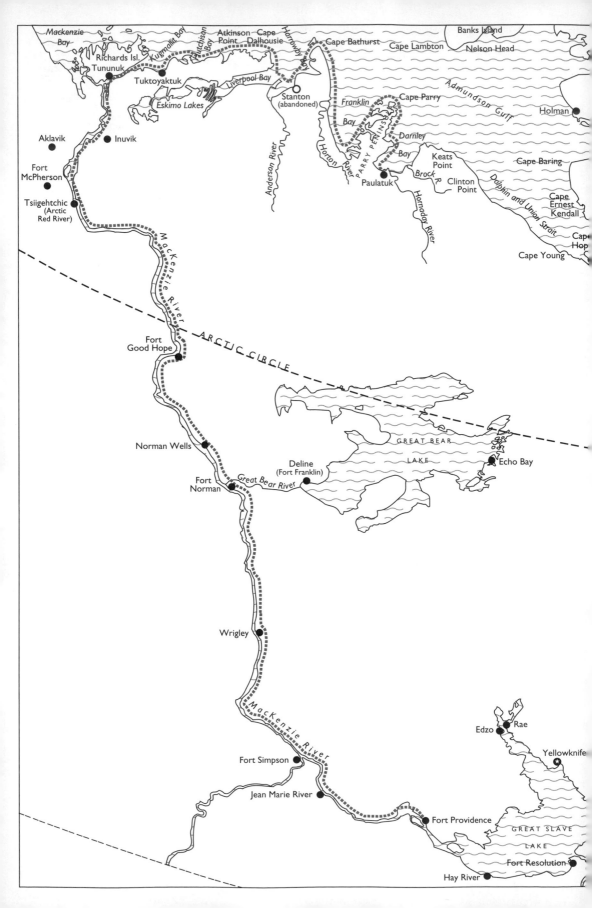

It should have been enough to have lived, to have been able to hope and dream, but the Arctic had captured my heart. Try as I might, I could not make a serious commitment to another. All I could concentrate on was returning again, on my own terms.

I would travel alone. I would go from west to east.

My original plan had been to buy a truck and, with my kayak on board, drive the Dempster Highway to Inuvik. There I would look for employment for the following year. My job at the C.N.R. was scheduled to disappear during my absence due to technological change.

However, on a bright spring day, I went onto the roof of my house to clean the eavestroughs and discovered the shingles would not last another year. My truck money ended up on the roof of my house, and I had to find another, less expensive way to get to the Arctic. I asked my friend Steve Hawyluk to help me drive to Fort Providence on the Mackenzie River at Great Slave Lake and return my car to Winnipeg. From there I would paddle down the Mackenzie to the Arctic Ocean.

On June 6, 1993, Steve and I left Winnipeg. Excitement was running high the next day at 6:00 p.m. when we crossed into the Northwest Territories at latitude 60° north, directly north of Peace River, Alberta.

We took time out to see the spectacular Alexandra Falls plunging 33 metres and, further along, the Louise Falls dropping fifteen metres in a series of steps. We camped at the Lady Evelynn Falls on the Kakisa River for the night. We were the only occupants of the excellent campgrounds, and spent the time exploring the falls. We followed a nature trail that led to a lookout where the Kakisa River drops over a limestone escarpment. This was Steve's first adventure into the Northwest Territories and he marvelled at the absence of darkness.

Morning found us waiting for the ferry to take us across the ice-choked Mackenzie River. Glistening floes came out of Great Slave Lake and rode the dark blue river's swift current. Neither of us spoke. Steve probably suspected he would have a passenger on the way home.

During the crossing the floes collided with the ferry with tremendous force. I recalled the trip on the Hudson Bay and my confidence began to falter. All spring I had been writing the first draft of my book and had not had time to train. I had planned to use the Mackenzie River as a warm-up before heading onto the Arctic Ocean. I hadn't counted on dodging fast-moving ice.

We unloaded the kayak on the east shore of the river in front of the R.C.M.P. station in town. Steve went on to discover Yellowknife 180 miles away, but promised to check on me on the way back, in case I had surplus gear. After setting up my tent and sorting my gear I walked into town for coffee.

Latitude 61°20′58″ N and longtitude 117°38′48″ W. Fort Providence, which is Mile 50 on the Mackenzie River, is a neat, sleepy town. The Northern Store holds a prominent spot and was stocked with everything from groceries to hardware. I spotted a burgundy babushka with large bright flowers on it. I bought it because it brought back special memories of my mother. At the craft store I enjoyed looking at the exquisitely made native crafts on display. There were many things I would have liked, but travelling in a kayak limits the amount one can purchase.

Later while drinking my coffee in the restaurant and day-dreaming, I was interrupted by a native fellow from the next table.

"Where are you from?" he asked.

Before answering, I picked up my coffee and moved to his table. "From Winnipeg," I said.

"What are you doing here?" he inquired.

"Well, I plan to kayak down the Mackenzie River to Tuk and also do some paddling on the Arctic coast before winter comes," I answered.

"How long will that take?" he asked.

"Three months, if I'm lucky," I replied.

His next statement stunned me. "I wish my people could have that much time off and afford to do that," he said.

I felt a flash of anger. Already the trip had cost me more than I could readily afford and I hadn't even started. Their advantage of already living on the river had to be a bonus.

Calmly, I answered, "It really isn't that hard. I've worked for the last 26 years of my life. I didn't have enough money saved, so I went to see my bank manager and borrowed $5000.00 for the trip. My employer allowed me leave of absence without pay and here I am."

"You must have a stupid bank manager," he replied.

"No, he's not stupid," I answered. "He knows I'll pay the loan back, because if I don't, he will take my house."

Our gaze met and held a long time. It developed into a silent stand-off.

Finally he spoke. "I want to go with you to see your kayak. I'll drive you back."

I answered all his questions about the kayak.

He wished me a safe journey. We shook hands and parted.

Inwardly, I was still seething that someone would begrudge me the hard-earned fulfilment of my dreams. My romanticism was of the most innocent sort. I craved to leave no mark other than footsteps in the sand and the trailing wake of the kayak.

Water has a way of soothing my feelings. I sat on the bank of the river most of the evening, watching the ice streaming past in the current. Two days ago I had been caught up in the hectic, high-geared city life, and now I had slipped back many cogs to a slow-moving pace on the edge of the wilderness. The time had come to smell the flowers and listen to nature's music again.

Morning came quickly. To my surprise, the river was completely free of ice. I hurried to the Renewable Resources office.

"What happened to the ice?" I asked.

"The ice is jammed up on the lake shore. It happens sometimes," the officer explained. The timing couldn't have been better.

I filed a Wilderness Pursuit Form with the R.C.M.P. on the way back to the tent. I would be reporting to them at each of their detachments as I proceeded along the river. That way, they would find it easier to track me down in case of an emergency. If I was overdue, it would also make the search easier.

Maggie and Cocktail, the hotel owner's dogs, adopted me. They sunned themselves among the dandelions as I worked. When I went to town to phone my family, they followed along and guarded the phone booth while I talked, cocking their heads as though eavesdropping.

Steve returned from Yellowknife at noon. He helped me carry my kayak and gear down to the river's edge. I appreciated his help and concern. As we kissed goodbye, he seemed very precious to me. He was my last link to the safety of the South. I didn't know what lay ahead. The outcome would depend on me and the decisions I would make.

With clenched fists deep in my pockets, I watched as my car disappeared down the road, trailed by a cloud of dust. I couldn't stop the leaden yo-yo from bouncing around in my stomach. I hurried to the river to pack.

One thousand thirty-nine miles to the north lay the Arctic Ocean. I bent to the task at hand.

If it is possible to love material things, then I love my kayak. I was still using Windsong. I had total confidence in her ability to handle extreme water conditions. The deep, wide rudder gave me maximum control in strong currents. My double-blades were expertly made by Bill Brigden, a legend in the paddling world. Every time I picked up the beautiful, lightweight blades, I thought of him. My spare double-blade was secured under the deck elastics within easy reach. I certainly didn't want to be going down that big creek without a paddle.

The roses I received from my family and friends I arranged around my Sailor II deck compass. It seemed fitting, since it is love that makes the world go round. I vowed to set the petals free in the Arctic.

It had taken me 2½ hours to pack, normal for the first day of a long trip. Everything was arranged in the order it would be used. My winter clothes were packed deep into the tips of the bow and stern. I hoped I would not need them for a long time.

I had neglected to send a huge hockey bag back with Steve. Into it I put some surplus food, extra tie-down straps, paper towels and such, and walked down the beach to where a native family was getting ready to go fishing. "If you can use these things, they are yours." I handed the bag to them and they accepted. We chatted a minute and parted. Little did I know this simple act would bring a reward some miles down the river.

"Time to go, Windsong. It's just you and I!"

June 9th. 4:00 p.m. I pushed away from shore and ruddered into the current. Anxiety over what I might have forgotten slipped away. Whatever had been left behind I would learn to do without. The Arctic was waiting.

I settled into an easy, rhythmic paddle stroke. The current was going to be a big help. Fort Providence vanished from sight. The sounds of civilization diminished. The river was between two and three miles wide, and full of islands. The only topographical maps I had of the river were of the delta area 900 miles to the north, so I had no way of knowing my exact location. However, I had the current and the channel markers on shore. I did have a Northwest Territories Official Explorers Map that I had obtained from the tourist office. The Mackenzie River showed plainly, but the scale wasn't accurate. The river went north and that is where I wanted to go.

I decided to favour the east shore. Thirty miles northwest of Fort

Providence, according to the wall map at the Renewable Resources office, the Mackenzie would widen into a bulge called Mills Lake which is about twelve miles wide and fifteen miles long. Due to my late start, I had planned to paddle only as far as the edge of the lake. It seemed no time had passed when I rounded a bend to find the river take on a different look. Ahead were small dark islands with no horizon behind them. They wavered, mirage-like, on the edge of the earth. Lifting my binoculars, I tried to make sense of what I was seeing. My kayak drifted around the bend while I scanned the scene.

Suddenly I heard voices. Not fifty feet away was the native family I had given the hockey bag to. I paddled over. They were busy having a fish-bake over an open fire. It smelled delicious.

"Hello!" The surprise was mutual.

"What's behind those islands?" I asked the father.

"That is Mills Lake," he replied. "You should cross the river to the west shore now and stay on that side until you pass the lake. If the wind comes up, get to shore fast. The lake is wide and the waves can get very wild."

I had not realized I had come so far, so quickly. I accepted the advice with thanks.

"I should get past the lake with the weather this calm. This will give me a good chance to stay ahead of the ice, if the wind changes," I said.

"Yes," he answered, "it will drift around the lake and partly melt before it finds the channel into the river once more."

I graciously declined their invitation to stay for fresh fish. My stomach grumbled for the rest of the evening. After explaining the kayak and demonstrating the use of the rudder to their twelve-year-old son, I said goodbye and headed across the river.

Once past the islands, there was nothing but water to my right. The sky joined the water and stayed that way for the next three hours. It might as well have been the ocean. A good part of the west shore was swampy, but I could have ducked into it if necessary. By the time the wind started to rise I was in sight of a solid shoreline, and I landed at the end of the lake just as the sun dipped behind the trees.

I had done well. This was my first solo campsite on a major expedition. The only thing that marred my confidence were the bear tracks in the mud. There was no point in moving camp. I was in the wilderness and I might as well become used to being alert. I set the noise-makers and shotgun within reach, hoping I would never have to use them.

I drifted off to sleep, thankful for the calm. Early morning found me working my way into the main channel and crossing back to the right-hand side of the river. Right-handed, I feel more comfortable with the shore to my right, although I did switch where conditions indicated the need.

The day was calm, the sun hot. The sky was mirrored in the still water.

I ruddered into the main current to generate a breeze. By noon I was down to a skimpy tank top. The spray skirt held too much heat in the cockpit, so I had to undo it. The heat felt good on my back, where a few sore muscles had shown up overnight.

It was wonderful to be so alone, to have so much time to think.

I wondered what Alexander Mackenzie thought when he started down this river in 1789. He had no way of knowing he was on North America's second-longest river. A fur trader and explorer, he went down in history as the first white man to chart and travel the entire length of the river from its source to the Arctic Ocean. How was he to know then that it would become the historic trade route to the North? Two hundred and four years later, I was paddling the mighty river that bears his name. Except for the eight villages along its 1089-mile course, it probably has not changed a great deal from when he viewed it.

Eagles soared above the river. Their high-pitched calls to one another could be heard long before I could pick them out of the sky. One pair had its large nest in a treetop on the river's edge. I watched one come in with legs outstretched, wings and tail fully spread to break the flight, then land gracefully on the nest. The partner then left and, within minutes, became a mere speck in the sky.

The compass needle showed the river dipping in a southwesterly direction. It wasn't until the third day that it swung toward north again.

A beached boat caught my attention. A makeshift tent was on shore. I stopped to see if there was a problem. Three men came out of the tent when I climbed out of the kayak. They had a problem with the outboard motor. They had already radioed in to Fort Providence and were waiting for parts to be sent out.

"Do you have enough food?" I inquired.

"Yes, we caught some fish," they replied.

"There will be a camp on the other side of the river, if you want to stop. It is near the mouth of the Trout River," one added.

"I'll watch for it," I promised, and ruddered back into the current.

By noon I had the camp in sight. In the middle of the river, riding a very swift current, I debated whether I should paddle the mile to shore and visit. At the last minute I turned toward shore. Caught in the current, I was drifting sideways faster than I was paddling forward. I would have overshot the camp if Peter Cazon had not come to retrieve me with his motorboat. I held on to the side while he steered me in to shore. The beach was long and sandy. A trail led to the top of the slope, where a log cabin stood among the pines.

"Come and meet my woman," he invited. Already he had introduced me to fifteen-year-old Peter Jr. and his adorable two-year-old son. Peter reminded me of Jeremiah Johnson, the mountain man of movie fame. He was rugged, dark, and handsome, as outgoing and friendly as his "woman," Dora, was shy. Peter's father also lived with them. He was busy cutting up a moose Peter had shot the previous night.

"You must take some moose meat," Peter said. "It's good. If you want it any fresher you'd have to shoot one yourself."

Dora brought me tea and we chatted for an hour. The visit was pleasant and comfortable. We sat at a handmade table in the shade of a pine tree. Being out of the sun revived me, and a breeze sprang up. Peter's father expressed their wish to set up a permanent tourist camp. I could see they would have made excellent hosts and guides. Dreams are important. I hope they realize theirs.

"You'll be the first one to sign my guest book this year," Peter said. He brought out a writing pad and pencil. "This is last year's book."

"Did all those people come by in 1992?" I asked.

"Yes, and look at this. Most of the paddlers were from Japan," he pointed out.

The majority of the signatures I couldn't pronounce. The Japanese were seconded by Germans and, surprisingly, one crew came from Argentina.

"You're early," Peter told me. "One canoe and one boat have gone by already, but they didn't stop. You must stop at the hunting camps. How else will we get news of the river?"

He was a very sweet person and I assured him it would be my pleasure to stop and visit.

"You can stay for a week and you'll see how I hunt," he offered. Hunting is still so vital to their lifestyle and he was proud of his skill. It would have been a most interesting week, but I wasn't certain how much time I needed to get to Tuktoyaktuk, so I declined with thanks.

Mr. Cazon handed me a large piece of moose meat as I rose to leave at 1:00 p.m.

"I'm sorry I cannot take so much," I apologized. "My kayak is very full. I will take a smaller piece." I ended up with a piece large enough for three meals.

Peter and the boys walked me back to the river bank. In order to make room for the meat, I gave them all my coffee, a box of Del Monte fruit cups, and a package of candy.

Peter was as thrilled with the coffee as I was with the fresh meat.

"You'll be in Jean Marie River in five hours' time," Peter assured me.

"Five hours?" I repeated. The distance on the map looked too far.

"Yes, on the button. Once you head around the curve at Willow Island, the river will become narrow and very fast. You'll be in Jean Marie in time to cook moose meat for supper," he laughed. "Radio back to me and let me know," he added.

Within the hour this family had captured my heart. I hated to leave. They gently pushed the kayak free from the sand. Willow Island appeared quickly and I had only a few moments to decide on the right or left channel.

The river changed dramatically. For the past 2½ days it had flowed wide and still through low, forested country. Here the banks were steep and high, the water swift and turbulent. Strange noises were coming from the water. I traced the source of the noise to big boils on the surface. I double-checked my rudder to see that it was working freely. This would not be a good place for it to fail. The channel markers were straining wildly at their moorings in the current. The roar of the water was deafening.

A high clay island stood in the channel, defying the river. It was losing the battle, and evidence showed the force of the erosive power of the ice. The high cliffs were scraped clear so that trees crowned only the highest reaches.

Four hours later the river widened again and Windsong and I came off the roller-coaster to placid waters. I worked my way to the left shore once again in anticipation of Jean Marie. The first indication was a net-float stretching across a small creek, and then the stern of a beached canoe. Mile 165, Jean Marie. The time, 6:00 p.m. Exactly five hours!

I went into the village to find a radiophone to call Peter. There was so much interference I had to relay the message through others on the line.

My family in Winnipeg was just as surprised as I at the miles I had made in three days, and it was good to talk to them. My daughters had a difficult time believing I was suffering from the heat. Winnipeg weather was cold and wet.

I was anxious to try the moose meat. I dug out my only onion, and soon stew was simmering in the fry pan. A young native chap, Rufus Sanquez, came by to see the kayak. He declined an invitation to supper but stayed for tea. We spent a lazy evening on the shore, talking.

I had spotted a small store in the village and headed there, hoping to buy a man's cotton work shirt to cover my arms. The manager, Don, approached me as I entered.

"May I help with something?" he asked.

"I hope so," I said. "I've just come off the river and am suffering from sunburn. I'd like to buy a cotton work shirt to cover my arms."

"I'm sorry," he replied. "We have only groceries, but you can have mine." He proceeded to take it off and handed it to me.

"Oh, I can't take the shirt off your back!" I answered.

"Yes, you must," he insisted. "It's all right. I have another one upstairs."

Emotions made it hard to keep the tears back. I accepted with gratitude. The episode set a wonderful mood for the trip. The river was beautiful, but it was the people I met who made it unforgettable. I paddled away early on the 12th of June while the village slept. I was very comfortable in Don's shirt.

It was tied loosely at my waist, the buttons undone. Without a bra, it was so cool. My arms were protected. All was well. I was enjoying the solitude and the freedom, and was totally at peace with the world. I had an idea I might even be in Fort Simpson the same day. It was only 42 miles away. The scenery became more varied. Islands dotted the river. Unfamiliar noises would draw my attention. I was cautious enough to stay far away from conditions I didn't understand. Natural curiosity about what was around the next bend kept me paddling happily.

My stomach reminded me I had forgotten about lunch. That wasn't my only complaint. I had been drinking the water directly from the river as I went along. The effects of my blunder were about to start. I didn't have time to think about either problem at the moment. The wind changed and I paddled headlong into a wicked summer storm. At the same time I spotted red and white buildings. "Can that be Fort Simpson already?" I asked myself. I judged the distance to be four or five miles.

I needed to get off the water, but the wind came directly across the mile width of the river, and landing would be very tricky. Paddling on, I hoped to find a more suitable spot with less of a slope. Time ran out and I was facing the mouth of the Liard River. Ahead lay the conflicting forces of the Liard River, the Mackenzie, and the storm from the east.

I had only a split second to evaluate the situation. I couldn't turn back against the current and wind. There was no going into the Liard. The current was too swift. My only chance was the sand bar in the middle of the mouth of the Liard. If I didn't make the sand bar, the end would come dramatically and quickly.

We were sucked into the silt-laden, four-foot standing waves. "We can make it, Windsong!" Her saucy, determined look made me grin. She always seemed ready. I kept the double-blade as low as possible to keep the wind and waves from wrenching it from my hands. Methodically, I put varying levels of force on the blade and adjusted to the wave action. We were tossed and slapped around, but gaining on the sand bar. I was much relieved when the bottom of the kayak connected with the sand shallows of the island. Using pieces of driftwood as rollers, I pulled Windsong to safety. Exhaustion overtook me. I wrapped myself in a tarp and lay down in the willows to wait out the storm.

The rain woke me three hours later. The wind had calmed. I slipped Windsong off the sand bar and prepared to cross the last mile of the Liard to Fort Simpson at the junction of the Mackenzie and Liard Rivers. I had better direction on the waves this time and landed safely on the muddy river bank below town.

Without changing clothes I trudged up a steep path ripe with mosquitoes to find a phone. As I stood at the phone booth talking to my daughter, a tour bus parked in front.

Angie's concerned questions were, "Are you going to be okay? Will you be able to get help if you need it? What's the town like?"

"Didn't see much of the town yet, but I'll tell you what I see from this phone booth. Right now there is a bus-load of tourists coming at me. They're all in Bermuda shorts and T-shirts, with sparkling white knee-high socks and runners. Most are wearing Tilley hats and sunglasses, and all have cameras hanging from their necks. They're giving me the lifted brow as they pass. My hair is wet and hanging from the rain. I'm dirty from the river mud, but I feel just great."

"You're kidding, Mom. A tour bus?" came Angie's reply.

"Yes, a tour bus!" Those days on the river had made me forget how quickly civilization was catching up with the wilderness.

July 12th. It was my youngest grandson Keith's second birthday. Tomorrow, the 13th, would be my oldest grandson Garrett's seventh birthday. I thought of them so much as I paddled. What kind of grandmother was I? This was the third year I had missed their birthdays. I was thankful I could at least speak to them on the phone. They were busy at their grandparent Davey's cottage at the Big Whiteshell Lake, enjoying the summer.

Fort Simpson is a modern Slavey-Dene community of about 1150 people. Noted for being the oldest continuously occupied trading post on the Mackenzie River, it was the terminus of the Mackenzie Highway in 1993. It is perched high on the towering banks of the junction of the rivers. I was amazed at the varieties of vibrant flowers growing in the neatly fenced yards. The meadows were lush and green. Everything smelled clean and fresh after the rain.

I stayed the weekend to do laundry and rest. Rest didn't come easily. A chap out joyriding spotted my camp and proceeded to spy on me on the hour.

I would hear the deep throb of the truck's motor as he approached, then the gears jamming as he turned around on the dead-end road. Finally, I preferred the noise to the silence. It wasn't as creepy. I was thankful for the long, steep, mosquito-infested path separating the road from the river's edge.

I brought my shotgun into the tent and switched the slugs for bird shot, hoping I would not have to shatter any kneecaps before morning.

Windsong was packed and ready to leave early Sunday morning. I decided to try and obtain some topographic maps at the Tourist Centre. When I tried the door, it was locked. A fellow called to me from across the street to tell me it only opened for tours on the weekends during the month of June.

"Was there something you needed?" he asked kindly.

I mentioned the maps.

"Let's have coffee," he offered. "Then we'll go to my office and see what I have."

Peter Shaw had a way with words. "Paddling the Mackenzie," he told me, "is like hitting your fingers with a hammer. It sure feels good when you stop." He did get me a topographic map showing the river from Fort Simpson to Fort Norman and navigational information all the way to Tuk. Departure was delayed until 3:00 p.m., but it was well worth the friendship. Peter drove me back to the kayak and saw me on my way.

Toward evening the sound of a powerful motor caught my attention. It was a tug ferrying construction equipment across the river. Once the highway to Wrigley was open in 1994, there would be a permanent ferry crossing. The crew waiting on shore called a greeting, but the water was too swift and the banks were too muddy to land.

Evening found me past Burnt Island. A bend in the river exposed the faint blue outline of Nahanni Mountain over the treetops behind the far western shore. I relaxed beside the campfire, enjoying the view. No one interrupted the silence of the wilderness.

The river became more scenic. Mount Camsell and the Camsell Range occupied my attention all the next morning. I heard the sound of the North Nahanni River before I spotted it. Islands obscured the mouth somewhat, and I had paddled too far past to cross over in time. The current of the river picked up with the extra volume. I glanced back in time to see its mouth, choked by silt islands and a tangle of trees and roots. The mere word "Nahanni" conjures up seductive wilderness and mystery.

Dreamily, I paddled along. The river was crowded with islands, the largest of which was McGern Island, 100 feet high and fourteen miles long. The sun was hot. Relief came from the cool breeze from the mountains.

At Willowlake River I stopped at a very old, traditional Indian village. The only person who could speak English was away hunting. His wife and sister-in-law came down to the river to greet me. Through various motions, they encouraged me to share samples of most of my supplies. My herbal teas were a source of interest. Peach, apricot, mountain berry, blackberry. We passed them back and forth, deciding which flavour smelled the best. The decision was hard, so they took two of each. The chewing tobacco I was taking to a friend in Coppermine brought the most giggles.

"You don't use this, do you?" I asked.

Both heads nodded "yes." I put a can in each upturned palm and we all had a good laugh over it.

"Are you going to share with your husband?" I inquired. They tucked the cans down deep into their sweaters. No, he would not see it, that was certain. We all felt like children sharing a secret. They ran up the path to check their treasure. I paddled away.

I stopped to say hello to three people enjoying lunch on shore. Max was from Smithers, British Columbia, and Irene and Ben from Juneau, Alaska. They had put in at Fort Simpson and were leaving the Mackenzie at Fort Norman to go by way of Great Bear River to Great Bear Lake. There they would cross into the Anderson River system, paddle to the bottom of Liverpool Bay on the Arctic Ocean, and double back into Inuvik by way of the Eskimo (Husky) Lakes. They had a long trip ahead.

At a hunting camp I stopped to borrow a Robertson screwdriver. A couple of screws were loosening on my double-blade. The elderly Indian fellow didn't speak English, but he soon realized what I needed and pointed to tools spread on a table. He had a grand view of the river. The camp was perched high on the bank. A table stood on the edge. Over it hung a tarpaulin canopy. The ever-present binoculars lay on the table. He explained in sign that his sons had just spotted a moose on the other side of the river and had gone after it by motorboat. Sitting in the shade, we enjoyed the silence together. I fixed my blade and returned the screwdriver and two pounds of macaroni in exchange for its use.

At the "River Between Two Mountains," I spotted Max, Irene, and Ben again. As I went by, Max was reeling in a large fish.

Around the bend, I spotted another hunting camp. A young woman waved and called down to me. Her name has slipped my mind, but she and her husband were from Hay River. They had come to visit her elderly folks at the camp. She had two little children, and I was glad to have handfuls of candy in my pocket. From youngest to oldest, we all shared the taffy caramels Angela had tucked into my supplies.

"You must cross the river to the other side now," the woman warned. "The waters are very turbulent around the bend. I'm frightened to go through there in a motorboat. You may even see a black wolf. It passed on the far shore."

I appreciated the advice I received from the wonderful people I met, whether they were in camp or in town. Of course you never know if advice is good or bad until you follow it. Still, I always had confidence it was given in good faith.

The current increased rapidly even as I crossed. There was a visible drop in the river. I spotted the wolf before the crossing was complete. I expected him to bolt for the forest as soon as he spotted me. He surprised me by breaking into a pace that would keep him alongside me. I paddled twenty feet from shore, unable to keep my eyes from this beautiful creature. He was long and black with grey in his ruff. The most riveting feature was his wild, mysterious eyes.

"Hi! Aren't you a beauty," I commented. "How has the hunting been? Where's your family? Where are you off to?" He was curious and unafraid. He cocked his head from side to side, listening intently just like a family pet.

The kayak was caught up in the grip of the current, and I had to focus all attention on the whirlpools, eddies, and the waves that were folding back on me. The wolf increased his pace, trying to keep up. I glanced back whenever I had a chance. He was bounding over everything in his path in a full-out sprint, not wanting to give up. Something deep inside me was touched by this brief encounter. I felt we had shared a kinship in the freedom of the moment. Unfortunately the tie between wolves and humans has not always been so innocent. I glanced back one more time. He was a mere speck, still running full out.

I paddled on humming the song, "Wild Thing, You Make My Heart Sing."

A wide gravel swath through the forest looked like a roadbed. I pushed it from my mind. I spotted three Indian fellows on the river bank. The sleeves on their white dress shirts were rolled up, the collars open. Their jeans looked freshly pressed, their cowboy boots polished. I paddled alongside. "Hi! Where are you from?" I asked.

"Wrigley," they replied.

"How far is Wrigley? How did you get here?" I asked.

"About 35 miles," they answered. "We came by truck."

"Truck? Then it was a road I saw back there," I said.

"Yes, as soon as the ferry crossing is complete and one more bridge goes in, the road to Wrigley will be open," they commented proudly.

Man's fickle finger of progress was still following me.

"See you in Wrigley," they called.

"Not tonight," I thought. I needed a calm, secluded campsite.

I enjoyed my tea as the last of the campfire died out. Before the zipper on my sleeping bag was all the way up I drifted off to sleep. From the water came the haunting call of a loon.

Two hours of paddling brought me into Wrigley. If it hadn't been for a large fuel tank and a bit of secluded road showing, I would easily have passed without seeing the town. Large floes of dirty, tumbled ice jammed the shore. The cool breeze coming off the ice made me shiver in the shadows of the steep bank. Hurriedly, I started up to where the town must be. From the road I switched to a narrow trail heading up through the trees. It took two rest stops before I managed to scale the bank. I ended up in a back yard among tethered huskies. Awakened from their sleep, they started howling in unison. Ten o'clock, and not a soul stirred as I gained the main street, wondering if I should go left or right. Out of nowhere a beautiful Indian girl appeared.

"Can I help you?" she asked.

Explaining that I had come by way of the river, I asked, "Is there a phone nearby? I'd like to phone my family."

"Come with me," Mary beckoned. "There's a phone at the hotel. I am meeting my cousin there. She's flown in from Trout Lake and has brought me fresh fish."

"Do you know Peter Cazon of the Trout River camp?" I inquired. Yes, she did, and went on to ask of his welfare.

The girls invited me to have breakfast with them once my calls were done. Bacon and eggs sounded grand, but I had left my money in the cockpit of the kayak and didn't relish the thought of the climb once more.

I was enjoying the village on the way down the rise. The modern log cabins nestled in the pines. A pickup truck slowed and stopped.

"Do you need help?" the young man asked.

"I'm heading back to the river," I answered.

"Jump in, I'll drive you there," he offered. We chatted on the way down. He turned out to be Mary's husband.

The river was narrow and fast. There were huge chunks of ice on the bank, making the shoreline wet with the melt. I had set my sights on the mouth of the Blackwater River as my next camp. Too many pit-stops slowed me down. My stomach was starting to react to the Mackenzie River water with a vengeance, even though I had stopped using it a few days back. Gut-wrenching pain would signal "time out." I became adept at making leaping dismounts the minute the kayak hit the shore.

Once the Johnson River came into sight I crossed over to the west shore and half paddled, half dragged Windsong over the gravel shoals in the mouth to camp on its bank. The water was clean and warmer than the Mackenzie. It was a good place to swim, wash my hair, and do laundry. Large moose tracks crisscrossed the large sand beach. I set up the tent with the door facing across the Mackenzie to where the McConnell Range of the Franklin Mountains showed above the tree line. The McConnell Range gradually rises out of the lowland east of the Mackenzie River and parallels the river for 200 miles. Even without darkness, the hush and peacefulness of a world ready for rest was noticeable.

The Blackwater River at last. I rested Windsong against a gravel ledge in the mouth and refilled my drinking-water bottles. The water was clear and very cold. I drank as much as possible, hoping to get the Mackenzie's revenge out of my system. The Blackwater River is appropriately named. As it enters the Mackenzie a long black wedge pushes into the milky, silt-laden Mackenzie and flows distinctly separate until the volume of the Mackenzie overpowers it and they merge. It was a joy paddling in clear water for a few moments.

At Old Fort Point the river demanded all my attention. Not only was the current strong and turbulent, but I was facing a strong head wind. The sky was dark and overcast. Gravel shoals extended first from one shore, then the other. Nothing keeps you more alert than the sound of the rudder biting bottom. Grounding on bars with the current still coming full force makes for a tough battle. The silt meant there was no way of distinguishing the shallow water from the deep. A good clue came from the seagulls. If they were standing ankle deep in water, I headed for the channel markers. Here and there, otters rose vertically from the water, quite seal-like in their play. They let out sharp little snorts and carried on with their game of tag.

Fourteen miles short of Fort Norman the wind forced me off the water. It wasn't a choice camp spot. It required some landscaping among the rocks to smooth an area for the tent. After the twelve-hour paddle, I was ready for rest. Lumps didn't matter much.

Storm clouds still threatened as I set out in the morning. Before long the rain came. My rain jacket did little to keep me dry. The humidity was high and perspiration soaked my clothes beneath it. I hate setting a tent on a muddy shore. Thinking the sun might come out, I decided to keep paddling. The sun didn't show. The wind increased, folding the waves back upon themselves. My progress was not worth the effort. My arms ached from gripping the double-blade in the sudden gusts. I headed in. I gathered long poles of driftwood and laid them at right angles along the length of the kayak. By lifting first the bow and then the stern, I was able to slide it clear of the water. A large tree trunk made a good hitching post.

Looking for a good spot to sit out the storm, I spotted the frame of a teepee on the edge of the towering bank. The path that led to it would have been best left to experienced mountain goats. I scrambled over the edge. Not only was there a teepee frame, but half a cabin too. The cabin had a door and a floor, but the walls were only four feet high. The roof and the rest of the walls were probably covered by a tarpaulin when it was occupied. To me it was a luxury. I gathered scraps of plywood and made a shelter across one corner of the cabin.

Over a campfire on the river bank I heated a Magic Pantry beef-stew dinner. Hot cups of tea made me forget the drizzle. After collecting my sleeping bag, air mattress, bivouac sack, gun, and whistle, I moved into my temporary home. I had only been on the water 3½ hours. I wasn't tired. There were many trails to explore. The soft moss underfoot was soothing to the feet. The woods were filled with the heavenly aroma of wild roses. There was an abundance of other flowers. At the end of the trail was an outdoor toilet made of plywood. The front was open to the elements. The view was terrific. After playing catch as catch can along the river, that plywood seat felt like fine porcelain.

I was roused from a deep sleep by a terrible ruckus beneath the cabin floor. With gun in hand I tiptoed to the wall and looked over. It couldn't be a bear. There was not enough space underneath. Not even thinking it could be a wolverine, I went back to sleep. Again, the racket woke me. This time I whacked the floor as hard as I could with a length of 2"x 4". From then until I left, silence prevailed.

The sky was overcast. Heavy clouds shifted back and forth. Up ahead puffs of smoke belched out of the river bank. As I neared, I could see the interesting patterns the coal seams had made in the high clay banks. These must have been the ones Alexander Mackenzie in 1789 and Sir John Franklin in 1825 mentioned in their journals. They were still burning.

The head wind became much stronger, but now mud cliffs edged the river. There was nowhere to pull out. The current became swift and the water very choppy. There was no good place to paddle. If I had been wearing a life-jacket, I might have tried the main current, but I chose to be near the shore, such as it was. The shoreline itself was full of irregularities causing back eddies strong enough to bring me to a stop or even propel me backwards. The eddies might have served as a place to rest if it hadn't been for the chunks of mud cascading into the water from the cliffs. I'd rudder hard to break out of the eddy and back into the current.

I rounded a bend to find a friendlier shoreline and the village of Fort Norman. The red and white buildings of the North West Company showed among the dark green of the trees on the high bank. Behind it, Great Bear Rock rose 1400 feet in height. It has been an obvious landmark for generations of travellers. Between Great Bear Rock and Fort Norman the mouth of the Great Bear River empties into the Mackenzie.

Even setting up the tent on the muddy shore didn't dampen my spirits. I was at Mile 514, halfway to Tuktoyaktuk. It was only 10:00 a.m., Saturday the 19th of June. Nine and one-half days had brought me this far. I had averaged fifty miles per day. It was hard to believe.

Gradually I had developed self-reliance and a confidence in myself and my judgment in virtually any situation. I was proud. I tumbled into my sleeping bag to wait out the rain.

The Mackenzie's disagreeable effect on my system woke me. I would have to get some medication soon. The nursing station was closed for the weekend. My next hope would be the Northern Store. On the shelf I spotted Fowler's Wild Strawberry Extract. I didn't even know it was still being sold. As a little girl, I remember it being one of the medications in our pantry. It had worked well for diarrhea then. I bought two bottles just in case.

I made my way through town towards the Great Bear River. Walking ahead of me, three young Indian girls were giggling and talking. As a man approached them, they hurriedly switched to the opposite side of the road. I walked straight into trouble. He was wildly swinging both arms above his head, swatting imaginary mosquitoes and talking to himself. As we came face to face he stopped me.

"Are you one of the tourists?" he inquired.

"Yes, I've been called that," I answered.

"I've got some brochures for you," he told me.

At this point I didn't want to tell him I would rather go to the river by myself, so I went with him. He had something to do with the Band Council. He unlocked the office door. I followed him up a long flight of stairs, already dubious about the situation. He really did have an office. My guard was still up. He switched the conversation to the sexually explicit cartoon on the wall. "I've seen that one before," I answered, to make light of it.

"Aren't you afraid to travel alone?" he asked.

"Yes, I would be, if I came to a frightening situation," I replied.

"Yeah, but what about, you know, what about –" he stumbled. I waited, playing dumb.

"You know, the one with the 'Big Feet,' " he said.

The whole time he kept fidgeting and raising himself from the chair to above desk level. Whether this was supposed to be a clue or a come-on, I wasn't sure. I did, however, know what he was heading at.

"You mean the Sasquatch? I didn't see any," I answered. "May I see the brochure?" I asked.

He handed me one. It was titled "Tulit'a," translating to "where the rivers meet" in Slavey. It was a hiking trail brochure.

"Where's the one on the San Sault Rapids?" I asked.

"You don't want to go there," he replied. "I don't want to be going to hunt for your body."

I didn't want him to either. I was getting angry. He was wasting my time, but only diplomacy would get me through this one.

"Two Japanese girls came through here in a canoe," he told me. "One was really horny, the other wasn't."

"That goes to show you all people aren't the same," I replied.

"Yeah, but it's hard. All the people here are related." He kept referring to this at every chance.

I thanked him for the brochure and rose to leave. He blocked my way. My temper was rising. I had no way of knowing if the door at the bottom of the stairs would open without a key. So, I sat down again.

"Aren't you afraid of, you know –" he persisted again.

"Of what?" I couldn't keep my voice from rising.

"Of, of people, you know," he insisted.

"No, I am not afraid of people! I trust people!" I answered.

I knew he wanted me to say "rape." I was sure it would set him off. I was tired of looking at his rotten, fungus-covered teeth. He sensed my anger. His only recourse, without losing face, was to back off.

"I want you to make coffee for me at your tent," he insisted.

"I don't have coffee. I gave it away," I replied.

"Then we will have coffee on the town," he answered. He went to the coffee machine and took a package of Nabob coffee.

173

At least this might get me outside. "I only have Mackenzie River water," I told him, hoping he would give up.

"I will get some from my cousin. You cannot drink water from that river," he said.

Didn't I know it!

Before I put the coffee on, Max paddled up in his kayak. I could have kissed this gorgeous stranger I had only seen once. Max had handcrafted his own kayak of wood and reinforced it with kevlar. It had a unique shape and was truly a thing of beauty. Michael, a young man from Germany, paddled up to shore in a Feathercraft kayak. Of course, the conversation got carried away. The local backed away, but not before he told me not to let anyone sleep in my tent. I refrained from being nasty. He still had the upper hand if I was alone along the river.

Max's paddling partners, Ben and Irene, arrived before evening. Now we had our own settlement on the river bank. While we waited out the storm, we compared equipment, exchanged paddling stories, and thoroughly enjoyed the company. Max gave me a hot tip for extending the bottom of my fly with extra flaps. This would work well in the Arctic, where tent pegs wouldn't hold the tent down. I would be able to use driftwood, sand, or rocks to pin the flaps against the ground and prevent the wind from getting under the fly and floor. It turned out to be a blessing.

Michael had put in at Fort Nelson, British Columbia. He had come by way of the Nelson and Liard Rivers to the Mackenzie at Fort Simpson. His plan was to paddle to Inuvik, resupply, then head back to the Point of Separation, where the Mackenzie divides into numerous channels. From there he would head west up the Peel and Rat Rivers to Summit Lake on the Great Divide. The rest would be downhill on the Bell and Porcupine Rivers to Fort Yukon, Alaska. Talk about a major undertaking!

Max, Ben, and Irene were leaving the Mackenzie at Fort Norman.

June 21st. Monday morning, Michael and I left together. We dipped into the mouth of the Great Bear River to fill our water bottles. The cold, clear water followed the north bank of the Mackenzie several miles downstream before it lost its identity in the Mackenzie's muddy waters.

Michael was a very pleasant paddling companion. We learned to compromise. He tolerated the pace I set and I tolerated his long lunch and supper breaks. We enjoyed the scenery together. The snow-capped Mackenzie Mountains rose in the west, the Norman and Franklin Ranges to the east. It pleased me to see someone enjoy my country so intensely. The vastness intrigued him. Why wouldn't it? The Northwest Territories alone are thirteen times larger than West Germany. Having someone to talk and laugh with was nice too.

The river widened and the current slowed as we approached Norman Wells. We had seen the flame over the oil derrick for the last eighteen miles. We hurried to the Northern Store before it closed for the evening. The day had been very hot. I looked forward to a cold drink. I had more than enough food to get me to Tuk, but I enjoyed treats like apples, oranges, and ice-cream bars.

We were on our way back to the tents when country music caught our attention. It was coming from the open door of the local pub. "Let's stop for a beer, Michael," I said.

"Oh, no! It will be too expensive," he replied.

"Just one each. I'll buy," I offered. His eyes lit up. The interior was dark and cool. The cold wood of the chair felt good against my back. We toasted the first day of summer.

Norman Wells owes its success to the oil in the area. Six huge artificial islands dot the river, providing access to the oilfield below. Imperial Oil has been extracting oil since 1921. In 1789, Alexander Mackenzie had recorded seeing oil near Bosworth Creek, where it was later rediscovered by geologists in the early 1900s.

The North was alive. Powerful tugs, pushing heavy barges, were plying the waters, carrying vehicles, fuel, pre-fab houses, groceries, and supplies to the settlements on the river and onward to the Arctic coastline. The Coast Guard ship *Eckaloo* was carrying out its duties along the route. There was always a wave or a friendly toot on the whistle as we passed one another.

It was a delight to smell the snow from the Mackenzie Mountains. The currents of cool air reached out across the water. Michael paddled in the middle of the river, getting as much help as possible from the current. I preferred the shoreline. The scents from the forest wafted down to the river. Tossing my head back, taking a deep breath, I would become intoxicated by the smell of the wild roses on the banks. Often a stray breeze would lift the hair off my neck.

In the mouth of the Mountain River a large black bear rocked on his haunches each time he tore a chunk off a rotting moose carcass at the water's edge. The seagulls were all lined up, waiting for him to finish.

Already we could hear the roar of the San Sault Rapids. Two mountains, called East and West Mountain, guarded the entrance to the rapids. The Mackenzie River narrowed to three-quarters of a mile and changed direction abruptly to the north. We had inquired about the rapids at the visitors' centre in Norman Wells. Following excellent instructions, we favoured the west shore and had no problems. Although we could hear the tremendous roar of the main rapids, we were left only with turbulent water and an increase in the current.

North of the rapids the river widened to three miles. It looked more like a huge lake.

"Let's try fishing," Michael suggested eagerly.

"Good idea," I answered. "Let's try at the next incoming river."

We landed in the mud at the Tsintu River. The bank was covered in bear and wolf tracks. Nothing could discourage Michael from his mission. He was handing me his fishing rod before I had my kayak beached.

"Michael, I don't know how to cast," I told him.

"Well, I practised casting, but I won't know what to do if I catch a fish. You see, there are very few fish left in Germany. I cannot afford to fish there. I've never seen a fish caught," he explained.

"Okay, then. You catch one and I'll show you," I replied.

On the first cast, he snagged a fish and lost it. On the third, a huge jackfish struck hard. Michael's eyes were as large as saucers with question marks in them. I knew he would lose his lure if those big jaws closed, because he had no leader on the line. "Don't try to reel him in," I suggested. "Back up and pull him out."

I was able to grab the fish behind the gills and hold on just as the line snapped. Meantime, I was sinking to my knees in mud. It had been a long time since I had seen such excitement. First came the picture taking. The first fish of Michael's lifetime. He was 36 years old. No one could outdo the size of his grin. We had caused such a commotion I was sure we would attract a bear. "Watch for bears, Michael," I told him.

"If I do that, I wouldn't see how you clean the fish," he replied. "Besides, I don't have to outrun the bear. I just have to outrun you." With those long legs there was a good chance he would.

He watched like a hawk while I filleted. It wasn't a great job, but he got the idea. He proudly arranged enough for both of us in my fry pan. It was delicious. We had enough left for two more meals. We ended up dirty, smelling of fish, and very happy. I would have liked to leave quickly, but a sudden squall sent large muddy waves to shore and prevented us from launching. Michael snoozed and read. I watched for bears.

"You're fun to travel with," he stated.

"And you're not hard to please," I retorted.

By early morning, we approached the entrance to the Ramparts. Here the Mackenzie narrows from two miles in width to a quarter of a mile, and hurries through a seven-mile-long canyon carved through a limestone plateau. The main difficulty was the strong crosscurrent and numerous whirlpools and eddies at the entrance. Michael seemed a little uneasy and gladly gave me the lead. It was a magical ride. Peregrine falcons screamed from the heights, and in the clay banks the swallows chirped from their little burrows. All too soon the river expanded. Straight ahead was Fort Good Hope. We stopped only long enough to get some supplies. At the R.C.M.P. detachment I checked in and phoned home. The day was hot and we had our minds on paddling another two miles to the Hare Indian River for a swim.

As we strolled to our kayaks, we spotted a fellow in a rowboat. We spoke briefly. Mike Bailey was from California. He had put in at Fort Providence on June 1st and was rowing his way to Inuvik. He had built the boat himself and had enjoyed rowing so much that he had chosen it over his kayak. I couldn't imagine doing 1000 miles facing backwards, but I was happy for him.

Twenty-seven miles downstream, at latitude 66°30′ north, lay the Arctic Circle. I had a Global Positioning System with me. We were going to record our exact time and film each other at the precise spot. We planned to leave at 8:00 a.m. However, at 11:00 a.m. Michael was still sleeping. I left a note and continued on my own. We had no commitment to each other.

Another hot, calm day. One hour past the Loon River, at Mile 710, I crossed into the Arctic Circle. I paddled with renewed enthusiasm.

By evening huge thunderstorms were forming in the east. I would need a good camp spot soon. A young man was poling a canoe along shore.

"Do you live here?" I asked.

"No," he answered, "I'm staying in the cabin up there." He pointed to the top of the steep bank. "Come share it with me."

I should have guessed from the leather knee and bum patches that Willy was from Germany too. Willy was very energetic and enthusiastic. I liked him immediately. We secured kayak and canoe. With Willy's help, I got my gear to the cabin. On the stove he had onions and garlic sautéing in a frying pan. He boiled four large potatoes, peeled them, and smothered them with the onions and garlic. An extra dab of butter went over it all. He offered me some, but I had already fixed a flaked-turkey sandwich.

"Do you always eat this well?" I asked.

"No, usually much better," he answered. "I have lots of food."

We had time to explore trails, fetch water from a creek, and take pictures before the rain came. This cabin was the first solid roof I'd had over my head since Winnipeg. I relished the luxury of a thick mattress and the sound of the rain on the roof. Again and again from the river came the melancholy yodel of the loon.

Willy worked on his maps and journals late into the night. In the morning we cleaned the cabin and left together. Willy was paddling a thirteen-foot canoe that was almost as wide as it was long. It was very stable but had no keel, so he could only manage on very calm days.

He had come from Germany to Boston, Massachusetts, in April. From Boston he had travelled by bus to Fort Providence. After a week of searching he was able to buy the second-hand canoe. On May 9th he had started out. The river had barely broken up and was in full flood at the time. It was too early to be on the river. He used hip-waders to get over muddy shores and through the willows to camp. I admired the courage of this young lad and the degree of tolerance he showed just to be able to live his dream. He had averaged ten miles per day on the days he was able to paddle and was very content with the pace.

His plan was to leave the Mackenzie at Arctic Red River and hitchhike to Fort McPherson. There he had a Coleman canoe waiting and arrangements to charter into Summit Lake. As with Michael, he would take the Bell and Porcupine into Fort Yukon, Alaska.

I was hoping the two could meet. We spotted Michael once during the day. He was barely visible on the opposite shore, where he had stopped for lunch. By the time we crossed, we had overshot the spot by more than a mile, and neither of us could paddle against the current.

The wind came up, but Willy hung in.

"If we get separated, let's meet at a place marked 'Sawmill' on my map," I offered. Willy agreed. We headed for the west bank. Just before the Ontaratue River, a large sand bar and shoal area extended three-quarters of the way across the Mackenzie, forcing us diagonally across the river to within a quarter mile of the east bank. We had come to the part of the Mackenzie known as "The Grand View." The river flows between low-lying wooded banks of willow, spruce, and tamarack. Many long, sparsely wooded islands dot the river. We both spotted the sawdust pile in the distance. The rising wind was giving Willy a few problems. "You go on," he said. "It'll take me longer, but I will meet you there."

I beached Windsong near a boat on shore and hurried up a path through the woods. Two huge dogs came bounding down the path, barking for all they were worth. My first thought was, "Victoria, you have come a long way to end up as dog food." Then I noticed their tails wagging.

Next came a disarmingly attractive man. He was carrying a long rifle and closed the space between us in long, running steps.

Out came his hand. "Hi! I'm Fred Sorensen. Go on up, Irene is expecting you."

I stood dazed. "Expecting me?"

"I think I saw a moose swimming across the river. I'm going to check it out. I'll be right back," Fred told me.

Hurriedly I said, "If that moose turns out to be my friend Willy, please don't shoot him."

At the top of the path stood a beautiful cabin. The porch was crowded with boxes of blooming plants. There among the flowers was a large telescope mounted on a tripod.

Irene came out the door. "Come in. Bring your boots. The dogs may cart them off." I had no fear of that. No animal would want that pair of boots between its teeth. Fred returned. The moose turned out to be a large tree root tumbling in the current. Willy had refused a tow and was happily making his way in. I watched him through the telescope. One could almost see clear down to Yellowknife.

Big bowls of hot, thick soup were put in front of us, along with homemade bread and plates of fresh, fried fish. It was the most wonderful way to end a paddling day. It was easy to feel at home with Fred and Irene. Pictures of their family were displayed on the walls. They had a right to be proud of their six children and 21 grandchildren. Fred showed me their wedding picture. Irene looked like a fragile porcelain doll in her wedding dress.

"Fred, do you mean to tell me you married this beautiful lady, brought her to the North, and kept her here all these years?" I asked.

"Yep! Did just that," he answered, "and it was a good life."

It must have been in spite of the hardships. They both looked to be in their early fifties. Fred claimed to be 78. They are both legends in the North. All the way to Tuk people would ask about them, once they knew I had come by way of the river.

After a breakfast of bacon, eggs, and biscuits, Irene showed me her tomato and strawberry garden. I went to pull the fish net in with Fred, while Willy went to work turning the soil for a vegetable garden. I watched, fascinated, as Fred deftly removed the fish. It was the first time I had seen inconnu, a very large fish with big scales.

Fred mentioned seeing an odd contraption on the river the day before.

"It looked like the guy was going backwards," he said.

"Oh, that was Mike in the rowboat," I explained.

Fred gave me some excellent smoked white fish and I prepared to leave at 1:00 p.m.

"Are you coming with me?" I asked of Willy.

"Oh no," he answered. "You made me paddle 46 miles yesterday. I can afford to rest for four days. I'll write to you many times," he promised. And he did. When I called back from Inuvik a week later, he was still with Fred and Irene.

Little Chicago, an abandoned trading post, was perched high on the east shore. My heart was pounding by the time I had scaled the bank. The reward was a spectacular view of the mighty Mackenzie. I tried to imagine what it had been like to live here so long ago. Did the scent of the wild roses come through the window, as it did this day?

The river wound its way northward. Shoal areas kept me meandering from east bank to west and back. I watched carefully for any change in the water's surface, but it flowed swiftly, never changing, over deep or shallow.

The threat of rain sent me to shore at 1:00 a.m. As I sat by the fire, I cleaned my gun to rid it of condensation. The low rumble of distant thunder came from the west. I looked forward to the sound of rain on the tent. Just as I was about to crawl in for the night, a blast from an air horn came from the river. It was Michael.

"Hi!" I called. "You ready to quit for tonight?"

"Is it 2:30 yet?" he asked.

"No, it's 2:15," I answered.

"Close enough." He headed in.

Within minutes he had set up and had gone to sleep. The night was hot. I left both the door and window undone. I lay on top of my sleeping bag in a T-shirt and panties. The thunder was nearer now. I drifted off, wondering if we would be safe enough on this exposed ledge if the storm increased.

I awoke to the sound of a high-pitched roar coming from the south. "My god, if that's the wind funnelling down the river, we'll have to flatten the tents," I thought. I fell out of the tent in haste. I was so relieved to see a massive barge that, in my stupor, I forgot I was not dressed. There was no time to go back. A big wake was rolling onto shore. I dashed over to steady my kayak. Bedlam struck. The hoots, hollering, and whistling were magnified over the water. All I could do was laugh and wave.

Back in the tent I discovered everything covered in a film of very fine dust. My carefully cleaned gun was grey. My face and hair were full of grit too. Finally, the rain came.

The alarm sounded much too early. I listened for Michael stirring, but there was nothing from his tent. Instantly I fell asleep. Just as quickly I awakened myself with one ear-splitting, inhaled snore. It struck me funny and I burst out laughing. Just as suddenly I was asleep again. I could have sworn I heard a blast from Michael's air horn. "Now you're dreaming, Victoria," I chastised myself.

Michael was preparing his breakfast when I came to.

"What are you making today?" I asked.

"Oatmeal," he answered. Often he had oatmeal three times a day. It was a different colour each time. It was not until Inuvik that I realized he was adding Kool-aid powder to flavour it. Lime-green oatmeal is not a visual prize-winner to me. I stuck to granola.

"Did you hear the thunder during the night?" I asked.

"No."

"Did you hear the barge come through?"

"No," he answered. He volunteered no more information. I waited a few more minutes.

"Michael, did you lean on your air horn accidentally or was I dreaming?" I quizzed.

"It wasn't accidental," he admitted. "I heard this awful noise. I thought it was a bear until I heard you laughing. I was too embarrassed to mention it."

"You didn't hear the thunder, you didn't hear the commotion from the barge, you didn't hear the alarm, but you heard my snore. It is I who am embarrassed." We both laughed.

We left in the rain. A day's paddle brought us past the Lower Ramparts, eight miles above Arctic Red River. The 300-foot, shale river banks shielded us from the sun until we rounded the last bend before the village. The red and white Roman Catholic mission beckoned from the hill. Flowing in a northwesterly direction from its source close to the Yukon border, the 250-mile-long Arctic Red River joins the Mackenzie at the settlement. A ferry plied the waters between the river banks, carrying the Dempster Highway traffic to the opposite shores. It was a most picturesque scene.

The horseflies made our visit very brief. A decent conversation with my daughter Angela in Winnipeg was nearly impossible.

"Hi! I'm calling from (ouch!) Arctic Red (damn horseflies) River."

"Where?" she asked.

"A pay phone (ouch, ouch!) at Arctic Red River. The horseflies are killing me. Gotta go. (Ouch, ouch!)"

Michael and I dashed down the hill to the kayaks with the horseflies in pursuit. We crossed the river and I lazed on the sandy beach, looking back at the village.

In the winter of 1932 the first detachment of R.C.M.P. left Arctic Red River to arrest Albert Johnson, the Mad Trapper of Rat River. He became the subject of Canada's greatest manhunt, and his mysterious legend lives on. He lies buried in the village of Aklavik, on the banks of the Peel Channel in the Mackenzie River Delta.

Across the water drifted the melody of ducks and an eerie yodel of a loon. It was time to rest.

At Mile 912, the Point of Separation, the Mackenzie River divides into numerous channels, which form the delta. The Mackenzie Delta stretches 150 miles to the north to empty into the Beaufort Sea. It is a major flyway for migrating birds, and I couldn't begin to decipher the many different bird calls echoing from the sky and water. In the distance to the west we could occasionally glimpse a huge barge making its way through the main channels between the islands. After resupplying in Inuvik, Michael would be making his way back here to follow the Peel and Rat Rivers westward. I wondered how he would manage to paddle against the current.

Michael called for a lunch break. He was having difficulty in the short chop generated by the wind.

"My kayak feels like it's bending in the middle," he said. "Let's wait for the wind to calm out."

I admired his easygoing manner. Nothing seemed to rile him, not the mud, not even the mosquitoes or black flies. He seldom slapped or brushed them away, even though I did not see him use repellent. He would write in his journals or read for hours in the hot sun without stirring. He prepared his meals methodically – not that much can go wrong with oatmeal. He would put everything away neatly and have a nap. I began to appreciate this unhurried pace, although I did want to be in Inuvik for the Canada Day celebrations on July 1st.

The current eased to about two miles per hour once we entered the narrow, winding East Channel at Mile 925 that would take us the 57 miles to Inuvik.

After the width of the main channel it seemed claustrophobic. Willows covered the tops of the six-foot banks. Their roots hung like tangled tentacles down the mud banks where the vicious action of the moving ice had gouged away the shore. Miles later, I was relieved to see level mud ledges covered in sparse green shoots on the inside of the river bends. They would make ideal camp spots. The prints and droppings of thousands of geese marked the ledges. No wonder the grass was such a brilliant emerald green.

Michael decided he would rest for a day. I planned to leave at 6:00 a.m. and make a sprint for Inuvik.

Morning brought a stiff head wind funnelling down the channel. What should have been a seven-hour paddle turned into eleven hours. I ruddered diagonally back and forth across the channel, cutting the curves short and using the current as much as possible to make up time. Gusts of wind would catch my blade, straining my wrists and arms. Break time was a relief. A silt bar provided the perch, but the view wasn't much. On a point across the river, what looked like garbage was defacing the river bank. I looked more carefully and realized that the ice had eroded the shore so much that one-half of a trapper's cabin and most of its contents had spilled down the bank. A pair of long-johns had snagged on the way down, displaying a grotesque shape.

Rounding a bend, I saw an occupied camp. I was hailed from shore. Lucille Adams immediately took me under her wing in a motherly way. She brushed away my apologies for my uncivilized appearance and sat me at an outdoor table. A steaming mug of coffee was in my hand before I knew it. Along with it came hot, buttered bannock biscuits full of raisins, then delicate strips of freshly smoked fish. More fish was being cured in the smokehouse nearby. Daintily covered by tea towels, large trays of bannock biscuits covered the table. Steaming pots of coffee were ready, alongside bowls of sugar and cans of milk. Curiosity was getting the best of me. Counting myself, there were only five of us.

Sounds from the river made me look up. Coming to shore was a 45-passenger catamaran. It had come out of Inuvik for Lucille's Tea and Bannock Tour.

"Oh, Lucille, I'd better go. I'm so dirty," I told her.

"You will not. You are my guest," she insisted.

It was ladies' night by the look of it. They paraded onto shore in Bermuda shorts and white runners. How they could tour for weeks and keep their runners so clean was beyond me. I looked at the beautifully coiffured hairdos and remembered how badly I needed to shampoo mine. Everyone had a million questions about my trip. I was invited to visit homes once I reached Inuvik. They were very kind. Lucille was busy giving a tour of her camp, pouring coffee, and making all of us feel at home and welcome. What a nice way to celebrate Canada's birthday. She explained that she and her late husband had lived at the camp year-round, hunting, fishing, and trapping. Now she came only in the summertime.

Two long straight stretches brought me into Inuvik at 5:00 p.m. on July 1st, just as the Canada Day celebrations came to a close. After checking in at the R.C.M.P. detachment, I phoned home from the lobby of the Mackenzie Hotel.

"Mom, are you all right? Will you be okay? What's Inuvik like?" Angie questioned.

"Do you want me to tell you what I see from the phone booth?" I asked.

"Not a tour bus?" she asked again.

"Yes, a tour bus, Bermuda shorts, white runners – you know the rest!" I answered.

I set my tent on the bank of the Mackenzie below town, too tired to eat. The mosquitoes weren't. They bombarded the tent long after I'd settled into my sleeping bag.

Michael's tent was pitched not far from mine when I awoke. He had paddled in at 4:00 a.m. The mosquitoes had been horrible even over water, he said. It was the only complaint I ever heard from him.

Mike Bailey rowed in during the day. He also had trouble with the mosquitoes.

It was a treat to shop at the Northern Store bakery for goodies like brownies and New York slice. Michael was busy shopping for two months' supply of food. I wondered where he would put it all.

The biggest treat was the chance to do laundry and get cleaned up. Inuvik is a modern town with a full range of services. A tour brought us past Our Lady of Victory Church, commonly called the Igloo Church because of its shape. At the visitors' centre I heard of two men in a tandem kayak heading for the Northwest Passage. They were ten days ahead of me. I didn't suppose I would meet up with them.

I spent time sponging out my kayak, trying to rid it of the mud. Michael completely dismantled his to clean it properly.

"Weren't you rather tired of all the mud?" I asked him.

"No. That's the way it is," he answered.

Many times on the rest of the trip his words would come to me. I stopped fretting about things I could not change.

I rested for 4½ days in Inuvik. The heat and the rain drove the mosquitoes and black flies into a frenzy. They kept me tent-bound most of the time.

July 3rd. On Sunday Gary and Craig Hamilton of Winnipeg paddled up in front of my tent in a Grumman canoe. Father and son were on their way to a leisurely trip from Inuvik to Tuk, a distance of 108 miles. Gary's wife, Pat, was staying behind to do some exploring of her own.

"I'll see you somewhere on the river," I promised.

They were a sharp-looking team as they paddled away in perfect style.

My parcel from home was at the post office on Monday. My grandson told me of his summer adventures. Everyone was well.

Angela wrote, "Mom, We were worried about you until you phoned for hair colour. If that was your greatest need, we knew you were fine."

Pat and I met for breakfast. After browsing through the stores, we celebrated her and Gary's 24th wedding anniversary by going out for musk-ox burgers. The nerve of the man, leaving his wife and paddling off to Tuktoyaktuk!

Another Mackenzie squall moved in and kept me tent-bound for 24 hours.

July 6th, Tuesday. 1:00 p.m. Windsong was packed and pointing north.

Michael was ready. His kayak pointed south.

Goodbyes were tender. I worried about him. He had 200 miles of paddling against the current before Summit Lake, if there was enough water to paddle in the last 50 miles of the Rat. He was big, strong, and healthy, but he was still some mother's son and she didn't even know he was in Canada, much less striking out into the Arctic wilderness alone, with only an air horn for protection.

"There's nothing but sand ahead," a chap on the river bank promised as I prepared to launch. I neglected to ask how far ahead. If that was so, I vowed I would not camp in mud again. Around each bend I hoped to see sand.

I had enjoyed the rest in Inuvik. For a moment I had been lulled by the comforts, but the restless feeling had returned. I longed to be on my way. I had missed the solitude terribly.

At Reindeer Depot, Mile 1003, I pulled up to a makeshift dock to make my supper. There was much history associated with the area, but now it stands abandoned. In 1931 a Laplander by the name of Andrew Barr was hired by the government to drive a herd of 2300 reindeer from Alaska to the Tuktoyaktuk area. Four years and 2000 miles later they arrived at what is still called Reindeer Depot. The purpose of the project was to keep a constant supply of meat on hand for the settlements.

Exploring the site was out of the question. Swarms of black flies pelted me so viciously I could barely stay on my feet. Even with repellent, it was hard to keep them out of my nose, eyes, and ears. I couldn't begin to imagine the torment of the animals in the area.

Twelve hours of hard paddling had brought me up against the foot of the Caribou Hills, near the mouth of a creek. Sand, beautiful, clean, fine sand, and clear, clean water. Even though it was 2:00 a.m., I swam, shampooed my hair, and did some exploring. Gary and Craig had enjoyed this spot too. Their footprints were visible on the beach and on the high sloping banks of the shore.

I had made it to the tundra, "the land beyond the trees." I had come so far for this. I went to sleep contented and pleased.

I had seen bear, wolf, and moose tracks, or a combination of them, at most of my campsites, but except for one large wolf, a few shy foxes, and an occasional hare, I had encountered little wildlife.

I slowed to admire a beautiful sandy beach. It would be grand, I thought, to land and get an all-over suntan. My sixth sense warned me otherwise. Movement caught my eye. Heading toward my beach was a large cinnamon-coloured grizzly. I decided the suntan could wait.

The head wind regulated my days more and more. I paddled when I could and stopped when forced to. It was wonderful! High sand hills rose from wide beaches. Magenta fireweed flaunted its blossoms from the slopes. Large tundra swans kept me company on the water.

July 8th. One day before Tuk, I spotted Gary and Craig ahead of me. They had grounded on a shallow sand bar and were in the process of reloading. Without warning, I grounded too. However, I was able to drag my kayak through. I followed silently behind them as they towed the canoe toward shore.

"Back in Winnipeg we paddle those things," I said jokingly.

We had a most enjoyable lunch together. They pampered me and even did the dishes.

The Mackenzie Delta was behind us. We toasted the mighty Mackenzie, the tundra, and the Arctic Ocean. Our spirits were soaring. The wide-open ocean lay ahead.

Craig took his gun and climbed the steep hill to the plateau above. He called excitedly, "Come up here, you've got to see this!"

I looked at the wall in front of us and groaned. It had been a tough day, but the view from the top was worth it. Craig had also discovered a large burial ground. The skeletons and skulls lay in their sites. Unlike the graves I had seen on the Hudson Bay coast, these had at one time been covered by driftwood instead of rocks. It didn't seem like a sad place. The end of the delta and the beginnings of the ocean lay to the west and north. To the east was lush tundra and many sapphire lakes. Flowers, freedom, and space. A place for spirits to roam.

Already, the water levels were being affected by the tide, so we headed back, digging our heels in to descend the steep bank. We pulled kayak and canoe to solid shore and packed up.

We struggled against the current, incoming tide, and a strong head wind until 6:00 p.m.

All of us were excited about paddling on the ocean. We didn't fall asleep until midnight.

The wind calmed, Gary roused us, and we were on the way again at 3:00 a.m. The quarter moon hung in the sky as we paddled past Whitefish Station on the east shore of Kugmallit Bay. Whitefish Station is a traditional hunting camp of the whale-hunting Inuvialuit. It spans hundreds of years of history. The beluga has always been an important source of food for the native people.

For breakfast we stopped at Whitefish Pingo. Pingos are symmetrical, ice-cored domes forced up out of the tundra permafrost, and one of the world's rare geological formations. With the tundra now so flat, the pingos were the only distinguishable landmarks. There are about 1500 pingos along Canada's western Arctic coast, most of them concentrated on the Tuk Peninsula and Richard's Island.

My leg muscles were burning by the time we reached the top of the pingo. From the summit we could see Tuk wavering mirage-like on the horizon, at least eighteen miles distant. I could barely eat my breakfast for the excitement. Gary and Craig felt the same way.

The mosquitoes had followed us down to the campfire and were using every opportunity to indulge. At least we didn't have to worry about snakes, scorpions, spiders, killer bees, malaria-carrying mosquitoes, lizards, or alligators.

The tide was on the way in. The water was getting rougher by the minute. I was paddling ahead of Gary and Craig. The wind wasn't affecting the kayak as much as it did the canoe. Periodically, I would glance back to see how the fellows were doing. I slipped into a day-dream, and, when I came to, I was unable to see them. Paddling back as fast as I could, I scanned the water and coast for sight of them. A long grey object got my attention. Had they gone over? Why couldn't I see them swimming? My eyes were glued to that object. In my haste I paddled past the mouth of an inlet. Hearing voices, I glanced back. One cannot imagine the relief I felt seeing Craig coming into view, pulling up his pants. The silver object turned out to be a bleached tree trunk.

At noon, Gary and Craig went to shore to wait out the wind. I paddled on, concentrating on the confused short chop that was common when the current was running over shallows and against the wind. I got a good soaking. Strange optical effects were occurring over the water. The big spheres of the DEW Line station in Tuk would shift far out onto the water. Then they would rise, sink, advance, and recede. Nothing was constant except the shoreline, so I kept my eyes on it.

July 9th. I beached the kayak in Tuktoyaktuk, Mile 1089, at 3:00 p.m., exactly one month after leaving Fort Providence. The Mackenzie had been a good warm-up trip. Now, I felt my real journey was going to start.

There was much rejoicing when I called home. I finally sensed my family had confidence I could survive on my own. A pretty Inuvialuit lady stopped to give me a lift back to my kayak.

"There's another kayaker on shore," she said, and pointed to a tent set near the research facility of the Polar Continental Shelf Project, near the airstrip.

I met Phil Torrens.

"Do you know anything about two kayakers heading for the Northwest Passage?" I asked.

"Yes, that's us," he answered. "My friend, Mark, is back in Vancouver settling some personal problems, and I'm waiting for him to return." I was very surprised to find them in Tuk.

Gary and Craig paddled in later in the evening. They were thrilled. It was easy to see and feel their triumph as a father-and-son team. I was so pleased for them. We had enjoyed an excellent, fun-filled 24 hours together. Gary stood on the shore, looking north over the Arctic Ocean. His face was beaming, but there was a hint of moisture in his eye.

"This is some all right, Gary, isn't it?" I volunteered.

One deep sigh came before the answer, "Yes, it is."

I smiled. Another victim had succumbed to the lure of the Arctic.

I left him with his thoughts.

Gary and Craig explored Tuk and spent an enjoyable morning with Alphonse Voudrach before returning to Inuvik.

Phil and Mark had kayaked in from Inuvik in a custom-made 23-foot tandem. They were planning to get through the Northwest Passage to Cambridge Bay. When Mark delayed his return, the plans were shortened to Coppermine. My plan was to try for Coppermine too. Phil suggested we travel together. They had a marine radio and emergency beeper along. I didn't have either, so it seemed like a good idea. We both waited.

Phil was a friendly sort. Before long we had many friends in Tuk. They all thought we were crazy nevertheless. I really started chafing at the bit as Mark delayed his return. Precious days were slipping by, nine in total.

They were enjoyable, though. I felt strong and well. I had already lost twenty pounds. With the fat gone, my body reserves were low, making me feel the cold wind more. I forced myself to eat to replenish some calories before I carried on. With the well-stocked Northern Store and the Tuk Inn restaurant, it wasn't hard to do.

We met Don Gardner from Calgary and Eliza Hart from Yellowknife. They were working on a project for the Yellowknife Museum. They were interviewing the Inuvialuit elders for information on the type of ancient tools they remembered. Don was skilfully duplicating them. I admired the fine detail of the harpoon, scraping tools, spear heads, and the kudlik, which is a seal-oil lamp used for cooking and heat.

I was also honoured to meet Eleanor Elias and her father Jordan. Eleanor has the reputation of being one of the best hunters and trappers in the area. Whenever someone would mention it, she deferred the compliment to her father by saying, "I learned from the best." She runs a powerful dog team in wintertime and takes sports hunters out to hunt polar bear and grizzlies. After midnight she and her father would come down to the ocean to pull in the fish net to feed the dog team. The huskies were tethered near our tents, and howled in unison at the sight of her. She also helped me with my maps, pointing out the locations of out-camps and areas of concern along the Arctic coastline.

"There are polar bears on Cape Bathurst," she told me. "That is where I go to hunt. There's a shack there, but it's very old and probably smelly."

"That's okay," I answered. "I probably will be too by the time I get there."

There was an air of excitement in Tuk. It was white whale-hunting season. The Inuvialuit use the whale to replenish and vary their food supply. The flesh was cut in strips and hung on drying racks.

Tuk is a combination of the old ways and the new. People live in tents in view of their modern, pre-fab homes. *Our Lady of Lourdes,* a schooner displayed near the Northern Store, is a reminder of the steam-powered boats that plied the waters of the Mackenzie and the Arctic, delivering supplies to isolated trading posts and missions. Across the harbour is the DEW Line station, built hurriedly in the mid-1950s in response to the threat of enemy planes coming from the north. Native people go about their lives as hundreds of tourists fly to Tuk to dip their toes in the Arctic Ocean.

I sensed a special freedom in Tuk because it is nearly surrounded by water. It is built on a narrow sandspit curving into the sea. The spit protects a natural harbour four miles long that has been used for countless years as a transfer point for river and ocean traffic supplying the Arctic outposts.

Often Phil and I were joined by campers who had flown in from Inuvik for a day or two. Two young girls were from New Zealand and Australia. A married couple from Switzerland had cycled up the Dempster to Inuvik. A fellow from Spain, living in Vancouver, used a free weekend to satisfy his desire to see the Nahanni and Tuk. Another two came from Dawson Creek in the Yukon. The company made for varied conversation.

The colony of sik-siks didn't mind us. They would stand on tiptoes, twitch their noses, and head for the supper smells that appealed to them most. One sneaky little devil discovered my chocolate-chip cookies. When he returned to find them gone, he really gave me what for. His fat little cheeks trembled with anger.

The Polar Shelf Project helicopter pad was near our campsite. The pilots told us the ice was out of sight. As I was sorting gear in my kayak, I heard a chopper coming in to land. I looked up in time to see Don Starkell's kayak in a sling, swinging from the helicopter. They had retrieved it from the Hutchinson Bay area, where he had abandoned it after being rescued at the end of his fateful trip in 1992. I knew then I couldn't keep the skeletons from rattling in my closet.

Using Max's idea, I got Christina, a seamstress, to sew extra strips of material to extend the bottom of my tent fly. This kept the tent stable in the Arctic winds.

July 17th. Mark returned on Saturday morning. Within the first hour, I had a hint I had made a mistake. He was the opposite of Phil. An air of arrogance reigned about him. I chalked it up to immaturity.

"With two of us paddling in one kayak, you may not be able to keep up," he started.

"It's no big deal," I answered. "We aren't committed to each other. We can go our separate ways." The fact I had just paddled 1039 miles in 22 days didn't seem to count.

"We're expert kayakers," he went on. "Phil and I are both instructors. Do you know how to brace?" Blah, blah, blah, etc.

I didn't have names for my paddle strokes. I had learned to respect and recognize many conditions on the water. My self-taught skills were geared for survival on the ocean and, under tense conditions, I wouldn't be worrying about names for my paddle strokes anyway.

"Do you have a sail?" he continued.

"No, I have no intentions of sailing," I answered.

"Do you have a sea anchor?" he asked.

"What's that?" I asked.

"You throw it out behind the kayak to keep you from surfing in rough water," he informed me.

"If conditions are that rough, you won't have time to rummage around for it. You'll be too busy," I answered.

"Do you have a life-jacket?" he continued.

"No," I answered, "I haven't paddled in one yet."

"What good will you be to us if you're not wearing a life-jacket? You won't be able to help us," he said.

It would be foolish for me to jump into the water if they went over. I let it slide.

My confidence was beginning to take a beating. Was I really unprepared? "Do you paddle in a gale?" he kept on.

"I don't go looking for gales to paddle in," I replied. "If I get caught in one, due to no fault of my own, I can ride one out safely."

"With our kayak," he said, "we might just be starting to have fun in a gale and you'll be wanting to go to shore."

"You little twirp," I thought to myself. "There is no such thing as having fun in an Arctic gale!"

With commendable self-control I answered, "No one says you'll have to go to shore because I do. With luck, that's where I will be, before the gale strikes."

My confidence was restored. God had granted me more than my share of patience. If I could travel with Don Starkell, then I surely should be able to tolerate Mark.

"Victoria, did you really need this?" I reprimanded myself silently.

Sunday came. Phil and Mark made no move to leave.

July 19th. Monday came. My kayak was packed and ready. Ten o'clock and they were still sleeping, so I walked to the Northern Store to buy a life-jacket.

Phil and Mark were wearing excellent-looking dry-suits with rubber gaskets at the neck and wrists. Even the boots were attached. They were a sharp-looking pair. I was suffocating just thinking about how hot they would be. Then came their tight neoprene spray skirts and their life-jackets.

I was wondering how they would keep from overheating. They were probably wondering how I was going to stay warm. I had on neoprene boots – new ones from my sister Wilma – wind pants, a polyester turtleneck sweater, an unlined Sierra jacket, neoprene paddling gloves, and a sun visor.

At 2:00 p.m. all was ready. The wind was rising, but at least we were leaving.

Ahead lay the Northwest Passage. For so long it has been immortalized in the journals of explorers and adventurers. Now I would see it for myself. My dream was beginning to take shape.

It felt good to be on the ocean. The water became clear and blue as the silt of the Mackenzie disappeared.

Phil and Mark were using a waterproof Magellan Global Positioning System for navigating. The bearing was set for Tibjak Point, eight miles north of Tuk. I was confident we would make up some time. I was wrong. Their kayak was grossly overloaded. They had every piece of high-tech equipment imaginable. Along with the Magellan, there were solar panels the length of the kayak, a twelve-volt battery to store the power, a dual stereo system, a sail, sea anchor, Dutch-oven-sized pressure-cooker, heat exchanger, camcorder, cameras, thermoses. A camera tripod was mounted on the back of the kayak. It swayed back and forth with each stroke. Phil's passion was reading, and he carried many books. They also carried a shotgun and ammo.

The water became rough. The wave direction was still good, but Phil and Mark weren't. They were both flushed with the exertion and Mark was complaining about a sore wrist. They called a halt for the day at Tibjak Point, two hours from Tuk.

I was disappointed. I was counting on thirty-mile days in order to get to Coppermine on time. However, I was determined to remain flexible. The beaches were littered with driftwood. I made a fire to soothe my nerves. I had work to do. My new life-jacket was too long. It pushed down on my spray skirt and made a well for the drips to collect in. I opened the bottom seam, cut off a width of foam, and made it shorter. Tomorrow will be better, I promised myself.

When the tide came in I was surprised to see jellyfish on the sand. They were at least one foot in diameter. They probably were harmless, but I put my booties back on just in case. There was always a chance one could get an allergic reaction from them. I wasn't taking any chances.

The following day wasn't much better mileage-wise. The fellows were short of drinking water. We turned into a bay to search for some. Looking at a map of the Tuk Peninsula, one would expect fresh water wouldn't be hard to find, but it is. The shoreline is low and sandy, so pools are contaminated by salt water. Within the entrance of the bay we were surprised to see a powerboat. Elvis and Robin Raddi had been seal hunting, but had come into the bay for shelter.

"Is there fresh water nearby?" we asked.

"No," they told us, "but don't leave the bay. The wind is coming from the northwest. The storm will be here soon. We cannot get back to Tuk today."

"Do you have a tent?" I asked.

"We have lots of food, but no tent," Elvis said.

"We have two tents. We can figure something out," I said. "Is that a snow-bank across the bay?"

"Yes," Elvis told us. "Go to the next point and set up the tents. Robin and I will bring the snow." I handed them a large garbage bag and they were off.

We camped on a long point of an island at the west end of Hutchinson Bay.

"We can't afford to use our fuel to melt snow," Mark said.

"Why would you use fuel with all this driftwood around?" I asked.

The storm came quickly. We were protected by the high sandy shore. The mosquitoes were vicious after the rain. Elvis and Robin used my tent and I bunked in with the boys.

We woke to fog in the morning. As it lifted, the day turned hot and very calm.

I was anxious to be on the way. Elvis and Raddi left to go seal hunting. I waited for Mark and Phil to wake up.

"Watch the wind," Elvis had warned before he left. "If it switches to the northwest, get off the water in a hurry. That is a bad wind. The storm will come very quickly." I respected and appreciated his advice. It served me well.

The tide was coming in when we left at 2:00 p.m. The wind was also rising. We cut across Hutchinson Bay. To our delight we spotted a pod of beluga whales heading toward us. Their sleek white bodies contrasted sharply with the blue of the water.

"Raft the two kayaks together," Mark yelled. "I want to stand up and take some film."

I wasn't fond of the idea. Phil and I tried to hold the kayaks together in the waves while Mark attempted to stand with one foot on each. He quickly discovered the camcorder wasn't working. I was glad to get away from the situation. More belugas came. Mark and Phil went chasing after them.

"We had better head for shore," I called after them. "The wind is changing to the northwest."

"That's good," Mark yelled back. "You go on and we'll use the sail and catch up to you."

I headed for the east shore of Hutchinson Bay. A female beluga came by with a calf at her side. They rose to blow in unison. Shrill whistles were exchanged between mother and baby as they went on their way.

The far shore was just a mirage. I didn't waste any time. I was soaked from the spray by the time I beached. I made a cozy fire and dried my clothes. In the distance I could see Mark and Phil, but no sail.

When they finally arrived, I asked, "Where's your sail?"

"The wind changed before I could set it up," Mark said sheepishly.

That fellow in Inuvik was certainly right. There was nothing but sand out here. The beaches were wide. Sand dunes piled up wherever there was an obstruction. The shoreline was sparsely covered by moss and grass. I felt at home in the treeless landscape.

We set camp at the eastern edge of Hutchinson Bay. The tide went out and we were a long way from the water because of the shallow shore. We had only gone eight miles.

"We'll have to leave on the high tide at 3:00 a.m.," I told the fellows.

Mark gave me a dirty look.

"We have no choice," I continued. "We can't get our kayaks to deeper water any other way." Theirs especially, because of the weight.

The shore was littered with an astonishing abundance of driftwood. Not only on shore, but out on the tundra too. It was evidence of the powerful Arctic storms. Also amazing were the curls of birch bark I found at every stop. They must have come hundreds of miles down the Mackenzie, to be caught up and distributed along the Arctic coast by the current. It became a game with me as I travelled.

"There won't be birch bark here," I would tell myself. "It's too far." Still, there would be. It made an excellent fire starter. I was using open fires to make my meals. Long after I had eaten, I would watch the flames and relax. I was chafing at the slow pace. Every delay would bring us closer to the autumn storms. I decided I would try one more day with Mark and Phil. If things didn't improve, I would leave on my own.

We did leave on the 3:00 a.m. tide. Mark seemed resentful that I had taken control, and poor Phil was caught in the middle. We passed the sand bar Don got swamped on in the last couple of days of his fateful trip. Ahead stretched a twelve-mile strip of shoal area. I wanted to get through as quickly as possible. If the wind were to rise, the waves over the shallow water would be dangerous.

Three hours later we spotted oil derricks and buildings. We headed in along a beautiful sand bar, two miles long. Through a break in the bar, we entered a shallow bay at Atkinson Point. A twenty-mile day!

We had to stake the kayaks in the shallows and bring them up as the tide rose.

"We'll have to leave with the high tide at 3:15 a.m.," I volunteered. They glanced at each other but didn't say a word.

The buildings turned out to be an abandoned DEW Line station and an oil-drilling camp. The derricks we had seen were on ships docked at a man-made island in McKinley Bay.

We went in search of fresh water. All we found were water-filled depressions with a black film on top. We were surprised to see a Honda quad all-terrain-vehicle in the distance.

Mark called a meeting. We enjoyed the Scotch he passed around. I brought the crackers, peanut butter, and honey. "My wrist is sore and we need our sleep," Mark started. "We are going to stay and rest."

"That's okay with me," I answered. "I'm leaving on the tide." They went to sleep.

I was too excited to rest. I took my binoculars and walked toward the lightless beacon at the tip of Atkinson Point. It stood high on the sand dunes. I climbed as high as I could onto the supports to see what lay ahead for the early morning. A long sandspit stretched toward McKinley Bay. I could paddle the four miles of its length before I came to the open water of the bay. In the other direction I could see a Zodiac boat moored on the bar. Someone was here.

As I looked down for footing, movement caught my eye. Below me was an adorable caribou calf. No other caribou could be seen. I found a perch and watched until it disappeared in the dunes.

193

There were tire tracks in the sand. I decided to investigate a run-down shack on the tundra. I called out as I neared the door. Two young men and a young woman appeared. They were as surprised as I. They invited me in. They were all from McGill University in Montreal. They were busy writing their dissertations on marine biology and oceanography. I had to laugh at the stacks of Magic Pantry dinners they had along.

"Where do you get water from?" I asked.

"Past the buildings there's a big lake," one said. "You can fill your containers here. We can get more tomorrow." They were kind enough to give me two extra containers for water.

"Would you like to come back to the tents?" I asked. "You can meet Phil and Mark."

We chatted all the way back. "What a wonderful way to spend a summer," I thought. More young people need experiences like this. In another three weeks they would be heading back to Tuk by helicopter and then home.

We all sat around the campfire and talked until 1:00 a.m. Mark disappeared into the tent. I had been awake for 23 hours already. Phil and I said our goodbyes. Phil had been the driving force behind their project. It had been his dream. I knew how important dreams are. We faced each other holding hands. We both knew they wouldn't be going much farther.

"I'm so sorry your plans aren't turning out for you, Phil," was all I could manage.

"Good luck, Victoria," he said. With a big hug and a kiss on both cheeks we parted.

I set the alarm for 2:00 a.m. After only an hour's sleep, I left silently on the high tide.

Delighted with the solitude and the freedom, I paddled with renewed energy across McKinley Bay. The beaches on the east shore were marvellous. I stopped to make breakfast on one that would rival any in the South Pacific.

A flash of blue on the beach caught my attention. It turned out to be a huge, tangled skein of cordage. It must have slipped from the deck of a ship.

The sun was hot, the wind light. Bays and inlets cut into the shoreline. I'd peek into them as I passed the entrances, wishing I had more time to explore. Access to shore was easy, which made for an even more relaxed paddle.

I had lots of company. Seals would bob up nearby. After a few curious looks they seemed to accept me amongst them. I liked the feeling of being low in the water beside them. Windsong was just as much at home in the water as their little bodies were.

The ducks would come winging in nearby. I would hear the rush of the wind through their wing feathers as they came in for a landing. Gulls would settle close by. They would swim out of my way without taking flight. The terns were up to their usual racket. They circled above, elegant as swallows.

Sometimes they'd take a dive at my head, but most times it was into the water for whatever waited there. Twenty feet from me, on the beach, the little shore birds with their long legs and beaks were busy discussing with each other the tasty morsels the tide was bringing in.

The sky was clear blue, except for a long, narrow, streaky cloud-curtain in the northwest. A feeling of foreboding came over me as I watched the shifting cloud. Oppressive stillness surrounded me. The seals and birds had sensed it too. A moment earlier they had romped near the kayak. Now they had disappeared! I wasn't sure what was happening. I would pull the kayak out of the water to wait and watch. Not a living thing stirred. The only sound was the hiss of foam as it ran down the beach after each wave.

I was standing on a four-mile-long sand bar. The only protection was a huge log at least four feet in diameter. The thick bark was polished smooth by the abrasion of the sand. After tying Windsong securely to the log, I pulled out a tarp for myself, thinking I could wrap myself in it and lie alongside the tree trunk.

The wind switched to the northwest. I had sensed the coming of the storm and now I watched in fascination. First came the ground wind, running along the surface of the sand. The sand was lifting knee-high and belting my shins. The whole sand bar was in motion. Then came the cloud just as if someone had cancelled the pause button. Stretching, reaching, stretching, the curtain of cloud advanced with overwhelming suddenness. Then it quickly veered to the southwest in a huge arc and sped by, sucking the water into pointed waves. I started to shiver as an eerie cold blast enveloped me in passing. To my mind came the lyrics of Frankie Laine's song, "Ghost Riders in the Sky."

Just as quickly all was normal. The birds came back. I guided Windsong to the end of the sandspit and ruddered right into Seal Bay. The tide was rising, but with every stroke my double-blade would connect with the ocean floor. I was anxious to get across before the wind rose. I picked the south shore of a long, flat-topped island for my camp. I couldn't chance getting stranded in the shallows, if the tide reversed. My time was flexible, since I was determined not to make specific plans for each day. I would travel only as far as conditions allowed.

Bunches of daisies grew in profusion out of cracks in the exposed bank. A trail made by caribou led to the top of the steep bank. Many kinds of little flowers grew there, keeping a low profile to avoid the wind. To the north was nothing but the blue, blue water of the Beaufort Sea. The caribou grazed contentedly in the breeze.

Weariness slowly enveloped my whole body. I reminded myself I only had one hour of sleep to my credit in the last 36 hours. After double-checking my kayak, I set the alarm for high tide and fell into a dreamless sleep.

A thick fog blanketed the bay when I awoke. Every fifteen minutes I would restake Windsong in the retreating tide. I would be ready if the chance came. Eventually the sun burnt through the fog, sending shafts of light to pierce the gloom. It evaporated the dew from the daisies, and it was time to go.

The soft, moist wind felt good against my skin as I headed around the island and into the open sea. In no time I had passed the beacon on Nuvorak Point, and ahead of me lay the sixteen-mile crossing of Russell Inlet. The opposite shore was not visible, but strange optical effects were occurring over the water where it should have been. Two hours into the crossing the mirages disappeared. The deck compass showed me the bearing was still good. A backward glance at the fast-disappearing beacon confirmed I was not side-drifting.

"Patience, lady," I told myself.

I finally spotted land. I was only eight miles from Cape Dalhousie when I stopped on an island and checked my position on the Global Positioning System.

The sea was starting to build. Dark clouds were starting to fill the sky to the northwest. Hugging the main coast, I made it to the northernmost point of the Tuktoyaktuk Peninsula before the wind forced me to the shallow shore. I secured the tent firmly on the tundra by rolling logs of driftwood into the fly extensions.

The shores around the cape were etched by the broad-edged hooves of hundreds of caribou. The sand was packed to the hardness of concrete. They must have run the course countless times to try to escape the mosquitoes. I buried the tow rope in the sand to keep them from tripping should they return.

I planned to wait for the tide to help me bring Windsong closer to high ground. The west wind had other plans. Within minutes even the shallows were churning. Hurriedly I collected two small fuel drums from an assortment on shore. Lifting first the front, then the back of the kayak, I got the drums underneath and used them as rollers to bring Windsong to safety against the crumbling bank. White bands of breakers were already forming on the wildly pitching seas.

A crescent-shaped sandspit a quarter mile from my shore was taking the brunt of the waves. I could hear the violent crash of the surf. Before long, the onslaught of the waves was covering my beach, erasing the evidence of the caribous' torment. Gusts of wind whipped the foam from the top of the waves and streaked it far ahead of the breakers. The storm surge undercut hunks of shoreline, causing the slopes to avalanche and slump into the ocean. At this rate, how long would this peninsula be here?

The caribou were taking advantage of the wind, grazing peacefully on the tundra. We shared a kinship. They enjoyed the wind and were wanderers like I.

The tent extensions proved their worth before the wind exhausted its fury 24 hours later. It took the sea another twelve hours to settle down.

A large metal shack hung precariously over the edge of a cliff not far away. The windows and door were missing. One more ice movement and it would be in the sea. Empty 45-gallon drums littered the area. A shiny object caught my attention. I bent to pick up an aluminum plate. Apparently Archie Krill had canoed from Inuvik to Cape Dalhousie years ago. The engraving was still legible, but a bullet hole marred its surface. I set it down and stepped back. In a horrifying moment, I felt the brush of fur against my bare ankle. One hand flew to my heart, the other to my mouth to stifle the scream rising from within. I looked down at the body of a huge husky. There was no smell of deomposition, but the eyes were filmed over and the fangs bared, depicting the agony of the dog's death. It took a few moments before my wobbly knees would carry me back to the tent.

The door-zipper of my tent had separated. The underside of my tent was crawling with black flies and mosquitoes. After many tries, the zipper stayed closed. I squashed all my company and fell asleep to the drone of their relatives outside.

A check at midnight showed a sky tinged in red.

A Danish seemed like a good idea for a midnight snack. I buttered bread liberally on both sides. After browning it in the fry pan, I sprinkled it with brown sugar and cinnamon. I sat with my feet hanging over the bank, with the wind in my hair and face. The wind was slowly switching to the west after its last futile attempts to move the distant sandspit.

Nine in the morning found me paddling into the shimmering path of the sun. Although my eyes had bulged at the sights, I was ready to put the shallow, Swiss-cheese shores of the Tuk Peninsula behind me and paddle a more solid coastline. "Once you pass Cape Dalhousie, things will be better," Elvis Raddi had promised.

The beacon at Char Point came into sight four hours later. From the beacon, the radar globes of the Nicholson Island DEW Line station were clearly visible halfway across Liverpool Bay. For a moment, I was intimidated by the sixteen-mile crossing ahead. Liverpool Bay is exposed to the breadth of the Beaufort Sea. Much can happen in four hours. I decided to go to shore, find fresh water, have lunch, and think this one through. My clothes dried nicely by the fire. The big white globes were tempting me. It was too much. Once the decision was made the rest was easy. I took a bearing that would give me the best advantage over the waves and headed across. I found supreme satisfaction in depending solely on myself. I was confident that with careful observation I would learn to read the wind and it would become more friend than foe. It was not my desire to conquer the elements of the Arctic, but to adapt to, and abide by, them.

The sea was running tremendously high as I neared Nicholson Island. I saw sand beaches against the hills. The tricky part was getting there. Two sand bars ran parallel to the shore. Waves were breaking over the first one. My only chance was to ride a wave over it into calmer water. Timing was crucial. Pick a wave, now or never! The kayak picked up speed and height with the surging wave. I was jarred momentarily as Windsong skinned the top of the first sand bar. There was only a slight rattle from the rudder when a following wave lifted me up and over. The second sand bar protected me as I towed Windsong to the beach.

July 26th. Once the tent was set up I climbed the cliff and walked the 1½ miles to the station. I carried neither my shotgun nor the camera, as I was unfamiliar with the security routine of the stations. Caribou were peacefully grazing in the valley. A large male with a magnificent set of antlers lay near the buildings.

One of the employees walked toward me. He didn't seem surprised to see me.

"Is the big buck still lying there?" he asked. His camera was ready.

"Yes," I answered. "Do you suppose I could use a phone?"

"Talk to the station manager," he said, and left.

The manager was very polite. I made my calls and got two answering machines. I was invited for coffee. Some of the men were from Winnipeg. They had been at the site when Don Starkell had paddled in, in 1992. They warmed up as we talked. I rose to leave.

"Do you need anything? You can have whatever you like," they said, pointing to the counter. I would have given my eyeteeth for an orange and a handful of fresh cherries, but I couldn't bring myself to ask.

"No, thanks, I have everything I need. I appreciate the coffee. Perhaps we'll meet in Winnipeg someday."

Unfortunately, as with government cutbacks all over the country, the Nicholson Island Station was scheduled to close within the next five weeks.

To celebrate the crossing, I made Magic Pantry chicken à la king over instant rice. Lots of hot sweet tea helped settle me. The beach, as far as I could see, was wide and flat. The evening sun was hot against the backdrop of the cliffs. No foreign sounds marred the picture. I was somewhat solitary, but I was never lonely. I was developing a deep appreciation for expedition paddling. It was marvellous to be living according to the whim of the moment.

I checked my gun, even though the fellows said no grizzlies had been seen on the island. They had mentioned wolverines. I think I would rather face a grizz than a wolverine, so I laid my gun within reach of my sleeping bag.

Sixteen days later, when I arrived in Paulatuk, I was surprised to hear Phil and Mark were attacked by a bear on this same stretch of beach. Perhaps it had something to do with their cooking within the vestibule of their tent. The bear had ripped through the side of the tent and raked Phil across the forehead and shoulder blade. Then he grabbed Phil's ankle and tried to drag him from the tent, shaking him all the while. Mark, thinking quickly, had fired the shotgun through the roof, frightening the bear into letting go and leaving. Fortunately, they were near the DEW Line station.

I paddled around the bottom of Nicholson Island to see more caribou. I also toyed with the idea of paddling to the mouth of the Anderson River. Lorran and Terry, biologists whom I had met in Tuk, were working on a Polar Shelf project at the Goose Camp near the mouth of the river. Lorran had invited me to join them if I was in the vicinity. I was also wondering if Irene, Ben, and Max had made it safely through the Anderson River system from Great Bear Lake.

When the wind started to rise, I decided to head east across the last of Liverpool Bay to Stanton. My chance for fresh water came at the bottom of the island. A big lake was draining by way of a stream, across the beach. Caribou, intent on getting rid of mosquitoes, barely noticed me on the shore. The mosquitoes were driving them berserk. A lone, exhausted caribou stood motionless between the cliff and the water. Clouds of mosquitoes surrounded him. He didn't have the strength to wiggle his ears. I could not bear to photograph him in his misery. Tears would not have allowed me to focus. It wasn't the fact that he was going to die that caused my heartbreak. It was the hopelessness in his stance and the droop of his head and shoulders. Misery had caused him to give up completely. It hurt to see the fatalistic submission. Whether displayed in humans or in animals, it is the saddest emotion possible.

Coming out from behind the island, I noticed black objects far out in the water. They were caribou, silhouetted majestically against the morning sun. The sand bar was so low they seemed to be walking on water a mile from shore. More were making their way to the bar. The large male noticed me first. Soon they became uneasy about this strange intrusion from the ocean. They stood spraddle-legged and wide-eyed, a little reluctant to return to the mosquito-infested tundra. Windsong grounded and they spooked.

I got out quickly and dragged Windsong to deeper water. I was rewarded with two waves in the cockpit before I arrested the bucking kayak long enough to get back in.

Stanton, on the east shore of Liverpool Bay, was scenic as a postcard. From what I understood, it is an abandoned mission post. It sits nestled at the bottom of high green hills. Beautiful high gravel beaches ran north and south of it as far as I could see. My greeting came from a rascally raven. Its resonant, bell-like call seemed to roll out of its beak and bind it closer to the bell tower where it had its nest. I had promised Jordon Elias that I would hunt for the snow-knife which he had lost near the building during the winter. Search as I did, I could not find it in the tangle of grass and willow.

The doors of the house were not locked. It was rumoured to be haunted. I tiptoed in. I didn't find any ghosts, but in an upstairs bedroom a cute homemade card was tacked to the wall. In it, a little girl, in all her wisdom, had written:

Your heart is not a plaything
Your heart is not a toy
But if you want it broken
Just give it to a boy!

The post had been abandoned for a long while, but there were still clothes hanging out of dresser drawers, as though someone had left in a hurry. The windows were intact. An airtight heater stood ready for use. I closed the door carefully. The secrets it held stayed behind.

I paddled close to the coast. The water lapped gently against the beaches that wormed their way along the bottom of green hills.

Turbulent brown-coloured water slowed me down at the two-mile-wide mouth of the Mason River. The river comes from deep within the interior of the Cape Bathurst Peninsula. The swift current, deflected by a few islands as it joins the sea, called for complete attention. I felt elation each time my body responded to the added demands. I landed happily at the foot of the cliffs on Cape Wolki. A large snowdrift supplied fresh water for cooking my supper and filling my water bottles.

Early morning took me past the four miles of cliffs to the expanse of Harrowby Bay. It lies at the mouth of the Old Horton River channel. The tail wind was strong from the southeast and the seas were high. I dipped into the bay only far enough to get a better angle on the waves, and started across. In a record one hour and fifteen minutes, I put the eight-mile crossing behind me. It had been one wild ride, but nothing like the treacherous seas waiting for me at the mouth of the Cy Peck Inlet, the last big gouge in the shoreline for a while. After that, the shores would be smooth for at least 120 miles.

Perhaps I let my guard down, perhaps I was just tired. Too late I heard the unmistakable gurgle of surf over gravel. What normally would be an exposed gravel bar was now covered by six inches of rough water, because of the wind and rising tide. The rudder rang like a cowbell over the stones as I turned back into the four-footers coming at me. I had to get to deeper water. More and more I was hampered by the gusting wind. I called on every skill I possessed.

Windsong rose to the challenge, one moment dodging the sweeping breakers, the next mocking the ocean bottom in the troughs. We gained some deeper water, but it wasn't over yet. The water streaming into Cy Peck Inlet was now streaming outward, against wind and tide, through a weak spot in the bar. There was nowhere to go but through this turbulent, thrashing zone. I've been in riptides that were kinder. For some reason, the water was muddy. The night before I'd had a nightmare. In my dream, I lost my hatch covers, and all my supplies were floating in muddy water.

I wouldn't let it happen. I concentrated on every chop. Not for a moment did I break the rhythm of my paddle stroke. Slowly I gained ground. With relief I felt the tug of the current subside. Now, if I had a problem, I would be carried to shore by the wind. Through this whole dilemma I had a persistent feeling that someone was hovering over my left shoulder. I looked up and smiled.

I paddled another two hours to get the muddy water out of my sight and to unwind.

Six miles of cliffs lay ahead. The wind and current were right, but I needed rest. It had been quite a day. I was assured of fresh water by a snowdrift against the cliff. Landing would be tricky. It was obvious, too, that once I landed, I would have to wait for the sea to settle and the high tide to come in before I could launch again. The beach sloped out to the sea very gradually. Shallow waters make beach approaches very difficult, because the waves break far from shore and come rolling in with tremendous force. Grounding in these conditions is serious business. If the force of the waves turns the kayak broadside, it will roll many times before the wave's energy is spent.

I chose a shore-bound wave, lifted the rudder, and skidded onto the beach. I catapulted out of the cockpit, landing on my hands and knees. It wasn't my most graceful landing. I rolled over on the sand for a good laugh. "Yes, Windsong, we did it!"

I changed into dry clothes and pitched the tent on the beach, against the mud bank. As usual, I tried to be as close to my kayak as possible. It was my link to the outside world. Once the fire was going well, I collected my cooking pot, coffee pot, and water containers, and headed for the snowdrift at the foot of the cliffs, a half mile from camp.

As I walked along the water's edge, the ripples of water flowed over my feet. My neoprene booties were life-savers, but they became too warm by the end of a ten-hour paddle. The cold water felt good. I would change to runners when I returned to camp. Crossing the beach to the drift, I became absorbed in scraping the crystallized snow into the containers. Handfuls went into my mouth. I relished the cold freshness of it. A craving for rum and Coke, loaded with ice, came over me. I could make iced tea and pretend. I slid down from the drift, happy as a lark, but not for long. At the bottom were fresh polar bear tracks. Worse, they were heading down the centre of the beach in the direction of my camp. Had I been so careless that I had let him get by without noticing? The hairs at the base of my neck were standing erect. I had learned many times to trust my fear, but to control the panic. This would be the ultimate test. I wished I had not left the shotgun behind. Setting the containers down, I broke into a full run alongside the tracks. "I can't let him get to the kayak first!"

Rounding the bend in the shoreline I could see the tent and kayak were safe. No polar bear either. I slowed to catch my breath and followed the prints until they disappeared into the waves before they reached my landing spot. No wonder I hadn't seen them sooner. Past my tent, they continued higher up on the beach. He was heading south toward Cy Peck Inlet, his nose into the wind. "Well, Bruin," I said, "there'd better be room for both of us, 'cause I'm not leaving just yet!"

Picking up my shotgun, I returned for the containers. My plans for fresh-baked bannock went down the drain. I ate cold baked beans with crackers to minimize food odours, after which I burned the can to a crisp in the fire. The tundra was at eye level from the beach. I made a habit of scanning the horizon. Alongside my sleeping bag lay my shotgun, bear crackers, hatchet, whistle, flare gun, and knife. As I surveyed my arsenal, I felt sorry for the bear. I had done everything I could to lower the odds. My remaining chore was to discipline my mind to shut out the events of the day and get the rest I so badly needed. Sleep came quickly.

The alarm rang at 3:00 a.m. Windsong was safe. The water was quite rough, but the tide was in. Not anxious to spend another twelve hours so near a bear, I guided Windsong along a channel protected by a sand bar, punched through the surf in an opening, and I was on my way.

A heavily overcast sky kept the sheer face of the cliffs in shadow. Wave action had undercut cylindrical hollows in their base, at water level. As my eyes became accustomed to the darkness, I could make out caribou standing single file in the hollows, their massive antlers barely clearing the top of the overhang. They were enjoying some respite from the mosquitoes. I could sense the uneasiness my presence caused. Their only escape to the tundra would be at either end of the six miles of cliffs. I widened the gap between myself and shore to keep them from bolting into the water. I wasn't the only danger. At frequent intervals, long stretches of the overhang would collapse and go crashing into the water. I suspected a number of their kin had lost their lives to this natural disaster.

The sea calmed. Giant swells carried me northward at a terrific pace toward the top of the Cape Bathurst Peninsula. Ahead was the Snowgoose Passage, reputed to possess very strong currents. It separates the Baillie Islands from the tip of a two-mile-long sandspit connected to the mainland of the Cape Bathurst Peninsula.

When I had been in Gjoa Haven in 1992, I had met Eddie Kikoak. He had spoken fondly of the Baillie Islands. As a child he had lived there with his parents Edward Sr. and Violet, brothers Billy and Douglas, and a sister, Molly. When I told him someday I would paddle the Arctic coast, he asked me to stop at the cape and take a picture of his home.

"If it's possible, I will do that," I promised him. I wanted terribly to fulfil his wish. In Tuk, I had inquired about the Kikoak home. The news was not good. Yes, a village including Eskimo homes, a church, and R.C.M.P. buildings had once stood on the shores. Now there was nothing. The erosive forces of the Beaufort Sea had claimed it all.

Large black shapes appeared on the shore to my right. I hoped they would be musk-oxen. They turned out to be parts of large tree trunks or mounds of some sort. One was a large iron boiler from an ancient steamship. Not knowing what lay ahead, I paddled on. Similar to turning the pages of a book, one never knows what will be found there.

A long sandspit took me away from the mainland once more. The water was rougher as I came near the end of its length. Peculiar things were happening on the horizon in the distance. I blamed my strained eyes, then the grey light of an overcast sky. White clouds, tinged with pink from the rising sun, were billowing into the sky. Seconds later they slid below the horizon, only to rise again. I rubbed my eyes. I looked away. Up, down, up, down. It can't be waves! Eddie said they would be huge, but this was ridiculous. I steadied Windsong against the sand bar. With binoculars I scanned the scene.

The flat-topped Baillie Islands were solid and dark to the northwest, but the opening of the Snow Goose passage had turned into a river of hurtling water. The rhythmic rise and fall of the clouds continued. "It must be waves." The wind was whistling into my hood. I loosened the drawstring and flipped the hood back to listen. According to the map I was still three miles from the Cape Bathurst spit, but the unmistakable sound of crashing surf echoed through the morning air. The sandspit was keeping the sea at bay.

I left the security of my sand bar and proceeded cautiously. I could always return if need be. The water was very shallow. Normally I would skirt the shallows at a respectful distance, but today I preferred to stay behind the protection of the sandspit. An hour later, with help from the storm surge, I grounded firmly on the mud flats at Cape Bathurst. Windsong was still 100 feet from the beach. I stepped out into six inches of water and oozing mud. I hurried to get the kayak free before the suction became too strong. Like a miracle, there were a few small fuel drums scattered on shore. I picked three of the best ones. If it worked on Cape Dalhousie, it would work here. Lifting the kayak was the hardest part. The weight forced me into the muck, ankle deep. Once the drums were under, it was a matter of pulling, then going to the back to bring the last drum to the front each time.

By 7:30 a.m., exhausted, covered in mud, but safely on solid ground, I plunked down on the shore of the lagoon to rest, right next to a huge set of polar bear tracks. Out came the shotgun.

The roar of the surf was deafening. Unimpeded by any land, huge, angry combers came lunging in and crashed against the sandspit. The impact would send them shooting into the sky, only to crash back down. Torrents of water slid across thirty feet of spit and into a channel that drained back into the ocean through a weak spot next to the mainland cliffs. Never have I seen a more powerful display of nature at work. If this continued, I would need to be on higher ground.

I would see what the polar bear was up to. Shotgun in hand, I traced his prints. He had milled around on the beach, then retreated around the point of the cape from which I had come. I hoped he had business elsewhere. My size 8½ shoe was dwarfed by the prints. At least they didn't look as wicked as the grizzly tracks on the Mackenzie. Polar bears have a growth of hair on the soles of their feet. This padding means the prints aren't as deep, and only little dents show in the sand, where the tips of the claws touch.

July 29th, Thursday. Next was a campsite. I chose the northernmost tip of the Cape Bathurst Peninsula, latitude 70°33′ 44″ north, longtitude 128°00′ 04″ west, between the drainage channel and the cliffs.

Loaded, Windsong was 300 pounds plus. The campsite was at least a quarter mile away. I made three trips with the heavier gear.

Using driftwood logs, I skidded Windsong across the beach to the drainage channel. Avoiding the spray from the waves, I lined her along the length of the channel to my chosen spot. I built a very comforting fire. Windsong was nearby. It was peaceful indeed. Peaceful and simple, for I had only necessities to worry about and not the luxuries that often complicate our lives.

A late breakfast of hot, steaming bannock covered in margarine and raspberry jam, washed down with hot sweetened tea, made me sleepy and lazy. There was no need to hurry. I would be here for a while. I thought back to the trials of the eary morning.

The resounding boom of the surf came from the full two-mile length of the sandspit. The spectacular display continued through the day. I climbed the steep mud embankment to the tundra above. With binoculars I scanned the meadows and the beach for movement. Polar bears are stealthy animals. If he didn't want to be seen, then it was not likely that I would see him, but that didn't keep me from looking.

The stillness and the space were comforting to me. Flowers in the lush meadow stretched beyond the horizon to the south. The map showed a large lake eight miles in that direction. If I couldn't find water nearby, I could always trek to it. Having plenty of water is important. The worst effect of dehydration is the feeling of confusion. I couldn't afford to be confused. To conserve water, I would use canned foods that already contained their own moisture.

An old shack stood on the tundra surrounded by empty, rusting sections of an aluminum tower. This must be the shack Eleanor Elias had meant. The windows and door were missing and half the roof was gone. It smelled of decay. Raised ridges in the tundra showed the perimeters of older buildings. One even had a ladder leading to a water-filled cellar.

At midday, I drifted off to sleep to an array of beautifully orchestrated sounds made by the ever-changing pulse of the ocean. The sound of collapsing breakers was followed by a rush of foam and then the backwash clawing at the pebbles on its way back to join the ocean. I loved the sounds of the sea, but I resented it for making a prisoner of me.

A lull in the storm during the night made me start planning for a possible launch. I stood on the sandspit, studying the wave pattern for hours. I walked long stretches of the beach, searching for the perfect spot. My only chance was to go over the sandspit. I could no longer leave the way I had paddled in, since the storm surge turned the lagoon behind the spit into a mud flat as it receded.

I was sure I could handle the ocean if I got through the surf. First I needed a good meal. If I was lucky enough to launch, I would be paddling for a long while. The first accessible beach was twelve miles down the coast. If the conditions were too rough for landing, I would have to paddle to Trail Point, 24 miles away. I stuffed myself with pasta and corned beef, cookies for dessert, and hot tea. A snack of peanut butter sandwiches and chocolate bars went under the deck elastic. Two litres of drinking water were handy in the cockpit. If I had to stay in the kayak longer than expected, I wouldn't starve.

When all was ready, I half dragged, half zigzagged Windsong across the beach, and waded across the drainage channel, over the sandspit, to the oceans' edge. Then I returned to the beach to build up the campfire. This may seem strange, but I had to be sure I could warm up quickly if I had an accident launching. The fire pit was surrounded by fifty feet of sand in every direction, so I wasn't afraid of the fire spreading if I had to leave it behind.

With Windsong pointed northwest into the waves, I waited. The waves were coming in sets of two. First two large ones, then two smaller ones broke in perfect rhythm on the beach. There was an abundance of volume in the backwash. If I could shoot down the beach in the backwash, after the last large one, I would have time to get a few good power strokes in before the next large ones came. Better plans have gone awry.

I shoved Windsong into the backwash, running alongside. Just as I hopped into the cockpit, a rogue cylindrical wave came rolling along the beach and slapped the bow, sending it broadside into the beach. Before I could scramble out a large wave soaked me to the skin, filling the cockpit half full of water and marble-sized stones. At 62 pounds per cubic foot, water adds weight quickly even without rocks in it.

Finding it impossible to move the kayak with the extra weight, I started bailing frantically. To keep the ocean from sucking it away, I stood between Windsong and the waves, bracing the kayak against my legs while I bailed. Just as I thought I was fighting a losing battle, I emptied enough water to drag the kayak clear of the surf. I plunked down on the sand, dejected and exhausted. The ocean seemed to be warning me. It sent a volley of spray towards me. My shins started turning black and blue from the force they had absorbed. Lessons like this keep one humble.

The fire was comforting. There was nothing to do but wait and watch. The hours melted into each other. The wind increased once more. I used the padded earphones of my cassette player to seal out some of the surf's roar.

The heat of the sun warmed the inside of the tent. I lay on top of the sleeping bag and succumbed to dreams of my children, who had done so much to enrich my life. I awoke homesick for them and restless.

Slowly options started to form in my mind. How about using the drainage channel for an exit to the sea? I set about studying the possibilities.

The water was still moving fairly well in the channel, through the weak spot in the sandspit, and back into the ocean. If I could gather enough speed before the opening I might be able to punch through the surf. I walked the sandspit towards the opening. Where it narrowed, the sea-soaked sand had turned to mush. It was like quicksand! Across the narrow channel the steep mud cliffs rose sheer from the water's edge. I was quite aware that this land rarely offers a second chance. Here that was certain. If I had trouble in the opening, there would be nowhere to go.

I strolled the tundra and beach to settle my plans firmly in my mind. At the same time, I was pleased not to find any more fresh bear tracks. Again, preparations began. I would eat and rest. When I felt confident, I would leave. I slept fitfully, for how long I don't know. It seemed unimportant to know the time. Day and night blended as one. The only reason I checked my watch was for the date.

I awoke to the feeling of a clammy coldness creeping through the air mattress. The water table in the sand must be rising, but why? With eyes tightly closed, I cautiously extended my hand past the edge of the air mattress to see if the tent floor was wet. No, it wasn't. Hurriedly I exited the tent to find the problem. Sure enough, the water was only two feet away. The stern of the kayak was already sitting in water. Something had caused the drainage channel to expand from twenty feet to over one hundred feet wide.

I bounded to the top of the steep bank. My heart sank. The cliff at the mouth of the drainage channel had split apart, and a wall of mud had cascaded down across my escape route, blocking it completely. A strange feeling crept up my back and into my neck! Was this a coincidence or was it my guardian angel's handiwork? To whom did I owe my life?

The beach was quickly turning into a lagoon. My next chore was to get both tent and kayak to higher ground. I knew I would have trouble setting up the tent on the exposed tundra. A strong wind was coming from the northwest. The fuel drums came in handy again. I rolled seven drums to the cliff's edge, where I righted and arranged them in a semicircle large enough to accommodate my tent. Within their protection the tent set up cozily. Carefully I moved Windsong to the first terrace of the crumbled bank, just below the tent site. I had to be prepared to wait indefinitely and to discipline my mind to cope with the delay.

The Coast Guard boat was ahead of me on its way to Cambridge Bay. It would be returning past Cape Bathurst. Tugs pushing barges would be making their way to villages along the Arctic coast in two or three weeks' time. If I had to wait that long, there was a good chance I would be able to signal them. I set up a section of the aluminum tower, climbed to the top, and wrapped my life jacket around it just in case.

I was amazed at the number of polar bear skulls around. I picked up at least a dozen before I found one with the teeth intact. If I could remove them, they would make a good souvenir. In the debris around the shack I found part of a pocket book. The front and back pages were missing, but at least I would have something to read. I discovered a pool of water. Not more than two feet wide and six feet long, but fresh water nevertheless. One of my problems was solved.

As I wandered, I mused and reflected. I found it refreshing to know it is unlikely a skyscraper will ever stand on this shore due to the permafrost. Perhaps it was meant from the beginning to be a wonderful way to preserve this incredible wilderness.

July 31st, Saturday. It was still overcast. I longed to see the sun again. The wind continued, but at least it switched to the north. I had become accustomed to the ceaseless sound of the surf, and drifted in and out of sleep through the day. Brief rain showers added to the peace.

As I slept, I dreamt warm pleasant dreams of my parents. They seemed to be sitting side by side at the edge of my sleeping bag. They spoke softly in Ukrainian. Their voices had been stilled by heart attacks thirteen and fifteen years ago. In my dreams, they were as vivid as the last time we had spoken. Their conversation was jovial and they were so kind to each other, something that was not so in the latter years of their lives. I awoke feeling secure and loved.

I awoke again with a start and was instantly alert. Missing was the percussion of the thunderous surf. All I could hear in the great silence was the wild beating of my heart. No longer able to contain the excitement, I forgot to scan for polar bears, but fell out of my tent and half slid, half tumbled down the bank. I waded across the lagoon and up and over the sandspit to the ocean's edge. Yes!

Within thirty minutes the tent was down, the kayak loaded and waiting at the water's edge. Automatically, my glance was to the heavens in appreciation. The door was open. It was all up to me. With a slight caress from the sand, Windsong slipped to freedom. The satin swells and the incoming tide welcomed me.

There and then, I realized the most valuable asset one can take to the Arctic is *patience*.

I love the water. I love to paddle. It was sheer pleasure to be on the way again.

I glanced back at my camp. From the top of the cliff, perched on the fuel drum, my polar bear skull, fangs extended, bid farewell. I had forgotten it in my rush. I noticed I had also forgotten to secure my extra double-blades properly. One end was under the deck elastic, but the tops of the handles were loose. I berated myself for being careless. There was nothing I could do, and, as long as the water remained calm, they would be okay.

The sky was heavily overcast, the air calm and humid. I was caught up quickly in the long powerful swells. Paddling was effortless. The Horton River was 52 miles away. I needed at least ten hours of good weather. In the excitement, I barely noticed the formidable expanse of cliffs extending from the water. Twelve miles later I passed the beach Eleanor Elias had mentioned to me. I didn't need to stop, neither did I want to. Forty miles of cliffs lay ahead, with one break at Trail Point, twelve miles away. The map showed a small river entering the ocean there. I would stop for water.

From the ocean to my right, the cliffs rose stark and bold. Slabs of permafrost were working their way out of the steep sides. Erosion caused huge patches to plunge into the ocean and send the backwash towards me.

I focused on the sounds around me. Then came a different sound. I strained my eyes and ears for the source. A swoosh and a hiss. I heard them before I could see them.

Whales. Bowhead whales were coming towards me. They swam in staggered formation. The water slid off their broad backs in a rush of foam. Explosive gusts of vapour came from their blowholes. The warm mist drifted across my face. They were swimming hard.

Windsong was dwarfed by the length of their bodies. At first I was intimidated by them. They came so close that if they had lifted their flukes, I would have been in serious trouble. My kayak did not seem to be a threat to them, but they would yield for me. If we were meeting head on, they would sound and go below me. The surge in the water from their eighty-ton-plus bodies would bring Windsong to a near standstill. I kept paddling so they would know where I was. I would have loved to photograph them, but staying upright was more important. It would have been wonderful to beach the kayak and watch from shore, but the cliffs didn't offer that choice.

They lacked a dorsal fin, and had what I thought were two blowholes. Actually, they have one blowhole divided by a membrane such as we have between our nostrils.

"Hi! Where are you going?" I called to them. "Stay away from Alaska!"

Unfortunately, bowhead whale hunting has resumed in Alaska. I am proud that Canada has protected the bowhead since 1937 and that this docile whale, hunted so heavily for its baleen and blubber, is slowly recovering from near extinction. In the western Arctic their summer home is in the Beaufort Sea and Amundsen Gulf area. I was thrilled to be there for this unforgettable encounter. What novel paddling companions!

The opening in the cliff at Trail Point caught me off guard. Landing was carefree and easy. I shivered with the sheer excitement of having been among so many whales.

"Windsong, what do you think of that?" I asked. I would have liked to share times like this with a companion.

Even the sight of fresh grizzly tracks didn't dull the elation. The long curved claws left five distinctive marks in the sand. He seemed to have bolted. The prints were deep, the sand within them still wet. They led up and over a mud rise to the south.

I started a cooking fire and went to check the cabin in the ravine, next to the creek. Snow-machine parts were scattered about. The back room of the shack was carefully swept out. It was empty except for a ghetto-blaster hanging from a nail on the wall. The orange tarp that had once covered the windows was shredded by the claws of a grizzly. I refilled my water bottles and headed back to the beach to make a pot of soup. I kept my eyes and ears open and my shotgun across my knees.

I paddled on.

The black menacing cliffs turned to steep-tiered mountainsides rising to the tundra. Slivers of beach appeared at their foot now that the tide was dropping, but the banks were unstable, and I would only have landed in an extreme emergency.

A lone gull seemed to take on the responsibility of keeping me from daydreaming. When my paddle stroke slowed he appeared, hovering overhead, squawking.

"Okay, okay! I'm coming," I called to him. Away he'd wing toward the cliffs, and far ahead of me he'd wait on the water. Again and again, the stunt was repeated. Was he really warning me not to linger?

The novelty of the terrain kept me fascinated. I'm sure I paddled the whole stretch with a perpetual smile on my face. Thick puffs of smoke belched from the hills along the shore. I was puzzled because the Smoking Hills on my map were marked south of the Horton River. I was still hours north of its mouth. Time sped by as this unusual sight led me on. The wind came fair and easterly, blowing the smoke up and over the cliffs. I wondered if the caribou on the tundra above were taking advantage of the smoke as protection from mosquitoes.

Nature had sculptured intricate mosaic patterns in the cliffs. Some of the shapes resembled chess players, hoodoos, even biblical statues in long flowing gowns, in colours of burgundy, red, pink, orange, rust, rose, brown, and yellow. The smoke billowed out from their bases, changing the shapes in mysterious ways. I landed on an exposed beach. I had to see if this was real. The beach was a mass of smooth, rounded pebbles that had crumbled from the forms. My grandchildren could have a ball here, collecting all the coloured stones. I wanted more time to explore, but the incoming tide would soon cover the beach.

A raucous call from my seagull reminded me I still had miles to go.

I spotted the sand bar enclosing the eight-mile-wide Horton River delta long before I got to it. It jutted out in a large semicircle. Serenity settled over me as Windsong snuggled against the sand bar near a perfect camp spot.

What a day this had been! I had slipped away from Cape Bathurst. I was halfway down Franklin Bay. I had seen bowhead whales, grizzly bear tracks, the famous Smoking Hills. I was past the worst stretch of cliffs and camping on the Horton. I should have been exhausted. Instead, I was alive with energy.

I would make pancakes for supper so I could share some with my seagull friend, who was now waddling about the beach near my tent. When I went to toss him some, he was not there. I didn't get a chance to thank him. He had guided me for forty miles.

Three buildings stood nearby. One was a quaint little frame house covered with shingles. The windows were broken. The floor was littered with garbage brought in by a storm tide. History has it that it was built by a whaler, Fritz Wolkie, and was used as a trading post in 1905. Stacked high in front were row upon row of empty, rusting, 45-gallon drums. I hoped they were the result of a beach clean-up project.

As I looked back toward the north, I realized I had passed beneath Maloch Hill. At its summit the large radar globe of a DEW Line station was visible against the horizon. To the east, the sky and water united as one. Somewhere below the horizon was the Cape Parry Peninsula.

The morning remained overcast. With gun in hand, I headed 1½ miles back toward Maloch Hill, hoping to call home. I started the climb but soon gave up the idea. The sand was soft. For every three steps up, I slid back two. I sat down, puffing. The hill rose only to 427 feet, but it seemed more like a mile. I couldn't afford the energy or the time. I headed back, following large

Fantastic Smoking Hills on the west shore of Franklin Bay.

Colony of nesting Murre birds on the cliffs of Cape Parry Peninsula.

Forced to shore by the incoming ice near the Hornaday River.

Waiting for the ice to move.

One of the incredible ice formations in Darnley Bay.

House Point on the Arctic coast.

Snowbanks were a good source of fresh water.

Maze of cliffs on the shoreline, east of House Point.

Miles of inaccessible shore, east of Keats Point.

Nechilak, a landmark on the Arctic coast.

Jenny, Nellie, Shannon and Eric at Glen and Bella Ekhoihina's camp.

Ada Ogina setting caribou meat to dry.
Couper Islands, north of Coppermine.

Near-disaster in the Queen Maud Gulf.

Inukshuk on the shores of King
William Island.
A delightful moment for me.

World renowned carver Judas
Ooloolak, Gjoa Haven.

My precious family.
L. to r., back row: Gregg, Grant and Brian. Middle row: Teresa, Debbie and
Angela. Front: myself with Keith, Garrett, Mickey the dog, and Denine.

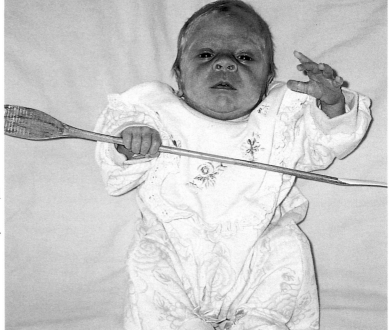

Aleia
Victoria,
born 4 days
after my
arrival in
Gjoa Haven.
She is
holding a Bill
Brigden
double-blade.

wolf tracks. By spreading my fingers as wide as possible, I could almost cover the prints. A story was displayed in the mud. The wolf had met a bear. Apparently they had done some sparring before the wolf retreated, chased by the bear. The bear tracks doubled back to the starting-point. Perhaps he had been disturbed in the middle of a meal. I was pleased that neither was nearby.

I was tempted to cross the mouth of the Horton within the confines of the sand bar. Intuition suggested otherwise. I paddled the eight miles around its perimeter. Later in the fall, when I talked to Don Starkell in Winnipeg, he related how he had to do much wading and towing of his kayak because he had taken the shortcut.

Through breaks in the bar I could see the mouth of the Horton. The bordering high sand hills, crowned in green, made a beautiful scene. I must come back to kayak the Horton's length. There were many places worth returning for. I was able to fill my water bottles from the kayak as I paddled past one of the channels cutting through the sand bar. The water remained fresh for some distance before it mingled with the salty water of Franklin Bay.

Past the delta the cliffs again rose directly from the water, but were not as threatening. Tiny streams cut gullies in the mud cliffs and across the gravel beach. The silt they carried turned the clear blue water to grey, until it dispersed in the ocean. I had hoped to use the streams as a water supply, but it was impossible to strain the water.

The wind had switched from the west this day, bringing the smoke out over the water. Early explorers had related in their journals how the sulphur dioxide fumes had burnt their eyes and throats, but I wasn't affected that way.

The bottom of Franklin Bay does an expansive sweep to the southeast. The coastal plain stretched to the smoke-shrouded hilltops. Sturdy grasses covered the tundra valleys. Everything was green as far as I could see. It reminded me of the foothills of the Rockies. The gravel and sand shoreline was readily accessible.

I paddled along, too absorbed in the shoreline, the wind, and the waves to feel the sense of being alone. Truly, I wasn't. A huge grizzly came into sight. He was digging with fierce intensity at the burrow of a ground squirrel. His powerful forelegs were like a miniature backhoe as he ripped out chunks of turf and tossed them behind him. He was impressive and beautiful. I noticed the prominent hump on his shoulders, formed by the muscles of his powerful forelegs. The wind stirred the long hairs of his ruff as he ripped at the burrow. I could only imagine the terror of the ground squirrel at the end of it. From the water I watched, undetected. I was not interested in attracting his attention since I would have to camp before long. It was a stirring sight to see this animal going about surviving in its wilderness environment.

The sun broke through the cloud cover. The water that had been dark from the overcast sky was now a transparent blue. I felt like I was kayaking over cellophane, like I had become part of the ocean. No longer was I gliding over it. I was accepted. I would trail my fingers in the water just to make sure my kayak was actually touching it. The tide was coming in. I was swept along the shore by the swift current but the sea remained smooth as glass.

Another grizzly came into view, busy poking around hummocks on a ridge. I was not surprised to see bears, for I knew the barrenlands grizzlies' territory lies between Inuvik and Coppermine. The element of danger tunes one's senses. I would be careful in camp this night. Bears have an excellent sense of smell and can locate food at tremendous distances. The wind was in my favour. It was blowing off the land onto the sea.

The yellow of my kayak attracted many bumblebees. They flew around it erratically, then dove into the water. Some I rescued with my double-blade and set them on the deck to dry. They seemed very dopey. After exploring the kayak while their wings dried, they'd fly off, only to dive into the ocean again. After that, I decided not to disrupt the process of nature and let them be.

Visibility was down to a mile when I stopped for the day. I knew the Cape Parry Peninsula lay to the east, but the smoke shroud hid it from view. Weariness caught up to me.

I set the tent on a narrow beach, its back against a clay bank in case the wind increased. A cheeky little sik-sik berated me for camping on his doorstep. With much gnashing of teeth and indignant chatter, he chastised me for my choice of a site. I passed him a chocolate-chip cookie to soothe his nerves. It worked for a while. There were so many of them. Their heads were bobbing up all over as they dashed around the tundra filling their fat little cheeks with food.

I collected driftwood, made a fire, hung my clothes on sticks, and went in search of water. The arctic terns screamed in defiance at my intrusion at their watering hole. The plucky little devils hovered overhead, ready to swoop down and peck me on the head while I filled my water bottles. Before long the neighbours joined in and the racket was deafening. "Why don't you just fly over and tell the grizzly I'm here?" I asked.

Even though the arctic terns are nasty when protecting their territory, one can only admire this graceful bird for its stamina. Before August was out, they would be returning to the Antarctic for the winter. A round trip of 22,000 miles in one year.

A halo surrounded the sun. Through the smoke haze it tinted the popcorn clouds to pinks, violets, and baby blues. I hoped the halo didn't signify a weather change. An evening hush settled over the tundra, even though the midnight sun was still shining, but I felt no need for sleep.

I went up to the tundra and broke into a run to feel the wind in my hair. The sounds of the ocean dimmed. I was enveloped by the silence of miles and miles of tundra. Hills rose behind hills, stretched southward, beckoning.

I ran, lifted my arms, and twirled. I loved this space and freedom. If I had been seen, I would surely have been committed. My solitude was so over-whelming. Deeply relaxed, I was floating through the meadow, in the hills, and over the ocean. The sik-siks watched in bewilderment as I danced all the way back to the tent. Maybe I am crazy. If I am, then I'm glad of it, for it allows me to do the things dreams are made of. I wish there was more time.

The sik-sik's chattering, magnified within the hollow of my tent, woke me shortly after I had drifted off to sleep. "Be quiet," I told him, "I'm only here for a few more hours. You're not getting any more cookies either. Go to sleep or the grizzly will get us both." The threat didn't work. He woke me routinely through the night.

Visibility was down to half a mile by morning. I followed the shoreline and the smoke to the bottom of Franklin Bay. I had the company of a flock of Brant's geese. A mottled brown colour, they were slightly smaller than the Canada goose. They were feeding along the tide line.

At the mouth of Langton Bay I beached Windsong and made up a package of Knorr's soup. I looked forward to this treat, especially the taste of the vegetables in the cream of asparagus, broccoli, spinach, and cauliflower varieties. If I was in a hurry, I would thicken the soup with instant potatoes or minute rice. It would be a very filling meal and it satisfied the craving for fresh vegetables.

Part of an abandoned cabin stood on the sand promontory jutting into the entrance. The R.C.M.P., long ago, had their winter quarters in Langton Bay. I wondered if this was part of their camp.

I had to paddle across the entrance to the outside of the Langton Bay Harbour sandspit in order to start up the west shore of the Cape Parry Peninsula, but the smoke was so thick I could not see the spit. I took a bearing off the map and started across, singing favourite old songs. The overcast and smoky skies didn't deter me. As the crow flies, I was only 36 miles from Paulatuk. In order to paddle there, I had to go up and over the Cape Parry Peninsula and down the east shore to the bottom of Darnley Bay. The distance would be 160 miles. I wasn't worried. If I had a problem, I would trek there overland.

To my left, movement caught my eye. I turned to see a dark head sliding through the water towards me. It wasn't acting like a seal. I started paddling in overdrive. I vividly remembered the polar bears chasing Don and me in 1991. This was too dark for a polar bear. Could grizzlies swim this fast?

It is hard to paddle when fear has the upper hand. I should at least find out what I was afraid of. I ruddered to face it and stopped. It wasn't a bear. A walrus would be even worse. The animal stopped too, then dived. From the flippers, I could tell it was a very large black seal. It had been at least 250 miles since I'd seen one. He bobbed up nearby, looking normal at last.

"Hi! What are you doing here? You sure gave me a good scare. Don't you ever do that again and I promise I won't sing again."

He snorted and shook his head. Before long, I discovered he had a personality of his own. He bobbed up nearer and nearer, first on one side, then the other.

"I see you, you silly goose," I teased him. If I pretended not see him, he did exaggerated back flips, landing with greater splashes than necessary. The harder I laughed the sillier he became. He frolicked and teased until I became concerned he might flip my kayak. I wasn't sure how to call off this game. If I ignored him, he strove harder to get my attention. I decided to keep talking to him. I told him where I was heading and asked him why he was alone.

The smoke cleared. I had paddled far off my bearing during the game. I was a couple of miles into Langton Bay, inside the sandspit. Turning, I paddled back out. I wasn't worried about the extra four miles. It was worth it.

I left my friend behind once I got to shallow water. If a seal can have a disappointed look on his face, then this one did. The wind increased. I stopped on shore to check my position on the G.P.S. Launching again proved difficult. After a couple of attempts I set up camp and called it a day. The fog rolled in; then came the rain. I fell asleep to the patter on the tent roof.

The west coast of the Cape Parry Peninsula is gouged deeply by many bays. Tom Cox Bay, Wright Bay, Sellwood Bay all contributed to the irregularities. Fog masked the shape of the shore, and I found it eerie to be kayaking in it. Every so often, the heavy fog turned into a cold rain. On August 3rd, I stopped and set camp three times. Even with a roaring fire, it became harder to dry my clothes.

At the entrance to Sellwood Bay the sun burnt through the fog and a welcome scene came slowly into focus, the Cape Parry DEW Line installation. I checked the map. Overland, as the crow flies, it was 26 miles away. I could be there for supper.

I still had to go out and about the promontories before I could head towards it. I started across the eight-mile-wide entrance with renewed energy. For the first time since leaving Tuk I began seeing boulders and rocks. Up to this point it had been nothing but sand, mud cliffs, and gravel. Crumbling limestone cliffs bulged out into the ocean. The pounding surf rebounded off the cliffs or sloshed around inside the caverns within. Between the outcrops, four-foot-high ledges of coarse gravel made landing inaccessible. The gravel was packed hard as concrete by the wind and waves coming across the breadth of Franklin Bay. The water was crystal clear and a beautiful turquoise. Clumps of fog rode the wind currents, adding a hushed silence and a silvery sheen to the waves. I sat there in my kayak and contemplated the fascinating, unpredictable realm I'd been paddling through.

From Diamond Rock, I glimpsed the Booth Islands through the drifting fog. Soon I would be turning eastward towards the tip of Cape Parry.

I turned around the next point and again spotted the DEW Line station, but only for a moment. The fog came down thick and solid. As much as I looked forward to the sound of human voices, I couldn't take the chance of becoming disoriented in the fog and paddling into the open ocean between the Booth Islands and Cape Parry.

I landed on the shore of Balaena Bay near a rusty boiler from a ship. Probably it was from the whaling steamship *Alexander*, which ran aground on Cape Parry in the early 1900s and was wrecked. I thought of exploring nearby, but I was too chilled. I already had two sets of wet clothes to pack. If I wasn't careful, I'd have to paddle in my long pink underwear. I certainly didn't want to be found dead in those.

I checked my position on the G.P.S. I was on Balaena Bay, ten miles across water from the DEW Line station.

I had navigated well in fog and all. Then immediately I was humbled. Long ago, men had traversed this area without maps. Explorers' names adorned the maps I was using. The bay, capes, straits, rivers, and islands all paid tribute to their courage.

Sometime in the future their names will disappear, to be changed to original native names. In my mind they will never disappear. Each time my eye wanders across the top of a Canadian map their names will come to life. I travel here this day, indebted to them for showing me the way, as they were to the Inuit who guided them!

At 3:00 a.m. I crawled outside. The fog was dark and thick. I shivered. I spotted a flash of light to the northeast.

"A beacon, it's the airport beacon at Cape Parry!" I yelled.

I moved Windsong closer to the water. Back in the tent I fixed my hair and makeup. If the fog lifted high enough for me to see the waves, I would be ready to leave.

At 5:00 a.m. I had Windsong on the water. I took a bearing on the beacon. To the east, the rising sun turned the fog to a lighter shade. I would keep that to my right, for there was land in that direction. The waves were coming from the southwest. As long as they came from behind I would be on track.

I double-checked the time. In two hours and fifteen minutes I should be at the beacon. I pushed away into the waves. Except for my pulse, silence reigned. My eyes were riveted to the flash of the beacon. I checked my watch often and ticked the miles off. Except for the Mackenzie River, I calculated my average travelling speed at 4½ miles per hour. It seemed to work out right.

The fog started to lift. I could see a long line of shore ahead, and the shape of a building. Headlights dropped out of the overhead fog. The truck stopped at the building. Minutes later it disappeared up the road into the fog again.

Seconds later the fog dropped back to the wave tops and the beacon went out. I checked my watch. I was still two miles from shore. I kept my eyes on the deck compass. I could barely see beyond Windsong's proud bow as she sliced through the waves.

"Just you and me, Babe!"

The shore popped out of the gloom suddenly. To my dismay, I found I couldn't land. The steep gravel banks were four feet above my head. I ruddered along the shore and around the bend to a cove protected by a rock reef. Windsong lined up for a large wave and glided across the reef into calm water. The time was 7:15 a.m.

The fog and lack of sleep had chilled me. The tent went up. Dry clothes and shoes made me feel much better. Instead of walking up the winding road to the top of the hill, I crossed the runway to the airport terminal. The door at the weather station was unlocked. I walked in and called out. No one answered. It was warm inside. The coffee was on. I sat down to wait for someone to show. Before long a young woman pulled up in a truck. I walked outside, so as not to frighten her. She was surprised. Roberta was the weather gal at the airport.

"Have a seat," she invited. "I'll drive you to the top of the hill after I do my nine o'clock report. In the meantime call Fred Smith, the site supervisor, and tell him you're here."

I dialled the number she gave me. The voice at the other end was silent as I explained who I was and how I came to be there. The sweetest words in the world came over the line. "Bet you could use a hot meal and a shower. Get Roberta to drive you up."

"We'll be there after 9:00," I replied. I fell in love with Fred Smith before I even met him. I'll remember his greeting forever.

I called my family to let them know I was safe and in good hands. I was pleased to know all was well on the home front. I reported my whereabouts to the R.C.M.P. in Tuk also.

"Are we ever glad you called," they said. "Are your friends with you?"

"If you mean Phil and Mark, no, they aren't," I replied. "We parted company three days out of Tuk at McKinley Bay. They told me they would probably be turning back. Why?"

"We haven't heard from them," the officer replied. "We were becoming worried."

"I'm sorry, I can't be of more help," I apologized.

The DEW Line installation is perched at the top of a 300-foot hill. We stopped at my tent to collect my laundry and wound our way to the top. Everyone was friendly, helpful, and curious. To them the idea of someone kayaking for enjoyment on the Arctic coast was incomprehensible.

From Fred Smith's office we looked down upon the aquamarine sea, where the waves were developed into pounding breakers that crashed into the limestone cliffs. White foam exploded high into the air. I shivered, glad I wasn't on the water. Even without the breakers, the map showed serious currents coming round the cape. Thick fog drifted by the windows on gusts of wind. Soon it blanketed the whole hilltop. How long would I be waiting this time?

"How long do weather conditions like this last?" I asked Fred.

"Sometimes for weeks," he replied. Cape Parry is notorious for fog.

I didn't have weeks left. Already the air carried the chill of an early autumn.

Of the 35 employees, three were women. Marge Strano and Shelly Wood directed me to the showers, laundry, and dining hall. Many introductions were made. Fred Martin's big brown eyes captured my attention. I was very impressed by Fred Benson, the jovial chef. His amazing meals and desserts combined with the warmth was great too! I hadn't minded the discomforts of travelling because I was enjoying my trip, but I did appreciate the comforts when they were available.

With map in hand I went to question Fred Smith about the narrow neck of land connecting the tip of Cape Parry to the mainland. If I could cross over it, I would not have to paddle around the top of the cape. I would save twenty miles.

"Where's your kayak?" Fred asked.

"At the bottom of the hill in the lagoon," I answered. "Can I cross over the sandspit?"

"Most certainly," came the answer. "As soon as Doug and Fred are finished their chores, they'll help you." Perhaps my wait wouldn't be very long after all.

As promised, Windsong was transported to the east side of the spit into the shelter of Gillet Bay. I relaxed completely. There was a great deal of interest in my maps. I relived the route as I described the scenery.

"We had a fellow here last year by the name of Don Starkell. He was kayaking too. We found him shivering to death at our party shack," they told me.

"Yes, I travelled with him part way," I said, and told them briefly of the trip.

"So you're the one he talked about!" they said, amazed. "You don't have to be nice about what you say. He had nothing nice to say about you."

I found that comical. I was surprised he had even mentioned me.

After dinner Fred Martin came by to escort me on a tour of the hill. Fred was not only extremely handsome, but charismatic and great fun to be with.

He showed me the murre bird colonies on the cliffs. The three peninsulas jutting into the ocean off the cape are now designated bird sanctuaries set aside to protect the summer nesting sites of thousands of murre birds. The narrow neck of the west peninsula stretched a half mile into the ocean. The cliffs dropped far down to the ocean below where the waves were thrashing wildly. I felt like we were walking a gangplank into the sea. This would be my first sight of murre birds. Looking down the cliff side, I could see hundreds and hundreds of them. They looked like miniature penguins as they perched on the very narrow ledges of the cliffs. They jostled each other in excited groups, vying for their space. If alarmed, they abandoned their perch and hurtled through the air to the water far below. The tumult was deafening. The stench from the droppings was intense.

They didn't have nests. Their eggs were laid directly on the edge of the rock ledges. We managed to spot some of the large, blotched, pale green eggs exposed beneath the adults, and even a little ball of fluff, which was a newly hatched chick. How they ever managed to keep themselves, the eggs, and the babies on those narrow ledges, in such high winds, I could not understand. We didn't disturb them. They would sit straight up, cock their heads from side to side, and go back to chastising the neighbours, looking for all the world like ushers in black and white tuxedos.

When the seagulls came too close, it was a different story. They stopped their squabbling and screamed in unison. The wave of sound would travel the length of the cliffs as the warning was passed on. What a rare sight this had been.

At the top of the hill we met Pat, Marge, Doug, and Shelly. They had confiscated a club-cab 4 x 4 truck and were on their way down to photograph the birds. Fred and I returned with them. Shelly was as nimble as a mountain goat on the cliff's edge. I couldn't bear to watch her. It was a long way down to the water. I had to return to the truck and wait there to keep from sounding like an old mother hen.

I would get a grand tour of Cape Parry, I was told. Up and over the hill to the south side we went, past the derelict red and white buildings of the Hudson's Bay Co. At one time this was a trading post. There had also been an Inuit village here. Unfortunately many children died of illness at this site. Solemn rows of white crosses mark their graves in a nearby cemetery. The village was deserted one night long ago, and many people moved to Paulatuk.

Along the road the tundra had heaved and cracked open. A solid slab of ice four feet thick was exposed. A carpet of lush green turf still clung to its sloping side. I'll never be able to understand how anything can grow on a solid bed of ice.

Pat carried on down a single track meandering across the tundra. Everyone here is very conscious of the tundra's delicate nature. No one strays from this trail. The tour took us to "Five Mile Lake" and "Seven Mile Lake," where the employees go for a break to do some fishing. The lakes are surrounded by greenery, rocks, and cliffs.

The gang stopped to check on a gyrfalcon. She had her nest in the cliff above the lake. In the nest sat three little balls of down with huge eyes. My new friends had a special interest in the chicks. When they had hatched, one was very weak and was being forced out of the nest by its siblings. Everyone had taken turns to bring it hamburger meat to keep it from starving. Now it was healthy and strong, ready to defend its place. The mother resented our presence. I was fascinated by the speed of her dive as she feigned an attack, stalled at the last minute, and screamed in defiance. We left quickly.

On the way back to the truck we noticed fox kits playing on a ledge. Shelly had been leaving leftovers from the kitchen on the tundra for the adult, when hunting was lean. This must be her den and family.

The Party Shack adorned a rise facing west over the ocean. Most of the employees have contracts for three- to six-month stints, so diversions are necessary to keep things running smoothly. The Cape Parry site is a dry site, which means no alcohol is allowed. This doesn't seem to stop people from having a good time without it. The building was assembled by employees with scraps of building materials. A fellow by the name of John made a walkway of carefully laid, flat stones.

"This is where we found your friend Don," they told me.

"Don't use that word loosely," I warned.

Back at the site, at 2:00 a.m. we gathered in the dining area for tea and toast. The fog moved in again. I snuggled into the soft warm bed among fluffy pillows. My mind wouldn't shut off. I listened to the rain pelting on the window until breakfast call at 6:45. Six of us were drinking black coffee that morning. Fred and Doug left to wait for a plane that was expected, Marge had work in the office, and Shelly was hurrying through her chores.

I took the time to pack my gear, in case the fog lifted. By 10:00 a.m. there was hope. The plane brought a nurse among the passengers. I had been concerned about my thumb. A large blister had healed poorly. The thumb was swollen and blue. When Joan was finished her meeting, she had a look at it. There didn't seem to be anything to worry about. She made up a prescription, just in case the pain started up my arm, but I was pleased it healed on its own. She asked about my trip.

"I'll say a prayer for you," Joan told me as we parted.

"I'd like that," I replied.

By 11:00 a.m. parts of the sky were blue. The sun was out.

"Guys and gals, I have to go," I announced.

"Have lunch with us first," they asked. "Then we can all see you off. Fred Benson wants to bring his camcorder."

At 1:00 p.m. the announcement came over the loudspeaker, "Victoria is leaving. The bus is waiting for anyone wishing to watch her departure." I was bashful. They were treating me like a celebrity!

Everyone was in a jovial mood. The sun does that. It had been a long, long time since I had felt its glow. Down at the bottom of the hill it glinted off the fragmented wreckage of a plane that had landed a few feet short of the runway, probably in fog.

"There's my kayak," I exclaimed. I had missed Windsong, not realizing how much until I spotted her.

"Where?" asked Phil, who was sitting next to me.

I pointed to the beach.

"I don't see it," he replied.

We were upon it before he noticed it. "You came in that?" he asked incredulously.

"Yep! And the good Lord willing, I'll leave in it too."

Shelly and the cook had put together a care package for me – grapefruit, apples, tiny cans of tomato juice, and two loaves of bread. Shelly slipped a crystal heart into my palm, and Marge, a Cape Parry pin.

It is impossible not to be affected emotionally by such caring people. Within 1½ days they had become my family. With hugs and kisses and a few tears all around, we parted. Windsong slipped back into the ocean.

"If you have trouble, look for a whaling camp ten miles south," Fred Smith called after me. "There may still be people there."

"Thanks everyone, I'll never forget you. Come and see me in Winnipeg."

I ruddered east towards the open ocean. The structure of the DEW Line station faded into the distance. I was alone once more.

An hour out, the rain came, hard and steady. I spied the whaling camp on Boldon Bay and ruddered into the protective cove. Three Inuit men came to greet me. I met brothers Tony and Nelson Green and Tony's son, John, from Paulatuk.

"Come in for coffee and caribou stew," they invited. They lifted Windsong to safety on the beach, beside a complete skeleton of a beluga whale.

They were concerned about my wet clothes.

"Please don't worry," I told them. "I'm used to being cold and wet."

Nelson started the oil heater. He was busy stirring the stew. It smelled delicious. It was full of onions, something I hadn't tasted for a while. The hot coffee was a treat.

They were the last of the whaling crew. The water had been rough. Hunting was poor. They had only managed to get three belugas for the entire hamlet.

"Did you see any whales?" they asked.

I told them about the belugas in Hutchinson Bay and the whales off Cape Bathurst and how close they had come to the kayak. They were amazed.

"We're hunting from the wrong boat," they concluded.

If the weather didn't improve, they would be heading to Paulatuk within a few days.

Tony was not convinced I was okay in my wet clothes. He gave me his duffel socks for my bare feet. "How about I give you my jeans?" he offered.

"No," I answered, "I can't let the word get round that I got into your pants." For a second, silence. John burst out laughing before the rest of us. That broke the ice. They didn't worry about me as much after that.

"Do you have enough food, if the weather holds you here for a while?" I asked. "I have extra."

"Yes, we'll be okay," they answered. "We have been able to get a few ducks. Now we have a caribou too."

Full of stew and coffee, I headed out feeling very grateful.

"We'll call Paulatuk on the radio and tell them you're coming," Tony called.

The sky cleared. The wind and sea calmed. A narrow channel separated a large, wedge-shaped island from the shore. Its west beach was at water level. The east side, facing the ocean, rose to hundreds of feet. I chose the cliff side to paddle on. I wasn't disappointed. The cliff was hollowed out into large caverns that were connected by arched openings. The swells I was paddling on sloshed softly against the inside walls from one cavern to the next. Meandering through by kayak would be a dream, but I was concerned about rocks dropping from the ceilings.

As I approached Letty Harbour, the sea was absolutely still. The clear sky was mirrored in the water. There are few days like this in the Arctic. I was tempted to paddle on, but my body refused to cooperate. It was midnight. I had been awake for 45 hours. No wonder I wasn't focusing properly. I only had energy to concentrate on one thing at a time. It wasn't a good condition to be in. I promised myself it wouldn't happen again. Here I was in Letty Harbour, once a safe haven for sailing and steam ships. Tonight, a haven for one lone kayak. Nearby the campfire crackled. I lay on the smooth white rocks with hands clasped behind my head, relaxed, content, at peace with myself, and very thankful for all that was granted me this day. I was humbled too. I will live and I will die. These shores and scenes will still be here. I'd like to see so much more, but I cannot linger. Mother Nature has a date with the changing season. For now, it is good to think of nothing but what is before me at this moment. My eyelids became heavy. I tiptoed to my tent. Breaking the silence would have been a harsh thing to do.

My next objective was to get around Bennett Point while the weather held. Bennett Point is at the tip of a twelve-mile-long peninsula that juts east into Darnley Bay at a 90° angle. Once I got to the south side, the shores would protect me from the worst of the north winds.

I was on the way early. How quickly the conditions had changed from the glass calm of midnight. The waves were already moderate. The sound sleep had done me a lot of good. I paddled hard and watched the advancing storm front building in the west. The thick clouds loomed menacingly, repeatedly advanced and stalled. I knew I wouldn't clear Bennett Point.

The wind was still favourable from due north. The waves were getting steeper and closer together. I searched the shore for a safe takeout. I could see nothing but cliffs ahead. Before long the waves were reflecting violently off the cliffs and slapping the bow around. It was becoming harder to decipher the complexity of the waves. A break in the cliffs exposed a tiny beach 100 feet long. Breakers were hitting the terraced gravel shore. I had no choice but to try for a landing.

The water was very deep along the shore. I decided to come in on an angle and turn broadside at the last minute to get deposited on one of the ledges. I timed the waves like a child ready to enter into the arc of a twirling skipping-rope. There was no room to miscalculate the timing or angle of the kayak. A big wave was building. Now! I yanked the spray skirt off and lined up. The lift was good. The second Windsong touched gravel I catapulted from the cockpit, grabbing for the tow rope. Windsong caught part of the following wave in the cockpit. It was a small price to pay for safety. I lifted her out of harm's way.

I located the tent against the cliff for protection. The wind switched to the northwest. The temperature dropped dramatically. The storm turned the sky dark and ominous. Within minutes, it matched the violence and power of the ocean. The tops of the waves were whipped off by the wind. Then the rain came in stinging pellets. I was snug in my sleeping bag when the snow started to fall.

August 8th. For me the smell of snow was the smell of adventure. I blew a few breaths into the air just for fun. The puffs floated in the dome of the tent, then disappeared. I drifted in and out of sleep, wakened by the changing wind and water.

When mist from the crashing waves began drenching my tent, I moved it and Windsong to higher ground. It was strange to be fumbling around in the dark. I had last seen darkness in Winnipeg. Autumn, the season of squalls and high winds, was here.

An arctic fox came out of curiosity, probably drawn by the smell of peanut butter. I had left my sandwich in a double ziploc bag under my deck elastic. He was ready to pilfer my sandwich, but accidentally snagged his tooth on the elastic. When he pulled his head back the elastic snapped against the kayak with a terrific noise. He sat back debating another try, thought better of it, and went around exploring the rest of my camp. He blended so well with the surroundings it was difficult to keep him in sight.

Among the driftwood I found curls of birch bark to start my fire. I sat on a heavy log, ate my supper, and enjoyed the view while my clothes dried. That I was not bored with my own company worked in my favour. It was 36 hours before I could paddle again.

I made camp once more before I paddled to the bottom of Darnley Bay. The shores were fine sand. Paulatuk was in sight. The deep, dark blue water was in sharp contrast with the lighter tints of the shallow water. I travelled on the margin, but couldn't get a good angle on the waves. They broke over the bow and slammed into my chest, drenching me. I would have to go two miles past the town to get around the sandspit and come into the harbour. I paddled in unnoticed. No one expected me to arrive in such conditions.

August 10th. 3:00 p.m. As soon as Windsong was safely beached, I headed for the hamlet office. I had estimated three days from Cape Parry to Paulatuk, but it had been five. I felt guilty about the worry I caused. At the hamlet office I removed my booties, as is customary even in government buildings, because of the sand. I couldn't do much about my dripping clothes. A puddle was forming at my feet as I asked to use a phone.

A handsome, curly-headed fellow came toward me, extended his hand, and introduced himself as Ken Thompson.

I apologized for my cold, wet hands. I detected amusement in his eyes.

"We weren't expecting you until tomorrow," he said. "Do you have a place to stay?"

"Yes, I have my tent, but I'd like to call my family first," I answered.

He handed me a set of keys. The amusement never left his face. "These are the keys to my house. There is an apartment upstairs. No one will bother you there. There is a shower and phone, and don't be shy about raiding the fridge. My foreman, Keith, will drive you there. I'll be home at 7:30." He caught me off guard. I was amazed one could be so hospitable and trusting of a stranger.

As Keith let me off at the house, I was pleased to see a helicopter pilot I recognized from Tuk.

"Hi," he said. "I'm surprised to see you here. We heard you were already in Coppermine."

"I only need ten more days," I answered. "Do you think the weather will calm?"

"Hard to say. Those nine days in Tuk may do you in," he answered. "By the way, Phil and Mark were attacked by a grizzly at Nicholson Island."

"What?" I didn't believe him.

"Yes, they've been medi-vaced to Inuvik. Listen to the radio. They've been on the news," he replied.

He continued, "I met two people in a canoe and one in a kayak coming out of the Anderson River. They were at the Goose Camp with Loran and Terry."

"That must be Irene and Ben and Max," I said.

I was relieved they had safely come that far. "I met them in Fort Norman," I told Eric.

"Yep. Same ones," he replied.

All of a sudden, I was chilled to the bone. Inside, it was an unexpected pleasure to find such excellent accommodations. A hot shower was first on my mind.

Ken was an easygoing sort of fellow. After work we loaded Windsong on his truck and brought her near the house. I wanted to repack and be ready to leave for Coppermine once the wind settled down. I was pleased to discover I had plenty of food left to get there.

The weather forecast was not good, but I expected my break would come. Perhaps it was too much to ask. I had been granted more than my share of breaks already.

The heavy pounding of the surf continued into the third and fourth day. The thought of ending my trip formed a heavy cloud around my heart. How would I live without the smell of the ocean, without to the wind and wild places? My tent had been my home for 2½ months. With an intensity that amazed me, I already missed the sound of the surf, the chill of the evening, and the flapping of the tent in the wind. The lack of sleep showed on my face.

Ken and Keith offered to gather rocks to spread under my sheets and proposed to stay near my bed and pour water from one bucket to another all night.

"That's what friends are for!" they informed me.

My Inuit friends advised against paddling on. I respected their opinion. The midnight sun was starting to caress the ocean. Each day it would sink a little lower. The season was getting on. Once the decision was made it became easier to cope. I unloaded Windsong, gave away the food, got rid of my fuel, and discarded the well-worn clothes with the many holes left by campfire embers.

Windsong was made ready for the trip home. I dismantled the rudder and wrapped her in cardboard for protection. Ken would see she was loaded on the barge, to be transported back to Hay River.

I had so much to be thankful for. Already, I had seen much of this land's varied geographic conditions. I had witnessed the moods of the Arctic. The people, the animals, the heat, the cold, the calm, the tumult. I had come to know each day's struggle held a reward and usually a lesson or two. I felt privileged.

It was easy to enjoy the last of the jubilant summer days in Paulatuk. Ken made me feel welcome. Everything was done with care and kindness. One morning I found a fluffy terry robe and slippers and a note wishing me a good day waiting for me at the bottom of the stairs. He took me on a tour of the hamlet. Home to 206 people, it is located at the south end of Darnley Bay near the mouth of the Hornaday River on the Arctic coast. Many well-known Inuvialuit sculptors and tapestry artists live in Paulatuk. Billy Ruben makes graceful swan sculptures out of musk-ox horns, and his wife, Bertha, fashions wall hangings on duffel. They depict life on the land. I am proud to own these priceless pieces.

Next on the tour was a trip down Lover's Lane. It wasn't very romantic. There was no darkness and no trees, the only music was from the seagulls, and it ended at the dump. It was the company that counted.

The children were always full of spirit and energy. They would call on me at least three times a day. Off we would go on walks. They chattered constantly. I tried learning some new words. They would end up laughing at my blunders.

One day the girls came by to invite me for a swim.

"Do you have a swimming pool in Paulatuk?" I asked.

"Oh yes! A big one!" came the reply as we headed for the ocean.

I couldn't bring myself to go in.

The girls had no problem. "Aren't you cold?" I asked.

"No, we are not cold," they said in unison. "We are Eskimos!"

They showed me how to find blueberries. Without glasses I could barely see the single berries beneath the green leaves. They always picked more than I, but would divide them so we all had an equal amount. They told me of a yellow berry, a sort of watery, low bush raspberry that is very sweet. "We'll have to go far back to the lakes for them," I was told.

At the Catholic Grotto they would all kneel to say prayers. Before we left, they pointed to the rust-coloured lichens on the rocks. "We have to be good. The spirit of our ancestors is coming out to watch us," they solemnly told me.

It is tragic that many traditional spiritual beliefs are lost to religion as some know it today. The old way seems more interesting. From the innocence of children I was allowed a brief glimpse of the past. It is certainly with humility and respect that I travel through their land.

For the first time I heard of the Little People. Legend has it that the people are very small, wear animal clothing, are helpful to strangers in distress, and live on Cape Bathurst. The smoke of the Smoking Hills was once said to come from their cooking fires.

"Did the Little People help you?" I was asked, when they heard I had been on Cape Bathurst.

"I didn't see anyone," I answered. My mind went back to the cliff collapsing into the drainage channel on cue. "But perhaps they did help me after all."

At 10:15 p.m. a blast from the siren signals curfew for the children. They all scamper out of sight. Fifteen minutes later they were all outside playing again. My heart went out to one little boy. He screamed hysterically. Each night he relived the horror of the loss of his family home by fire.

I was very pleased to meet Renee. She and Keith lived next door to Ken. Renee's family was originally from Cape Parry. She was taken from her mother at the age of seven and kept at the school in Inuvik. She didn't see her mother for seventeen years. It is hard to imagine the trauma a mother and child endure in those conditions, and survive. Tragedy continues for her mother, Mona. She lost her husband in a boating accident. She still searches the shores for some trace of him.

Renee helped me find all the ingredients to make a birthday cake for Ken. It is not a simple matter in Paulatuk. Things like eggs, icing, and candles aren't always available. My attempt at making bread didn't fare as well. The bread smelled good, but it made concrete look soft. I had forgotten to check the expiry date on the yeast package.

All too soon it was time to leave. The weather turned hot and still. If all my gear hadn't been packed, I might have been tempted to try for Coppermine and make a foolish error.

Ken saw me off at the plane. I found it hard to express my gratitude for his making my stay in Paulatuk so enjoyable and interesting. Happiness and heartbreak clouded my eyes. I left with a treasure trove of memories.

From the plane I could identify the Darnley Bay coast, Langton Bay, the south shore of Franklin Bay, the Horton River snaking its way north, the Smoking Hills. I wanted to absorb as much as possible. I might never be able to afford another trip. By the time I reached Inuvik, I was fighting terrible pangs of loneliness. My soul had stayed behind on the coast.

August 19th, as my flight circled Winnipeg airport for the landing, a fierce rebellion built inside. "I will go back!"

The joy of seeing my family wiped out some hurt. We were caught up in the reunion. I had missed them so much.

Just to confirm my decision, I phoned Ken. "Hold my kayak, Ken. I'm coming back!"

Strangely enough, he wasn't surprised.

1994

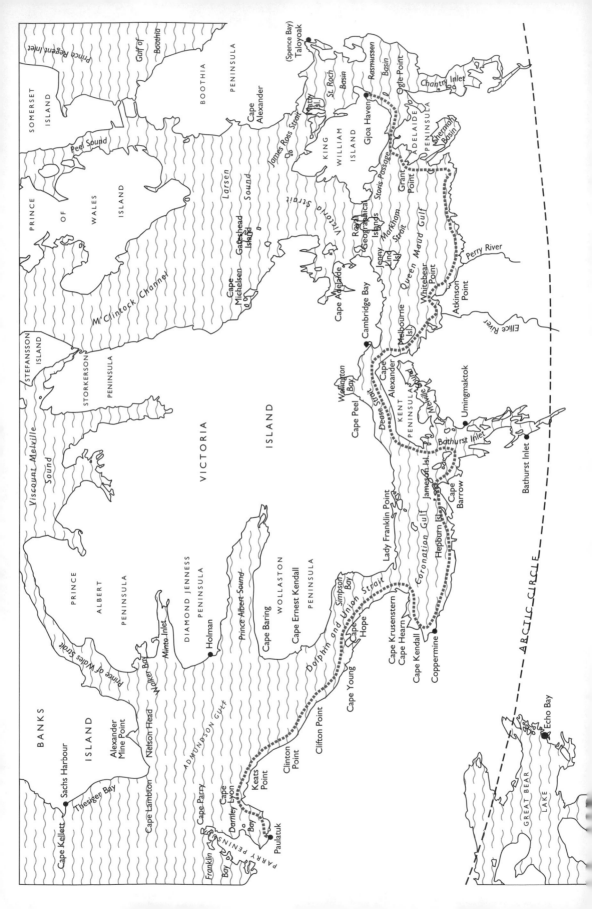

The early spring of 1994 found me making arrangements for another trip. I planned to return to Paulatuk and continue eastward through the Northwest Passage to Gjoa Haven, approximately 1500 miles of Arctic coastline. If the weather allowed, I would paddle an extra 109 miles to Taloyoak (Spence Bay). Don and I had walked over the ice from Spence to Gjoa in 1992. I just thought it would be interesting to see it in the summertime.

There were those who encouraged me and, as before, those who questioned my sanity. So strong was my desire to return to the North that nothing could blunt my determination.

Ken and I had kept in contact throughout the winter. He had stored my kayak in Paulatuk. He had teased me by saying the children in town had enjoyed using it as a toboggan during the winter. The ice had gone out very early in 1993. There had been open water by July 1st. I set my sights on July 1st, since the Arctic summer season is very brief.

The bulk of my food supplies were mailed through Canada Post. It was much cheaper than paying excess baggage on the airlines. There was gear to replace, arrangements for more life insurance, health insurance, airline tickets, and last-minute duties around the house and yard.

My friend Yvonne Maxim was busy promoting my trip. The staff at Urban Trail became interested and supplied a comfortable pair of hiking boots; Mark's Work Wearhouse offered a cozy fleece sweater; and Kodak Canada supplied the film. It was exciting to know they wanted to be part of the journey. I enjoyed the comradeship of my friends and family at the going-away parties. Their unfailing support was important.

My biggest surprise came when my daughter Angela and her husband Brian announced the coming arrival of their first baby. With bated breath, I asked for the due date. I was relieved to hear it was October 16th. Surely I would be home.

Every free moment was spent writing my memoirs of the last three years in the Arctic. I realized I had a 50/50 chance of coming through this adventure alive. Leaving the manuscript up to date meant much to me. My children would have part of the story were I to meet with disaster. As harsh as it may sound, it never hurts to be realistic. I was never one to hide my head in the sand.

My flight was scheduled for June 20th. I wanted to spend a week in Paulatuk with Ken and the friends I had made in 1993. Leaving children and friends behind never gets easier, but the Arctic beckoned.

The evening found me sharing a taxi into Inuvik with a fellow traveller by the name of Harry Wehrens from Oshawa, Ontario. We both had rooms at the Mackenzie Hotel in downtown Inuvik. Harry went to get some rest while I did a quick tour of the town before it closed for the night. We had planned to meet at the Brass Rail, the lounge at the hotel, but I fell into an exhausted sleep upon returning to my room. I slept until morning.

Fog hung heavily over Inuvik on the 21st. From the lobby I phoned Aklak Air to inquire about the flight to Paulatuk at noon. Despite the fog, they would leave as scheduled.

A good-looking, dark-haired fellow overheard my call. "You are luckier than I," he said. "Norman Wells is fogged in so badly that I have to wait until tomorrow." Introductions were made. Dave Wilton, a helicopter pilot, was stationed out of Yellowknife. He had been delayed in Inuvik for yet another day, because of the weather.

"I'm waiting for my friend, Harry," I explained. "Would you like to join us for coffee?"

They couldn't believe what I was attempting to do. Dave insisted on seeing the route I was to take. He carefully studied the map I had in my room and discreetly kept his comments to himself. From the puzzled look he gave me, I understood they weren't all favourable, but I did have some merit for paddling from Fort Providence to Paulatuk on my own.

I studied his face. A chord was struck deep in my heart. He was sure of himself without being the least bit conceited. His gentle, helpful manner pleased me as well. It did not hurt that he had a face that would stop a chorus line.

I hurried away to attend to a list of chores. First it was to the Northern Store for the rest of my supplies. After my attempts at renting an HF radio failed, I was referred to the Coast Guard station. Brian, Kathy, and Wayne were in the office. They suggested I purchase an Emergency Locating Transmitter (ELT). They got me in touch with a company in Vancouver that sold the units. They could send one to Paulatuk for me. I accepted Brian's offer to drive me to the airport. We made a quick stop at the Mackenzie Inn. Dave helped load my gear. At that time I had no way of knowing I would hear from Harry and Dave again. I promised Brian and the rest of the crew at the Coast Guard station that I would inform them of my progress.

I had hoped the fog would clear to allow me to see the landscape below. Only over Franklin Bay did the clouds start to break up. What I saw wasn't promising. The ocean was still solid with ice, except for a narrow open lead here and there. Darnley Bay was the same. The harbour at Paulatuk was open. As we circled for a landing, the butterflies in my stomach started acting up. I stepped off the plane and at once my eyes were drawn to the massive icebergs outside the harbour.

June 21st. The first day of summer. I tilted my head back to smell the ice and the ocean, the true smells of adventure. Through tears of happiness, I saw Ken coming across the tarmac towards me. At last I felt at home again.

The news spread quickly. "Ken's woman is back in town!"

Before long my little friends were at the door. We walked to the Old Lake and they were all chattering at once. We caught up on all their news of the past winter and looked for flounder in Flounder Creek. The fish were too fast for us.

Ken and I had an invitation for dinner at Kelly's apartment. Kelly McVittie was the nurse at the Health Centre.

"I wonder what time it is," I said.

"It's 6:30," Christina, one of my little companions, answered.

"Do you have a watch?" I asked

"Yes," she replied, "in my eyeballs." She was only out by ten minutes.

Supper at Kelly's was a lovely affair. She and her girlfriend, Linda, had made the pasta noodles. To top this treat there was delicious, thick sauce. Homemade bread accompanied the meal. For dessert we enjoyed homemade ice-cream, which we all helped make.

Back at his home Ken presented me with a large package. "This is for you," he said, with a wicked twinkle in his eye. It was an automatic bread-making machine, a reminder of the disastrous results of my bread-making efforts of the previous year. Excited, I was awake long into the night, listening to the heavy rain pelting the window pane.

Fog shrouded the hamlet the next morning. As it lifted, the snow came thick and heavy. The next three days were the same. I was safe and warm, but couldn't ignore the restless pull inside of me. I blamed the wind and the sea for the wanderlust creeping into my soul.

Each day Ken would drive me to the end of the airport runway to check the bergs and the ice-pack. "There is ice out there, Victoria. Why would you want to leave?"

Windsong was hauled out of storage, polished up, and repaired with help from my friends. I was anxious to get on the water. So were the kids. We compromised. I got in some training by taking them for rides up and down the beach in the harbour. They would take turns sitting in the front hatch. Their little faces would light up and make me laugh. The teenagers would do their own paddling. I held on to a safety rope tied to the kayak and ran up and down the beach as they practised. Even Valerie, the R.C.M.P. officer's wife, tried her hand at kayaking. From the start I could tell she wouldn't need the safety rope.

On June 27th I did a test run in the direction of the Hornaday River. I needed to prepare myself mentally for what lay ahead.

Once out of the harbour, there was a narrow swath of open water between the ice-pack and the shoreline. That would be the case for at least twenty miles. The local people were getting through with their powerboats during high tide, travelling to fish camps to do their char fishing.

The nearer I paddled to the icebergs, the more magnificent they looked. They had broken off the polar ice cap and came drifting south. The sun glinted off their transparent, turquoise faces. One can easily be lulled by the serenity of it all, but the lack of total concentration can be lethal in the moving pack ice. I enjoyed the excursion, but the next morning my shoulders ached from the constant jarring as my double-blade connected with the ocean floor on nearly every stroke. Until I passed the Hornaday and Brock River deltas, I would have to follow the tide tables religiously.

I planned my departure for Wednesday, June 29th. I hoped two more days and nights of sunlight would keep the temperature above freezing.

The media caught up with me in Paulatuk. Lynn Nicol of CBC Radio phoned for an interview, as did Ronna Bremer of *News North*, a widely read paper in the North. A simple trip for my own pleasure had now blossomed and involved many people who would be following the progress closely. I could sense the extra pressure, but vowed that safety alone would be my guideline. I accepted the responsibility for the consequences of my decisions, whether it be defeat or success.

June 29th. The weather cooperated. The day dawned sunny and hot. I wasn't in such grand shape. I awoke tired and hung-over. Ken and I had toasted and talked into the wee hours. On his coffee break Ken delivered my kayak and

350 pounds of gear to the harbour shore. "That can't possibly fit into your kayak," were his parting words.

The news got around. Various people came by to see the pile of gear. They all left with mirth around their eyes. Amazingly enough, everything fit. Every cubic inch of space was used. Can the red-headed Kabloona pack or what? I got a few warm handshakes after that feat.

Windsong was ready. The wind rose, sending whitecaps across the harbour. There was nothing to do but wait. Renee and her nephews Lee and Michael Wolki came over for tea. Sadie and her children Bobbi and Michael dropped by after Ken came home from work. It was a warm parting from some very special friends. Ken went to power-nap. I paced the floor and watched the ocean and the sky. By 11:00 p.m. the water was settling. Instinct told me the time was right. Windsong slipped heavily into the water but managed to stay afloat, to Ken's utter amazement.

I wasn't allowed to say goodbye, because it would sound too permanent. Instead, it was "until we meet again." I paddled away from Paulatuk at 11:30 p.m. on the 29th of June. Ken was left standing on the shore. It was too hard to look back. We had been drawn together by the mysterious bond of comfort and kindness. His wonderful characteristics and support were a shelter to my soul during my stay. I paddled hard, seeking to bring my emotions under some semblance of control.

Icebergs were glowing in the light of the midnight sun. Two hours later I spotted the landmark of the first fish camp. It was the tail of an Air Canada plane that had stopped short of the Paulatuk runway. It stands upright, embedded on a sand bar in the ocean.

A white canvas tent was set up on the beach. Joe and Lynn Illasiak, a young couple with three little girls, were busy cleaning their day's catch. Already filleted char, red as sunset, hung in uniform rows to dry in the wind. I asked for permission to camp nearby. They welcomed me and invited me for coffee and char. We talked late into the morning. I was thankful to crawl into my sleeping bag and warm up. A cold wind was blowing from the edge of the ice-field a couple of hundred feet away.

Joe helped me with the maps. "Stay fifty feet to the inside of the sand bars," he instructed. "That is where you'll find the deepest water." How thankful I was for that information. It served me well.

I pushed away from shore amid best wishes for a safe journey and flying kisses from the little girls. A present of dried char was safely stored in the cockpit.

Near the Hornaday River the water became even more shallow. The sand bars were some distance apart and barely showed above the water. The heat rising from the sand bars was creating a mist when it mixed with the cold air from the ice. Although I couldn't see the bars, I would head toward the patches of mist and this way was able to navigate to the north end of the Hornaday delta.

Deeper water was a relief. Twelve miles of shallows was enough. My shoulders ached. Deeper water and fewer sand bars also meant that the pack-ice could come in closer to shore. I had just spotted the second fish camp when the ice started moving in. I began weaving my way in and out of the pancakes until I was even with the camp. Ahead the ice-field was jammed hard against the shore and stretched to the horizon. There was nothing to do but pull out.

It wasn't the best place to stop. Grizzly bear tracks were all over the beach. Long claw marks showed on the steep bank leading to the open den. With shotgun in hand, I climbed the bank to the white canvas tent above. The door was open. Nothing inside was disturbed. Even a pat of margarine still remained on the table. Half of the back wall was missing. A quick check showed it had been ripped open by the grizzly. I kept my eyes peeled. I gained some comfort from the caribou who were grazing peacefully nearby. With their incredible eyesight, they would surely spot the grizzly before I did.

I retreated a half mile to the mouth of a little creek. From there it would be easier to scan the tundra. The ice was moving in quickly on the rising tide. Half paddling, half dragging Windsong, I made it back to the creek. I set up the tent, watched, and waited for the ice to move or the grizzly to show.

Fresh tracks led southward along the beach. I followed them as they meandered from the water's edge across the beach to the four-foot bank and back. He was obviously scavenging and ripping at the ground squirrels' burrows as he went. More than likely he would be returning from that direction. I counted off fifty paces from the tent. I laid a line of driftwood across the beach. This would serve as a marker if I needed to use the flare gun. I found it to be quite accurate at that range. I explored the tundra some. Oil cans, old boots, rusty stoves, and just plain old garbage were scattered about. Obviously the area was well used.

I memorized all the dark objects. Having them in my mind gave me a better chance to distinguish the grizzly, should he appear. On the way back I found parts of an airtight stove. I hauled it to my campsite and assembled it. There was only one lid missing. It would be great for cooking. The beach was strewn with driftwood. I could save my fuel. The half litre of oil I found would serve as lighter fuel. Once camp was set it appeared very homey. A white plastic pail was my chair, a piece of plywood my table. The crackling flames inside the stove relaxed me and the smoke kept the mosquitoes away. The south wind cooperated by blowing all the scents to the sea. The south wind was also good news. Perhaps by morning a lead would open near shore.

July 1st. Happy birthday, Canada!

There had been significant ice movement during the night. By 5:30 a.m. Windsong was back in the water. Through binoculars I could see open water toward the Brock River. Two miles later I was cut off by the jammed ice-pack. Lack of an accessible landing spot forced me to return to the original camp.

The reversing tide brought the ice back thicker and tighter. Wait again and watch. This was grizzly country. The question was not whether I would meet a grizzly, but when, and under what circumstances.

The heat lulled me into a deep sleep. I came to with a jolt. I held my breath and listened. I was surrounded by a totally unnatural stillness. The tent stood motionless. The ice was stilled, not a ripple licked the shore, not a cloud moved. Not a ground squirrel scolded, not a bird chirped, nor did a blade of grass move. It was deathly quiet.

"This must be what it's like to be deaf," I thought to myself.

I found the silence unnerving. I decided to make tea, just for the sake of activity. I had bent to gather driftwood when my eyes locked on to movement a quarter mile away.

Grizzly!

I watched him. Old, powerful, huge, the undisputed master of the tundra.

I had no desire to shoot him, but I readied my shotgun by pumping a slug into the chamber. I dropped extra shells into my pocket, as per instructions from my coach. I assembled the rest of my arsenal. The flare gun was loaded with a noise-maker. My air horn and bear spray were within reach. Then I added my hatchet.

I was prepared to stake my life to see the Arctic, but I didn't want it to end two days out of Paulatuk. There was still so much to see.

Windsong was at the water's edge. While there wasn't enough open water for an escape, the kayak would be safer floating free of shore. I tied a long rope to her and gave her a shove out to sea. The tent was left standing to give me more size.

The grizzly was still approaching, stopping to tear at the burrows of the ground squirrels. Before long he discovered the scent of my footprints. Whether it would give me an advantage or disadvantage, I was not sure. He followed them onto the tundra, inspecting articles I had handled. He lifted his head and swung it from side to side, trying to pick up my scent.

He returned to the beach. His manner changed. He became more intense and came on with a purpose. I had to wait for him to get into range.

"Take a deep breath, Victoria," I commanded myself. I couldn't have my hands shaking if I had to use the shotgun.

He approached the driftwood marker. When he stepped over it, I fired the first flare. Nothing. I tightened it. Silence! "Oh Lord, a dud."

With fumbling fingers I reloaded, one eye on the advancing grizzly.

I aimed the flare between him and the water, hoping to drive him onto the tundra, away from the tent. He stopped for a moment and glanced toward the ocean. It was apparent he was accustomed to the crack and explosion of sea-ice. He was not startled in the least.

I sent out a silent prayer, "Please don't make me shoot you!"

I fired the second flare closer to his front feet. He reared back, swivelled, and scrambled up the bank to the tundra and disappeared.

Tense moments passed. My heart was pounding in my ears. One, two, three deep breaths and wait. Would he take the draw southward to the hills or would he come at me over the rise? I waited one excruciating minute after another until I spotted him ambling the hollows towards the hills.

I sank to the sand to keep my knees from knocking. I noticed I was covered by mosquitoes. I wished it were as easy to get rid of them.

I was enjoying a leisurely breakfast in the stifling heat of morning when I noticed a lane of water opening between the pack and the shore. I was on the way, glad to leave the grizzly to his territory. As I approached the Brock River Delta, the water became extremely shallow. Often heavily-laden Windsong grounded out. It was either tow her through or search for deeper channels. I was thankful to have my ski pole along to lean on. The movement of the water and Windsong bouncing against my leg made me dizzy.

Once I turned northeast across the top of the delta the water became deeper. A mile of stranded bergs made for an incredible sight. They contrasted sharply with the sand dunes on shore and the royal blue of the water. I wound in and out amongst them, my mouth open in awe. Loons kept me company. I pulled to shore just to stand on the sand and make sure it wasn't an illusion. On the opposite side of the sand bar the Brock Lagoon stretched for miles to the rolling hills that framed it. Heat waves were rising from the land, making everything look fuzzy. I settled near the ice with my lunch.

I carried on in T-shirt and shorts. Two miles past the opening to the Brock Lagoon I caught up with the ice-pack. There was great movement within the pack. I was certain I would soon continue. I backtracked a mile and set up camp on the fine sand. It was much too hot for clothes. The sun beat down with such fierce intensity that even the mosquitoes disappeared. The tundra stretched flat and wide. No object rose high enough to cast shade. For relief, I'd wade out amid the ice for a quick swim.

The blinding glare off the white ice-field was causing my eyes to water. Having all that ice around meant I didn't have to search for fresh water. Gravity pulls the salt brine from the surface of the ice. The fresh layer can be safely used for drinking water. A pot of ice melted quickly in the heat of the day.

A piece of birch bark, a beaver-chewed log, and a ladybug on my arm all made me miss my home and family. My daughters would be attending my nephew Owen's wedding in Norquay, Saskatchewan, this day. I was missing the family gathering.

By midnight I was on the water again. The ice was moving quickly now. Six miles later it came to a standstill once more. I had to do some landscaping in order to set up the tent. The wind rose and I slept soundly in the coolness.

Silence awoke me. The ice was out of sight, the ocean absolutely still. The paddling was fine. I wove in and out among the stragglers from the ice-pack. Before long it was back to T-shirt and rad-pants in the heat. The scenery changed dramatically from low tundra to massive cliffs at the water's edge. The water was mirror-like. The cliffs stood on the edge of their own inverted images in perfect reflection. The stranded floes were a variety of blues and greens. The droplets of water falling off their edges supplied the only sound. So perfect was the scene that I rested my paddle. To disturb this tranquillity would have been a sin.

Ahead, Halcro Point jutted far into the ocean. I had hoped to pass it within the hour, but the tide had stabilized and the ice-pack was jammed solidly against the point. I had to retreat to the first accessible beach, two miles back, and wait once more. The pack was on the move again with help from a strong south wind. For the third time that day, I dismantled the tent and followed. ice-floes were piled high at the base of the rugged cliffs bordering Halcro Point. I paddled in the coolness of their shadow. Once the ice-pack passed the point, it dispersed into the open ocean. In another hour I would be out of Darnley Bay.

July 3rd. At midnight I was rounding Cape Lyon, the most northerly point in my 1994 trip. From now on I would be heading eastward.

The cliffs surrounding the cape were stunning, as were the icebergs offshore. The low midnight sun fired their glistening edges blood red. The waves picked up the colour, making the ocean dance with energy and life. Meltwater from a berg's crown was cascading over the edge to drop in an arc to the ocean below in a supreme example of nature's artwork. I was spell-bound, but I couldn't linger. The wicked current and increasing wind soon had all my attention.

A five-mile-wide bay lay behind the cape. The friendly beaches beckoned. I landed and lay on the gravel, dwelling on the wonders I had witnessed. By 4:30 a.m. I was forced to seek shelter from the wind in a small gravel cove bordered by high, crumbling buttes. From my door I could see the towering arch of Pearce Point.

Every day nature determined how much time I would be granted on the water. I awoke when the surf and wind were stilled, and slept soundly when it was too rough to travel. My mind was geared to the changing sounds in the environment. I began to trust my intuition. I developed an acute sense of awareness. It was reassuring since my survival depended on it.

July 4th. After a hurried lunch I paddled through the arch on my way around Pearce Point. I wanted to take advantage of the offshore winds. I would have the warmth off the tundra and calm waters near shore. Pearce Harbour caught me by surprise. I didn't realize I was so near. Half of it was still locked in ice. The island in the harbour that had a tunnel through its midst was inaccessible. I had planned years ago to paddle through it if I ever got the chance.

In the next cove I stopped to watch a small herd of caribou pass. Sharing the tundra were Canada geese. Each pair had a couple of fluffy yellow goslings to tend. My presence caused quite a ruckus. I left quickly and followed the long sandy beaches all the way to House Point. A couple of abandoned houses made a picturesque scene. The offshore islands were towering and stark, bordered by brilliant white bergs floating in the turquoise waters. Beautiful but so isolated.

Many polar bear skulls lay on the tundra. My grandson Garrett would have been interested in them. House Point is connected to the islands by a narrow reef at low tide. I removed a few rocks and pulled Windsong through to open water on the other side. There were many jellyfish in the cold water. One lone seal led me away from House Point. I had to stop and glance back. What sort of person did it take to live in a place like that?

Caribou browsed along the shore. Their bodies blended completely with the tundra, but their magnificent racks gave them away. Sand beaches gave way to cliffs. Nature had whittled fanciful shapes in their walls. Waves sloshed within the caverns, while narrow clefts formed an intricate network of passages. The child in me enticed me to follow the passages. Small, secluded caves held the last of the winter's snow. As my eyes became accustomed to the shadows, I spotted movement in a cave. My double-blade scraped the canyon wall as I drifted nearer. The noise startled the caribou inside. He had been seeking relief from the mosquitoes. He slipped silently into an obscure passage and disappeared. Each section of cliffs seemed more spectacular than the last. Their colours and textures varied, but the arches and caverns amazed me the most. Then came the not-so-friendly stretch past Keat's Point. The weather held, but for miles and miles there weren't any landing spots. The cliffs were not high, but the snow made them dangerous. It was hard-packed from the water's edge to the top of the cliff. I don't imagine it ever completely melts away.

Streaks of clouds were building in the northwest. I spotted a narrow crevasse in the snowbank. It was only about twelve feet wide, but it would do. A fair-sized iceberg was stranded in front. It would calm the water for the takeout. A ledge of flat rock provided easy access. Three tiers formed the bank. The first was covered in slippery rocks, the second in driftwood, and the third was tundra. I chose the second and cleared enough driftwood to make room for the tent. The kayak had to stay at water level. I didn't like the set-up, but that's all there was.

Caribou grazed peacefully nearby, their young at their sides. A tour didn't reveal any bear tracks. Down below, the icebergs reflected the sun's glow. Far to the north the pack ice lined the horizon in white. The notorious Northwest Passage lay at my feet.

I set the alarm on the hour for every hour. One quick peek at the kayak, and I would fall asleep again. Morning found me with a case of the slows. I blamed it on the interrupted sleep. I sat half in and half out of my tent, contemplating breakfast. I glanced down between my feet at a flower that had opened overnight. As I reached back into the tent for the camera, movement caught my eye.

A huge grizzly was no more that 25 feet away. His mind was on ripping apart the row of driftwood, or maybe it was a show of strength to get a reaction from the blue blob in his path.

Quickly, I loaded a noise-maker and fired. Not even a pop. It dawned on me that I had dropped the dud back in with the good flares. The shotgun was out of the question. If he decided to charge, he would close the distance before the slug left the barrel. Truthfully, I did not know if I possessed the will to pull the trigger on that magnificent beast.

I reloaded and paused for two deep breaths. I only had one chance. I knew the flares shouldn't be fired into the ground, but I had no choice. If I put a flare past him, he would come towards me. I aimed for the pile of driftwood in front of him. The explosion sent him reeling backwards. In a split second he vanished. Shotgun in hand, I dashed to the tundra above. His brown rump was just a blur in the distance. My grandson Keith would have been proud of me.

My appetite disappeared with the bear. Instead of relaxing and regaining my composure, I started packing up to leave. As soon as I removed all the stones holding the tent down, a gust of wind picked the fully-set-up tent off the ledge and sent it careening down toward the ocean. Barefoot, with double-blade in hand, I sprinted after it, swatting at it with my blade. Over the wood, over the slippery rocks, over the snow. How I survived the descent without broken limbs or neck I'll never figure out. The tent landed right side up in the water. The suction on the floor held it down until I retrieved it. That episode scared me more than the bear had. All it took was one moment of carelessness.

Water has a way of relaxing me. Back in the kayak the tension slowly left my muscles. Two miles later I rounded a point. Spread for miles ahead was a shallow bay with gravel beaches. The wretched stretch of cliffs was behind me. At the end of the bay were more cliffs. Those rose sheer out of the water. Caves, caverns, and an arch at the distant point adorned the face. A waterfall cascaded over rocks and down to the beach. It was a wonderful, peaceful place for breakfast and refilling my water bottles. If I had had a little more faith, I wouldn't have spent the night on that lousy ledge.

With a peanut-butter-and-jam sandwich in hand I went to lean against the cliff. I revelled in the shade, sensing the texture of the rock, feeling the coolness through my clothes. I leaned my head back to absorb some of the strength, to stand firm like a rock. I closed my eyes and the troubles melted away.

The sea remained calm. I passed through the arch and in and out of the caverns. There's more kid in me than I thought. The cliffs were spaced apart now, with good beaches in between. I started singing just to hear the echo bounce off the walls. Further down the shore I came upon another grizzly chewing on a smelly carcass. I was glad it wasn't mine. He noticed me at once. Rearing onto his hind legs, he maneuvered to catch my scent.

"Ah, buzz off!" I yelled. I had had enough of grizzlies for one day.

Rounding Deas Thompson Point I changed my direction abruptly to southeast. I was dropping down into the Dolphin and Union Strait. A few minor cliffs bordered the shore, then nothing but long stretches of high-banked gravel shores. Small streams spilled into the ocean. Through the breaks I would get a glimpse of the lush tundra valleys and rolling hills behind them. Mount Hooker, veiled in haze, was visible on the southern horizon for most of the day. I pulled out to make supper at 6:30. No sooner had I set out my gear than two caribou came at a full trot towards me from opposite directions. I wasn't sure what to expect. I grabbed the air horn just in case. When they were only a foot apart they each took a long pee and immediately bolted back in the direction from which they had come. They had been so close I could have slapped their rumps. I wondered if that was how they treated all trespassers.

At 8:00 p.m. I beached in front of the Clinton Point DEW Line Station.

After changing into dry clothes, I climbed the hill to the site. I hoped someone might be there so I might call home, but the complex was boarded up tightly. It was eerie to walk past the silent buildings where so many people had worked. The hilltop view left me speechless. Caribou roamed freely across the roads. A lone arctic fox limped through the grounds. My hopes dashed, I walked back to my camp. The wind changed direction, and before long the heavy surf was crashing onto the shore.

Through the night the sea kept rising. By morning I had to move both tent and kayak to higher ground. I was shore-bound for the day. The time was spent washing my hair, doing chores, and listening to cassettes to dull the roar of the surf. I had been lucky so far. The offshore ice pack had kept the sea fairly calm, although this day the ice was not visible on the horizon. I was sure I hadn't seen the last of it, since I could smell it in the wind. I would have to make better time too. The scenery had been so fascinating that I had spent too much time stopping and gawking. I would have to pick up the pace if I were to make it to Coppermine by the 15th of July.

The surf had calmed somewhat by 5:00 a.m. and I decided to chance a launch. As far as I could see the beaches looked friendly enough. I could always pull out if I had trouble. I timed the waves and only got part of a wave into the cockpit before I fastened the spray skirt. It was no big deal. I'd been wet before.

A twelve-hour paddle took me past a multitude of small creeks and rivers to within eight miles of the Crocker River. The openings to the tundra never ceased to astound me. I hoped to spy musk-oxen on the land, but there were only caribou. The short chop on the water had taken a toll on my energy. The waves were hitting hard on the shore. I scanned the beaches, mile after mile, for a takeout. Then my chance came. A long iceberg was wedged against the beach. Windsong glided in behind, to still water.

A perfect landing and a beautiful spot. I was at the mouth of a small, unnamed river. The beach was of warm sand. A mat of purple and white flowers covered the tundra. Erosion had cut deep gorges in the sand. It was a spectacular contrast between delicate and rugged! A tour of the campsite showed many caribou tracks and those of geese and polar bears. I had been watching for grizzlies in the last while. The sight of polar bear tracks stunned me at first. I shouldn't have been surprised, since the ice was not far away. If one was riding the pack, a stop on shore was not out of the question.

My cold supper of granola, cheese, and a chocolate bar kept food odours to a minimum. I fell asleep to the sound of the waves hitting the undercut of the berg. The violent explosion of the berg splitting woke me. In one swift motion I was out of my sleeping bag and through the door. That whittled a few years off my life.

The Crocker River was fast and wild. The many channels of the delta spread to a four-mile width, carrying much silt and discolouring the ocean. I skirted the mouth at a distance to avoid the sand bars. It was the first river to have such volume and strength.

July 8th. The sea was calm and a haze veiled the horizon. It was a perfect paddling day. I was happy about the accessible gravel shores. They were high enough to block my view of the low tundra behind. When curiosity would get the best of me, I would land, walk up, and scan the area.

The pack ice was back on the northern horizon, but only a number of bergs or large floes floated freely nearby. They added to the seascape. In the afternoon, dark, threatening storm clouds loomed in the south. The claps of thunder spooked the caribou, causing them to dash erratically about the tundra. Caribou were very plentiful in the area. Most had young at their sides and spent much time at the water's edge to gain some relief from the flies and mosquitoes. They would run for great distances along the edge of the water to splash the bugs off their legs, then promptly flop down with their legs under their bodies. Although they'd spot me from a great distance, they barely gave me a second thought. Abandoned buildings caught my attention. A derelict schooner was beached nearby. Fuel drums littered the area. I hoped to outrun the storm, so I didn't stop to explore. I set camp minutes before the deluge came. Large heavy drops made the ocean's surface vibrate. Between showers I refilled my water containers from a small pond on the tundra, made my supper, and burned all my garbage. The caribou were taking advantage of the smoke so I tossed extra seaweed on the fire. As the fire died I covered the pit with sand.

Flat tundra and gravel stretched to the horizon in three directions. I fell asleep to the comforting patter of rain on the tent. Caribou milled around. Calves cavorted playfully among the adults. I became accustomed to the sharp, quick raps of their hooves on the gravel.

I was brought out of my slumber by the scrunch of heavy footsteps on gravel, inches from my head. The skin at the back of my neck began to tighten. Long ago I had learned to awaken without moving, opening my eyes to orient myself and tuning my ears to the sounds around me. I held my breath, heart pounding, all senses alert.

It is best to trust your fear. With one hand on the air horn, I quietly unzipped the door. A glance at the kayak showed nothing amiss. I relaxed for a second. "You had to be dreaming, Victoria," I told myself.

Then came a disgusted snort, and the scrunch, scrunch came nearer again. Slowly, I unzipped the rear window. The big rump of a grizzly passed by a few feet away.

Knowing that only a thin wall of nylon separated me from a grizzly's claws galvanized me into action. I went out the front, pronto, on hands and knees. A glance over the tent showed the huge grizzly heading back to the tundra. His blank, backward stare will be indelible in my mind. The situation was not entirely comfortable. I watched as he blended back into the tundra as silently as he had come.

The fire pit was torn apart. It had been three hours since I had put the fire out, and it had been rained on too. He had come directly to it to satisfy his curiosity, but his only reward was a scorched paw. And maybe the satisfaction of nearly making me crap my undies. I didn't linger any longer than necessary.

The Inman is another powerful river entering the ocean. It flows through a very scenic valley of towering canyon walls, and divides into many channels near its mouth. A cabin sat high on one of the branches. It would have been an interesting place to stop. The fishing would have been excellent, but I couldn't even attempt to tackle the current. Besides, I was counting on making it to Cape Young forty miles away. I understood the DEW Line station there was still operational. It would be nice to phone the girls. I had so much to tell them.

The ocean was calm after the storm. I could see free-floating jellyfish and the landscape of the ocean's floor. The ice-field was moving closer. More bergs rode the currents. My spirits were high.

I caught sight of the *Nechilak,* an iron-bodied vessel, at the foot of a section of high, crumbling buttes. Tossed ashore and wrecked many years ago by a vicious Arctic storm, it made for a very scenic, although tragic, photograph. Its rusty hull added colour to the landscape. From the cliffs falcons screamed at the intrusion into their territory.

Rounding Cape Young was a battle. I had to maneuver among shallows, rocks, and stranded floes. The wind had increased and I was soaked to the skin, chilled, and tired. I landed at the foot of the site. The station was boarded up and silent. The disappointment was heavy. I consoled myself with the fact that six more good paddling days would bring me into Coppermine. Mother Nature had her own ideas.

The ice-pack started crowding the shore when I left Cape Young. I was worried about Stapleton Bay at Cape Hope and South Bay at Cape Bexley. Both very deep bays, they face northwest into the Dolphin and Union Strait. They could be jammed full of ice.

Ice blocked the mouth of Stapleton but was moving out slowly. I squeezed my way into the bay along the shoreline and dipped down for about four miles. Once I got behind the pack I made the six-mile crossing, allowing plenty of room for the huge floes to pass. Clinging to the opposite shore, I made my way to the top and rounded Cape Hope.

That was easy, but when I reached the entrance to South Bay the pack was streaming out heavier and tighter. I climbed a cliff. There was open water behind the pack. I started making my way in, weaving in and out among the floes near shore, even dragging Windsong over some. I got to the bottom of the pack, but not before the fickle Arctic wind reversed and the ice all moved back in. There was nothing to do but get out of its way and wait.

The northwest wind brought cold temperatures and overcast skies. The ice churned, growled, and packed tighter and tighter. The temperature dropped. The ocean started to congeal between the cakes of ice. For 2½ days I waited for the right combination of wind and tide. Many seals appeared. I watched carefully for polar bears.

On the third day, I decided to walk the four miles back to Cape Hope. With Windsong in tow, I hopped from floe to floe. She sure is one tough little craft. My double-blade took a beating too as I used it to push cakes out of the way or slow them down. Whenever I could, I'd walk the beach and line the kayak through the shallows. The sun had come out. My clothes dried quickly and my neoprene booties kept my feet warm even on the ice. At the front of the pack I used driftwood logs to skid Windsong to high ground.

The tent was set securely against a cliff and heavily weighed down by rocks. I didn't like the look of the sky to the northwest. I made my campfire inside a small alcove in the cliff. What I needed was tea, hot and sweet. For supper I chose Knorr's cream of asparagus soup. When it was hot and thick, I added half a cup of couscous. Like an eagle, I sat on my perch in the cliff, ate, and watched my kingdom below.

The breakers came rolling in. Loose floes were lifting and grinding into the shore rocks. At the point the waves were splitting, sending foam hurtling through the air in an astonishing display of power.

I planned my strategy. I would need at least one hour and fifteen minutes to make the six-mile crossing to Cape Bexley. I would need a west wind to keep the ice in the bay. I couldn't risk having it move out while I was in front of it. An incoming tide would also help.

By the time I undressed for bed, my legs were turning black and blue – the price to pay for misjudging the distance between ice-floes and the length of tow rope in my hand.

The water was still fairly rough at 4:00 a.m., but the tide and wind were right. "Hang in there, Windsong. We are going to make it." Pushing off from shore, I set my sights on the beacon at Cape Bexley.

As I passed the cape I gave wide berth to the icebergs stranded there. It was good to be on the way and heading southeast. The coast was lined with broken ice-floes, but there was plenty of open water among the pack ice. I was thankful the ice was keeping the water fairly calm, since landing spots were at a premium. Concentration and good lift from the water made the forty miles pass quickly. Before I knew it, I was paddling into Bernard Harbour. I held my breath and paddled slowly, trying to picture what it was like when it was the cherished home of the Coppermine Eskimo. Then the missionaries came, bringing frightening diseases to which the people had no immunity. Those who survived moved to the present sight of Coppermine to save what was left of their race.

I chose a long, narrow gravel island at the south entrance of the harbour for my camp. The flightless Canada geese waddled off to the far end of the island and settled down once they realized I meant no harm. My clothes dried quickly in the heat. They were becoming stiffer by the day from the caked salt in them. Tomorrow I could be at Locker Point, if I could manage 45 miles.

Then another sixty to Coppermine. Only 2½ days more. I drifted off to sleep, smiling to myself.

The varied scenery kept me fascinated mile after mile. As I entered the Lambert Channel the current increased. The ice was moving fast, but was still far enough off shore not to be a threat to me. Rounding a bend I caught sight of a beautiful waterfall. It tumbled through a little canyon over rocks to the ocean's edge. Hanging gardens drooped from the ledges. It was a little oasis in the midst of gravel and rock. To wash the salt off my face, drink my fill, and replenish my water supply was refreshing. I climbed to the top of the waterfall to find it originated from a huge lake on the tundra. Lush and green, the ground was covered in dazzling meadow flowers. Paradise was made for fools like me. Should I linger? No, Locker Point was waiting.

Past Cape Lambert the water was more congested with ice. It choked the entrance to Pasley Cove. I chanced a crossing. Many tries and many retreats brought me to the opposite shore. Caribou glanced with curiosity at the strange contraption in the water.

I was making good time along the coast of Cape Krusenstern. The sound of a powerboat captured my attention. I spied the boat and waved. The boat swerved. The man at the outboard stood up and grabbed a gun, and the boat disappeared behind the bend.

"How bad do I look? Is this an ambush?" I slowed my pace and cautiously proceeded. The boat was snugged up to a rock ledge at the base of some cliffs. A family was getting out. The man waved me in.

"Come join us for tea," he called. "I just shot a caribou. I'm going up on the cliff to butcher it." I paddled closer, relieved. He steadied the kayak while I got out.

I glanced up at his face. "Jerry?"

"Yes," he answered.

"In 1992 you offered me an arctic char when I was leaving Coppermine," I reminded him.

"Of course, the Kabloona in the yellow kayak. What a surprise! Come and meet my wife and family," he said.

Jerry's wife, Susan, was a dear lady. In moments she made me feel welcome. Miranda, about eight or nine, was their oldest daughter. She was still giggling from the caribou episode. She had seen the caribou first and turned in her seat and shouted "Tuktu" into her father's face. In one fluid motion he had swerved the boat, stood up with gun in hand, fired from the wildly pitching vessel, and of course brought the caribou down.

"You're quite a marksman," I complimented him.

He downplayed it. "I'm used to it."

The other children were two-year-old Andrew and Robin, who was one. I tried to keep them occupied while Susan made tea and Jerry and Miranda disappeared over the cliff to dress the caribou. Their warm company took the chill out of my bones, as did the hot tea. It was good to hear a human voice again.

Jerry set up his radio and called Coppermine to let the R.C.M.P. know I was alive and well. Word about the Kabloona in the kayak spread quickly over the radio waves. I couldn't understand what was said except for "Kabloona" and "kayak," but I could see the amusement in Jerry's face as he repeated the story time and again. "Paulatuk, eiyah, Paulatuk!"

I was due in Coppermine this day according to my plans, but it wasn't important any more. My family would get the news that I was only 1½ days away.

Susan was busy dressing the children warmly in winter parkas and pants. They would be heading eighteen miles across the Dolphin and Union Straits to Lady Franklin Point on Victoria Island. Then they would visit family at a hunting camp. I looked at the swiftly moving pack ice in the Northwest Passage and the faintly visible domes of the Lady Franklin DEW Line Station on the distant coast of Victoria Island and marvelled at their courage. Jerry presented me with a choice piece of caribou as we said goodbye.

The Atatahak family disappeared into the field of ice. As the sound of the boat's motor faded, I bowed my head for a moment to pray for their safe journey.

I gently pushed Windsong away from the rock ledge. She was sucked quickly into the incredible current and I paddled hard to match the speed. A shoulder-check revealed floes overtaking me in the passing lane. Not a comfortable situation, to say the least. I was ready for relief by the time the end of the cliffs came into view. A large bay opened to the right. I ruddered out of the current, rested my double-blade across the cockpit, and watched the current veer off across the bay, sucking the ice along with it. A few cakes were jostled out of the current, to be left behind, twirling in the calmer water.

I set my sights on Locker Point twelve miles away. Three hours of paddling would get me there by midnight, giving me a 45-mile day. I was tired. Paddling leisurely, I enjoyed the friendly landscape to the fullest. Sight of the beacon at Locker Point brought renewed energy. As I neared the point, to my dismay I found ice blocking my route. There was nothing to do but retreat westward, find a break, and try to get in between the pack and shore. This I did, but it involved wading and towing. Getting in and out so many times was the most tiring. My cramped leg muscles would barely cooperate.

Dark objects appeared on the tundra in line with the beacon. Musk-oxen? No, probably fuel drums. My eyes weren't focusing too well. I had to pay full attention to my footing on the floes. There was open water ahead. I settled into the cockpit for the paddle around the point. In my enthusiasm I cut it too sharply and grounded in the shallows. With more moans and groans I exited the cockpit, picked up the tow rope, and started wading again.

Movement caught my attention. The pillars at the base of the beacon tower all started to move. Nausea started to crowd me. The ice was moving, the water was rippling, Windsong was rocking against my leg, the storm clouds were moving, and now the pillars were moving. I brushed my sleeve across my eyes and looked again toward the midnight sun and the pillars. Not pillars, people!

One stepped forward from the group.

I beached Windsong as he spoke. "You must be the paddling grand-mother."

"How do you know I'm a grandmother?" I retorted in surprise.

Something familiar about his voice made me look more carefully.

"Joe? Joe Allan from Coppermine?" I asked incredulously.

It was his turn to be surprised. "In 1992 on the beach at Coppermine, you helped me with my maps and told me about your own kayak," I reminded him. Recognition flooded his face. Our hands met in mid-air, clasping warm and hard. "The same Kabloona and the yellow kayak," he uttered.

"Yep! The same," I agreed, as he led me to meet his family.

I was pleased to meet Allan's wife, Suzy, his two little daughters, and Joe Junior, his son. Suzy's parents, Roy and Kate Inuptaliak, were also travelling with them. They were on their way to Bernard Harbour to do some caribou hunting and had stopped for tea on the shore of Locker Point. Within minutes my hands were full of delicious bannock and dried char, and a mug of steaming, sweet tea was balanced between my knees. With big smiles they kept encouraging me to eat. I must have looked half-starved. I had forgotten to stop for supper and now it was already midnight.

"Did you see the musk-ox?" they asked.

"No, where?" I wondered.

"Here, on the rise. We could see you coming through the ice and thought you would see them better than we could," they answered.

"I did see something I thought was fuel drums," I told them. I was disappointed at missing my first encounter with musk-oxen. Perhaps I would see them, come morning.

Both big boats were readied for the continuation of the hunting trip. Goodbyes were warm. What a coincidence it had been to meet two special people whom I knew, in such a short space of time.

The alarm clock sounded much too early. Thick, heavy fog hung low over tundra and ocean, obscuring the shoreline. With a sigh of relief I curled up in my sleeping bag and dozed off to sleep again.

Morning tea in hand, I sat on the beach and watched the fog rise to expose a serene turquoise sea, frosted with ice. Across 36 miles of open water lay my destination of Coppermine, but I couldn't chance it. I would rather do the 52 miles along the coast and be in a better position to pull out in case of trouble.

A check of the tundra revealed no sign of musk-oxen, although fresh droppings were numerous. Clumps of fog still floated by. I set Windsong on a course that would keep me within sight of land at all times. The morning breeze shifted, bringing heavier fog. I didn't like paddling in it. Suddenly a helicopter emerged out of the fog. I headed in. Three or four cabins and a tent popped out next. A long-legged fellow sat on an overturned pail, enjoying his coffee. He seemed lost in his thoughts. I beached and called out as I approached, so as not to alarm him.

"Care for coffee?" he asked. How good that sounded. It would be my first cup of coffee since Paulatuk. Coffee and peanut butter cookies.

I met the rest of the team. They were on a goose-banding project. Marc was the pilot of the Bell Jet Ranger and Murch the engineer. In the cabin I met Dr. Bob Bromley, a waterfowl biologist for the Northwest Territories. Mike Johnson, a Game and Fish migratory game-bird management supervisor, was all the way from Bismarck, North Dakota. Roy and Isaac Klengenberg were their two guides from Coppermine.

The two hours I spent with them were a pleasure. The sun burnt its way through the fog as they walked me to the kayak. Roy tried it out for size. His grin extended the full width of his face. If his ancestors could see him now!

As I turned to leave, an Inuit fellow from another camp extended his hand silently and placed an orange in my palm. Our eyes met and held. He could understand how grateful I was. He nodded slightly in acknowledgement. Kindness like this tugs strongly on the heartstrings. I paddled away amid the click of camera shutters.

Riding the current and making terrific time, I came upon Cape Hearne without realizing it. I recognized the familiar snowplough formation of the height of land, the familiar coves, and the river where I resupplied my drinking water and saw my first grizzly tracks. All this rekindled the affectionate and later heartbreaking memories of my attempt to reach Tuktoyaktuk in 1992. From here to Coppermine I would not need the map. It was all recorded in my head.

I was heading into serious pack ice again. Some of it I skirted, some I wove through. Klengenberg Bay was packed solid, as was most of the bay behind Cape Kendall. I had two choices. I could camp and wait or work my way through the pack in a direct line to Cape Kendall twelve miles away. Beyond the cape, eleven miles to the south, lay Coppermine. The lure was too strong. Against my better judgment, I started to snake my way through the narrow passages. I was encouraged when the lanes between the ice became more spacious. The sea lay calm, stilled by the weight of the ice. The coolness was refreshing. Seals raised their heads from the floes only long enough to watch me pass. They didn't even seem to mind my singing. Two hours later the floes were more tightly packed. It became more and more difficult to find a way through. Then one-quarter mile from Cape Kendall the ice became a solid mass. I searched for a break in the pack but found none. I was so close.

I anxiously watched a disturbance in the western sky that might develop into trouble. The seals were becoming skittish. Something was brewing. Gut instinct told me not to waste any time making a fast retreat. The closest shore with a possible landing spot was four miles back. By 2:00 a.m. Windsong was safely on shore. Huge clouds spread across the sky, hiding the sun. I had only enough time to set up the tent and make a quick cup of tea over the campfire before the rain came. I fell asleep to the sound of it sizzling on the hot embers.

An hour later I was rudely awakened by wet nylon slapping my face. Even with the geodesic dome design, the tent was folding in on itself, the poles creaking with the abuse. I went out to shore it up with heavier rocks. A blast of ice-cold air from the northwest enveloped me, driving the sleep from my brain. By the time I had collected enough rocks, my hands were ice-cold. I blew on them to keep them flexible. I glanced at the ocean and froze, except for my heart, which was ricocheting off my chest wall. The scene before me was alarming. Pancakes of ice were pitching wildly and piling up over each other. The impact was sending shards of ice high into the air. Others were rafting up on shore, sliding over each other, as quickly as a card player deals cards. A wide, hurtling swath of open water was heading in a huge arc toward the cape. I couldn't control the shudder that shook my body. A one-hour delay on the water would have meant disaster. I moved Windsong next to the tent, out of harm's way.

The sun was well into the sky when I awoke. I lingered in the sleeping bag until the heat penetrated the tent. It was one of those rare Arctic days. Not even a ripple creased the ocean's surface, not a breath stirred the air. The sun shone full-strength from a cloudless sky. The bay that yesterday was crammed solid with ice was now a placid blue. Only a margin of white remained along the cape.

I was in no hurry. Four hours would bring me into Coppermine. Windsong skidded easily over the ice on the beach, her bow in the direction of Cape Kendall. An hour later I approached the margin of white at the base. To my dismay, there was no way through. I had been so sure that the night's shake-up would have left the ice loose. I retreated along the outward edge of the pack all the way to shore again. Fortunately, I found a channel between the beach and the ice stranded in the shallows. With only a foot of water below me, I easily passed in front of the pack and hugged the rock wall all the way around the cape.

I had an appointment with a silk rose in a ziploc bag. I had hidden it in a cavern on the bank of a special cove on the south side of Cape Kendall. Eagerly I scanned the banks. Over the two years the weather had changed the shape of the surface, but pure instinct brought me to the secret spot. I removed the rocks and reached inside. Yes! As beautiful as ever. I clutched it in my hand. A flood of emotions and memories filled my head. How sick, physically and emotionally, I had been. How my dreams had been shattered when I laid it there so carefully, knowing I couldn't paddle any further. How my hopes had hinged on not having to return for it alone.

Realizations came full force. I had recovered my health, I had carried on with my desire to see the North. Now I had to carry on with my life. If I didn't change it, I would forever be doing things alone. With a heavy heart but an open mind, I stowed the rose safely in the kayak. I was going to be fine.

Around the bend, Glen and Bella Ekhiohina's camp came into view. Four children came running down the hill to the water's edge to greet me.

Jenny, Nellie, Shannon, and Eric all had questions about the kayak. I was pleased to see them. The little girls were adorable in their Mother Hubbard parka covers. The flounce at the bottom spread in a circle around them as they crouched near the kayak. Watching their eager little faces made me homesick for my grandchildren. Luckily, I still had enough Dipps bars to go around. We shared them on the walk up the hill to their camp. Lunch and tea were served immediately. We sat cross-legged on the ground, balancing plate and teacup. The view was magnificent. Below lay the ocean capped in white. Beyond, the Couper Islands in the Coronation Gulf stood guard duty over Coppermine, and, behind Coppermine, the mauve hills were shrouded in a haze. No wonder Glen and Bella had chosen this spot for their holidays.

"What are my chances of getting through the pack today?" I asked Glen.

"It's pretty solid now," he answered. " I made it in from Coppermine early this morning, but I had to go to the bottom of Richardson Bay to get behind and around it. That will be your best bet."

I found the eight-mile length of Richardson Bay plugged with ice. There was no longer a way in. From the top of the cliffs at its entrance I sat and watched for movement in the ice-field.

My mind drifted back to Winnipeg. Eileen Smerchanski was having a kayaking and sailboarding party at her lovely resort on Lake Winnipeg. If I could reach Coppermine, I could contact the whole gang. It would be fun to say hello.

The tide came and with it more ice. It looked hopeless. Down to the kayak I went. I might as well set up the tent and stay the night. While I searched the beach for a good camp spot, I discovered a dead seal in the water. I wasn't sure if it had been shot or crushed in the ice. I certainly did not want to be near it if a grizzly came.

I climbed to the top of the cliff again to watch and wait. I hoped the reversing tide would start the ice moving. Then my chance came. The ice-field pulled apart. Half of it remained in the bay; the other half moved with the outgoing tide. In one fluid motion I slid to the bottom of the cliff. Minutes later Windsong was heading for the break. The current was strong but the pack was loose. I yielded willingly to the half-mile-wide floes coming at me. Even after all the ice I had seen, I could not help but be impressed by its movement.

Late evening found me through the pack with free sailing to the Couper Islands. The wind was beginning to raise the surface of the water as I approached. I ducked between some islands for shelter and was hailed from shore. "Come for tea. Come for tea."

Joe Ogina steadied Windsong against the rocks while I got out. We hauled her to safety next to his boat. "Sure is getting rough out there in a hurry," I commented.

"You're better off staying here for the night," Joe replied. In the direction of Coppermine the breakers were already capped in foam.

Joe's wife, Ada, came down to help me up the hill. She had tears in her eyes. I hoped I hadn't come at a bad time. Later I learned she had spotted me on the open water through binoculars. She started to cry because the kayak looked so small. She was not only strikingly beautiful because of her flawless complexion and high cheekbones, but inwardly beautiful as well.

Halfway up, Ada's friend held out her hand.

"Hello again," she greeted me.

"Again?" I asked. I peered closer at her face.

She kept hold of my hand. "Locker Point. We met at Locker Point."

"Oh shoot, Kate, forgive me. I didn't recognize you with your big parka hood on," I replied. Kate's husband Roy came to stand beside his wife.

"Hi, Roy. I'm surprised to see you back from Bernard Harbour so soon," I said.

"We had a good trip," he answered. "We shot four caribou. Two for Joe Allan and two for us."

Tea time at Joe and Ada's was like a homecoming. The five of us sat around the radio with hot mugs of tea in hand, listening to the socializing going on over the airwaves. I spent the night in Joe and Ada's snug cabin. During the night, the northwest wind had been wicked. By morning all traces of ice had disappeared. I would not see ice again for the rest of the trip.

July 18th, Monday. The day was spent on the island in the company of the two Inuit couples. It was impossible to be on the water. The wind kept switching direction quickly, churning the sea into a wild mass of breakers.

Outdoors, under Roy's work table, I spotted part of a musk-ox horn.

"Roy, are you a carver?" I asked. He said indeed he was.

"What will this be?" I continued.

"It will be a narwhal," he told me. " I have one of them finished at home."

"When you finish this one, may I buy them both?" I asked.

"I will finish it today," he promised. "On Tuesday I'll bring them to Coppermine."

He set to work at once.

Ada and Kate were busy cutting up the two caribou. The meat was stripped from the bones and hung to dry in the wind and sun. I marvelled at their skill with the ulu and the anatomical knowledge they possessed. They dismembered the caribou without a saw and without breaking a bone.

At first they spoke in English to each other. I could see it was awkward for them. "Please use your own language," I suggested. "I won't mind at all. I am very content just to be here."

They slipped into Inuktitut, two good friends enjoying their time together. Often they stopped to interpret a funny episode for me. It was a pleasant, peaceful time. Even Kate's husky pup enjoyed it. He curled up and fell asleep in my arms.

For lunch Kate served goose soup with lots of meat. We sat on the floor around the huge pot and enjoyed it. For me, time stood still.

The wind died down in the late evening. Windsong could handle the last of the waves. At 11:00 p.m. I departed the little island. By midnight I was paddling past the roped-off swimming area in Coppermine. I was soaked to the skin, exhausted, and relieved to have arrived at last. It was midnight, July 18th.

Phoning my family and a cup of hot coffee were on my mind when I awoke. I headed for the hotel only to find it locked. I stopped a young lady on the road to ask about the restaurant.

"Oh no, they only serve meals to guests," she informed me. "Are you the paddling grandmother?"

"My name is Victoria Jason," I replied. "How does everyone know I'm a grandmother?"

Anna Claire MacAdam introduced herself and replied, "*News North* has an article on you this week. I'm on my way to work, but I will unlock the door to my house. You may make yourself some coffee, have a shower, and relax. Lock the door when you leave."

I was speechless.

"It's okay," she assured me. "I know what it's like. I used to travel a lot. I must go or I'll be late for work."

I walked across the street and opened the door to her lovely home. With the luxury of a shower at hand, I forgot all about coffee.

I was anxious to see Ron, Julie, and Brielle Morrison, whom I had last seen in Spence Bay in 1992. Also Ann Whittaker, a nurse at the Health Centre who in 1992 had tried so hard to ease some of my hurt. I tried surprising Ron at the office, but he had already heard I was in town. He handed me the newspaper and pointed me in the direction of his home, making me promise to return for supper. Julie and I had coffee while Brielle ate her breakfast. She had grown into an adorable three-year-old.

Chores kept me busy all day – parcels to pick up at the post office, thanks to Julie's help; letters to write; phone calls to make; supplies to buy; laundry to do; and repairs to make. I hurried to the First Air depot to see if my Emergency Locating Transmitter had arrived from Vancouver. Its lithium battery had caused it to be labelled "Dangerous Goods" and it had been rerouted from the original destination of Paulatuk to Coppermine. It had arrived. I was relieved. I had dreaded going into the Queen Maud Gulf without any means of signalling for help, should the need arise. The Northern Store staff handed me a fax from Jan and Mike Riley and the rest of the gang. It was a treat to hear from them.

On the way back to my tent I stopped to talk to a group of five camped in the churchyard. They were all from Denmark and had spent the last month paddling the Coppermine River in two canoes and one kayak. They looked tanned and healthy.

Supper at Ron and Julie's was a lovely affair. Barbecued arctic char, new potatoes, and salad. Julie understood the craving one can develop for fresh vegetables after lack of them over an extended period. Ron delivered me to the beach on the back of his Honda ATV. Visitors already had gathered to inspect Windsong. The Danish group was there; John Nishi, a biologist from Ron's office; Gerry Ruygrok, a geologist from a special project in the Coronation Gulf; the minister and his wife. I'm always pleased to show off my kayak and am fascinated at the types of people the sport of kayaking can involve, be they adventurers, daredevils, soul-searchers, or dreamers like me, male, female or child.

Before long Windsong was on the way to the beach for test runs. John went first. I could tell he was a natural. He sat relaxed and comfortable. I couldn't adjust the rudder cables for Jerry's long legs, but he was very powerful, with good canoeing skills. He could easily turn Windsong without the rudder.

A long line of teenaged boys formed out of nowhere. "Us too, us too!" came the chorus.

I saw a young boy watching me. Recognition flooded over me. The dimple in his cheek, I knew that dimple.

"Victoria?" he said shyly. "Victoria from Manitoba?"

"Oh my God, Ryan, is that really you?" I asked. The hug was spontaneous.

At arm's length I could see he had filled out to become a very handsome lad.

"Where are your friend David and your sister Nicole?" I inquired. In 1992 all three of them had showed me how to fish for tomcod from the edge of a cliff on one of the Couper Islands.

"And your grandparents, are they well?"

"Yes, I'll tell them you're here," he answered, and disappeared.

It was well after midnight when I returned to the tent. The midnight sun was dipping its bottom edge into the ocean. This was the height of summer. Each day it would sink lower. As much as I was enjoying Coppermine, I knew I couldn't linger. The season was getting shorter. One more day and I would leave.

Gerry came by in the morning to invite me for breakfast at the geologists' camp. "Our chef will make you the most delicious eggs Benedict you have ever had," he promised.

At noon, Julie, Ron and Brielle, and Ann Whittaker and her two sons Steven and Thomas, showed up with a full-fledged picnic. David, Ann's oldest son, was too shy to join us.

We sat on the sand around a red-checkered tablecloth and enjoyed salads loaded with fresh vegetables, freshly baked biscuits, sandwiches, grapes, and soda pop. It was difficult to express my thanks adequately. Meanwhile, back home, my children were worried about my suffering in the wilderness!

Ron was curious about the gear I carried in the kayak. I rattled off a multitude of supplies. I got to the Braun curling iron, mascara, and hair colour.

"Hair colour?" Ann exclaimed. "You carry hair colour?"

"I have to," I replied. "This 24-hour sun bleaches my hair." It had already turned a flaming copper colour.

"How do you manage to do your hair when you are travelling?" she continued.

"Well, on the days I'm shore-bound I find a pond, heat some water, and, with a mirror balanced between my knees and through much trial and error, I manage," I told her.

They laughed at the picture it brought to mind.

"I'd love to help you with your hair," Ann volunteered.

"You would?" I was thrilled.

Ann laughed, "Just wait until I tell the girls at the nursing station on our next coffee break."

We went on to discuss the fact that in this day and age no one had to live with grey hair if they didn't want to. Ron bowed out of the conversation by saying he had to get back to the office.

I love getting my hair done and being fussed over. Ann was just a charm. It was fun to be doing girlie things with a good friend. We talked about the business of our lives, agreeing that we don't make time for small talk and silliness. I liked the closeness. I floated back to the tent, my shiny, silky hair swaying in the breeze.

David appeared silently on the beach path. We shared a big hug. He was now thirteen years old. He was tall, long-legged, extremely good-looking, with a dashing smile and jet-black hair, but there was a hint of sadness in his big brown eyes.

"Do you still live in Manitoba?" was his first question.

I knew of the hurt and hope he and Ryan held inside. Their white fathers both live in Manitoba, and the boys cling to the hope that they may one day be contacted. I pray they will. They are such good boys. Ryan joined us. Together we walked up the hill to Ryan's grandparents' house. Ryan's grandparents have accepted David as their own, and both boys live with them. I had met Millie and Andrew Nivingalok at their camp on the Couper Islands in 1992. When my fishing expedition with the boys and Nicole had only yielded a three-inch tomcod, they supplied a large, dried arctic char.

We sat in their living-room, catching up on the two years that had slipped by so quickly. They praised the boys for being such hard workers and for looking after them so well. Andrew had passed on his hunting skills. David had already shot his first caribou. Ryan, now twelve, would be able to take the Hunter's Safety Course. Soon he would be hunting too. They talked about some of the old times, of the upheaval they had seen in their lives. My heart went out to them. They had one thing left. It was the love that radiated between the four of them and the protectiveness they had for each other.

At the R.C.M.P. office I filed another Wilderness Pursuit Plan. My next contact would be 1100 miles away at Gjoa Haven. I set my arrival at Gjoa for August 25th.

Windsong was repacked, and last-minute purchases like bread, margarine, cheese, and eggs were stowed away. My friend Yvonne Maxim had forwarded eight pounds of Nutri-Bars supplied by the Nutri-Bar Company. I tucked them in wherever I could. They would prove to be a great addition to my food supply before the trip was over. John Nishi came to say goodbye just as I was finishing the last of the postcards and letters. He would mail them, since I planned to leave early on the morrow. I was pleased and honoured to autograph his book on sea kayaking instruction. I felt like a celebrity. It hadn't taken him long to get hooked on kayaking. Good luck, John. Meet you on the water some day!

Last phone calls to my daughters and Ken were difficult. I didn't know what lay ahead. At times like that one clings to the phone long after there is nothing left to say. I could only promise to be careful and keep the emergency transmitter on me at all times.

July 21st. Eight a.m. found me heading across the mouth of the Coppermine River.

"Victoria-a-a" came loud and clear across the water. Gerry stood on shore, camera in hand. I should have returned, but Windsong was already caught up by the current. I turned only enough to wave. I headed eastward past the islands in the mouth. Ahead stretched the mighty sweep of the Arctic coast. I was absorbed into its beauty – wide green valleys, hills, sandy beaches, cliffs, and rivers entering the ocean. To my left, in the Coronation Gulf, the string of Couper, Berens, and Sir Graham Moore Islands stood stark and bold. The hue of the cliffs changed with the passing clouds. I had hoped to reach the Kugaryuak River the first day. That would have brought me halfway to the Tree River, but the northwest wind had other ideas. In no time a heavy surf was building. Two white tents appeared across the bay. I headed in. Glad for the invitation to camp nearby, I circled for a better chance at a decent landing. I was eleven miles short of the river.

George and Teddy were doing repairs to a boat that had been abandoned earlier because of motor trouble. Meanwhile, members of the family scouted for caribou. Instead of caribou they spotted a grizzly in the area.

I had time to give my shotgun a good cleaning and to catch up on the sleep I missed in Coppermine. The storm blew itself out by 4:00 p.m. the next day. I left, carrying a message for Colin Hayiak at the Tree River Surveying Camp.

My eyes were riveted to the constantly changing shoreline. The contours of the topographic map led me to day-dreaming about what lay further inland. The flat, smooth, terraced rock ledges near the entrance to Tree River fascinated me. I have always enjoyed going for walks on just such terrain and for a moment contemplated camping for the night. Instead, I decided to try for the survey camp.

The wind had been coming off the land, keeping the ocean fairly calm. When I turned south into the two-mile-wide mouth of the river, I got the full blast of the wind funnelling down the valley. A three-foot short chop came at me on a swift current. Jumbled, jagged rocks lined the shore at the base of sloping rock cliffs. Gusts of wind took my breath away. The spray stung my face. There was no way to turn Windsong in that mess. I had to go on. As I kept the double-blade low, it was brace, paddle, brace – every nerve alert, eyes already bulging from the strain and pain of paddling into the glare of the early morning sun for the last few hours. My shoulders and arms were screaming for mercy by the time I found a sheltered cove an hour later. Fifty-six miles in fourteen hours had delivered me to this spot. It was 6:00 a.m. when I set up the tent, stripped off my clothes, and crawled into my sleeping bag, too exhausted to eat.

A quick scan with binoculars revealed the surveyors' camp in a bay three miles away on the opposite shore. If it hadn't been for the message, I would have crossed over and out of the Tree River instead of making the extra miles to the camp.

Shirley Hatogina from Coppermine was the cook at the camp. I handed her the note for Colin. In minutes she had me sitting in front of a ham, tomato, cheese, and lettuce sandwich. Topped off with coffee, it was a good way to start the afternoon. Her son was interested in the kayak. It wasn't until a few days later, after some totally frustrating compass bearings, that I realized he had turned the deck compass 45° off its centre mark.

Many long open water crossings brought me to a twelve-foot-high cairn erected on a solid rock shore. A semblance of a cross crowned its height. Nothing in the vicinity gave me any clues to its purpose. The undisturbed lichens growing on the rock surfaces testified to its age. What kind of grand history would it reveal, were it able to speak? I tiptoed away, silently sending my regards to those who had preceded me through these waters. I filled my water bottles from a small pond on the way back to the kayak and decided on a few extra miles.

A short time later I rounded a towering headland and realized I didn't have a clue to where I was. Nothing I could see ahead corresponded to the area of the map I thought I was in. At least two miles across the water, cliffs loomed high out of the sea. The perpendicular walls on the southeast face were cast in shadow by the lowering midnight sun. Could that be Hepburn Island? Could I possibly have come this far? The deck compass was no help. The screwy reading confused me more. What I needed was to check the G.P.S., but landing spots at the base of the cliffs didn't look promising. From the location of the midnight sun I could tell where east was. I had to go east and I had to keep all land to my right. I watched and waited until a stronger ray of sun broke through the cloud bank and revealed a copper-coloured island across the water to the east. A faint outline of shore lingered on the horizon behind it. The breeze was light, the ocean gently rolling. Focusing on the island, I started across. An hour later, as I neared the island, a large sphere appeared over the hills on the mainland.

I was awestruck. "It's the full moon."

The man in the moon seemed to have an extra-big smile. I don't think that wink was my imagination either! It buoyed up my spirits. I didn't care if I was lost. The full moon was on my right shoulder, the midnight sun on my left. It was fabulous.

Even the lack of a takeout spot on the island didn't dampen my spirits. I turned Windsong in the direction of a light-coloured spot on the mainland. Sand was always lucky for me. I headed across. A wide, soft sand beach welcomed me at the mouth of a large, unnamed river. A boarded-up summer camp stood at the junction. The G.P.S. reading astonished me even more.

I had been at Agiak Headland. I had crossed ten miles across the top of Gray's Bay, and those really were the high palisades of Hepburn Island to the north. Tired as I was, I could not sleep. I lay on the sand, hands clasped behind my head, and watched the moon and sun weave their magic over land and sea. I could not stop grinning. Tomorrow I would see Bathurst Inlet.

I set off in high spirits. I still couldn't believe my good fortune. "There had to have been a guardian angel over my shoulder last night," I thought.

Out to sea, Hepburn Island stayed with me for part of the day. Ann Whittaker had told me how lovely it was at its summit. I could imagine the view one would get from its majestic height. I plied a shoreline etched with enchanted little coves. Meadows meandered from lofty rock ridges to sandy beaches, each more wondrous than the last.

"Wow, would you look at that!" escaped from my lips many times during the day.

Then came the exquisitely-coloured rocks around Inman Harbour. Reds, rose, and burgundy were set off by the turquoise water and the emerald greens of the meadows. Across the open water to my left the lofty 32-mile-long chain of the Jameson Islands had begun. Their flat tops and walls falling sheer to the sea guarded the mouth of Bathurst Inlet. I could use all the protection they offered. At Cape Barrow I would start across the 36-mile stretch of open water to Cape Flinders on the east side of the inlet.

The wind picked up as I approached Cape Barrow. In the shelter of some small islands I set ashore to assess the situation. I had hoped to see the Chapman Islands lying in the middle of the inlet, but all I could make out was a dark margin on the horizon. Never constant, it would shift back and forth, rise and fall. A curtain of haze shrouded it. I could wait for morning and hope the early sun would make things clearer, or I could dip down into the inlet for fourteen miles to the Galena Islands and do some island-hopping across to the Chapmans, then the Wilmot Islands, and reach Cape Flinders that way. I sat on the rose-coloured gravel, snacking on Nutri-Bars and dried fruit. Next to me lay a magnificent set of bleached caribou antlers. Garrett would have loved to see them. Only eight years old, he already had a strong interest in bones and could remember the exact number in a human skeleton and their placement in the body.

By the time I finished my lunch I had decided on the longer, safer way across. "What's an extra four hours of my life anyway?" I told myself. Pointing Windsong southward, I headed into the inlet. The offshore wind left the water calmer. I relished the coolness as I paddled in the shadows of the cliffs. Stopping only to top my water containers up with snow from the remaining drifts, I continued until, at midnight, I was even with the first of the Galena Islands. By then the ocean had stilled to a glass finish.

"Can't waste this fine paddling weather, Windsong. I promise we'll rest on the first island we come to." Determined little craft that she is, in no time her bow was cutting a smooth path eastward. The nagging sensation that I was being watched made me glance back. I looked down into the inquiring eyes of a sleek black seal. His trailing wake, parallel to Windsong's, showed that he had been with us a while.

"Hi, pal! Is this your home?" I asked.

He stalled for a minute, reconsidered, and decided to accompany me a little further. As long as I didn't break the rhythm of my stroke, he confidently swam alongside. For the first three miles, the current was strong and favourable. We glided effortlessly. Then came heavy water. My speed was reduced by half. A gale struck at the same time. I bent to the task of riding it out for the last mile, not even noticing that my companion had abandoned me.

I paused on the highest island only long enough to climb a ridge and orient myself for the crossing to the Chapmans. I could go no further this night. Crossing a narrow channel to a crumbling, black shale island, I pulled into shore. The sky was turning ugly. Quickly, I kicked the fresh goose droppings out of the way. Struggling in the wind, I erected the tent and hurriedly shored it up with extra rocks. A wall of rain was advancing across the water. I dived for cover seconds before it struck. Two a.m. It had been quite a day. Thankful to be safe, I fell asleep to the sound of thunder ripping the sky apart.

The storm kept me tent-bound for the next full day. It was a good time for planning my route, making notes, and enjoying the pictures of my family. From the photos they returned my smile. How I missed them. I'd close my eyes and try to imagine what they might be doing at that moment.

July 26th. Gale-force winds continued through the night. By noon the sky had cleared, but the whitecaps kept rushing to shore. With stove, pots, and shampoo in hand, I headed to the freshwater pond for a birdbath and shampoo. A huge swan had claimed the pond. He just swam in circles at the opposite edge and watched my antics.

By 10:00 p.m. there seemed to be a lull in the waves. If I could get through the shore-surf, I could paddle. Using my double-blade to steady Windsong against the shore, I had just dropped into the cockpit when I heard the sickening crack of my blade breaking in two. A few frantic moments ensued. I jumped into thigh-deep water and grabbed the tow rope. The next wave slammed Windsong hard into my legs. The backwash pulled her away far enough for me to scramble to shore and haul her in. Fearing I might lose my nerve if I didn't act quickly, I assembled the spare blade and placed the broken one under the deck elastics. Watch. Time the waves. Go. Seconds later,

Windsong was free of the surf and pointing toward the first of a string of islands heading towards the Chapmans.

It took me some hours to become accustomed to the new blade. I would have preferred to have done it in calmer conditions, but the choice was not mine. My familiar old blade had taken me to the Arctic four times. My fingers recognized each little imperfection in the shaft. Now it rode unceremoniously under the deck elastic.

My new blade was sleekly varnished, smooth, slightly finer in circumference, and a few ounces lighter. Before long it was cutting wind and water with rhythmic precision.

Navigation became increasingly difficult as I neared the cluster of islands. The setting sun cast shadows over them, causing them to blend into a solid dark mass. Increasing wind and current forced me to change my direction to the leeward of an available island. Pleased to be a third of the way across, I used the first accessible beach for my camp. Tomorrow I would figure things out.

The islands looked different in the morning light. I was certain I was not on the chain of islands heading for Cape Flinders, but which island was I on? The G.P.S. reading did not help. It pinpointed me in open water. My best bet was to return to the point at which I had turned eastward. It was easier said than done. I could not hold my own against the current. My only hope was to run with the current and pick a different channel. A quick four miles brought me to the tip of the long island and out of the strongest part of the current, only to be faced with gusting winds from the north. With only one hour's paddling to my credit, I headed in to set camp and wait out the wind.

Again the G.P.S. reading placed me in open water. Not only on the nautical chart, but also on the topographical map. With G.P.S., map, and emergency beeper in hand, I hiked two miles to the centre of the island to get a better reading and a good look from a ridge located there. To my great relief, I spotted the largest of the Chapman Islands. The towering, tell-tale spine that made up its eastern shore coincided with the contours of the map. I was back in the game again. The G.P.S. confirmed my location at the top of the ridge.

I would have to backtrack a full five miles, but I also had a choice of four different channels for the trip back to the main island.

A strenuous paddle against the current and four-foot waves brought me near the largest island in the northeast chain. The worst wasn't over. Violent gusts of wind struck in erratic patterns. The only warnings were slight ripples on the water. Then came the blast. In order to hold on to my double-blade, I had to lower it close to the cockpit. Windsong skidded helplessly ahead of the gusts. My full concentration was focused on keeping the kayak from being blasted broadside. She responded faithfully, levelling out in the lulls and standing fast in the gusts. "We can make it, Windsong," I encouraged her.

My arms and lungs were aching by the time we literally hit the shore. I needed to get my breath back. The G.P.S. reading confirmed I was on the right shore.

In order to relax, I put a pot of soup on to boil and watched the antics of the wind. For a moment the water's surface would be peaceful; then the ripples would start and the blast would hit, scooping water from the ocean's surface and flinging it far in advance of itself. The display was both frightening and impressive. I ate and watched. Should I wait? Perhaps it wouldn't get any better. Perhaps the wind always funnels through the islands like this. I decided to try again. My plan was to cling close to shore, but it was too dangerous. When the blasts struck, I would be hurled toward shore at an incredible speed. I needed more room to gain control and ride out the gusts. Before long, my lungs were taking too long to recover from the vacuum the gusts created. I headed in and set the tent up.

Scaling the backbone of the island was a waste of time. Once there, I could not stand erect in the force of the wind. The hood of my jacket was snapping violently against the side of my face. Half hopping, half slipping, I descended to the safety of my tent.

The display on the water continued through the evening, the night, and the next day.

Finally, a semblance of calm. Windsong slid obligingly into the ocean.

The cliffs along the shore were grand, and the problems of the last few days were forgotten. A torrent of waves greeted me between each of the islands as I crossed northeast toward the Wilmots. After resting for nearly two days, the challenge was refreshing.

July 29th. By 5:00 a.m. I had rounded the southeast end of the largest of the Wilmots and continued to a smaller island in the direction of Cape Flinders. A chute of gravel made a perfect landing spot. Stripping out of my wet clothes, I spread them on the gravel to drain.

A large arctic hare sprang into view. With mighty leaps he disappeared up a well-worn path to the top of the cliffs. Cozy in my dry clothes, I decided to follow. The path was narrow, but easy to climb. Surely he could not have trampled it so well on his own. I scanned the island with binoculars. Nothing else moved. A pond glistened in the meadow – fresh water. Tiny yellow flowers edged the path at my feet. Islands dotted the crystal blue water. I stood dazzled by the view. Six miles across the open water lay Cape Flinders and the mainland. A bad case of eyestrain and the direct rays of the early morning sun made it hard to focus on the cape. I would get some sleep and check the situation in the afternoon. I snuggled into my soft sleeping bag. No worries of grizzlies entered my head.

My thoughts wandered back to Ken. It was exactly one month since I had said so long to him on the shores of Paulatuk harbour.

I enjoyed breakfast at high noon. Although the wind was fairly stiff, it was from the southwest and would take me to the cape in style. Using the crudest of "eyeball" navigation, I headed for the cliffs at Cape Flinders. Touching mainland again was a milestone. Although the cliffs prevented me from landing, the fact that they were part of a large land mass gave me a sense of security. According to the map, the next eighty miles would be a fairly smooth shoreline. I looked forward to a more relaxed progress along the Kent Peninsula.

Rounding the cape came with a switch in the wind direction. With ever more persistence, the gusts started coming from the northwest. It was time to get off the water, but the boulders in the shallows posed too much risk, except for emergencies. The first accessible takeout came eighteen miles from my starting-point. Windsong nestled into a black gravel shore and I easily brought her clear of the high-tide mark, with extra room to spare in case of a storm surge.

Humps of black gravel sculptured the land as far back as I could see. Caribou drifted ghost-like from one to another, curious enough to get within close range. I scouted for grizzly tracks. With the sun setting lower, the mounds cast shadows that at a glance could be mistaken for bears, or bears could be mistaken for shadows. The tour produced nothing but caribou and goose tracks. One huge seagull appointed himself my watchdog. He watched with much interest as I spread my clothes to dry and prepared my meal. When I awoke at 2:00 a.m. he was still a permanent fixture on the bald rock.

I took advantage of the calm sea. The shoreline pointed north-northeast for the next four hours until, at 6:25 a.m., I came around Turnagain Point and headed due east into the brilliant morning sun. It was here that John Franklin in 1821 made his regrettable decision to turn back to Coppermine instead of continuing through the Northwest Passage. I laid my double-blade across the cockpit and paused to reflect for a while on the monumental longing that had driven me to see and feel this powerful land for myself. How many before me had paused and felt the thrill? I couldn't keep my hands from trembling as I resumed paddling.

Ahead of me the mighty sweep of the Arctic coast stretched to infinity. The beauty was overwhelming. A green carpet of lush tundra valley stretched to the foot of the ridge marking the point. Eastward, ho! Mile after mile, I paddled along shallow, sandy shores, enjoying the peaceful setting. To my left across Dease Strait I could finally see the shores of Victoria Island. The shallowness of the water kept me a quarter of a mile from shore. I day-dreamed much of the time, and it was either the drag on the kayak or a sharp jar of my paddle hitting the ocean floor that would signal that I had drifted too close to shore. Then it would be back to the deep-water line, where the dark blue met the turquoise. I could see the drift of the current a little further out, but I couldn't bear to pass by too quickly.

Movement inland captured my attention. What had looked from the distance like a grizzly turned out to be a musk-ox. I quickly headed in. This was my first sighting of musk-oxen in their natural setting. I had promised myself I would not leave the North without seeing musk-oxen, even if I had to pay someone to show me. Tracks in the sand, made by their sharp-edged hooves, greeted me. There were eleven of them, seven adults and four young ones. Some were lying down, while the others browsed. The calves, dark and glossy, were romping around the adults.

I was tempted to follow the gully to where they grazed, but caution ruled. My leg muscles were beginning to turn to jelly from the ten- to twelve-hour days in the kayak. If it came to a hasty retreat, I wasn't sure I would be a winner. Of course, one never knows one's own capabilities until charged by a half ton of animal with horns.

I contented myself with watching through binoculars. About four feet high, with their prominent shoulder humps and an area behind the withers that was shaded much lighter, they were hard to distinguish from grizzlies at a distance. The season was still early. Patches of shedded underfur clung to the long guard hairs, giving them an unkempt, tussled look. The long guard hairs of the skirt brushed the ground, parting and swaying in the wind.

It was hard for me to understand how this land could be called barren. Isolated maybe, but not barren.

Before descending the bank, I stopped to absorb the scene. My loyal little craft rested on the warm sand. Tapping gently against the beach was the water of the Northwest Passage, and to the north, Victoria Island. Although I had been paddling the Passage for the past five weeks, it was here that the impact of where I was actually hit home. I cannot express the force of my emotions at that moment.

The wind gently lifted the hair off my neck and brought me out of my trance. It was a timely warning that the calm would not last. Before long the sea was running high. The lack of a long sleep and the range of emotions that had possessed me had drained my energy. I made some obviously sloppy moves among the breakers, and common sense told me to call it a day. I rode the waves into shallow water and carefully walked Windsong in among the scattered rocks to a seaweed-strewn beach. The dried seaweed made a cushy mattress under my tent. An arctic fox and many sik-siks watched me and each other as I spread my clothes on the stiff grasses to dry in the hot midday sun. It had been quite a day.

The sound of a motorboat labouring in the waves woke me in the late evening. I hadn't seen a soul since Tree River, so I anxiously waited to get sight of the traveller. He came through the rough sea, the sixteen-foot Lund bucking and coming down hard. I kept my hands deep in my pockets so I wouldn't be tempted to wave. Landing would be treacherous. I didn't want him to think I needed help. He waved first. I happily waved back. It took three skilful attempts to get the boat to shore. I ran to the point to meet him. An Inuit fellow hopped overboard. His name was John. He was on his way from Bay Chimo to Cambridge Bay. He immediately inquired about my welfare. Did I have enough food?

Out loud, I wished I had written some letters to send home. "There are some people weathered out at Trap Point, below Cambridge," he told me. "They will take your letters to the post office." He evidently carried an HF radio.

I asked him to pass on a message of my whereabouts to the R.C.M.P. in Cambridge. My invitation to stay for tea was graciously declined.

"I would enjoy tea," John said, "but I can't anchor the boat and am afraid it will become damaged on the rocks." He poled his way through the rocks and shallows. Moments later the waves swept away all evidence of his visit. My spirits were high. I would find fresh water and get on with my letter writing. I followed the sandy flood plain southward, then turned into one of the gullies made by the run-off. I hoped to find a pothole that had retained water. The musk-oxen must have had the same idea. Their tracks circled the dry depressions. Sand dunes, crowned by stiff grasses, bordered the gullies. Sik-sik burrows peppered their sides. I sat on a tuft and laughed as I watched them make new ones. Their fat little rear quarters and their tails jerked rapidly to and fro as they worked. The head and upper body would be out of sight except when they would back out, take a look around, chastise me, and resume digging. They didn't judge me much of a threat.

After a fruitless search of the gullies, I climbed to the highest knoll I could find. With help from my binoculars I spotted a glint of blue on the tundra in the direction of the hills. Memorizing a few landmarks, I headed in. The lake was much larger than I expected. Three adult swans swam serenely on the still water. I talked to them while refilling my containers. The smell of the salt water in the wind guided me back. Two hours later I was glad to dump the pack in camp. My leg muscles were burning from the hike.

August 1st. All morning and afternoon I waited for a combination of calm water and the rising tide to get out of my shallow cove. The wind switched from northwest to northeast. I would have to contend with a head wind. I couldn't wait too long. If the weather calmed, the hunters at Trap Point would be heading across to Cambridge, without my letters. I decided to chance a launch. I walked Windsong part way out of the cove to meet the incoming tide. Using a rock to stabilize her, I dropped into the cockpit. The breakers demanded my undivided attention. They broke coming into the shallow water and I tried to stay out of range of this area. At the same time it was treacherous trying to kayak in the turbulence of the shallows. Two and a half hours later, I was exhausted both mentally and physically. I set camp due north of 600-foot Mt. George. I had gained ten miles.

August 2nd. 3:00 p.m. The wind and ocean began to settle. The last of the head wind felt good on my face. The shallow, sandy shores gave way to deep, dark waters. I paddled within forty feet of shore for a ten-mile stretch. The aroma from the meadows wafted over the water. I had heady expectations of rounding Cape Alexander by midnight.

I came upon a camp late in the evening. The boat looked a lot like John's, but I couldn't be sure. It was hauled part way up some rocks, and equipment was strewn all the way from the bow to a white canvas tent set at a crazy angle on a pile of boulders. The rock-strewn waters prevented me from landing. I called loudly as I went by. No one stirred. A half mile further, I hastily beached Windsong on the sand and started back at a run. Within earshot of the tent, I stopped and called out. John came through the flaps of the door. "Are you all right?" I gasped, totally out of breath.

He shook my hand and laughed. "Yes, I'm all right," he answered, "No, I don't have a problem. I was listening to the radio and didn't hear you. I'm waiting for the water to calm down to make the crossing. What are you doing out there in this weather?"

I assured him the kayak was very stable in the waves.

"Do you have enough food until you get to Cambridge?" I asked him. He confirmed he had.

"My nephew is just below the cape," he told me. "I've just talked to him on the radio. I'll tell him to watch for you." We shook hands again and parted.

My bladder was bursting. At the kayak I waved once more, got in, and paddled away in agony.

Once out of sight I hit the shore "double time" and shed my jumpsuit with but a second to spare. My kidneys were accustomed to ten- to twelve-hour stretches in the kayak, but the minute Windsong scraped the shore it was a signal for "time out."

I was in a good mood. I started to sing. The sensation of being followed made me turn around. A large black seal was only a few feet behind the kayak. Instead of sliding back into the water, this fellow came fully out of the water in a very powerful surge and landed broadside, causing a geyser that soaked my face, my shoulder, and part of my back. He was either perturbed that I hadn't acknowledged him or else he really hated the song. Just to be safe, I stopped singing and headed for very shallow water. He hadn't missed the kayak by much, and I didn't relish a repeat of his performance. I had to give him credit. He got his point across.

At midnight, right on cue, I rounded Cape Alexander below Cambridge and started southeast toward the bottom of the Queen Maud Gulf.

Rusty red pebbles bordered the water's edge. The water was deep and turquoise. I was only ten to twenty feet from shore except where rock slides had deposited rubble in the water. Rugged and awesome, the red sandstone buttes in the background rose to 400 feet and were highlighted by the rays from the midnight sun. I sped by on the swift current, expending very little energy.

I stopped at John's nephew's camp, thankful I had reached it in time. I asked if they would mail my letters.

"We are sorry," they told me. "We're heading to Bay Chimo for a two-week holiday. We were just weathered out here."

"Are there still people at Trap Point?" I asked.

"No, they all crossed over once the water calmed down," they answered.

I guess they sensed my disappointment. How I wished I had left the letters with John.

"There are still people coming across the portage at Elu Inlet," the nephew told me. "Get your map and I'll show you where they will be camped."

"That's 25 miles south of here," I said out loud.

"You can camp here," they told me, "and catch up to them tomorrow."

"Are there grizzlies in this area?" I asked.

The husband looked at the wife. "No," he answered. "You probably won't see any until Perry River."

Whether he said that for her benefit or mine, I wasn't sure. All the blood over the rocks from a freshly killed caribou was bad news anyway. I decided to try for Elu Inlet. Trap Point stood deserted as I passed. My eyes were strained and blurry from the half-twilight. Exhaustion was seeping in. Simple things, like a loon bobbing up from a dive, were beginning to startle me. It was 47 miles since I'd left camp the previous afternoon. I hated to give up the free ride on the current, but at 3:00 a.m. I turned to shore. The warm rays of the morning sun were already penetrating the breeze.

Lush, flat meadows, bordered by high ridges, stretched out along the shore. A deep canyon south of my camp still had snowdrifts in the shadows of the walls. This had to be musk-ox country. I wasn't disappointed. Within a mile I spotted a herd along the shore. If rocks and waves hadn't prevented me from landing, I could have scaled the bank and come up at their feet. I had to be content to watch, undetected, from the water.

There wasn't a soul left at the Elu Inlet crossing. My disappointment was absolute. I turned toward shore to make tea and give myself a good talking to.

A flash of silver caught my eye. I turned, astonished to see a boat behind me. The couple were just as surprised to see me.

John and Helen were from Cambridge Bay.

"Where are you going?" they asked.

"I'm on my way from Paulatuk to Gjoa Haven," I replied.

There was silence. They exchanged looks and smiled politely at me. If they thought me deplorably insane, they made no mention of it.

"May I ask you to take some letters to Cambridge for me?" I inquired. "My family always worries about me, so I want to let them know where I am," I explained.

"We can understand that," John said. "We'll be hunting here for a few days, but we'll take your letters to the post office when we get back."

I was so relieved I could have hugged them both. "I'm going to shore to make tea. Would you like some?" I invited. No, they decided to go further and make camp. We parted.

I felt so elated that I started to sing, after first checking for seals. I even forgot about the tea break. I was on my way to the bottom of the gulf and my letters were on the way to Winnipeg. The Minto Islands and the tip of huge Melbourne Island were now to my left.

The late evenings were becoming a little cooler now. The sun was dipping halfway below the horizon already. Soon there would be some darkness at midnight. I wasn't far from Cape Roxborough when I spotted a beach. I couldn't resist and stopped for the night. It was covered in thousands of rabbit tracks. There must have been a convention there during the last full moon. I strolled to the top of the rise, but couldn't spot a solitary hare.

The firewood had become sparse at the last few stops. This would be my last true campfire. I was still carrying my full supply of alcohol fuel for my stove. I would have more than I needed to get to Gjoa.

Labyrinth Bay lay ahead. I studied the map before falling asleep. Hundreds of islands dotted the bay. If the ocean was calm, I would keep all the islands to my right and travel on the open ocean. If not, I would use the islands for protection and wind my way among them.

Within the first hour of paddling, I passed John and Helen's camp. All was still, so I continued quietly by. At the same time, I crossed the boundary of the Queen Maud Gulf Bird Sanctuary. The water was rough in the bay. I headed in among the islands. So began my most frustrating day. I had miscalculated and wound up inside a four-mile-long peninsula jutting northeast from the mainland shore. Enclosed by the horseshoe shape, I paddled in and out among the countless islands for nearly two hours, looking for the exit.

I felt a presence again over my left shoulder. I landed to check the map. Subconsciously, I made room on the rock for my helper. I shifted the map to the left and caught myself asking, "How are we going to figure this out?" I shook my head, but couldn't deny the feeling of warmth and strength. Sheepishly I looked to the heavens and grinned. I could imagine the good Lord commanding my father to "get down there and straighten your daughter out." With help from the G.P.S. I found my position and headed north to the open sea, and turned eastward. I found I preferred the large waves to that claustrophobic mess.

A saddlebacked island caught my fancy. Progress-wise, the day was a disaster. Still, I was pleased the ten-mile stretch of the bay was behind me. I could now see Dease Point and the tip of the next chunk of mainland.

I stirred up two loon families in my quest for fresh water. They voiced their disapproval for hours and hours. The ponds had all been polluted by salt water, so I rationed what I had. From the look of the sky, I might have a long stay. In the evening the north wind howled harsh and cold. The rain began, and continued through the night, and the next day and night.

August 6th. The silence woke me at 4:00 a.m. I powered across Foggy Bay and through the channel between Brown Point and an offshore island. I hugged the west shore of Conolly Bay, heading south. Once I turned eastward at the bottom of the bay, I would have to watch carefully for one of the three narrow channels that would let me pass between the mainland and the fifteen-mile-long stretch of the Fitzgerald Islands to the north. Caribou were plentiful here. It had been a long while since I had seen any. Many had young ones at their sides. The calves were older now and nursed aggressively, butting the udders so violently as to lift the mother's hind legs off the ground.

I turned my full attention to finding the narrow channel. There was only one way to get through. I didn't want to miss the entrance. I explored behind each rock outcropping and carefully studied each cove for a break in the shoreline, progressing slowly. The channel caught me by surprise. I hadn't expected it to be that narrow. A number of boulders were strewn in the entrance. I held back and studied the situation. The water looked flat and deadly. The whirlpools spun their wicked course beyond the rocks. I circled and lined up with the current. I had to make this count. On approach there seemed to be resistance to my progress, then a near stall. Then came the suction. I was zapped through the opening with a mild case of whiplash. My main concern was to keep Windsong in a straight line. Not breaking the rhythm of my stroke, I was propelled helplessly forward until the whirlpool skidded us off the outer edge into less turbulent water. I hoped the next two channels were passable. I couldn't imagine trying to make it back against the current.

The time was getting on to midnight. It was difficult to see in the hazy twilight. Again, I hugged and scoured the shore for the next channel.

According to the map its entrance was narrower and longer. The full force of the gulf's water was funnelling through this shortcut. I spotted the current before the opening. I lined up, for better or for worse. For the first 100 feet or so, I had no control. The rudder seemed ineffective. I paddled more out of habit than for the good it did. It looked as though I was in for one wild ride, but before long the channel dumped into a wide bay and I eased out of the current. Many ducks rose from the water as I approached. Caribou dotted the shore.

The Nutri-Bar under the deck elastic tempted me. A good time for a break. I let Windsong drift. She certainly was one good little craft.

"One more chute, Windsong, and we'll be in the open ocean once more," I promised her. The exit was the least difficult. We sped through and the current took a sharp turn to the right, along the mainland. Twilight was deepening. I could no longer distinguish objects on shore. Windsong was slicing effortlessly through the water with incredible speed. The current had sucked the ripples from the water's surface. The last rays of the sun added a glint to the water. We passed silently over the sea of liquid silver. My greatest fear was of striking a hidden rock at that speed. I needed to find a good landing spot. It came more by chance than by choice. The land turned abruptly eastward and I realized I was at the very bottom of the Queen Maud Gulf. I set camp in a shallow cove in its extreme southwest corner. The cranes, loons, and geese set up a chorus on a nearby lake. Their day was beginning; mine had just ended.

For the first time I felt chilly in my sleeping bag. Whether it was from the temperature, the excitement, or just being plain tired, I wasn't sure. I fell asleep soundly as the first rays of the morning sun warmed the interior of the tent.

A quick check at 8:00 a.m. showed low, heavy fog. The tide was out. No point in rushing. Two more hours in the sleeping bag felt good. By 10:00 a.m. the tide was returning. The water trickled in among the raised clods of mud made by a caribou's passing. I shook the moisture off the tent and started breakfast, waiting for the water and fog to rise. I was excited this morning. For the last four days I had been heading south. Now that I was at the bottom of the Queen Maud Gulf, I would turn eastward. As the crow flies, it was approximately 160 miles across. Because I wanted to stay as close as possible to shore, I would tack on many extra miles. What lay ahead, I did not know. Of all the books and articles I had managed to find at the library, not one described the area.

I could see from the map that the brid sanctuary occupies the whole bottom of the gulf. I would guess it must be the largest in the world.

Gently, I pulled Windsong through the mud to meet the tide. I couldn't waste any of this gorgeous day. The deck compass showed east, but it was tilting at an awkward angle within its bubble. The magnetic North Pole was affecting it drastically.

"I'm on my way, girls!" I called into the wind. With a smooth rhythm I scooted from point to point, avoiding the rubble extending from each.

I counted on refilling my water containers at the Ellice River, but it was nearly impossible to find the deep channel into the mouth. I kept running into sand bars and very shallow water. The taupe-coloured sand of the shoreline extended as far as I could see. Heat waves distorted both the distance and the height.

Rather than tormenting myself and straining my eyes, I headed for the large island a mile north of the river's mouth. Stepping ashore had an immediate calming effect. Through binoculars I scanned the two-mile-wide delta and was thankful I hadn't been trapped within it. A pond of water glistened at the north tip of the island. My worries were over for the time being.

I had planned to do a relaxed paddle along the shoreline of eight-mile-wide Campbell Bay, but the dropping tide and the shallow shores forced me further and further into the ocean. At its east end I caught on to a swift current and the reversing tide. I'm not sure whether it was the speed at which I travelled, the gawking I did, or plain tiredness that caused me to lose my place on the map.

A group of islands I couldn't identify appeared ahead. I was skimming toward an opening between two of them when a rush of wind from behind made me duck. A large seagull barely missed my head. Feet forward and wing flaps down in a frantic braking maneuver, he landed a few feet ahead of Windsong's bow in ankle-deep water. Reaction set in. I ruddered hard to the left and brought Windsong to a skidding stop, broadside to a solid gravel reef covered by a couple of inches of water. Jonathan the gull never flinched, even though I could have touched him with my blade. We held a long, steady eye contact. A million thoughts entered my head. Who was this messenger?

I managed "Thanks, pal."

Suddenly I felt drained. I paddled back to an accessible island to set camp.

Overnight there was absolute calm, not a ripple, not a breeze. Every two hours I awoke to scan the horizon for a shoreline I could make sense of. Morning brought a heavily overcast sky and high humidity. The darker sky worked in my favour. I was able to distinguish land stretching due north on the horizon. That had to be White Bear Point at the tip of the eight-mile-long peninsula. The G.P.S. reading finally made sense.

August 10th. Low tide revealed many scattered gravel reefs. Blustery winds came with the reversing tide. The water rose, making it necessary to move Windsong many times. To make it easier I carried armfuls of soggy seaweed to slide her on. Before long it was necessary to move the tent too. Fond, melancholy thoughts of my family entered my head while I waited. It was only twelve days to Teresa's birthday. I hoped to be in Gjoa in time to call her.

Late evening brought calm. Heading north along the peninsula, I was confronted with much rubble along the shore. Squinting into the midnight sun brought on eyestrain. By 1:00 a.m. the sun dipped low enough to cast a deepening twilight. I rounded White Bear Point, and a deep, horseshoe-shaped cove welcomed me. Windsong glided in. The walls of the cove were like the inside of a mixing bowl. With ease I tramped down enough gravel to form a ledge for Windsong to rest on. I had only gained sixteen miles but I was jubilant. This night I knew my location and I was around the longest peninsula. Tomorrow I would be heading deeper into the gulf. The magenta sunset was spectacular.

The sound of swans brought me to my feet. From the top of a rise, I could see them on the pond. Miles of tundra stretched to the south. Perhaps I would take the day off, wash my hair, and explore. I draped my wet clothes over rocks, and crawled into the sleeping bag. The temperature was dropping. Before long I was searching my gear for an extra foil emergency blanket to cover my sleeping bag.

Frost covered my clothes, the tent, and the ground when I awoke. As tempting as a day of rest sounded, I could not chance wasting a day. My stiff clothes attested to that. I found a warm, dry turtleneck pullover, shook the frost off my pants and jumpsuit, gritted my teeth, and put them on. Ice-cold booties came next. From now on it would be harder to dry my clothes. It would take supreme willpower to dress in the mornings.

To generate heat I would increase fat intake. I had plenty of margarine along and a few cans of corned beef. I could use extra lard when I made bannock or pancakes. Nutri-Bars and halvah for snacks would help. Barring any drastic delays, my food situation was still excellent.

The water along the shoreline on the east side of White Bear Point was deeper. I hugged it for comfort and the scenery. It took two hours to drop the eight miles to the bottom of Gernon Bay. There I turned due east, keeping all the offshore islands to my right. I was anxious to keep far away from the maze of the six-mile-wide delta of two rivers entering the ocean west of Atkinson Point. Once I spotted the beacon on the Mulroak Islands, I headed south again towards the mainland. I overshot Atkinson Point by more miles than any navigator would want to admit to. Again, I could not place myself on the map.

Shivers would attack if I stopped to study the map, so I just continued paddling with all land to the right. When I spied a huge, high, dark island close to shore, I couldn't believe it. Four miles away was Perry Island. I had made terrific time.

A very narrow channel separated Perry Island from the mainland. I walked up the path into the abandoned Hudson Bay trading post. A ghostly silence greeted me. The cabins were open, windows broken, contents strewn about. Old steamer trunks gaped wide, half-filled with rusting articles. A baby's walker and an odd toy or two attested to the past presence of complete families. A boy's skate lay in the sand. Boat motor parts adorned flat rocks. A pile of traps lay rusting in the salt air. Many oil drums littered the grounds. The old red and white Hudson Bay building was still standing, though no longer proudly.

My eyes were burning from the strain of the day. I wished I had brought some Murine eyedrops in my first-aid kit. No sooner had the thought passed than I spotted an empty Murine bottle in the sand. The coincidence was eerie. I tiptoed from one cabin to the next in the shadow cast by the high cliffs bordering the clearing.

An object caught my attention. It was a grizzly bear's skull, heavy and mightily impressive. I could easily have fit my head between the molars. The sight must have affected me more than I cared to admit. When a piercing scream cut the stillness, my feet left the ground. Two falcons were dive-bombing an arctic fox that was carefully working the narrow ledges in the upper reaches of the cliffs. The fox neared the nest. I couldn't bear to hear the agonized screams as the parents defended the young. How can nature be so beautiful and still so cruel?

I had at first thought of camping at the settlement, but I found it too depressing. I also remembered the hunter's comment about grizzlies at Perry River. I wanted to be further offshore than this. I dug out my neoprene gloves. I needed them to protect my hands from the cold. Another hour of paddling brought me to an island on the western edge of Chester Bay. Deep in the bay was the Perry River delta.

The sound of heavy waves woke me in the morning. I lifted Windsong well above the high-tide line and went back to sleep, hoping a storm surge wouldn't hit. The island was not high enough for any drastic change in the level of the ocean. I enjoyed a leisurely breakfast of fat, fluffy pancakes. It was a luxury I saved for the days I stayed on offshore islands, because of the aroma that hung around the camp. I scrubbed the frying pan hard with fine sand for safety's sake.

The tide rose to within feet of the tent, then fell to low, and I caught the rising high at 5:30 p.m. The waves were fairly heavy, but the winds and current were right. The shoreline was still fairly clean. Each mile I gained meant one mile less for the next day. I passed far above the Perry River delta. Huge Winter Island stood in its mouth. At one time this area was used extensively for hunting and camping. I mused at how powerful and knowledgeable the Inuit had to be to survive here. It was difficult to fathom the courage they possessed. I would have liked to pause, but my better judgment urged me to carry on. So I passed by, but not without humility, admiration, and respect.

Heavy seas forced me off the water at the western edge of Ogden Bay. The sun had dipped below the horizon. The timeless evenings I had enjoyed so much were now replaced by the lengthening autumn night. Coolness came sharply with the decreasing daylight.

I preferred to leave the sixteen-mile crossing of Ogden Bay for morning. With relief I noted that it was the last crossing of such distance.

I was so thankful to have both nautical charts and topographical maps. In the last few days I had found it increasingly difficult to navigate within reasonable distance of the mainland, due to the jumble of islands. Still, the islands were good to me. They provided a safe place to camp. I slept much better knowing I was reasonably safe from grizzlies. There was a very slight chance of a stray polar bear, but I couldn't see them hanging around long on islands that had no food source. The last seal I had seen had been south of Cambridge. Some of the higher islands also had sparse freshwater basins in the rocks. I would share this precious supply with gulls and terns. Although I carried a water filtering system, I did not use it. I would simply strain the water through two layers of Kleenex paper towels. I had no problem with stomach upset.

Past McTavish Point the islands became more numerous and clustered closer together. They blended so well into one another that they looked like mainland. Nothing seemed to resemble the map. Navigation became a nightmare. I would spot a channel between the islands and head in, only to come to a dead end blocked by silt or rock rubble. Often I would waste time trying to retrace the route by which I'd entered. Finally, out of sheer frustration, I headed north for three miles to the open ocean. With relief I turned east, keeping all but the stragglers to my right.

My deck compass starting behaving strangely. It wandered erratically around in its bubble, tilting half over onto its side. I depended on the sun for direction. In the area of Johnson Point I cruised to a stop. It had been another successful day, another day of learning.

My lessons weren't over yet. My tent door faced east. I sat in the opening, rubbing my eyes. They were becoming more painful as the days wore on. The alarm hadn't sounded yet. Ahead, the sun was rising. A huge orange half-circle already sat above the horizon. The rays of the sun came stretching down a long, empty channel between the mainland and some very large islands right to my doorstop. Taunting, tempting. Hurriedly I scoured the map. I washed a Nutri-Bar down with hot tea and, lured by the light, headed into the channel. This sure-fire shortcut would save me many miles. Down in the bottom of the bay the many tributaries of the Simpson River emptied into the ocean. I counted off the islands as I passed. "Doing good, Victoria!"

Two hours later the channel narrowed. There was a definite drag on the kayak. The water became dark brown with silt, and occasionally my double-blade would connect with the bottom. I started paying more attention to the map. Halfway up the channel a river dumped into the ocean. A group of islands clustered around its mouth. Momentarily, the thought of retreating and heading for the open ocean crossed my mind. However, the map did show clear passage through, so I continued. Paddling became difficult. Moments later, I grounded. I was nearly opposite the mouth. A long, wide flood plain stretched inland. Silt from the river had filled the spaces between the islands. I could not see a deeper channel, so I yanked the spray skirt off and stepped out. Panic set in as I started to sink in the goo.

First, I had to control the panic. Next, I had to keep Windsong in motion to stop the suction from making it too difficult to move her. To get to solid ground, I would have to cross the river bed. Quickly I pulled the ski pole I carried from beneath the deck elastic. With tow rope in hand, I fixed my eyes on the opposite shore to keep from being thrown off balance by the hypnotic pull of the moving water which was fast disappearing with the dropping tide. My leg muscles were burning from the exertion, but I couldn't stop to rest. Even a slight pause would cause me to sink quickly. Reaching the opposite shore was a miracle. I fell to my knees. I looked back in amusement at the trail I had left. The silt was covered by a slippery, beige-coloured slime. The water was transparent. My footprints had left deep black gouges.

My bladder had been screaming for mercy from the moment I had stood up. With knees bent and crossed, I went through the routine. Zipper down, rip open the Velcro cuffs, shrug the jumpsuit off my shoulders and down to my knees, ball it all up, and pull it forward between my legs and into my lap to keep it off the ground. With knees grasping the wad of blue, my attention would turn to the rad-pants and underwear beneath. I had lost so much weight that they slipped off easily. Relief at last! Now the toilet tissue. Inevitably it would be in a ziploc bag in one of the zippered pockets of the balled-up suit in my lap.

If there is reincarnation, I am coming back as a man, no question about it!

I was safe for the moment and comfortable. Next, I needed a way out of this mess. The possibility of lining the kayak along shore and continuing eastward through the channel crossed my mind. I could always step ashore and rest my legs. The kayak seemed to slip easily over the slime in only a couple of inches of water. The other solution would be to head for the open ocean. From the top of a ridge of rocks, I could see the beautiful blue about half a mile to the north.

Where was the channel? All I could see were islands crowded one upon the other, the spaces in between clogged with silt and slime.

I got a pot of soup going while I mulled things over. I could empty Windsong and portage. If I followed the river bed, I would need to get my nerve back first. Now I could rightly understand why people panic in quicksand. It is not a pleasant feeling at all.

The warmth buoyed my spirits, and my energy returned. I sat eating, occasionally scanning the river bed with binoculars. For a second I thought I had seen a hint of blue about fifty feet from shore. Deeper water? I summoned the courage to pick up the ski pole and a handful of moss and walked out. Sure enough, the water was at least six inches deep. I sprinkled the moss on the water and to my delight found it drifting in a winding path towards an opening between some rubble islands. The muck slurped away at my feet as I struggled back. I would try it.

I towed Windsong towards the "deep" water. A full chorus rose from the snow geese that had been watching.

"Easy for you to say," I muttered.

I slogged on. I threw another handful of debris onto the water, got in, and ruddered a winding course after it. Windsong was dragging on the bottom, but the slime and the current let her slip through. Rounding each island was an adventure. Soon, the low rubble islands with their silt-filled coves gave way to high, solid rock ones. The water became deeper and finally I spotted the ocean. The channel I was in meandered on. Instead of following further, I ruddered across to the solid sand bar that held back the ocean. Windsong was hauled up. I skidded her over to the ocean's edge and set about washing the slime off her little body. I sponged the cockpit and then waded into the ocean to wash the last traces of the near disaster from my clothes. With a shudder of relief I pushed away from shore into rough waters. I ruddered due north for three miles to the outside edge of all the islands. For the rest of the trip I stayed with the open ocean to my left, even if it meant I had to be four or five miles from the mainland.

I always liked to be within reach of a larger island. I played a game I called "I Can Land There, If I Have To." I always kept in memory the last suitable island, in case I had to return. I could no longer orient myself on the map. The islands were far too numerous. I could no longer see the major points on the mainland, but I was satisfied. If I headed due east, I would run into the Klutschak Peninsula, the land mass pointing north at the east end of the gulf. At day's end I could see long black mirages scooting about on the horizon.

The G.P.S. reading left me ecstatic! Even with the delay through the shortcut I had managed 36 miles as the crow flies. That left me with only 24 miles to the Klutschak Peninsula. The archipelago of millions of isles scattered across the bottom of the Queen Maud Gulf had been an adventure by itself, but I yearned to paddle along a clean, solid mainland shore. Making plans during an Arctic trip is rather impractical, because the weather controls one's every move, but nothing could dull my anticipation of touching the peninsula and turning north the next day.

Fog delayed my departure. I sat on the beach and ate breakfast while the morning breeze did its best to whisk it away. The seagulls must have guessed I was leaving their territory. As I paddled, they delighted in tormenting me more than usual. They would take turns gliding in from behind, and, once directly over my head, they would utter a squawk that would lift me off the seat. Once they had my attention, they would dive-bomb me within inches of my head. If I made eye contact with them as they came towards me, they became more aggressive. It would be good for at least a few miles of company. Their favourite trick was to zero in from behind and try to bombard me with a load of whitewash. I'm sure they had saved up for such an occasion. There isn't a whole lot of room in the kayak for ducking. My best defence was to pull the hood of my jumpsuit over my visor. I wasn't geared to washing the splat out of my long hair, especially with cold salt water. After hours of it, the irritation would set in. Evil thoughts of landing on an island and blasting them out of the sky would enter my head. Then I would remember Jonathan and how he had saved me from a serious crack-up. My tolerance prevailed.

The headlands of the Klutschak Peninsula were now very prominent. I could distinguish the colours of the tundra, the rocks, and the sand beaches. I picked a spot and headed for it. The last five miles were sheer torture. The waves escalated in size as they rushed in from the north. I could adapt to that by heading into them at an angle, but their transparency was harder to deal with. For me, this was new. Except for a tinge of emerald in the foam, there was no colour or substance to the waves. It was extremely hard to judge them. Depth perception was totally missing. Time after time, I'd either get walloped in the chest or take a heavy one over my head. My shoulders screamed for mercy. I slowed the pace and methodically carried on.

The problems disappeared the minute my feet touched solid ground. I did a wild victory dance all over the beach. The G.P.S. printout read 67°50′ 42″ N, 98°23′ 38″ W. The north boundary of the bird sanctuary crossed my campsite.

Setting camp was a treat. The beach was long and wide and sheltered by a high rock ridge. The sound of geese filtered over the top. Probably there would be fresh water within walking distance. A generous portion of pancakes, smothered in margarine and maple syrup, appeased my hunger. I sat cross-legged on the sand and marvelled at the sights I witnessed in Mchouglin Bay and all the lessons the Arctic had taught me. I would remember them well. Tomorrow another adventure would begin. I would be heading north.

I stowed all the water bottles in my backpack and headed up the ridge. My leg muscles had turned to mush from the many weeks in the kayak.

Slowly and cautiously, I wove among the rocks and ledges to the top. My Emergency Locating Transmitter was safely tucked inside my shirt.

I stood dazzled by the view. My tent was a microscopic dot on the ocean's edge. Beyond lay the thousands of islands I had passed. An involuntary shiver coursed through my body. Had I really paddled through there?

I headed towards the two large ponds in the meadow. Snow geese, not quite ready for flight, half flew, half tiptoed to a safe distance and waited. Caribou had come to drink here. Their tracks were everywhere. I returned through the lowlands around the north end of the ridge and along the beach. My lung capacity was excellent, but my leg muscles ached with fatigue.

I made a half-decent launch at high tide. The wind and waves were from the north. I would angle my way through. At least today the water had colour to it. The shore was of a friendly nature. I could pull out safely anywhere I wished. I was soaked to the skin again. I produced so much heat when I paddled that I would have to keep the zipper down on the suit to keep from overheating. Inevitably, if a wave broke over the bow, the spray would find the zipper opening and drain down into my lap.

Halfway up the peninsula I stopped in sight of some cabins in a cove. I checked through binoculars for movement. No one was home. I was back among islands again. They calmed the water and I could proceed with a more relaxed grip on the blade. They were beautiful islands, huge, well spaced, and surrounded by sand beaches. Sand beaches lined the mainland too. My head swivelled from side to side. I was reluctant to miss any of the scenery.

I was at the tip of Klutschak Peninsula, ready to cross Sherman Inlet, when I packed it in for the day, hoping to dry my clothes in the last bit of heat from the sun. I chose a soft sand beach on a large, high island. Half a mile across the water I faced a three-mile-long island, which on the map looked like a goose in flight. Appropriate too, since snow geese crowded the shore. Caribou wandered down from the heights and browsed near the water's edge. It was peaceful. I erected the tent and weighed the fly flaps down with sand. I was pleased the aluminum poles had stood up so well. In fact the whole tent had fared well. Except for the slash I had made in the fly the morning the grizzly had visited, there was barely a mark on it. I chuckled as I looked at the slash mark. I had repaired it with white silicone seal. The kids in Coppermine had thought it was a seagull hit and had enjoyed quite a few giggles until one had found the courage to ask of its origin.

From the top of the island I plotted my course for the next day. For the first twelve miles I would work my way among the islands to the north where I would connect with the Adelaide Peninsula. Then it would be coastal paddling again.

The sand was soft beneath the tent floor. I lay down and wiggled enough to make perfect indentations for my hip and shoulder bones. Weight loss had erased the padding I normally had there.

A halo appeared around the sun. I hoped it was not a signal for a change in the weather. I could not dismiss the fact that the temperature was dropping quickly. I gathered my damp clothes and stuffed them into a large plastic bag to keep them from drawing moisture from the air. By dusk the wind was gusting from the north. Morning brought heavy fog. At 2:00 p.m. I was still shore-bound. Just as I was ready to give up on the day, the sun burnt its way through the fog. Navigating was easy. The islands were huge and spaced a mile or two apart. I could easily check them off as I passed. My only concern was drinking water. The map ahead showed nothing but sand plains. The ponds were dry.

I reached the mainland with no problem. The map showed a huge lake approximately two miles inland. I couldn't pass up this source of water. I started walking in. The sand was packed hard. Within a mile I came to an area of dunes. They were cut deeply by run-off. I began to follow the gullies among them. Musk-oxen and caribou tracks were numerous. No grizzly tracks so far. I was getting edgy. To confront a grizz or musk-ox would be a tricky business. I decided to retreat and watch for a spot of moist sand I had seen earlier. Caribou had milled at the spot. Perhaps it was a little reservoir blown in by sand. With the back of my heel, I etched a groove in the sand. Moisture showed at once. In seconds I was down on my knees scooping out a foot-square hollow with my bare hands. Water seeped into the groove. Quickly it accelerated to a trickle into my holding pond. Excited, I watched it fill to the brim. The silt sank to the bottom. I scooped the water out with a mug and filled all my containers without having to strain it. To thank Mother Nature for this treasure, I expanded the hole in case the caribou wandered back.

Five miles later I spotted a trench cutting through the sand to the ocean. It was filled with swift-flowing fresh water. A crazy notion made me land. I drank all the water I could possibly handle. I would not go to bed thirsty this day.

The wind was increasing. The sky was troubled in the northwest. I could see breakers building in the open ocean. The shoreline was trimmed in white foam. The beach was barely two feet above water level, the flood plain behind it even lower. I preferred higher ground for my campsite. My chance came 2½ miles south of Grant Point. A large offshore island would take the brunt of the waves. In the deepening twilight I headed in. I grounded, jumped out, and towed Windsong the rest of the way. If things got too rough the shallows would work in my favour. The waves would break there before hitting the shore. A narrow ridge of sand nearby would be my refuge if the water rose considerably. The wind was howling by this time. My hands were freezing.

With much difficulty the tent was erected. I piled loads of wet sand on the fly extensions. Windsong was staked firmly out of harm's way.

I had to make tea inside the tent. I lit a candle to cut the gloom. It was the 15th of August, Ken's birthday. I raised my cup in the direction of Paulatuk and made a toast to his day. Approximately ninety miles to Gjoa. Three good days and he could stop his worrying.

The winds increased to gale force. The sand was whipping around, clogging the zipper and chewing at the tent. Still no change by morning. The waves were collapsing in the shallows, sending heavy spray over kayak and tent. The thump and hiss continued all day. There would be no chance to dry my clothes this stop. I packed them into a black garbage bag and put them in the sunlight. Warm and wet was better than cold and wet.

I dug out my quilted winter jacket for the first time. I had at least four sets of dry clothes left, plus various articles that could be added or subtracted as conditions dictated. I suspected things would be getting worse instead of better.

I kept my tent clothes in a separate bundle. It consisted of knit pants, sweat shirt, panties, socks, runners, a dry jacket, and wind pants. I never entered the tent in wet clothes. To get the sleeping bag or mattress wet with salt water would have been a disaster. No matter how cold it was, I undressed outside.

By the time the day was out, there was sand in everything. It even penetrated under the elastic of the cockpit cover. I had forgotten to put the neoprene cover on under the rear hatch cover. My food packages were coated in sand.

August 17th. Slowly, the sea settled.

I set hopeful sights on a peninsula with a cabin marked on it, just past Cape Geddes. I passed Grant Point and crossed safely to Smith Point. There was so much sand. I was thankful I had eight litres of fresh water along. The prospects of finding more were faint. At Smith Point I turned due east into McGillivray Bay. It was filled with many well-spaced islands. I navigated by dead reckoning. It was crude. I'd pick a spot and say, "I reckon I want to go there."

It got me across the Arctic.

I counted off the islands as I passed. All was going gloriously well. One more island and I would turn to the north. Clouds moved in. At the same time all the islands melted together in the changing light. Now I was looking at a solid mass. I was so intent on finding the next channel that I cut the point of a small island too short. Before I could correct the mistake, I got caught up in the breakers. Windsong was lifted sideways. I ruddered hard but I couldn't keep her off the pointed rock that loomed out of the waves. From the solid, sickening thud I knew we had connected on the rear bulkhead seam. Perhaps it kept me from going over. I'm not sure. A couple of swift strokes brought us out to safety. At least we weren't sinking, yet!

I chastised myself for the stupid mistake and apologized to Windsong. I pulled to the shore to assess the damage. There was no water coming into the cockpit and none in the rear hatch. I breathed a sigh of relief. A broken pallet lay on the rocks. I lifted Windsong onto it and looked underneath. Despite the force she had absorbed, there was only a small gouge in her side. It hadn't penetrated the fibreglass.

The G.P.S. reading confirmed I was on the right island. I would sit and watch until things fell into place. The clouds floated by. The sun shone hard. I could see the end of one island and the correct shape of the next. Once more the area conformed to the map.

The waves were escalating in size and rushing the shore when I spotted my destination. I had to get around the north end of the peninsula somehow. The gusts of wind were taking my breath away. I came around to the east side and I could see the cabin. Actually, two. I got Windsong out of the surf and stabilized in the rocks. I went to check things out. One was a long shed with the centre ripped out. The roof was drooping halfway to the floor. The other was fairly solid. The windows were broken and the door was off. A wooden platform covered half the floor. It smelled old and musty. I certainly could use either as a windbreak if the weather became worse.

The cabin part was disappointing. It was marked so clearly on the map that I had thought it might be an outpost camp or such. What wasn't disappointing was the sheltered cove behind the cabins. I hurried to bring Windsong around the tip and into this haven before the waves got any worse. A perfect sand beach awaited us.

I shored the tent up with heavy rocks, spread my wet clothes on an old bed frame to drip dry, dressed warmly, including mitts, and went exploring. A large arctic hare watched me with curiosity. Satisfied that he had seen enough of this weird apparition, he bounded away. A small flock of snow geese occupied the north end of the island. I would check there for water later.

A family once lived here. A child's decayed duffel sock lay on the ground along with the torso of a doll. Parts of a windmill were scattered about. Odds and ends littered the ground, including many 45-gallon drums.

By late evening the wind was blowing from the south. It was warming up nicely. My clothes dried reasonably well.

Sixty miles to Gjoa. Two days. I might be able to phone my sister Christine on the 19th. It would be her birthday.

The wind increased to gale force by morning. My beach was being washed away at an alarming rate. Windsong had to be moved many times. I cherished my kayak fiercely. No amount of work was too much to keep her safe. Before long the tent had to be moved. It was starting to bow in on itself. I collected five drums and stood them up in a semicircle on the south side of the tent. It made a great difference. The skies cleared momentarily during the day. I could see the white globes of the Gladman Point DEW Line Station across Simpson Strait.

Simpson Strait is the narrowest part of the Northwest Passage. It separates King William Island from mainland Canada. I could plainly see King William Island. I would have to cross to its shores to get to Gjoa Haven. I was so excited my knees were wobbling.

I spent hours scanning the strait at different times of the day. The changing light gave me a new perspective on the islands in between. I plotted my course. From my location I would keep a bearing of due east if the current allowed. Twelve miles later I would run smack into King William Island, because it curved southward at that point.

For a short period the winds calmed. I was becoming hopeful. The humidity was high. I was perspiring freely. When a cool breeze sprang up from the west, I was relieved. Then the temperature started falling. I became uneasy for no real reason. I watched the skies. A storm bank was building in the northwest.

The squall struck with a vengeance. Massive breakers rushed the shore. Geysers of spray were hurled high into the air. I stood spellbound. The wrath and fury of the frigid northern sea were like nothing I had ever seen before. I felt very, very small. It took a moment to snap out of the shock. Quickly, I dashed back to the tent and rolled the drums to the north side of it, and on second thought added two more. I held the hatch cover tightly between my knees while I dug out candles. I pointed Windsong's bow directly into the wind and staked her front and back. As an extra precaution, I laid heavy rocks on the ropes. The storm was going to be a beauty. I dived for the tent as the rain struck. Then came the sleet. Then the snow.

Nothing to do but wait. I lay on my back in the sleeping bag and blew a few breaths into the air. They rose and clung below the ceiling for a moment. Yes, the Arctic summer was nearly over.

I had nothing to worry about yet. My biggest concern was my family. I knew they would be worrying soon. I only hoped my "below Cambridge" letter had made it to them. I later learned they received it while celebrating Christine's birthday on the 19th.

I had plenty of food and fuel, candles too. My friend Joe Halek at CN had given me a super one for the trip. It was a jam can filled with beeswax, sporting a wick in the middle. It burned well and I could always put the plastic lid on when I put it out. Bless you, Joe. I considered myself a very lucky person to have had so much help and love from family and friends.

Every time I opened my hatches one thing or another would remind me of a special person in my life, whether it was the double-blade made by Bill Brigden, the camp stove made by Freddie Reffler, the extra gloves from Jerry Zaste, the booties and neoprene gloves my sister Wilma had sent to me, the deck compass my son-in-law Brian and daughter Angie had mounted, the treats and safety equipment my children Angie, Debbie, Teresa and their families and my sister Christine had so lovingly put in my packs, or the Tilley hat from Alex Tilley. A warm glow of gratitude would radiate through me as I remembered.

I thought of my fellow employees at CN, male and female. Of the members of the Big Lake Touring Kayak Club and the Manitoba Recreational Canoeing Association. They were all caught up in this adventure with me.

I thought of Geoff Ball, the director of purchasing and materials at CN, who had the guts to sign my leave of absence form four years in a row, allowing me to keep my job.

I thought of Barry Pearson, also at CN, who put in a good word for me with Geoff, of his coaching efforts to make me confident and skilful with a shotgun.

I thought of Pilgrim and how he had recorded my favourite songs and a few dirty ditties on cassettes. I used them gratefully to drown out the wind and thunderous pounding of the surf as the storm continued through the 18th, 19th, and 20th of August.

I thought of my grandson Garrett. He was waiting anxiously to see my pictures of the North. I thought of three-year-old Keith and his concern about my meeting with grizzlies. "When you get him running away, Grandma, chase after him and blast him again." He considered my air horn a good weapon. I thought of my granddaughter, "Rosebud." "Come back safely, Baba," were her words to me. I thought of my new grandchild on the way. Just the preceding night, I had dreamt Angie and Brian would have a blonde, curly-headed girl. She would be very clever. But then, isn't every grandchild exceptional?

I thought of all the grand people I had met in the North. How their unique personalities and kindness had flavoured my adventure. Yes, I did have plenty to be thankful for.

The weather alternated between rain, sleet and snow for 2½ days. By noon of the 20th, I was getting the jitters of cabin fever. I decided to bundle up and go in search of water. I pulled the drawstring of the hood tightly around my face and put a scarf over my nose so the wind wouldn't take my breath away. With head bent into the wind, I walked toward the north end of the point. All that remained of the pond was a shallow pool in the very middle. Two steps forward and I started to sink. I came back to solid ground with feet that looked like they belonged to the Creature from the Black

Lagoon. I solved the problem. I found as many flat rocks as I could and laid a trail out. The trail was good for one trip to the pool. I would tiptoe there, scoop as much water as I could before the stones sank, and high-tail it back. Before I could strain it into the water bottles, the rocks would disappear. Make a new trail and repeat. What a workout! I was soaked with sweat. By the time I walked back, the wind had whipped me dry.

The sea was still running incredibly high. I would estimate the breakers were cresting around fifteen to twenty feet as they rushed in from the northwest. The pounding was deafening as they collided with shore and folded. At first I had found it absolutely fascinating. After being trapped for three days, I was beginning to avoid looking at them. How long would it take to settle the water? How long before my nerves snapped? The Arctic deals harshly with weakness, whether physical or mental. I didn't want to be carried off, a raving lunatic.

I kept busy between naps. I listened over and over to the cassettes, and I looked through my only source of reading material – a dictionary. Unlike a pocket book, it can be read over and over.

August 21st. The fog lay low and motionless upon the sea. My beach was back in place, as if it had never left. Rays of sun started to filter weakly through the haze. Little by little, I edged Windsong down to the water. I had studied the islands on my route so carefully I was sure I could get through blind-folded. Still, I would not risk it. I wanted the fog to lift enough to allow me to see what was happening on the open ocean. It definitely was much quieter.

By 4:00 a.m. the wind was blowing directly from the west, low and steady, scattering the fog. The water surface showed a strong current heading east. I ruddered Windsong out of the cove and followed. I navigated easily among the islands. At the beacon on Minor Island, I paused to check my bearings. Northeast of my position I could see two red beacons side by side. That had to be Amittuq Point on King William. A flashing light or the colour red is always an irresistible lure. I headed across.

At 8:00 a.m. on August 21st, I touched the shore of King William Island. It was exactly one month, to the hour, of my departure from Coppermine. I was elated. I stepped ashore to make sure it was real.

Sir John Franklin's men had traversed this very shore in a desperate attempt to survive. I built a little inukshuk on the beach to celebrate. It wouldn't live through the next tide, but at the moment it was monumental.

The current was strong along the shore. I could stay in close except for the odd shallows. By the time I reached Douglas Bay the water was mirror calm. How glorious it all was. I felt I could conquer the world. However, the Arctic has a way of keeping one humble.

I was tiring by the time I got to the Koka Lake and Booth Point area. My eyes were sore and blurry. I became confused. I beached Windsong and took a walk to stretch my legs and clear my mind. I climbed a sand ridge. Quite by accident I spotted large, white objects to the northeast. I hurried back for binoculars. Gjoa Haven! The DEW Line site at Gjoa! My energy returned in a split second. So did the wind. By the time I tumbled into the cockpit the waves were building. I motored around the island at Booth Point and back along the shore. Three miles later I was forced off the water. That had been happening a whole lot lately.

It took positive concentration to work through the shore-surf and rocks to a safe landing. At first I did not notice the dome-shaped pile on shore. Then I realized it was a meat or fish cache. Bears crossed my mind. I couldn't launch. I would stay. Besides, what bear would want the bag of bones I'd become, when there was this mound of goodies around? All along the shore was a hard-packed trail made by all-terrain vehicles. The tracks were very fresh. I would be phoning my daughter Teresa on her birthday tomorrow, even if I couldn't paddle. Heck! I could walk to Gjoa.

The G.P.S. reading confirmed that. Sixteen miles to Gjoa. I felt light as a feather, but when it came to setting up the tent every bone ached. I had earned every ache. It was 44 miles since I'd left the cabin. I did my chores erratically, too tired to think properly, or maybe it was just a tiredness brought on by great relief. I wouldn't bother with my wet clothes. I would wear a soft, dry set.

An arctic fox came to visit. He circled the cache and licked at the blood on the rocks and nibbled tidbits he found. I set a bowl of soup out for him and he didn't mind my cooking at all. With the deepening twilight came a definite chill. The full moon came calling, a ghostly white. It hung motionless, its image reflected in the dark sea. Back home we would call it the harvest moon. Where had the summer gone? I hated to miss any of the evening, but my eyes refused to stay open.

August 22nd. The sea was wild. It was also Teresa's birthday. That was all the incentive I needed. I got away on my third attempt to launch. I didn't really expect to get very far, but every mile paddled was one less to walk. I checked to see if the lanyard line from my E.L.T. was fastened securely to my jumpsuit. At least the waves were in my favour. If I went over I would likely get tossed up on shore. With undivided concentration, I paddled into the pitching swells. There wouldn't be time for sightseeing or day-dreaming this day. The swells ran higher and swifter. Before long they started to separate into breakers. I headed for deeper water. It seemed less violent out there. Every so often, I'd drop into a trough and be hit by a diagonally curling wave from a cross swell. That would slow me down enough for a breaker to connect and douse me with a spray of foaming ice-water. I was spitting out so much salt water that my lips hurt.

Windsong was lighter with my supplies depleted. With the centre of gravity higher, she was slapped around much more. The exhilaration of the challenge occupied my mind totally, and for a moment I forgot about the danger. It doesn't get better than this! It was a battle of wits. The ocean would not give up easily, but neither would I.

I started making promises to myself. I would go to the Northern Store and buy a McCain's Deep and Delicious chocolate cake, take it back to the tent, and eat it all myself. I would top it off with cappuccino coffee.

I was gaining on Gjoa. A final surge of adrenaline carried me through the last of the breakers into the relatively protected safety of Petersen Bay. There were many cabins along the shore. Fish nets extended out into the ocean. Not a soul was in the camps. I slowed down to enjoy the last of the trip.

By 2:00 p.m., I was paddling across the harbour towards the Northern Store. A range of emotions coursed through my body. I could clearly remember 4:00 a.m. on June 19, 1992, the day Don Starkell and I had walked into this harbour from Spence Bay.

I had made the connection!

I still couldn't fully understand what had set me towards this inconceivable goal.

However I could understand what an abundance of respect, determination, and humility could accomplish.

I was content.

Epilogue

Gjoa Haven

Being in Gjoa was another highlight of my incredible journey. I was so impressed by the wonderful hospitality shown by everyone with whom I came in contact. It started with the three Inuit families who spotted me as I crossed the harbour to the hamlet. I fell in love with their beaming faces in an instant. It was an emotional time. Although I was dripping wet, they hugged me silly and shook my hand, as if greeting a long lost family member. Their invitations to use their home to warm up were so appreciated.

I must be hungry after such a long trip. They would bring a char.

Indeed I was hungry. I could barely control myself long enough to set up the tent near the barge ramp in front of the Northern Store. My mind was on the McCain's Deep and Delicious chocolate cake I had been craving. Hurriedly I changed into dry clothes and climbed the bank to the store. Lucky for my hips, the cakes were out of stock. My minute of disappointment was erased by the open-hearted greeting from Terry McCallum, the store manager. He had heard I was heading for Gjoa and immediately recognized me from 1992. Within minutes he was asking Maxine Osmond and Ken Chaisson if they minded sharing the staff house with me for a few days. Their consent was spontaneous.

Phone calls home were thrilling. Angela reported all was well. Her pregnancy was progressing normally. I had to track Teresa down at Mel and Ann Davey's cottage on the Big Whiteshell Lake. I was pleased to have paddled in in time to wish her a happy birthday. My grandsons were busy enjoying the sunshine and water. Grant, Debbie, and my granddaughter Denine were away travelling and enjoying a camping vacation. I left a message. As the excitement peaked, a weariness took over.

An elderly Inuit fellow was waiting for me when I returned to my tent.

He spoke in Inuktitut and pointed to the tent.

My mind was foggy, but I watched his eyes and hands carefully. "Are you telling me this is not a good place for my tent?" I asked, shaking my head.

He spread his hands wide and motioned along the beach. "O-o-o-o," he commented.

"The tide will come up and I'll get wet?" I queried, using my hands to indicate the water rising.

"O-o-o-o," he replied.

Then his face broke out in the grandest smile. He grasped my elbow and shook my hand and walked away shaking his head and smiling.

I looked up from securing Windsong to see a young, curly-headed fellow approaching. He introduced himself as James Murphy from Fargo, North Dakota. We strolled the beach to where he and his friend Ivan Robertson from Calgary had pitched their tent. James and Ivan had just arrived in Gjoa the day previous. They had completed an incredible two-month journey on the Back River by Tripper canoe. A local guide, Paul Iquallaq, had picked them up at the mouth of the Back at the bottom of Chantry Inlet. They looked a bit tired, but totally and rightly proud of themselves. I accepted their invitation to supper with much pleasure.

My next task was to report in at the R.C.M.P. detachment. I knocked and stepped into the office. A tall officer was busy on the phone. He asked the caller to hold. I introduced myself and explained I had kayaked in. He told me to wait and returned to the phone.

"It's not my girl," he said. "She just walked in the door."

Rob Gillan introduced himself.

"What was that about?" I asked.

He told me it was the R.C.M.P. from Cambridge Bay. They were about to go searching for me. "But why?" I asked. "I'm three days early."

Apparently, someone in a plane had spotted an S.O.S. in the beach sand on the coast, along with a dash of yellow colour. They thought it was I.

Rob offered to find room in a garage for my kayak. Before long Windsong was safely inside, my wet clothes were unloaded, and the tent was spread out to dry. It was kindness and thoughtfulness beyond all calls of duty.

Ken and Maxine turned out to be an adorable couple. They were from the east coast and had newly arrived in Gjoa Haven.

As you can imagine, a hot shower was heavenly, as was the warm bed and soft pillows. I must admit that I didn't sleep well. I missed the sound of the surf. Quiet meant travel time. My mind wouldn't shut off. The ocean was still wild in the morning. I shuddered, glad I wasn't paddling that day. I hurried to have coffee with Jim and Ivan at the Renewable Resources office, before they left for the airport and the south. I really admired them.

Deanna Clugston, the principal of the school, called to invite me to chat with the students. What an enjoyable afternoon it became! The staff were marvellous, the children attentive and a little shy. They could easily relate to travelling and living on the land.

On my way to Deanna's for dinner I became lost. I asked a young chap for directions, not realizing he didn't understand me. He pointed to any open door. "Deanna's?" I asked.

He nodded yes. The front yard was full of tools and soapstone, some partially carved. I was puzzled, but I had only met Deanna a couple of hours earlier. Perhaps she had many talents.

I entered. An Inuit fellow answered my call with the biggest smile I could ever hope to see. He clasped my hand and repeated, "Kayak, kayak, kayak!" Unfortunately, it was the only word I understood. Judas Ooloolak was very special. He led me to a chair, poured tea, took frozen char from the freezer, and never took a breath between words. I didn't want to be late for dinner, but I could not hurt his feelings. We had tea. I told him I had kayaked from Paulatuk and described various events on the trip. He told me stories using much pantomime. Even though we each understood very little, it was an interesting visit.

His grandson came by. "Please tell your grandfather I must leave," I asked of him, "but I'll visit tomorrow."

The little guy interpreted my message. First came a frown, and then his face lit up like a starburst. "Eiyah, kayak!" were his parting words.

Deanna and her friend Vicki Racey had prepared a delicious Oriental dinner with mounds of stir-fried vegetables. Fantastic! This was the sort of meal I would dream about out on the tundra, while I ate beans and instant mashed potatoes.

Martha Pooyatuq was waiting for me when I returned to the staff house. Moses Pootogok had spared two arctic char from his catch and she had delivered them. I really must have looked hungry when I paddled in.

Ken and I cut them into large pieces and he took them to the freezer, except for one share which he prepared to perfection the next day. Fresh arctic char is definitely my favourite choice of fish.

I had hoped to visit with Margaret Tisiptsis, the kind nurse I had met in 1992, but she was not due back for another week.

I did, however, get to visit Eddie Kikoak and his wife Mary. They were now running Mary's Bed and Breakfast in Gjoa Haven. It was good to see Eddie had not lost his sense of humour. It was also my pleasure to be introduced to the film crew of *The Great Outdoorsman* TV series. John Summerfield (producer/show host), Paul Rozon, and Dave Lostracco were staying at Eddie's while filming a char-fishing segment for the show.

Florence, Eddie's daughter, had made excellent twisted bannock sticks. I couldn't resist them, even though I had a dinner date with Ken and Maxine. Ken had spent a whole lot of time fixing and slowly simmering a thick spaghetti sauce. I thought I had died and gone to heaven. My burnt campfire meals were a vague memory.

My second visit with Judas was as interesting as the first. He invited his daughter-in-law to translate for us. Judas is a world-renowned carver, although I doubt he realizes his fame. I yearned to have a couple of his works and he promised to carve two for me before I left. I also would have liked to have his energy.

I still clung to the hope of paddling to Taloyoak (Spence Bay), for it was only another 109 miles.

I would need good weather. The 27-mile crossing of Rae Strait lay ahead of me.

I was about to hurry off to a dinner invitation at Rob's house when the telephone rang. My daughter Angela was on the line.

"Mom, Brian and I want to tell you that you have a new granddaughter," she told me.

Well, you could have knocked me over with a feather.

Aleia Victoria had arrived seven weeks early. She was a mere four pounds, but holding her own. Angie was fine. Brian too. I floated to Rob and Gwen's house on cloud nine. I was still in shock when I apologized for being late. Under the circumstances I was pardoned.

I was introduced to Rob's wife, Gwen, and their tiny adorable daughter, Allyson, nurses Elsie Friesen and Sandra Lichter, Rob's Inuit partner, Simeoni, and Dr. Brian Defresne. The same doctor had diagnosed my edema in 1992. He happened to be in from Cambridge for a clinic.

The exceptional meal included hot-off-the-grill barbecued chicken and homemade bread. I was getting terribly spoiled.

A phone call from the film crew woke me early Friday morning.

Would I consent to an interview and meet them at the water's edge in fifteen minutes?

"I have to shower. Give me thirty," I bargained.

I expected a half-hour interview at most. Instead, they filmed for four hours.

All thoughts of continuing on disappeared with the news from home. There was nothing more important than returning to be with my family. I emptied Windsong, packed the gear, and sent it home parcel post. Windsong and I would leave on Sunday the 28th of August by First Air.

I had one more date in my black book. It was a dinner invitation at Dave White's and Grace Natano's house. Dave is a freelance photographer and Grace is a nurse at the Health Care Centre. Dave also worked part-time at the Northern Store. Again the dinner was exceptional. Spaghetti, fresh salad, and homemade garlic bread. I had lost 28 pounds on the trip. If I continued to feast the way I had in the past week, I would soon outgrow my new size-seven jeans. We ended up at the beach, with Grace, Dave, and Ken all giving Windsong a trial run.

Windsong was made ready for the trip home. Axel Hahling, the Kekertak Co-op store manager, supplied the foam that would protect her bow and stern. The double-blades were stowed inside and her hatches taped shut.

Jessie Kekinek sold me an ulu that her husband had handcrafted. It was a fitting symbol and souvenir of my travels in the Arctic. How quickly it was all coming to a close!

There was much excitement in Gjoa on Saturday morning. A Russian cruise ship was scheduled to dock in the harbour at noon. All sorts of activities were arranged for entertaining the passengers. Disappointing news arrived. Due to heavy ice in the straits, the ship would be diverted to Cambridge Bay.

My last night in Gjoa was exceptional. Friends gathered at Ken and Maxine's for dinner. Once more I met Doug Hodgert of the Northern Store staff. In 1992 his humour had been instrumental in preserving my sanity. I was pleased to know he was still in Gjoa and that he and his fiancée had major plans for 1995. I'm glad good things happen to nice people! The evening ended with the midnight sun tinting the harbour waters a brilliant pink.

Sunday, August 28th, was a blur of activity.

Judas had finished my carvings – a drum-dancing musk-ox and a spirit man. I hurried to pick them up.

My only regret was not seeing Martha and Simon Qirnik. They were the adorable elderly couple who had befriended me at the Canada Day celebrations in 1992. Unfortunately, Simon had since passed away and Martha was visiting relatives at Holman, on Victoria Island.

How does one adequately express the deep feelings and appreciation to such special people? They turned my trip into a truly memorable journey.

Windsong was loaded on a freight plane. I was on the scheduled run the same afternoon. From the top of the stairs I glanced back at wonderful faces and Gjoa in the background. The "Social Butterfly" was on the way home. The teasing had been partly the truth. I would return to the city to recuperate. I couldn't take the pace. The plane lifted off over Scwatka Bay. Below, the sea was calm as glass, the first time since my arrival.

I would see Taloyoak (Spence Bay) after all. This Sunday flight would extend to Taloyoak and return to Cambridge and Yellowknife, by-passing Gjoa on the way back.

My travelling partner turned out to be Ian McCrea.

"Coppermine, 1992!" Ian commented.

"Yes, the lifeguard," I answered. How could I forget? We had one hour to fill in two years.

The stop in Taloyoak was brief. I looked on in amusement as a farm tractor, pulling a trailer full of children, arrived at the terminal. Everyone was enjoying the ride.

I had my nose pressed against the window on the return to Cambridge. The view of the King William Island's north shore was stunning. Masses of ice were visible in the straits and along the coast. The idea of circumnavigating King William by kayak started blossoming in my mind. The lure of the Arctic tugged at my soul. Some day, some day soon, I promised myself.

First Air was late coming into Yellowknife. Elsie Friesen, the nurse from Gjoa, who had also been on the flight, dashed to collect my luggage while I lined up for my ticket to Edmonton. Thanks to her I made the connection.

I was thrilled to see Doug Cranston, a friend from Winnipeg, waiting for me at the Edmonton airport. In his big-hearted way he treated me to a tour of the West Edmonton Mall.

It was a traumatic experience after the silence of the North.

Then came the grand finale, the joyous reunion with my family and friends at the Winnipeg airport.

We hurried away to the intensive care nursery to see the little character who couldn't wait for Grandma to come home.

Supplies and Gear 1994

tent: Eureka Windriver II

Therma-Rest mattress

bivouac sack

inflatable pillow

down sleeping bag

extra duffel bag

space blanket

extra flysheet

12-gauge shotgun

flare gun: 12 noise-makers, 10 red flares

Bear Scare (spray)

hatchet

signalling mirror and whistle

slugs, S.S.G's and bird shot

air horn

red neon flag and red ribbon tape

Buck knife

Emergency Locating Transmitter

G.P.S. (Global Positioning System)

topographical maps

tide tables

Silva compass

2 watches

maps: nautical charts

2 map cases

ruler, pen, and marker

Sailor II deck compass

alarm clock

magnifying glass

various medications

sanitary pads

tampons

vitamins

strawberry extract

2 foil blankets

triangle bandage for sling

razor

first-aid kit

tensor bandage

wrist braces

scissors

mini flashlight

Hot-Shots

insect repellent

mosquito-netting hat

Carmex: lip balm

fibreglass repair kit

duct tape

tie wraps: plastic

wire

tools: vice grips, screwdriver

Velcro straps

5-minute epoxy

marine silicone seal

hacksaw blades

swivel clips

extra rudder cables and parts

bungee cords

electrical tape

extra nuts and bolts, screws

2 cameras

tripod

print film

extra batteries for camera

slide film

spray skirt	2 50-foot ropes
ski pole (without basket)	long-handled ice-pick
life-jacket	collapsible fishing rod
fish hooks and line	small backpack
fanny pack	extra sea-bag
extra double-blade	
journal	pens
writing pad	envelopes
stamps	dictionary
personal cassette player	2 cassette tapes
reading glasses	
Braun curling iron and butane	shampoo and conditioner
hair-pik	hair colour
brush	face cream
soap	hand lotion
sunscreen	mascara and eyelash curler
nail clippers and file	towel and facecloth
water filtering apparatus	alcohol stove and wind shield
extra ziploc bags	methyl hydrate fuel
garbage bags	coffee pot
kitchen catchers	cooking pot
mug	plate and bowl
fork, spoon, knife	candles
can opener	spatula
matches and Bic lighters	
neoprene booties	neoprene socks
Gortex socks	3 pair heavy socks
2 pair light socks	runners
hiking boots	quilted nylon socks
neoprene gloves (3 prs. of various weights)	Gortex gauntlet mitts
polar fleece liners	polar fleece gloves
rubber paddling mitts (gauntlet style)	work gloves for around camp
woollen mitts	Isotoner gloves
fur-lined mitts	2 sun visors
1 baseball cap	sunglasses
polar fleece toque	Tilley hat

2 pair rad-pants

1 pair cotton knit pants

2 pair wind pants

1 set of long underwear

1 pair polyester pants

nylon jogging suit

Gortex rain-suit with hood

panties

polyester-filled jacket

sweat shirt with hood and front pockets

tank top

2 short-sleeved T-shirts

bikini bathing suit

one-piece jumpsuit with hood (Mountain Equipment Co-op)

¾-length Sierra windproof unlined jacket with hood

fleece sweater

Rad paddling shirts

4 polyester turtleneck pullovers

nightgown

*All clothes were vacuum-packed in ziploc bags.

Food Supplies for 1994

Magic Pantry dinners	pancake mixes
pork and beans	bannock mixes
flaked turkey	Carnation Instant Breakfast
corned beef	pablum
salmon	instant oatmeal
luncheon meat	sardines
granola	Knorr soups
powdered milk	Lipton soups
hot chocolate	Kraft dinner
Horlitz drink	3-minute noodles
Oxo broth packets	macaroni
instant chicken broth	instant potatoes
tea	minute rice
Tang fruit drink mix	couscous
2 small cans of mandarin oranges	2 onions
3 lbs. carrots	2 garlic bulbs
Mazola oil	lard
margarine	peanut butter
dried fruit	honey
candies	jam
chocolate bars	fig cookies
gum	halvah
mixed nuts	peanuts
crackers (whole wheat)	salt
sugar	pepper
cayenne pepper	cinnamon
garlic powder	

3 loaves of bread (which I was able to store in the cockpit)
48 Nutri-Bars (between Coppermine and Gjoa)

*All food was vacuum-packed in ziploc bags.